Making work more equal

Manchester University Press

Making work more equal

A new labour market segmentation approach

EDITED BY DAMIAN GRIMSHAW,
COLETTE FAGAN, GAIL HEBSON
AND ISABEL TAVORA

Manchester University Press

Published by Manchester University Press
Altrincham Street, Manchester M1 7JA

www.manchesteruniversitypress.co.uk

British Library Cataloguing-in-Publication Data
A catalogue record for this book is available from the British Library

ISBN 9781526117069 paperback
ISBN 9781526125972 open access

First published 2017

Typeset by
Servis Filmsetting Ltd, Stockport, Cheshire
Printed in Great Britain by
CPI Group (UK) Ltd, Croydon, CR0 4YY

Contents

Figures

Tables

Contributors

Nurjk Agloni is a doctoral researcher at the Department of Sociology of the University of Cambridge and a sponsored PhD researcher of the Centre for Social Conflict and Cohesion – COES (Fondap Project Number 15130009)

Phil Almond is Professor of Comparative Employment Relations at De Montfort University, Leicester and Director of CERC, the Comparative Employment Research Centre, UK.

Dominique Anxo is Professor of Economics in the Department of Economics and Statistics at Linnaeus University, Sweden.

Eileen Appelbaum is a Senior Economist at the Centre for Economic and Policy Research, Washington DC, USA.

Marian Baird is Professor of Gender and Employment Relations at the University of Sydney Business School and Director of the University's Women and Work Research Group, Australia.

Josep Banyuls is Lecturer in Labour Economics and Employment Policy at Valencia University, Spain.

Rosemary Batt is the Alice Hanson Cook Professor of Women and Work at the ILR School, Cornell University. She is also Professor in Human Resource Studies and International and Comparative Labor, USA.

Francesca Bettio is Professor of Political Economy at the University of Siena and coordinating member of the SAAGE team (Scientific analysis and advice on gender equality in the EU).

Gerhard Bosch is Professor of Sociology and ex-Director of the Institute for Work Skills and Training (IAQ) at the University of Duisburg Essen, Germany.

Brendan Burchell is Reader in the Social Sciences at the University of Cambridge and Director of the Cambridge Undergraduate Quantitative Methods Centre, UK.

Iain Campbell is an Academic Visitor at the Centre for Employment and Labour Relations Law (CELRL), University of Melbourne, Melbourne, Australia.

Tony Dundon is Professor of Human Resource Management and Employment Relations at the University of Manchester, UK.

Christine Erhel is an economist at the University Paris I Panthéon-Sorbonne, Director of the Center for Employment and Labor Studies (CNAM) and a Researcher at the Centre d'étude de l'emploi (CEE), France.

Colette Fagan is Professor of Sociology, Associate Dean for Research and Deputy Dean of the Faculty of Humanities at the University of Manchester, UK.

Alan Felstead is Research Professor at Cardiff School of Social Sciences, Cardiff University, UK.

Francis Green is Professor of Work and Education Economics at UCL Institute of Education, University College London, UK.

Damian Grimshaw is Professor of Employment Studies and Director of the European Work and Employment Research Centre (EWERC) at the University of Manchester, UK.

Gail Hebson is Senior Lecturer in Employment Studies at the University of Manchester, UK.

Jane Humphries is Professor of Economic History at All Souls College, University of Oxford, UK.

Maria Karamessini is Professor of Labour Economics and Economics of the Welfare State at Panteion University of Social and Political Sciences, Athens. She is currently Governor of the Public Employment Agency (OAED), Greece.

Fang Lee Cooke is Associate Dean of Graduate Research and Professor of Human Resource Management and Asian Studies at Monash Business School, Australia.

Steffen Lehndorff is Research Fellow at the Institute for Work Skills and Training (IAQ), University of Duisburg-Essen, Germany.

Mick Marchington is Emeritus Professor of Human Resource Management at the University of Manchester, UK.

Miguel Martínez Lucio is Professor of International Human Resource Management and Comparative Industrial Relations at the University of Manchester, UK.

Alberto Mazzon is a PhD candidate at the joint program in Economics of the Universities of Florence, Pisa and Siena, Italy.

Jacqueline O'Reilly is Professor of Comparative Human Resource Management at the University of Sussex and Research Director of CROME, the Centre for Research on Management and Employment, at the University of Brighton, UK.

Agnieszka Piasna is a Senior Researcher at the European Trade Union Institute, Brussels.

Albert Recio is Professor in Applied Economics at the Universitat Autònoma de Barcelona and a member of the QUIT-Institut Estudis del Treball, Spain.

Kirsten Sehnbruch is the director of the Public Policy Institute at the Faculty of Economics and Business of the Universidad Diego Portales, and an associate researcher of the Centre for Social Conflict and Cohesion (Fondap Project Number 15130009). She also gratefully acknowledges funding from Fondecyt Project Number 1171025 for this research.

Annamaria Simonazzi is Professor of Economics at Sapienza University of Rome and is Chair of the Scientific Committee of the Fondazione Giacomo Brodolini, Italy.

Mark Smith is Dean of Faculty and Professor of Human Resource Management at the Grenoble Ecole de Management, France.

Isabel Tavora is Lecturer in Human Resource Management at the University of Manchester, UK.

Paola Villa is Professor at the University of Trento, Italy.

Preface

This book is inspired by, and dedicated to, Jill Rubery. Jill is a major figure in international debates on inequalities in work and employment. Her intellectual contributions are renowned for both their critical questioning of mainstream theoretical approaches, whether in economics, management, industrial relations or comparative systems, and their attention to real-world empirical detail. Jill's intellectual roots are with the influential Cambridge economics group researching labour market segmentation in the late 1970s and 1980s during a period when Keynesian economic thought was being eclipsed by neoclassical economics modelling. The research was inter-disciplinary, grounded in data (mostly involving case studies of firms) and driven by an ambitious intellectual agenda that developed theory while also illuminating practical matters of relevance to policy-makers and practitioners.

During these Cambridge years, Jill developed a very important network of international friends and colleagues who formed the backbone of the *International Working Party on Labour Market Segmentation*, which Jill co-founded in 1979, and who provided the impetus for Jill's intellectual interest in comparative employment systems. Collaboration was an important characteristic of Jill's work then and continued following her move to Manchester in 1989 where for nearly three decades many colleagues have benefited enormously from working with her on high-profile research projects, publications and policy advisory work. This book has therefore been a rather strange experience for many of us because we are so used to talking through ideas and our writing with Jill. Her absence, dictated by the tradition of the *Festschrift*, feels wrong!

We would like to say thank you to the 33 friends and colleagues of Jill who have contributed to this volume. We are very conscious that we were unable to invite many others due to MUP page-length restrictions, in particular many younger colleagues and ex-PhD students. We were able to expand the numbers somewhat by suggesting to several colleagues that they co-authored chapters in order to bring a greater number of Jill's friends into the book. These suggestions were generously accepted and we believe they have in fact proven very fruitful, especially in expanding the cross-national comparative scope of chapters.

We are also very grateful for the assistance in the production of this book by two Manchester colleagues, Nina Teasdale and Helen Norman, Damian's eldest daughter, Helena Grimshaw, Thomas Dark at MUP and an anonymous reviewer.

We hope the book serves as a clear expression of Jill's major research interests and also looks to the future by outlining the key principles of what we are calling a 'new labour market segmentation approach'. Jill's career is by no means complete and indeed this book will be launched at the 39th *International Working Party on Labour Market Segmentation* conference in Manchester in 2017, billed as a 'mid-way career celebration for Jill Rubery'. We look forward to Jill's criticisms!

Damian, Colette, Gail and Isabel

1

A new labour market segmentation approach for analysing inequalities: introduction and overview

Damian Grimshaw, Colette Fagan, Gail Hebson and Isabel Tavora

There is a real need for a new multi-dimensional approach to understanding inequalities in work and employment. Faced with the pressures of globalisation, liberalisation of markets and periodic economic crises, many societies around the world have forged fragile compromises that are fundamentally incompatible with the goals of making the distribution of employment and quality of work more equal. Various fiscal, labour market and social policy reforms risk creating or increasing inequalities, expanding precarious forms of employment and exacerbating the social exclusion of vulnerable workforce groups. Such reforms include the marginalisation of organised labour through changes to industrial relations, the marketisation and outsourcing of public services, the weakening of employment rights, cuts to welfare entitlements, and the privatisation of responsibilities for family and care provision. Moreover, employers may also play a role in constructing and sustaining inequalities, whether by lobbying for deregulatory reforms, unbundling production structures in ways that fragment work, or evading rules designed to secure fair and equal treatment and to enhance job quality.

Political and economic actions are thus continuously shaping the trajectory and country specificity of work and employment inequalities in the context of shifting international patterns of production organisation, industrial relations, gender relations and demographic changes such as population ageing or migration flows. While processes of competitive market allocation and technological change matter, as do long-term trends in economic growth, these cannot fully explain divergent inequality outcomes (Lee and Gerecke, 2015). Instead, international research points to labour market institutions (e.g. minimum wage rules, collective bargaining, vocational training, immigration rules); organisations and collective movements that can exercise countervailing power (especially trade unions and feminist and civil society organisations); the recurring conflict over what constitutes a job (the bundle of tasks and the overall quality, value and status); a raft of institutions that interact with labour markets (especially social and welfare policy rules and corporate governance systems); and changes in the national and global organisation of production (e.g. Berg, 2015; Bettio *et al.*, 2013; Gallie, 2007; Gautié and Schmitt, 2010; Karamessini and Rubery, 2014; Marino *et al.*, 2017; Muñoz de Bustillo *et al.*, 2011; Vaughan-Whitehead, 2011, 2016).

This book contributes to this international evidence by proposing a 'new labour market segmentation' approach for the investigation of work and employment inequalities. Our hope is that this meets an intellectual need for a multi-dimensional perspective and also confronts the challenge of a resurgent neoliberalism that is undermining the models of social citizenship and principles of labour market inclusion which have been forged through collective bargaining, protective and participative rights, and welfare state regimes. The first section identifies the intellectual basis for this approach in contributions from three theoretical traditions that inform its distinctive focus on the segmentation, gender and comparative institutional effects on inequalities. We describe a set of propositions, designed to illuminate the main threads of a new labour market segmentation approach, and review each in the subsequent sections against the rich evidence and arguments presented in Chapters 2 through 17 of this volume.

Theoretical elements of a new labour market segmentation approach

The proposed new labour market segmentation approach brings together key insights from three theoretical traditions that have proven valuable in articulating the causes, characteristics and consequences of inequalities in work and employment. Table 1.1 presents a summary with a focus on key forms of inequalities, namely low pay, gender pay inequality and patterns of segmentation between standard and non-standard forms of employment.

The first theoretical tradition is the labour market segmentation approach as conceived in the 1970s and early 1980s (Craig *et al.*, 1982; Doeringer and Piore, 1971; Edwards *et al.*, 1975; Gordon *et al.*, 1982; Rubery, 1978; Sengenberger, 1981; Wilkinson, 1981).[1] In a radical break from the economics orthodoxy at the time (which still prevails today), segmentation theory rejected the assumption that labour market divisions could be attributed mainly to inadequate levels of human capital or differences in productivity. Instead, it placed the demand side of the labour market centre stage in its analysis of divisions, inequalities and dualisms in capitalist employment structures. As Jill Rubery has argued:

> The attraction of segmentation theory is that it focuses on employing organisations, the architects of the employment system, in the shaping of labour market inequalities. ... The obscuring of the active role of employers in shaping employment outcomes is perhaps one of the main legacies of mainstream economics. (2007: 955, 960)

Its long-standing significance lies in its opposition to neoclassical economics, which assumes employers automatically adjust to supply-side shifts in education and skill so that they utilise all potential productivity in the labour market, albeit constrained by institutional 'imperfections' (so-called) in the labour market. Instead, drawing on empirical case studies of employer practices and worker experiences, labour market segmentation theorists argued that employers and the wider economic conditions play a key role in shaping inequalities in the labour market via selective access to career and training opportunities (as in Doeringer and Piore's (1971) model of primary and secondary labour market segments); changing responses to economic conditions that affect workers' job queue prospects (Rubery, 1988; Sengenberger, 1981); under-investment in productive structures leading to low-wage, low-skill vicious cycles (Wilkinson, 1983); and the undermining of worker resistance through divide-and-rule tactics (Edwards *et al.*, 1975; see further discussion in the section 'Employers as architects of inequalities'). The argument is that these practices contribute to a continuous regeneration of inequalities through the construction of 'non-competing groups' (Cairnes, 1874), variously based on personal attributes such as social class, race, gender, migrant status, age and disability, among others. In other words, inequalities are not fostered only on the supply side through exogenous societal or cultural rules and conventions but also, and perhaps predominantly, through formal and informal institutionalised policies and practices in labour markets and workplaces.

The approach thus decidedly breaks with the neat wage-productivity theorising of neoclassical economics, as well as with most econometric models of wage formation, since it injects the possibility that many employers who are able to pay high wages commensurate with investments in technology and productivity performance may nevertheless be unwilling to do so (Craypo, 2003). A further important contribution is the critique of simplistic, abstract notions of the representative firm and the emphasis instead on the real-world context of the uneven development of sectors, supply chains and organisations. Such uneven development arises from the unequal distribution of power among

capital and which fuels differential opportunities for workers' pay and employment prospects that are not determined by their potential productivity characteristics (Grimshaw and Rubery, 2005). Workers may be at the right or wrong
end of a supply chain, for example, and therefore more or less able to press
for a decent share of the employer's rent (Guy, 1999; Perraudin et al., 2013).

The second theoretical tradition summarised in Table 1.1 is feminist socio-
economics. This approach brings an explicit analytic focus on gender inequalities, which both advances beyond some of the inadequacies of the early labour
market segmentation approach and enriches our understanding of wider societal processes of inequality generation. It emphasises the ways that women's
labour market opportunities are limited and moulded by sex discrimination,
gender inequalities in domestic labour, and the interplay of household and
workplace power relations. Three insights are fundamental for our focus here.
Firstly, feminist socio-economics demonstrates that the interaction between
the spheres of production and social reproduction is central to the gendered
structuring of labour market segmentation (Folbre, 1994; Humphries and
Rubery, 1984). Early labour market segmentation theory usefully veered off
to the demand side in a rejection of neoclassical economists' assumed supply-
side logic, but failed to revisit the supply side and thus was criticised for not
questioning stylised assumptions about the matching of periphery jobs with
periphery workers.

Feminist research has made major critical advances here and shows how the
politics of social reproduction and the household division of labour directly
affects the delineation by employers of work into 'good jobs' and 'bad jobs'.
Historical investigations exposed the construction of the male breadwinner in
need of a family wage and the constraints imposed by the associated widespread
beliefs that women worked for 'pin money' (Humphries, 1977). These issues
still reverberate in contemporary accounts of sex discrimination in many countries, where women are still too often treated by employers, policy-makers and
men as secondary rather than dual or equal earners. Sex discrimination takes
many forms. There is evidence that employers exploit gender profiling and gendered wage practices in the belief that women are less committed to work than
their male counterparts. Also, many country studies point to the adverse consequences of underdeveloped and gender biased welfare and family support policies for women's wage penalties over the life course. Furthermore, employers'
exploitative practices towards female workers who are assumed to be locked
into local labour markets are found to hinder wage prospects and the exercise
of autonomy at work (Cooke and Xiao, 2014; Figart et al., 2005; Korpi et al.,
2013; Lewis et al., 2008; Merluzzi and Dobrev, 2015; Rubery et al., 1999;
Tavora and Rubery, 2013; Ugarte, 2017; Weinkopf, 2014).

Table 1.1 Three theoretical approaches to understanding inequalities in work and employment

	Causes of inequalities	Likely characteristics of inequalities	Theoretical implications for policy and practice
i) Labour market segmentation	– Employers' pay and employment practices (e.g. internal labour markets versus periphery segments) create endogenous conditions of segmentation – Employer divide and rule strategies – Limited employer investment in skill and technologies – Mix of internal organisational and external conditions, not primarily reflective of workers' productivity potential – Lower reservation wage for vulnerable groups (e.g. youth, black or minority ethnic workers, migrant workers) weakens wage bargaining power	*Low pay?* • Restricted job mobility + low-pay, no-pay cycle undermines secure income needs • Youth and other labour market entrants face high risk of dead-end/precarious jobs • Employer discrimination by class status, gender, race, ethnicity, age, disability, migrant group *Gender pay gap?* • Employers sort more women than men into periphery segments (feminised) due to biased perceptions of skills and motivation • Women concentrated in unstable jobs/unstable firms (private sector) and professional, more secure jobs (public sector), but economic restructuring and austerity measures change the character of these labour market segments *Standard versus non-standard segmentation?* • Periphery jobs function according to a low value-added dynamic that is out of synchronisation with core sector processes • Weak collective representation of workers in non-standard jobs for wage bargaining	Justification for policy and practice to target exploitative employers and to rebalance power via: ➤ Effective minimum wage legislation ➤ Protective and participative standards ➤ Equal treatment and anti-discrimination rules between standard and non-standard contracts and between worker groups according to personal characteristics ➤ Industrial policy for skill and technology investment ➤ Tax penalties for high labour turnover ➤ Social value procurement practices

Table 1.1 (Continued)

	Causes of inequalities	Likely characteristics of inequalities	Theoretical implications for policy and practice
ii) Feminist socio-economics	– Persistent gender division of domestic and care work – Interplay of workplace and household power relations shapes good/bad job segmentation – Gendered wage practices target first and second earners – Economic cycles (booms and busts) have gendered employment effects – Occupational sex segregation, including feminised part-time work, influences the accompanying job design, career tracks and wage value – Jobs associated with women ('women's work') are undervalued – Sex discrimination by employers, co-workers and customers is shaped by powerful stereotypes about motherhood – Different standards and gendered models of family support provision	*Low pay?* • Women universally over-represented in low-wage jobs • Sometimes sustained via state subsidies to (mostly male) primary earners • Lower reservation wage for women than men (gender bias in welfare benefit rules) undermines wage bargaining position *Gender pay gap?* • Long-term secular change in women's aspirations, their employment and the family economy • Undervaluation of women's work through inter alia weak visibility of skill, status, experience and discretion • Domestic labour restricts women's job choices and mobility • Considerable life-course gender wage penalties *Standard versus non-standard segmentation?* • Feminised non-standard job features (part-time, casual contracts) overlap with low pay and undervaluation • Discriminatory 'mommy career tracks' for part-time jobs	Actions on a wide set of policy agendas including mainstreaming gender equality into all fiscal, social and labour market policies. ➤ Policies to raise the value of jobs women do (care work, part-time work, etc.) ➤ New job design and evaluation practices to address undervaluation ➤ Transparent pay and promotion practices in organisations ➤ Investment in family support provision (child and elder care services, family-related leave and other working time adjustments which include measures to foster men's involvement in care) ➤ Support for stronger trade union mobilisation and representation ➤ Investment in public sector employment

| iii) Comparative-institutionalist | Variety of national models of employment organisation linked with different distributive outcomes ('regulatory indeterminacy')
 – Diverse structures, character and power resources of social actors
 – Wide-ranging set of institutions shape work and employment inequalities, including:
 ○ education and training
 ○ labour market regulations
 ○ social protection systems
 ○ gender relations and norms
 ○ family policies and welfare systems
 ○ industrial relations
 ○ corporate governance
 ○ innovation systems | *Low pay?*
 • Diverse minimum wage intersections with collective bargaining and social protection systems influence low wage inequalities
 • Varied 'participative standards' shape wage bargaining power
 • Low-wage workforce composition varies with household structures, VET systems and migration

 Gender pay gap?
 • Varied/changing patterns of industry and occupational sex segregation, links with pay and employment practices
 • Varied inclusion/exclusion from collective bargaining and social protection systems

 Standard versus non-standard segmentation?
 • Varying size and nature of 'protective gaps' associated with employment rights, representation, enforcement and social protection
 • Indeterminacy of inclusion/exclusion dynamics shaped by strategies of social actors and economic conditions | A shared feature of this theoretical approach is the rejection of uniform policy prescriptions and the need to acknowledge relevant societal institutions (current and legacy) in the following areas:
 ➤ Minimum wage rules that enable and respond to social dialogue
 ➤ Inclusive supply chain wage bargaining (national and pan-national)
 ➤ Gender mainstreaming of fiscal, social and labour market policy
 ➤ Close protective gaps among non-standard forms of employment workers via inclusive and enforceable employment rights and social protection rights
 ➤ Varied composition of non-standard forms of employment workforce requires distinctive policy approaches |

Notes: The term 'social actors' refers to employers, trade unions, governments (national and pan-national) and civil society organisations; VET = vocational education and training.

A second insight from feminist socio-economics concerns its critical analysis of the wage–skill nexus and an alternative theoretical development of the notion of undervaluation. The productive value of jobs done predominantly by women is likely to be undervalued because women have historically been less able than men to establish high status for those occupations and sectors of female-dominated work, such that for the same skill level the jobs occupied by women are more likely to be attributed periphery status and paid at a lower level than those carried out by men (e.g. Walsh, 1990). These complex gendered processes play out over long periods of time and as women make inroads into once male-dominated occupations, there is a risk the relative status and wage attached to the job falls (Cohn, 1995; Reskin and Roos, 1990). Because skill is a socially constructed concept, employers are likely to make a 'value association' between unpaid work performed in the home by women and similar work performed in the wage economy: if the tasks are widely undertaken outside the workplace without formal training then it is judged 'unskilled'. This gendered practice is reinforced in societies where 'cultural ideas deprecate work done by women' (England, 2005: 278), where fathers fail to take on an equal share of domestic work (Fagan and Norman, 2013) and where employers deny women discretion in their work (through for example 'job crafting', see Leana et al., 2009). The archetype example is care work, which remains invisible, low status and exploited in most societies (Hebson et al., 2015). For the employer, the outcome of undervaluation is access to a higher quality of labour for a given wage (Grimshaw and Rubery, 2007).

A feminist *life course* perspective on the labour market experiences of mothers brings a third valuable insight to our new labour market segmentation approach. Rejecting the neoclassical economics explanations,[2] feminist socio-economics research finds evidence in many countries of significant 'motherhood pay gaps' that cannot be explained by human capital depreciation, diminished experience, lower skill levels, women's concentration in jobs that offer family-compatible working hours, or measures of employment commitment (for a review, see Rubery and Grimshaw, 2015). Instead the feminist research advocates alternative explanations, including the persistence of traditional sexist stereotyping of mothers' employment commitment, which imposes a kind of 'negative externality' of childbirth to working mothers (Self, 2005), and country differences in levels of defamilialisation, such that highly developed childcare services and family-oriented working-time arrangements for men and women support women's economic activity after motherhood and provide a buffer against employer strategies of core–periphery segmentation (Anxo et al., 2007; 2010; Pettit and Hook, 2009; see also the section 'Households, welfare regimes and inequalities effects'). In many developing countries, women's relationship to paid work needs to be understood in terms of the relative stability of family and community systems (Abu Sharkh and Gough, 2010) leading to calls for family–work reconciliation policies to be designed around household and neighbourhood activities (Beneria, 2007). Overall, the point is not simply that women fall behind men in supply-side job queues. Rather there is a continuous restructuring of job, wage and skill structures shaped by employer gender bias, alongside family support provisions that shape the form and extent of gender inequality over the life course.

The third area of literature underpinning our new labour market segmentation approach is comparative institutionalist theory. This research reveals a rich diversity of employment arrangements around the world and a wide variety of distributive outcomes in wages, household income, job quality and lifetime prospects. Moreover, this theoretical tradition is premised on the ontological notion that labour markets are socially constructed, an idea accepted by some leading economists (e.g. Solow, 1990), but mostly forgotten or ignored by others. As Jill Rubery articulated in the preface to her well-known international textbook:

> We take labour markets to be social constructs, shaped and influenced by institutions and by social actors. Comparison of labour markets among nation states, where the institutional arrangements, the social conditions, the forms of economic organisation and the role and attitudes of social actors all vary, provides a very rich field for developing these concepts and alerting students to the variety of ways in which employment can be and is organised. (2003: xvii)

This approach rejects the universalist theorising common to neoclassical economics, as well as some strands of Marxist theories from the USA. Instead it incorporates into the analysis both the systemic forces for change that are characteristic of advanced capitalist development (such as financialisation, digitalisation, migration, liberalisation and internationalisation) and the potentially diverse 'societal effects' associated with institutionalised labour markets and the surrounding nexus of product market, innovation, corporate governance, industrial relations and welfare state arrangements (see Phil Almond's contribution, Chapter 3, in this volume for a detailed theoretical discussion). This approach does not mean we ought to rule out the possibility of future convergence say around an Anglo-American model of employment. Rather, it cautions against applying *universalist theorising* about processes of labour market segmentation and inequalities (Almond and Rubery, 2000). A comparative institutionalist approach has been especially valuable recently in knocking down neoclassical economics claims about the inefficiencies of regulated labour markets – including, for example, new ideas about 'regulatory indeterminacy' (Deakin and Sarwar, 2008;

Lee and McCann, 2014) – and confronting universal policy prescriptions of the sort associated with Troika interventions seeking to dismantle collective bargaining and cut minimum wages (Koukiadaki *et al.*, 2016; Marginson, 2014; and Karamessini and Grimshaw, Chapter 17 in this volume). But the onward, international assault by neoliberal ideas and practices means important questions remain about the balance of societal and global systemic factors in driving change in labour market segmentation and the resilience of countries to retain societal norms and rules governing inequalities. In her state-of-the-art labour market segmentation analysis of challenges facing Italy today, Annamaria Simonazzi (in Chapter 14) demonstrates the futility of applying stylised mainstream economics ideas of dualism and over-regulation to Italy's problems of low productivity and inequality – as she puts it: 'No degree of labour flexibility can provide an adequate response to the multiple challenges represented by technological, organisational and social changes.' Instead, Simonazzi argues for a new coordinated response designed around a long-term industrial strategy, joint regulation among employers and trade unions, and the recognition that good social policy can be a productive factor (see also Rubery *et al.*, 2003a).

An important insight from the comparative institutionalist tradition for our study of inequalities is therefore the need to widen the scope of enquiry beyond the narrow frame of supply, demand and price (labour economics) and beyond those social actors usually assumed to directly regulate the employment relationship (industrial relations). This wider lens encompasses the rules and norms underpinning education and training systems, welfare state and social protection systems, gender relations, family and household organisation, industrial relations, workplace behaviours and organisational cultures, corporate governance and innovation systems. Comparative research traces fundamental claims regarding a raft of two-way interlinkages with work and employment inequalities, including for example that:

- variation in social protection standards and gaps alters the meaning, experience and regulation of low-wage and precarious employment across countries and workforce groups (Esping-Andersen, 1999; Grimshaw *et al.*, 2016);
- shareholder value rules generate stronger pressures on companies towards high executive pay, use of temporary contracts and cost competitive subcontracting than found under stakeholder rules of corporate governance (Gospel and Pendleton, 2014; Lazonick, 2014);
- family and welfare policies shape household composition and members' attachments to paid employment with direct consequences for inequalities of socio-economic class and income (Esping-Andersen and Myles, 2009; Shildrick *et al.*, 2012);

- countries with more inclusive labour market institutions and more soli-daristic trade union strategies have a lower incidence of precarious work (Doellgast *et al.* 2018);
- varied success across countries in sustaining high-innovation performance via high-quality jobs relates in part to the degree of fair treatment, job secu-rity and 'discretionary learning' in employment (Holm and Lorenz, 2015);
- more centralised and coordinated wage bargaining on the whole reduces wage inequality, the gender wage gap and the incidence of low-wage employment (Hayter, 2015; Rubery *et al.*, 2005);
- concern for inequalities among workers needs to be complemented by attention to what is happening to the share of aggregate income earned by labour relative to capital at national and global levels (Appelbaum and Batt, 2014);
- education and training systems display a mutual dynamic with the path dependent evolution of production models and job structures, whether generating the 'redundant capacities' of Germany's diversified quality pro-duction or the polarised skills and 'hollowing out' of jobs in the USA (Dwyer and Olin Wright, 2012; Streeck,1991);
- and the feminisation of many areas of non-standard forms of employ-ment, such as zero-hours contracts, mini jobs and *'paato'* jobs (low-wage part-timers in Japan), coincides with a lowering of employment standards reflecting gender-unequal assumptions about employers' use of women as a reserve army of labour (Keizer, 2008; Rubery, 2014).

This wider constellation of institutional interlinkages with work and employ-ment inequalities undoubtedly generates a complex framework for analysis. However, the added complexity is essential for incorporating the range of pres-sures on the employment relationship that help us explain real-world changes, and identify the multiple options available to social actors. The inherent conflict of interests between labour and capital goes some way to explaining distribu-tive outcomes, but this wider comparative institutionalist focus is essential to encapsulate the varied pressures, levers and conditions faced in different soci-etal contexts, with their (still) distinctive forms of inter-capitalist competition, welfare states and gender relations, as well as differential structures and power resources of the major social actors.

When combined, the insights from the three theoretical traditions reviewed above provide a promising foundation for a new labour market segmentation approach that is capable of both identifying the changing character of inequal-ities in work and employment and investigating their associated causes and consequences. From this foundation, we derive six propositions listed below and elaborated in the following six sections of this chapter. The purpose of each section is to review the relevant literature, especially the contributions of Jill Rubery, and to relate the particular proposition to the arguments and evidence set out in the relevant chapters of this volume. The chapters were carefully selected to reflect contemporary thinking and new findings around each of the six propositions, but we have not sought to categorise chapters rigidly around propositions because the propositions are interlinked and overlapping. Instead, the chapters are organised into three parts of the book, loosely described as addressing conceptual issues (Part I), international evidence (Part II) and convergence/divergence (Part III). The six propositions are as follows:

1) Employers are major architects in the shaping of inequalities.
2) Participative standards, especially those exercised by trade unions, are an essential bulwark against employer (and state) power.
3) Households and welfare systems affect women's and men's attachment to, and participation in, work, the quality of employment and the gendered distribution of resources.
4) Employment and social protection regulations can protect against growing dualism in labour markets and precarious employment but it is a question of appropriate design.
5) Undervaluation of feminised occupations undermines women's wage prospects.
6) An intersectional approach reveals the causes and consequences of inequalities between and within different social categories.

Employers as architects of inequalities

While the role of employing organisations as key actors shaping employment outcomes has been underplayed in much of economics, political science and policy literature, it is a core plank of a labour market segmentation approach to understanding inequalities. Markets, legal and joint regulation and other institutions may place boundaries on their actions, but it is the employer who enjoys ultimate power in determining who they hire for what jobs and under what conditions.

Also, where women make inroads into male-dominated occupations, such as solicitors for example, employers may respond by gradually adapting work organisation in ways that enhance managerial control and limit worker autonomy (Tomlinson et al., 2013).

Early segmentation theories of the 1970s were important at the time for placing employing organisations at the centre of labour market analysis. Jill Rubery

(1978; 1994; 2007; Rubery and Wilkinson, 1994) developed and extended this framework in a way that advanced our understanding of not only how bad jobs are filled, but also, crucially, how bad jobs are constructed. While dualist theorists (Doeringer and Piore, 1971) explained segmentation mostly through the technical features of the production process and the strategic importance for the firm of the skills they required, Rubery noted the more complex interactions between demand and supply side segmentation. In particular, employers' decisions about the type of jobs they offer and the labour market segment where they are placed are not independent from the characteristics of the labour force they target (Rubery, 2007). For example, in companies, industries or occupations where workers are organised into powerful unions, employers are more likely to offer good jobs. In turn, where workers are more vulnerable, lacking voice and without alternative job opportunities, employers may decide to offer jobs of poorer quality and lower pay irrespective of workers' skills or productivity (Rubery, 1978). Feminised jobs, for example, are often located in secondary labour markets not because they do not require skills or commitment from workers, but because it is easy for employers to recruit women at low pay to do these jobs (Craig et al., 1985). Also, where women make inroads into male-dominated occupations, such as solicitors for example, employers may respond by gradually adapting work organisation in ways that enhance managerial control and limit worker autonomy (Tomlinson et al., 2013).

This conceptualisation of segmentation provides a more holistic framework for labour market analysis that considers the dynamic interactions of the demand and supply sides, integrating inter-capital relations and capital–labour struggles, as well as the role of gender and societal institutions in shaping employment outcomes for different groups of workers, without exonerating employers from their responsibility for employment outcomes. In doing so, this approach enables new understandings about how labour market inequalities are created and recreated especially when labour market change increases opportunities for employers to take advantage of low-cost labour. Chapter 9 by Agniescka Piasna, Brendan Burchell, Kirsten Sehnbruch and Nurjk Agloni draws attention to the key role which employers exercise in determining objective job quality, through deploying a road safety metaphor which differentiates between the characteristics and subjectivities of workers (drivers), the job design (vehicles) and the societal environment that employers operate in – namely, the legal framework (traffic laws) and welfare policy (road traffic safety and infrastructure). Chapter 10 by Alan Felstead and Francis Green examines trends in working-time and work intensity, both of which are central to the concept of job quality. They demonstrate that while working hours have declined for some segments of the workforce, for example, through the expansion of part-time work, employers have gained from the intensification of work effort while workers contend with the negative impact on their health and well-being.

In addition, as the chapter on Spain (Chapter 7) by Josep Banyuls and Albert Recio shows, Rubery's conceptualisation of labour market segmentation provides a useful lens to analyse the particular patterns of segmentation in specific national contexts. Challenging the conventional interpretation of the high levels of unemployment and labour market segmentation in Spain as resulting from excessively protective employment legislation and collective bargaining, Banyuls and Recio provide a compelling alternative argument based on evidence from several industries. In their perspective, these divisions result from the specific features of the Spanish productive system and employer strategies, which have been increasingly facilitated by legal changes that have in turn contributed to the growth of precarious employment. They discuss the highly intricate patterns of segmentation in Spain that result in inequities between those working in large and small firms, between permanent and temporary workers and between full-time and part-time workers. They show how temporary and part-time employment is used not only as an adjustment mechanism, but also as a way of reducing labour costs and in some cases intensifying effort.

The role of the employer in shaping inequalities is further complicated by the intersection with changing industrial organisation. Since the 1990s, this has been especially associated with the deverticalisation of the large firm, inter-firm contracting and the emergence of the networked organisation (Sturgeon, 2002). The employment implications of this changed employer role was the object of pioneering research by Rubery as part of a Manchester team led by Mick Marchington (Marchington *et al.*, 2005a; Rubery *et al.*, 2003b). This major project, based on extensive qualitative case studies in the UK, was among the first to shed light on how networks of organisations linked together through outsourcing, franchising, temporary agency work and public–private partnerships were changing the nature of employment relationships and the organisation of work. The research revealed that intensified and increasingly complex inter-organisational relations are associated with the fragmentation of work and the blurring of organisational boundaries. These processes diffuse employer accountability along the subcontracting chain and confuse power and trust relations between employers, employees and the self-employed (often in a state of 'false' self-employment). Moreover, opportunities and mechanisms for collective worker voice are frustrated, so that there are fewer possibilities to contest or resist new inequalities and tensions among workers employed in interconnected organisations. As Banyuls and Recio argue in Chapter 7, many employers use subcontracting to evade labour standards set by collective agreements (see Chapter 5 by Mick Marchington and Tony Dundon). The upbeat rhetoric of much of the management and innovation discourse on the networked organisation obscures tensions and risks for workers in terms of fair treatment and voice, as well as for employers who may want to reduce labour costs but still need to maintain workers' cooperation and organisational performance.

Chapter 4 by Rosemary Batt and Eileen Appelbaum reviews these issues and their significance in light of both the original work published by Rubery and her Manchester colleagues and subsequent research in the USA and Europe. Batt and Appelbaum discuss the problems of an employment policy framework that everywhere is based on the assumption of a standard employment relationship and equality rights which are bounded by an individual employer. The authors emphasise the need to rethink labour market regulation to account for the more complex organisational structures and subcontracting relations so that policy and practice can better ensure fair pay, conditions and voice for all workers. In addition, new approaches to accountability across domestic and global supply chain networks are needed to assign responsibility for poor labour standards (Barrientos et al., 2011; Wright and Brown, 2013), or to avoid placing it on the weakest parties in networks which are often under price pressures and control of dominant firms.

Participative standards as a bulwark

The second proposition is that more robust participative standards – defined as statutory support for collective representation at workplace and/or industry levels (Sengenberger, 1994) – are an essential bulwark against greater employer and (in many countries) state power. The need to promote voice and transparency has become particularly important in the context of widening protective gaps facing workers in both standard and non-standard forms of employment, fragmented production networks and, in some countries, the declining power resources of trade unions to enforce rights and ensure workers are protected against unfair treatment (Doellgast et al., 2018; Marchington et al., 2005b; Rubery, 2015). These themes are explored in the chapters by Gerhard Bosch and Steffen Lehndorff (Chapter 2), Mick Marchington and Tony Dundon (Chapter 5) and Maria Karamessini and Damian Grimshaw (Chapter 17).

Bosch and Lehndorff compare trends in national systems of wage determination in several European countries to argue that a combination of participatory rights and statutory minimum standards is essential for reducing employment inequalities. Examining recent developments, the authors show that where participatory rights are well-established, such as in Sweden and Germany, protective institutions are far less vulnerable to pro-cyclical economic pressures or to the withdrawal of state support. In turn, where participatory rights are less well embedded and the state withdraws support for collective bargaining, such as in Greece during the post-2008 recession, protective labour market institutions can be easily dismantled. For this reason, Bosch and Lehndorff argue that a more inclusive regulatory framework needs to be anchored not only to statutory protections and minimum standards but also to strong participatory rights and discuss the scope for national actors to move towards these goals under the new European economic governance framework.

Marchington and Dundon discuss the societal forces for 'fair voice' and the challenges workers face in liberal market economies (LMEs) such as the UK, Ireland, Australia and New Zealand. Due to the weaker legal underpinning of worker voice they discuss the greater tendency in LMEs for these mechanisms to be shaped mostly by 'softer' institutional forces and managerial prerogative compared to coordinated market economies (CMEs) in continental Europe. Under these conditions, where they are not well embedded with other human resource management practices all forms of voice in LMEs are more susceptible to pressures from adverse changes in the economic and political context and are seldom perceived as fair by employees or unions. These problems are exacerbated in the case of workers employed across organisational boundaries who enjoy less voice than their in-house counterparts. The authors discuss the limited prospects of these challenges being addressed by better forms of regulation in LMEs, particularly in a post-Brexit world.

Karamessini and Grimshaw argue that disengagement with participative processes of social dialogue has been a notable feature of recent minimum wage reforms in Greece and the UK. In Greece, the government actively dismantled collective bargaining institutions under pressures from international credit bodies represented by the Troika and replaced a long-standing tripartite process of minimum wage-fixing with unilateral statutory intervention, characterised by a vicious 22 per cent cut in 2012 and subsequent freeze. Post-2016 reforms under the Tsipras government promise to reassert tripartite autonomy in minimum wage-fixing in response to evidence that plummeting real wages have done nothing to reverse a crisis in falling levels of gross domestic product (GDP) per capita. In the UK, the minimum wage-fixing process has since its inception only had a weak element of tripartite decision-making, represented in the composition of members of the independent Low Pay Commission, the body that fixes the minimum wage each year. However, from 2016 this element of tripartism was questioned when the government changed its approach and announced a new unilateral approach to fixing an adult 'premium rate', reducing tripartite influence to workers aged under 25 years old only. The risk is that the minimum wage becomes further isolated from other wage-setting procedures in the economy, diminishing the prospects to address problems of wage inequality through social dialogue.

These tendencies of changing modes of state intervention, shaped by contradictory progressive and regressive political tendencies and shifting economic conditions and social tensions, are interpreted very well in Chapter 15 by our Manchester colleague Miguel Martinez Lucio. He argues there is a need for more careful and detailed analysis of the real-world shifts in labour market regulations and forms of social dialogue in order to clearly document the fact that state interventions are rarely straightforward and instead demand greater sensitivity to the historical and societal specific factors shaping the complex role of the state in labour markets.

Households, welfare regimes and inequalities effects

The third proposition concerns the interconnections between employment and the welfare system and the implications for work and employment inequalities, especially gender inequalities. Early theoretical work by Jane Humphries and Jill Rubery (1984) on the 'relative autonomy' of social reproduction (involving long-term transformations in the organisation of family and welfare models) was crucial in articulating its role in shaping labour market organisation and the rise of female employment. Even more critically, it followed that as women's employment had become a permanent feature of social and economic organisation, so too the sphere of social reproduction had to become a central feature of labour market analysis and employment studies.

The comparative institutionalist approach described above incorporates welfare state and gender regimes literature (e.g. Duncan and Pfau-Effinger, 2012; Esping-Andersen, 1990; Lewis, 1992) in order to understand the mutual interactions of employment, welfare and family systems as 'interlocking institutional and social arrangements which together determine the social and economic organisation in a particular society' (Rubery et al., 2001: 45). Rubery has used this lens to conduct extensive comparative research on gender and employment, which has contributed to wider knowledge of societal variations in levels and patterns of gender inequality especially concerning norms regarding gender roles and the division of domestic labour and paid employment (Rubery et al., 1999). Indeed, the programme of research into women's relative position in employment coordinated by Jill Rubery from 1992 to 2003 for the European Commission arguably developed the methodological framework of institutionalist analysis from its infancy into what is now the established starting point for comparative analysis of gender inequalities and gender regimes. This work included, for example, the first systematic comparison of gender segregated employment in Europe that used case studies to illuminate processes of exclusion and inclusion among occupations and industries otherwise not captured by summary index measures of sex segregation (Rubery and Fagan, 1995).

In light of evidence of the changing heterogeneity of men's and women's life courses, research has also analysed key life stages when welfare support is particularly needed in addition to, or instead of, employment and the family, including the transition from education to employment, surviving interruptions in employment in prime age due to parenthood, sickness or unemployment, and withdrawing from employment into retirement (Anxo et al., 2010; Crompton, 2006; Stier et al., 2001). Social protection systems play a key role in ameliorating or exacerbating work and employment inequalities through inclusive or exclusive models of eligibility. Social protection rules differ among countries and may explicitly discriminate by employment status (standard versus non-standard employment forms, for example) and employment continuity (biased against women, youth and temporary workers) (Grimshaw et al., 2016). Moreover, there are potentially complementary and contradictory interlinkages between social protection systems and employment organisation since inclusive social protection relies on high quantities of employment organised around decent standards in order to provide the fiscal base to fund the welfare state. The quality of employment matters, because when employment fails to provide an adequate income level and/or security, individuals must rely on support from the state or from their family to whom employers are effectively passing on the costs of providing a living wage; as such, exclusive labour markets inhibit the development of inclusive social protection systems (Rubery, 2015). Inclusive labour markets thus go hand in hand with inclusive welfare systems and these in turn need to be supported by employment regulations that promote responsible pay and employment practices.

These empirical and theoretical contributions are reflected in four chapters in this volume. In Chapter 11, Jane Humphries reveals the salience of a framework which integrates the relative autonomy of the household through her historical analysis of women's employment during the English plague. Humphries demonstrates the weaknesses of accounts of the economic implications of the Black Death because they either assert the absolute autonomy of the family system or emphasise its collapse to servicing the needs of the economy. A more nuanced analysis of the inter-relationship between family, economy and the state reveals a more satisfactory explanation of the agency of women and their families. In Chapter 16, Dominique Anxo, Marian Baird and Christine Erhel compare how care regimes interact with employment regimes to influence female employment outcomes across the life course in Sweden, France and Australia. They show that social context also matters, especially attitudes towards motherhood and women's increasing education qualifications in all three countries, as well as persistent norms of female caregiving. Fang Lee Cooke, in Chapter 12, questions the anticipated positive impact of the ending of the one-child policy in China by focusing on its implications for employment opportunities of female university graduates. Cooke argues that a lack of welfare state support for childcare combined with the two-child policy will exacerbate the discriminatory responses of employers towards mothers. Employers will be less likely to hire female graduates who are yet to have children and this will push more women into self-employment with limited protection and wages. Furthermore, it entrenches a model of privatised family support for childcare relying upon gendered caring roles, leaving older female grandparents with limited financial support. Cooke's analysis thus demonstrates the interconnections between employment and welfare systems, as well as the importance of bringing the employer back into the analysis of inequality.

In Chapter 13, Jacqueline O'Reilly, Mark Smith and Paola Villa elaborate the concept of the 'relative autonomy of social reproduction' (Humphries and Rubery, 1984) to explore the labour market prospects of young workers, the influence of employment status and family arrangements of their parental households and intersections with gender and ethnicity. By applying the conceptual frameworks developed by Rubery in new ways, to new problems and in different societal contexts, these chapters offer novel insights into how different welfare and family systems interact with employment organisation and support our proposition that these interactions produce varied patterns of segmentation and inequalities.

Employment and social protection regulations against dualism and precarity

While recognising that current employment regulation is failing to protect an increasing segment of workers in a myriad of precarious employment arrangements, some important studies are challenging arguments that claim strengthened regulations necessarily reinforce within-workforce inequalities and labour market dualism (Allen *et al.*, 2016; Crouch, 2015; Dieckhoff *et al.*, 2015; Rubery, 2011, 2015). Recent calls from the European Commission to reduce the supposed over-protection of workers in standard employment (or 'insiders') in relation to those in non-standard arrangements ('outsiders') have led to measures in several European countries that disproportionally harm workers in non-standard forms of employment through freezes and cuts to the minimum wage, relaxation of rules governing use of temporary work and the erosion of collective bargaining arrangements (ETUI, 2014; Koukiadaki *et al.,* 2016; Karamessini and Grimshaw, Chapter 17 in this volume; Piasna and Myant, 2017; Rubery, 2015; van Gyes and Schulten, 2015). In several cases, such reforms were implemented at the beginning of the 2008–09 economic crisis with the consequence, in the case of Spain for example, of a far higher destruction of jobs in response to falling GDP than would otherwise have been the case (Muñoz de Bustillo and Antón, 2015). For Rubery (2015), the problem is not the existence of employment regulations but their design, which places certain groups of workers at risk of exclusion. As such, policy reforms should be in the opposite direction to those advanced by new dualist thinking. Inclusive labour markets require the extension of the protections, voice and rights associated with standard employment relationships to all workers irrespective of specific work arrangements. In addition, better forms of regulation need to increase the responsibilities of employers for providing sufficient decent jobs.

As the analysis by Josep Banyuls and Albert Recio in Chapter 7 illustrates, in Spain, as in many countries, non-standard and flexible working arrangements are often presented as favourable to workers, especially women, through improved opportunities for work–life reconciliation. Yet in practice they are often designed to meet employers' flexibility needs, rather than those of employees, and associated with the most precarious conditions, with the most irregular schedules often involving unsocial hours (see also Fleetwood, 2007). In the context of an ageing population and high levels of employment of women, inclusive labour markets require employers to find ways of reconciling their business needs for flexibility with those of workers in a way that improves access to good quality employment of mothers and carers, older workers and those with disabilities. Otherwise, the risk is that societies are exposed to employer-oriented flexibility, which as Iain Campbell (Chapter 6) argues, risks a proliferation of 'fragmented time systems' that feature digital monitoring of minutes worked, minimisation of on-the-job periods of inactivity (such as paid breaks or travel time between activities), and redrawing of temporal boundaries between social and unsocial hours and between work and family life. It is precisely these issues which are at stake in debates about how to regulate new forms of worker status associated with technology platform firms such as Hermes, Deliveroo and Uber. High-tech firms seem to have developed a 'winner takes all' business model with enormous shareholder dividends paid for by denying basic employment rights to an on-call workforce (Newsome *et al.*, 2016). Chapter 8 by Francesca Bettio and Alberto Mazzon asks whether service vouchers in Italy herald a radical departure from a standard employment model towards a highly commodified, task and time-centred series of spot-market transactions for work. In fact, they find that the volume of use remained low and, therefore, while there is no evidence of substitution of standard employment, there is a possible case for vouchers having regularised some forms of informal paid work activities that supplement household income.

Undervalued, feminised work and women's pay and employment prospects

Many jobs traditionally carried out by women are undervalued. What this means is that employers (and society) can claim a higher quality of female labour for a given wage (Grimshaw and Rubery, 2007; Warren *et al.*, 2010). It also means that women's wage and employment prospects are significantly impaired and this produces an over-representation of women among low-paid employment in all countries for which we have reliable earnings data. The conclusion of many years of feminist socio-economics research is that this universal outcome is not an efficient allocation driven by competitive market forces, but a clear expression of labour market failure. The institutional factors shaping undervaluation are multiple and complex, in part relating to employer practices, cost-led subcontracting, working-time policies and practices, and welfare and family policy regimes (discussed above). Here we examine the organisational factors that play out in one area of feminised employment, namely care work.

   Care work is probably the area of employment where most theoretical and empirical research has been undertaken with a view to understanding the causes of undervaluation of women's work. Care work is emblematic of the market failure to balance pay with the value of women's work. Feminist economists have directly challenged the related neoclassical economics theory of compensating differentials, which takes for granted that the intrinsic rewards of the job compensate in part for the low wages on offer (see England *et al.*, 2002; Folbre, 2012). Of particular interest to our formulation of ideas here is Rubery and colleagues' (2011; 2015) focus on a set of organisational and institutional factors that perpetuate the low-paid and low-quality nature of this work. In an extensive study of care work, Jill Rubery and several Manchester colleagues investigated undervaluation using a novel analytical framework that incorporated data on fragmented subcontracting practices, triangular employment relations (between clients, subcontractors and care workers), cost-focused human resource management practices, weak employment regulations (especially concerning zero-hours contracts), largely absent trade unions and public spending restrictions. This wide analytical lens is important since it shifts the analysis of women's undervalued and low-paid work into a wider critique about how the blurring of organisational and work–life boundaries alongside weak collective representation creates ambiguities around the employment relationship. These ambiguities perpetuate low-quality jobs, make worker resistance more difficult, and seemingly diminish the capacity and/or willingness of employers (or clients) to address the problems of undervaluation.

The research on care work also confronts stylised assumptions that low-paid, feminised work can be presented as a trade-off with family friendly employment practices, such as enhanced work–life balance for example. Rubery and colleagues (2015) reveal how subcontracting arrangements generate such extreme patterns of fragmented working time in the UK context that it is rare to find care workers benefiting from working hours that might be construed as family friendly. Overall, this wider framing of gender issues shows that improving the value attached to care work requires reform and actions on many fronts including developing and enforcing employment rights, especially working-time rules (e.g. a new right to minimum hours, as found for example in France) and a higher statutory minimum wage, as well as subcontracting rules that incorporate social value clauses to force subcontractors to pay higher wages, pay for all working time not only so-called productive time, provide effective training and make family-friendly schedules available to all. This wider agenda is essential to tackle the undervaluation of women's work in terms of its low pay and low job quality generally.

Intersectionality

The sixth and final proposition argues that an intersectional approach is necessary to reveal the causes and consequences of multiple intersections of inequalities. For example, a new labour market segmentation approach to the analysis of gender inequalities must incorporate an analysis of class, as well as age, ethnicity and other variables. Interrogation of the multiple intersections shaping gender inequalities reveals the processes through which gender inequalities are perpetuated or softened at different rates and via different processes for different groups of women. As McBride and colleagues (2015) argue, an 'intersectional sensitivity' must recognise how multiple dimensions of inequalities can shape workers' experiences and opportunities. This approach brings intra-group differences within social categories to the fore and problematises the notion of 'the' female experience and 'the' male experience. Significantly, it involves the analysis of intersections of inequalities that goes beyond an additive approach that assumes multiple experiences of different dimensions of inequalities simply create more, multiple disadvantage (Woodhams et al., 2015). Rather, it explores how the nature of inequalities may be reconstructed into something different at the point of the intersection. An ongoing debate is whether and how to theorise this in ways that recognise that the original inequalities do not become something totally different (Walby, 2012: 235).

An intersectional approach has implicitly provided the backdrop to much of Rubery and colleagues' analysis of gender inequality. It is reflected in the prioritising of the minimum wage as a key mechanism of gender equality, thereby identifying the need for a targeted policy approach towards women in low-wage jobs (Rubery and Grimshaw, 2011), and also in research on care work that shows how educational and family backgrounds shape women's acceptance of many of the poor-quality aspects of low-status jobs (Hebson *et al.*, 2015). The implications of these and other studies (e.g. Brown *et al.*, 2012; Duffy, 2005; Macdonald and Merrill, 2008) are far-reaching. Use of an intersectional lens to theorise how class and gender shape women's working orientations in low-paid work immediately breaks down some of the stylised assumptions (particularly in the economics literature) that women are often satisfied with low pay. Gender relations in society provide a partial explanation, but class also shapes low-wage, female workers' subjective evaluations of their job and how they make sense of their working lives. With a combined understanding of the gendered and class-based processes of work, research can offer a clearer explanation of gendered disadvantage that situates workers' employment experiences in the social and economic context that shapes their opportunities, judgements and norms. Research on ethnic inequalities in employment (Duffy, 2005) further supports the value of an intersectional analysis for our understanding of gender inequality and the need to capture the complexity of disadvantage and inequalities for many feminised groups of workers.

An intersectional approach thus recognises multiple sources of disadvantage and the reconstitution of multi-layered inequalities (Walby, 2012). Several contributions in this volume highlight this potential. For example, by examining social and labour market policies in France, Sweden and Australia, Dominique Anxo, Marian Baird and Christine Erhel (Chapter 16) show that family policy in France exacerbates class inequality between women by encouraging low-qualified and low-paid women with two or more children to stop working or take part-time work through the parental leave programme. The analysis of job segmentation in Chapter 13 by Jacqueline O'Reilly, Mark Smith and Paola Villa also presents a fascinating application of labour market segmentation theory in a manner that captures intersectionality among youth. They develop an account of youth inequality that differentiates between gender, parental households and ethnicity in order to identify new lines of labour market segmentation among young people. They show how segmentation theory is a powerful tool both to interrogate intersectional inequalities and, crucially, to provide robust evidence in support of targeted employment and social policies for youth that can address these specific inequalities. These contributions to the book underline the

value of a new labour market segmentation approach as it provides the tools to
explore and challenge new mechanisms and dimensions of inequalities at work.

Conclusions

In developing a multi-dimensional analytical framework this introductory
chapter aimed to contribute to ongoing debates about the nature of work
and employment inequalities and how to address them. Other contemporary
accounts of inequalities, dualism and precariousness in employment sometimes
provide only a partial analysis and risk generating simplistic and/or inappropri-
ate prescriptions for policy and practice. The new labour market segmentation
approach is distinctive in seeking to place the changing international patterns and
experiences of labour market inequalities in the wider context of shifting gender
relations, regulatory regimes and production structures. This volume as a whole
reflects on contemporary debates and points to various challenges concerned
with future work and labour market agendas. We conclude here by drawing
out three key contributions to academic, policy and practitioner debates that
emerge from the chapters in this book.

The first is one that was always central to Jill Rubery's intellectual focus,
namely the need to bring employers back into academic and employment policy
debates about why labour markets fail in both their allocative and their distributive functions. Aside from the occasional naming and shaming of rogue employers, employers hardly appear in employment policy debates – in shaping the
number of good and bad jobs in the economy, in holding down women's pay
and careers relative to men, in refusing to play by the rules, in pushing workers into precarious false self-employment, or in failing to redesign jobs to serve
higher value-added markets. Moreover, in cutting costs by tapping into global
value chains (through offshoring for example), or in meeting shareholder (or
private equity) claims on profits, research shows that organisations risk destabilising necessary labour investments (Goergen et al., 2014; Lazonick, 2014).
Paradoxically, the push to deregulate labour market institutions in many countries ought to have raised the profile of individual employers, but instead the
policy narrative all too often rests on a notion of atomised, competitive markets
in which organisations and individuals are assumed to respond to push-and-pull
factors mostly tied up with market prices.

Secondly, the chapters contribute to our understanding of the gendered
character of work and of the principal social actors – management, unions
and the state. Gender relations permeate all the big job quality issues such as
pay, progression, job security, representation, dignity and working time. While

research has considerably advanced our knowledge of the patterning of gender inequalities, our knowledge of gendered processes is still lacking. The book adds further insight into the forms of gender bias shaping employer practices and experiences of 'fairness at work', the gender impacts of employment and welfare policy reforms, and the way the labour of social reproduction (caring for children and older people) shapes the gendered nature of jobs and the organisation of the labour market. Furthermore, building on ideas of intersectionality, several chapters explore problems of inequality among women and among men – including vulnerabilities associated with youth and ethnicity.

Thirdly, all chapters are united in developing the case for long-term, interventionist actions for promoting and sustaining productive, dignified and decent work. There is growing interest in developed and developing countries in how to respond to multiple challenges confronting the world of work today. These challenges include labour market reforms that are reducing the security of employment relations in the public, private and informal sectors; the polarising effects of many new technologies on occupational differences in job quality; complex and uncertain effects of reforms to welfare and citizenship rights when assessed for their impact by gender, ethnicity, sexuality, disability, age and generation on current circumstances and life course prospects; new forms of conflict, harassment, discrimination and unfair practices in the workplace, especially towards vulnerable workers; and new insecurities and inequalities caused by the fragile positioning of many businesses in global value chains, particularly those in less developed countries. The chapters shed new light on possible courses of action and highlight the need for both a multi-level approach (national, sector, supply chain, organisation and workplace/job levels) and a multi-stakeholder approach that embraces narrow and wide forms of social dialogue and social solidarity (trade unions, pan-national governance structures, civil society organisations and enforcement bodies among others).

We designed this volume as a tribute to Jill Rubery's highly influential theoretical and empirical contributions to our understanding of inequalities. With the proposed architecture for a new labour market segmentation approach we hope this volume inspires further multi-dimensional research and new policy approaches towards the ever-changing patterns of inequalities in work and employment in countries around the world.

Notes

1   For a comprehensive review of this early period, including its roots in rich case studies of the predominantly black urban poor in the USA, see Rosenberg (1989).

2 Neoclassical explanations include those related to mothers' depreciated human capital, reduced commitment to paid employment and employment concentration in less-
   productive jobs – ostensibly involving a trade-off for family-friendly working hours (see
   the review in Grimshaw and Rubery, 2015).

References

Abu Sharkh, M. and Gough, I. (2010), 'Global welfare regimes: a cluster analysis, *Global Social Policy*, 10:1, 27–58.

Allen, M. M., Liu, J., Allen, M. L. and Saqib, S. I. (2016), 'Establishments' use of tem-porary agency workers: the influence of institutions and establishments' employment strategies', *The International Journal of Human Resource Management*, http://dx.doi.org/10.1080/09585192.2016.1172655.

Almond, P. and Rubery, J. (2000), 'Deregulation and societal systems', in Maurice, M. and Sorge, A. (eds), *Embedding Organizations* (Amsterdam: John Benjamins Publishing Company).

Anxo, D., Bosch, G. and Rubery, J. (2010), 'Shaping the life course: a European perspec-tive', in Anxo, D., Bosch, G. and Rubery, J. (eds), *The Welfare State and Life Transitions: A European Perspective* (Cheltenham: Edward Elgar).

Anxo, D., Fagan, C., Cebrian, I. and Moreno, G. (2007), 'Patterns of labour market inte-gration in Europe: a life course perspective on time policies', *Socio-Economic Review*, 5:2, 233–60.

Barrientos, S., Gereffi, G. and Rossi, A. (2011). 'Economic and social upgrading in global production networks: A new paradigm for a changing world', *International Labour Review*, 150:3–4, 319–40.

Appelbaum, E. and Batt, R. (2014), *Private Equity at Work: When Wall Street Manages Main Street* (New York: Russell Sage Foundation).

Beneria, L. (2007), *The Crisis of Care, International Migration and the Capabilities Approach: Implications for Policy* (Mario Einaudi Center for International Studies: Ithaca, NY: Cornell University).

Berg, J. (ed.) (2015), *Labour Markets, Institutions and Inequality: Building Just Societies in the 21st Century* (Cheltenham: Edward Elgar and Geneva: International Labour Organization).

Bettio, F., Plantenga, J. and Smith, M. (eds) (2013), *Gender and the European Labour Market* (London: Routledge).

Beynon, H., Grimshaw, D., Rubery, D. and Ward, K. (2002), *Managing Employment Change: The New Realities of Work* (Oxford: Oxford University Press).

Brown, A., Charlwood, A. and Spencer, D. (2012), 'Not all that it might seem: why job satisfaction is worth studying despite it being a poor measure of job quality', *Work, Employment and Society*, 26:6, 1017–18.

Cairnes, J. E. (1874), *Some Leading Principles of Political Economy* (London: Macmillan).

Cohn, S. (1995), *The Process of Sex Typing* (Philadelphia: Temple University Press).

Cooke, F. L. and Xiao, Y. C. (2014), 'Gender roles and organisational HR practices: the case of women's careers in accountancy and consultancy firms in China', *Human Resource Management*, 53:1, 23–44.

Craig, C., Garnsey, E. and Rubery J. (1985), 'Labour market segmentation and women's employment: a case study from the United Kingdom', *International Labour Review*, 124:3, 267–80.

Craig, C., Rubery, J., Tarling, R. and Wilkinson, F. (1982), *Labour Market Structure, Industrial Organisation and Low Pay* (Cambridge: Cambridge University Press).

Craypo, C. (2003), 'The decline of union bargaining power in the United States: an "ability to pay, ability to make pay" analysis', in Burchell, B., Deakin, S., Michie, J. and Rubery, J. (eds), *Systems of Production: Markets, Organisations and Performance* (London: Routledge).

Crompton, R. (2006), *Employment and the Family: The Reconfiguration of Work and Family Life in Contemporary Societies* (Cambridge: Cambridge University Press).

Crouch, C. (2015), 'Labour market governance and the creation of outsiders', *British Journal of Industrial Relations*, 53:1, 27–48.

Deakin, S. and Sarwar, P. (2008), 'Assessing the long-run economic impact of labour law systems', *Industrial Relations Journal*, 39:6, 453–87.

Dieckhoff, M., Gash, V. and Steiber, N. (2015), 'Measuring the effect of institutional change on gender inequality in the labour market', *Research in Social Stratification and Mobility*, 39, 59–75.

Doellgast, V., Lillie, N. and V. Pulignano (eds.) (2018), *Reconstructing Solidarity: Labor Unions, Precarious Work and the Politics of Institutional Change in Europe*, Oxford: Oxford University Press, forthcoming.

Doeringer, P. and Piore, M. (1971), *Internal Labour Markets and Manpower Analysis* (Lexington, MA: Heath Lexington Books).

Duffy, M. (2005), 'Reproducing labor inequalities: challenges for feminist conceptualising care at the intersections of gender, race and class', *Gender and Society*, 19:1, 66–82.

Duncan, S. and Pfau-Effinger, B. (2012), *Gender, Economy and Culture in the European Union* (London: Routledge).

Dwyer, R. and Olin Wright, E. (2012), 'Job growth and job polarisation in the United states and Europe, 1995–2007', in Fernandez-Macias, D., Hurley, J. and Storrie, D. (eds), *Transformation of the Employment Structure in the EU and USA* (Palgrave) pp. 52–74.

Edwards, R., Reich, M. and Gordon, D. (1975), *Labor Market Segmentation* (Lexington MA: Heath Lexington Books).

England, P. (2005), 'Gender inequality in the labour market: the role of motherhood and segregation', *Social Politics*, 12:2, 264–88.

England, P., Budig, M. and Folbre, N. (2002), 'Wages of virtue: the relative pay of care work', *Social Problems*, 49:4, 455–73.

Esping-Andersen, G. (1990), *The Three Worlds of Welfare Capitalism* (Cambridge: Polity Press).

Esping-Andersen, G. (1999), *Social Foundations of Postindustrial Economies* (Oxford: Oxford University Press).

Esping-Andersen, G. and Myles, J. (2009), 'Economic inequality and the welfare state', in Salverda, W., Nolan, B. and Smeeding, T. M. (eds), *The Oxford Handbook of Economic Inequality* (Oxford: Oxford University Press).

ETUI (2014), *Benchmarking Working Europe 2014* (Brussels: European Trade Union Institute).

Fagan, C. and Norman, H. (2013), 'Men and gender equality: tackling gender segregation in family roles and in social care jobs', in Bettio, F., Plantenga, J. and Smith, M. (eds), *Gender and the European Labour Market* (London: Routledge).

Figart, D. M., Mutari, E. and Power, M. (2005), *Living Wages, Equal Wages: Gender and Labour Market Policies in the United States* (New York: Routledge).

Fleetwood, S. (2007), 'Why Work-life balance now?', *International Journal of Human Resource Management*, 18:3, 387–400.

Folbre, N. (1994), *Who Pays for the Kids? Gender and the Structures of Constraint* (New York: Taylor & Francis).

Folbre, N. (2012), 'Should women care less? Intrinsic motivation and gender inequality', *Journal of Industrial Relations,* 50:4, 597–619.

Gallie, D. (ed.) (2007), *Employment Regimes and the Quality of Work* (Oxford: Oxford University Press).

Gautié, J. and Schmitt, J. (eds) (2010), *Low-wage Work in the Wealthy World* (New York: Russell Sage Foundation).

Goergen, M., O'Sullivan, N. and Wood, G. (2014), 'The consequences of private equity acquisitions for employees: new evidence on the impact on wages, employment and productivity', *Human Resource Management Journal*, 24:2, 145–58.

Gordon, D., Edwards, R. and Reich, M. (1982), *Segmented Work, Divided Workers: The Historical Transformation of Work in the United States* (Cambridge: Cambridge University Press).

Gospel, H. and Pendleton, A. (2014), 'Financialisation, new investment funds and labour', in Gospel, H., Pendleton, A. and Vitols, S. (eds), *Financialization, New Investment Funds and Labour: An International Comparison* (Oxford: Oxford University Press).

Grimshaw, D. (ed.) (2013), *Minimum Wages, Pay Equity and Comparative Industrial Relations* (London: Routledge).

Grimshaw, D., Johnson, M., Rubery, J. and Keizer, A. (2016), 'Reducing precarious work: protective gaps and the role of social dialogue in Europe' (Report for the European Commission DG Employment) http://www.research.mbs.ac.uk/ewerc/Our-research/Current-projects/.

Grimshaw, D. and Rubery, J. (2005), 'Inter-capital relations and the network organization: redefining the issues concerning work and employment', *Cambridge Journal of Economics*, 29:6, 1027–51.

Grimshaw, D. and Rubery, J. (2007), *Undervaluing Women's Work*, Working Paper Series No. 53 (Manchester: Equal Opportunities Commission).

Grimshaw, D. and Rubery, J. (2015), *The Motherhood Pay Gap: A Review of the Issues, Theory and International Evidence*, Conditions of Work and Employment Series No. 57 (Geneva: International Labour Organization), at p. 82).

Guy, F. (1999), 'Information technology, organization structure and earnings inequality', Working Paper, Birkbeck College, Department of Management.

Hayter, S. (2015), 'Unions and collective bargaining', in Berg, J. (ed.), *Labour Markets, Institutions and Inequality: Building Just Societies in the 21st Century* (Cheltenham: Edward Elgar and Geneva: International Labour Organization).

Hebson, G., Rubery, J. and Grimshaw, D. (2015), 'Rethinking job satisfaction in care work: looking beyond the care debates', *Work, Employment and Society*, 29:2, 314–30.

Holm, J. R., and Lorenz, E. (2015), 'Has "discretionary learning" declined during the Lisbon Agenda? A cross-sectional and longitudinal study of work organization in European nations, *Industrial and Corporate Change*, 24:6, 1179–214.

Humphries, J. (1977), 'The working class family, women's liberation, and class struggle: the case of nineteenth century British history', *Review of Radical Political Economics*, 9:3, 25–41.

Humphries, J., and Rubery, J. (1984), 'The reconstruction of the supply side of the labour market: the relative autonomy of social reproduction', *Cambridge Journal of Economics,* 8:4, 331–46.

Karamessini, M. and Rubery, J. (eds) (2014), *Women and Austerity: The Economic Crisis and the Future for Gender Equality* (London: Routledge).

Keizer, A. (2008), 'Non-regular employment in Japan: continued and renewed dualities', *Work, Employment and Society*, 22:3, 407–25.

Korpi, W., Ferrarini, T. and Englund, S. (2013), 'Women's opportunities under different family policy constellations: gender, class, and inequality tradeoffs in western countries re-examined', *Social Politics: International Studies in Gender, State & Society*, 20:1, 1–40.

Koukiadaki, A., Tavora, I. and Martinez-Lucio, M. (eds) (2016), *Joint Regulation and Labour Market Policy in Europe during the Crisis: A Seven-Country Comparison* (Brussels: European Trade Union Institute).

Lazonick, W. (2014), 'Profits without prosperity', *Harvard Business Review*, 92:9, 46–55.

Leana, C., Appelbaum, E. and Shevchuk, I. (2009), 'Work process and quality of care in early childhood education: the role of job crafting', *Academy of Management Journal*, 52:6, 1169–92.

Lee, S. and Gerecke, M. (2015), 'Economic development and inequality: revisiting the Kuznets curve', in Berg, J. (ed.), *Labour Markets, Institutions and Inequality: Building Just Societies in the 21st Century* (Cheltenham: Edward Elgar and Geneva: International Labour Organization).

Lee, S. and McCann, D. (2014), 'Regulatory indeterminacy and protection in contemporary labour markets: innovation in research and policy', in McCann, D., Lee, S., Belser, P., Fenwick, C., Howe, J. and Luebker, M. (eds), *Creative Labour Regulation: Indeterminacy and Protection in an Uncertain World* (Basingstoke: Palgrave).

Lewis, J. (1992), 'Gender and the development of welfare regimes', *Journal of European social policy,* 2:3, 159–73.

Lewis, J., Campbell, M. and Huerta, C. (2008), 'Patterns of paid and unpaid work in Western Europe', *Journal of European Social Policy*, 18:1, 21–37.

McBride, A., Hebson, G. and Holgate, J. (2015), 'Intersectionality: are we taking enough notice in the field of work and employment relations?', *Work, Employment and Society*, 29:2, 331–41.

Macdonald, C. and Merrill, D. (2008), 'Intersectionality in the emotional proletariat: a new lens on employment discrimination in service work', in Korczynski, M. and Macdonald, C. (eds), *Service Work: Critical Perspectives* (New York: Routledge).

Marchington, M., Grimshaw, D., Rubery, J. and Willmott, H. (eds) (2005a) *Fragmenting Work: Blurring Organizational Boundaries and Disordering Hierarchies* (Oxford: Oxford University Press).

Marchington, M., Rubery, J. and Cooke, F. L. (2005b), 'Prospects for worker voice across organizational boundaries', in Marchington, M., Grimshaw, D., Rubery, J. and Willmott, H. (eds), *Fragmenting Work: Blurring Organizational Boundaries and Disordering Hierarchies* (Oxford: Oxford University Press).

Marino, S., Roosblad, J. and Penninx, R. (eds.) (2018), *Trade Unions, Immigration and Immigrants in Europe in the 21st Century: New Approaches under Changing Conditions* (Cheltenham: Edward Elgar).

Marginson, P. (2014), 'Coordinated bargaining in Europe: from incremental corrosion to frontal assault?', *European Journal of Industrial Relations*, 21:2, 97–114.

Merluzzi, J. and Dobrev, S. D. (2015), 'Unequal on top: gender profiling and the income gap among high earner male and female professionals', *Social Science Research*, 53, 45–58.

Muñoz de Bustillo, R. and Antón, J.-I. (2015), 'Turning back before arriving: the dismantling of the Spanish welfare state', in Vaughan-Whitehead, D. (ed.), *The European Social Model in Crisis: Is Europe Losing Its Soul?* (Cheltenham: Edward Elgar and Geneva: International Labour Organization).

Muñoz de Bustillo, R., Fernández-Macías, E., Antón, J.-I., and Esteve, F. (2011), *Measuring More Than Money: The Social Economics of Job Quality* (Cheltenham: Edward Elgar).

Newsome, K., Moore, S. and Ross, C. (2016), 'Supply chain capitalism: Parcel delivery workers and the degradation of work', *International Labour Process Conference*, Berlin.

Perraudin, C., Petit, H., Thèvenot, N., Tinel, B. and Valentin, J. (2014), 'Inter-firm dependency and employment inequalities: Theoretical hypotheses and empirical tests on French subcontracting relationships', *Review of Radical Political Economics*, 46:2, 199–220.

Pettit, B. and Hook, J. (2009), *Institutionalizing Inequality: Gender, Family, and Economic Inequality in Comparative Perspective* (New York: Russell Sage).

Reskin, B. and Roos, P. (1990), *Job Queues, Gender Queues: Explaining Women's Inroads into Male Occupations* (Philadelphia: Temple University Press).

Rosenberg, S. (1989), 'From segmentation to flexibility', *Labour and Society*, 14:4, 363–407.

Rubery, J. (1978), 'Structured labour markets, worker organization and low pay', *Cambridge Journal of Economics*, 2:1, 17–37.

Rubery, J. (ed.) (1988), *Women and Recession* (London: Routledge and Kegan Paul).

Rubery, J. (1994), 'Internal and external labour markets: towards an integrated analysis', in Rubery, J. and Wilkinson, F. (eds), *Employer Strategy and the Labour Market* (Oxford: Oxford University Press).

Rubery, J. (2003), 'Preface', in Rubery, J. and D. Grimshaw, D., *The Organisation of Employment: An International Perspective* (Basingstoke: Palgrave).

Rubery, J. (2007), 'Developing segmentation theory: a thirty year perspective', *Économies et Sociétés,* 41:6, 941–64.

Rubery, J. (2011), 'Towards a gendering of the labour market regulation debate', *Cambridge Journal of Economics,* 35:6, 1103–26.

Rubery, J. (2014), 'From "women and recession" to "women and austerity": a framework for analysis', in Karamessini, M. and Rubery, J. (eds), *Women and Austerity: The Economic Crisis and the Future for Gender Equality* (London: Routledge).

Rubery, J. (2015), *Re-regulating for Inclusive Labour Markets*, Conditions of Work and Employment Series No. 65 (Geneva: International Labour Office).

Rubery, J., Cooke, F., Earnshaw, J. and Marchington, M. (2003b), 'Inter-organisational relations and employment in a multi-employer environment', *British Journal of Industrial Relations*, 41:2, 1100–222.

Rubery, J. and Fagan, C. (1995), 'Gender segregation in societal context', *Work, Employment and Society*, 9:2, 213–40.

Rubery, J. and Grimshaw, D. (2011), 'Gender and the minimum wage', in Lee, S. and McCann, D. (eds), *Regulating for Decent Work: New Directions in Labour Market Regulation* (Basingstoke: Palgrave).

Rubery, J. and Grimshaw, D. (2015), 'The 40-year pursuit of equal pay: a case of constantly moving goalposts', *Cambridge Journal of Economics*, 39:2, 319–43.

Rubery, J., Grimshaw, D. and Figueiredo, H. (2005), 'How to close the gender pay gap in Europe: towards the gender mainstreaming of pay policy', *Industrial Relations Journal*, 36:3, 184–213.

Rubery, J., Grimshaw, D., Hebson, G. and Ugarte, S. M. (2015), '"It's all about time": time as contested terrain in the management and experience of domiciliary care work in England', *Human Resource Management*, 54:5, 753–72.

Rubery, J., Hebson, G., Grimshaw, D., Carroll, M., Marchington, L., Smith, L. and Ugarte, S. (2011), *The Recruitment and Retention of a Care Workforce for Older People* (London: Department of Health).

Rubery, J., Humphries, J., Fagan, C., Grimshaw, D., and Smith, M. (2003a), 'Equal Opportunities as a Productive Factor', in Burchell, B., Deakin, S., Michie J. and Rubery J. (eds), *Systems of Production: Markets, Organisations and Performance* (London: Routledge).

Rubery, J., Smith, M. and Fagan, C. (1999), *Women's Employment in Europe: Trends and Prospects* (London: Routledge).

Rubery, J. and Urwin, P. (2011), 'Bringing the employer back in: why social care needs a standard employment relationship', *Human Resource Management Journal*, 21:2, 122–37.

Rubery, J. and Wilkinson, F. (eds) (1994), *Employer Strategy and the Labour Market* (Oxford: Oxford University Press).

Self, S. (2005), 'What makes motherhood so expensive? The role of social expectations, interdependence, and coordination failure in explaining lower wages of mothers', *Journal of Socio-Economics*, 34:6, 850–65.

Sengenberger, W. (1981), 'Labour market segmentation and the business cycle', in Wilkinson, F. (ed.), *The Dynamics of Labor Market Segmentation* (London: Academic Press).

Sengenberger, W. (1994), 'Protection – participation – promotion: the systemic nature and effects of labour standards', in Sengenberger, W. and Campbell, D. (eds), *Creating*

Economic Opportunities: The Role of Labour Standards in Industrial Restructuring (Geneva: International Labour Office).

Solow, R. M. (1990), *The Labor Market as a Social Institution* (Oxford: Blackwell)

Stier, H., Lewin-Epstein, N. and Braun, M. (2001), 'Welfare regimes, family-supportive policies, and women's employment along the life-course', *American Journal of Sociology*, 106:6, 1731–60.

Streeck, W. (1991), 'On the institutional conditions of diversified quality production', in Matzner, E. and Streeck, W. (eds), *Beyond Keynesianism: The Socio-Economics of Production and Employment* (Cheltenham: Edward Elgar).

Sturgeon, T. J. (2002), 'Modular production networks: a new American model of industrial organization', *Industrial and Corporate Change*, 11:3, 451–96.

Tavora, I. and Rubery, J. (2013), 'Female employment, labour market institutions and gender culture in Portugal', *European Journal of Industrial Relations*, 19:3, 221–37.

Tomlinson, J., Muzio, D., Sommerlad, H., Webley, L. and Duff, L. (2013), 'Structure, agency and career strategies of white women and black and minority ethnic individuals in the legal profession', *Human Relations*, 66:2, 245–69.

Ugarte, S. M. (2017), 'The gender pay implications of institutional and organisational wage-setting practices in Banking–a case study of Argentina and Chile', *The International Journal of Human Resource Management*, http://dx.doi.org/10.1080/09585192.2016.1277363.

Van Gyes, G. and Schulten, T. (eds) (2015), *Wage Bargaining under the New European Economic Governance* (Brussels: European Trade Union Institute).

Vaughan-Whitehead, D. (ed.) (2011), *Work Inequalities in the Crisis: Evidence from Europe* (Cheltenham: Edward Elgar).

Vaughan-Whitehead, D. (ed.) (2016), *Europe's Disappearing Middle Class: Evidence from the World of Work* (Cheltenham: Edward Elgar and Geneva: International Labour Organization).

Walby, S. (2012), 'Intersectionality: multiple inequalities in social theory', *Sociology*, 46:2, 224–40.

Walsh, T. (1990), 'Flexible labour utilisation in the private services sector', *Work, Employment and Society*, 4:4, 517–30.

Warren, T., Pascall, G. and Fox, E. (2010), 'Gender equality in time: low-paid mothers' paid and unpaid work in the UK', *Feminist Economics*, 16:3, 193–219.

Weinkopf, C. (2014), 'Women's employment in Germany', *Revue de l'OFCE*, 2, 189–214.

Wilkinson, F. (ed.) (1981), *The Dynamics of Labor Market Segmentation* (London: Academic Press).

Wilkinson, F. (1983), 'Productive systems', *Cambridge Journal of Economics*, 7:4, 413–29.

Woodhams, C., Lupton, B., Perkins, G. and Cowling, M. (2015), 'Multiple disadvantage and wage growth: the effect of merit pay on pay gaps', *Human Resource Management*, 54:2, 283–301.

Wright, C. F. and Brown, W. (2013), 'The effectiveness of socially sustainable sourcing mechanisms: Assessing the prospects of a new form of joint regulation', *Industrial Relations Journal*, 44:1, 20–37.

Part I

Conceptual issues:
employment standards, networks
and worker voice

2

Autonomous bargaining in the shadow of the law: from an enabling towards a disabling state?

Gerhard Bosch and Steffen Lehndorff

Introduction

In the years following the Second World War, income inequality in most developed countries was significantly reduced by strong trade unions and high rates of coverage by collective agreement. In 1957, even in the USA, where coverage in 2011 was only 13 per cent (Visser, 2016), Dunlop could still assume that 'collective bargaining must be taken as the normal case' (Dunlop, 1957: 125). Since the 1990s, job quality in many countries has deteriorated considerably as a result of increasing income inequality, the increase in low-wage work and the constant fear of loss of income, even among well-paid workers.[1]

Jill Rubery has investigated these processes with us in several joint research projects with various thematic focal points (see, among others, Bosch *et al.*, 2009; Grimshaw *et al.*, 2014; Grimshaw and Rubery, 2015; Rubery, 2005). Rubery (2015) has concluded, on the basis of her wide-ranging experience, that the standard employment relationship must be strengthened and extended if we are to draw any closer to the goal of establishing 'inclusive labour markets'.[2] She argues in favour of 're-regulation', supported primarily by a 'proactive state' but combined with a strengthening of 'opportunities for workers and citizens to exercise voice'. In what follows, we elaborate on these thoughts by examining a number of European collective bargaining systems.

Earlier research has shown that structural changes, such as the decreasing demand for low-skilled workers and the growth of the service sector, and external shocks, such as the deregulation of product markets, the privatisation of public services or the freedom to provide services in other countries with a company's own workforce, are 'filtered' through national wage systems, thereby producing different outcomes in different countries. The increase in low wages can be almost fully explained by the weakening of these institutions (Bosch *et al.*, 2010; Salverda and Mayhew, 2009). We also know that a high rate of coverage by collective agreements reduces the share of low-wage workers to a much greater extent than minimum wages. In the EU the correlation between the rate of coverage and the share of low-wage workers is 0.77 (Figure 2.1), while it is only 0.34 for minimum wages (Bosch and Weinkopf, 2013; Grimshaw *et al.*, 2014). This is hardly surprising, since the pay scales negotiated by collective bargaining are generally higher than the minimum wage and extend into the intermediate or even higher pay brackets well above the minimum wage. They set not only lower limits but also norms for fair pay that ensure that skills, additional responsibilities and, in particular, difficult working conditions and unsocial hours attract extra remuneration. Their influence on the income distribution is all the greater the more inclusive they are. Decentralised bargaining at company level may even support the growth of dualistic labour markets, since negotiations only take place in big companies. National or industry-wide collective agreements are significantly more inclusive than company agreements, since the collectively agreed standards are extended to employees in companies

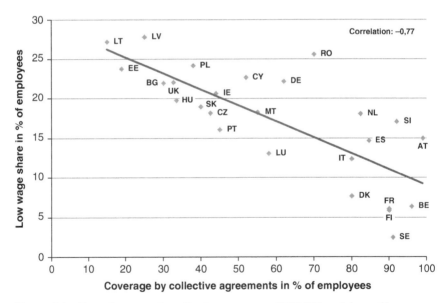

Figure 2.1   Rate of coverage by collective agreement (2008/09) and share of low-wage work (2010)

Source: Bernaciak *et al.* (2014); Bezzina (2012): share of low-wage workers 2010; ETUI (2015); Visser (2016); authors' compilation.

with weak bargaining power, such as small firms in particular. Minimum wages, on the other hand, are generally below the low-wage threshold (less than two-thirds of the median wage) and therefore compress wages only in the lower deciles of the income distribution.

Research in many countries has produced similar results. In their survey of 49 studies on collective agreements and wage inequality in recent decades in both developed and developing countries, Hayter and Weinberg (2011) show that wage inequality in the economy as a whole is reduced by collective agreements.

Certainly it would be desirable if the trade unions were in a position to increase the rate of unionisation through active organising to such an extent that they were able, through their own autonomous bargaining strength, to bring the employers to the negotiating table again and thereby increase the rate of coverage by collective agreement. This would seem at present to be more than unlikely. Furthermore, completely autonomous bargaining systems without state support are very vulnerable. Periods of trade union weakness, such as those in which rapid structural change and job losses begin to undermine the bastions of trade union power, can be exploited by firms intent on revoking collective agreements and setting wages unilaterally. The UK, where coverage by collective agreement in the private sector was once very high, is an example of such a development. The collective bargaining systems in several other European countries are currently exposed to similar threats.

The conclusion we draw is that, although trade union organising is important and should not be neglected, income inequality cannot be reduced without additional support from the state. This support can of course take several very different forms and is by no means confined to direct interventions in the wage-setting process. However, it also follows from this that the reduction or withdrawal of this state support can cause serious damage to wage-setting mechanisms. These interconnections are examined more closely in the next section.

The role of protective and participative labour standards in wage-setting

The distinction Sengenberger (1994) makes between protective and participative standards can help us to understand more clearly the differing kinds of state influence on wage-setting and other labour standards. Protective standards, such as minimum wages or maximum working times, directly establish norms governing employment conditions. Participative standards confer consultation or co-determination rights on employees or their representatives and organisations, who are protected from discrimination when they seek to exercise those

Table 2.1 Statutory protective and participative labour standards in five national
wage-setting systems (2010)

	Germany	Sweden	UK	France	Belgium	Greece	Spain
Statutory standards							
– protective	(X)*	–	X	XXX	XXX	XX	XXX
– participative	XX	XXX	–	X	XXX	–	X
Trade union density	19%	68%	27%	8%	52%	24%	20%
Rate of coverage by collective agreement (employees)	61%	91%	31%	92%	96%	64%	82%**
Share of low wage workers (<⅔ of median wage) 2010	22.2%	2.5%	22.1%	6.1%	6.4%	n.a.	14.7

Notes: * From 2007 with the introduction of industry minimum wage and 2015 with the statutory
national minimum wage; ** 2009; State-imposed standards: none, X weak, XX moderate, XXX strong.

Source: Bernaciak *et al.* (2014); Bezzina (2012): share of low-wage workers 2010; Visser (2016);
authors' compilation.

rights or equipped with resources (time and money). By establishing participative standards, the state can, as it were, enable others to influence working and
employment conditions in its stead.[3]

Table 2.1 presents considerable differences between seven EU member states
in the mix of these standards. In the two wage systems traditionally described
as autonomous – those of Germany (before 2007) and Sweden – the state does
not intervene directly in the wage-setting process with protective standards.
Rather, the weaker side of the labour market is strengthened by means of strong
co-determination rights at establishment and company level.

Sweden is one of the strong autonomous systems, since the state has also placed
the administration of the unemployment insurance funds in the hands of the trade
unions. The various funds cover largely the same territories as the unions' organising areas, which facilitates member recruitment (Lind, 2007). Consequently,
trade union density in Sweden is 70 per cent. The parties to collective bargaining
are able to conclude autonomous industry-level collective agreements that set
effective wage floors at between 50 and 70 per cent of the average wage (Eldring
and Alsos, 2012: 78), which is higher than the statutory minimum wages in most
European countries. Consequently, the share of low-wage workers, at 2.5 per
cent (2010), is lower than in any other European country.

The main threat to the system's stability comes from political and legal med-
dling with the union's power resources. In 2006, the conservative Swedish

government made membership of the unemployment insurance funds and the trade unions considerably more expensive. The extent to which contributions to the funds and union dues could be offset against tax was reduced and the level of contributions was made dependent on the unemployment rate in each sector. In Sweden, from 2007 to 2008, when these new regulations were introduced, trade union density fell by 6 per cent (Kjellberg, 2009: 502).

Germany used to be one of the weak autonomous systems. Even in the heyday of trade union strength in the 1970s, no more than 35.5 per cent of employees were trade union members in 1978 (Visser, 2016). Consequently, the German system was particularly dependent on the willingness of companies to become members of employers' associations. Until German reunification, the rate of coverage by collective agreements was around 85 per cent (Visser, 2016), several times greater than trade union density, since most companies belonged to an employers' association. The high levels of unemployment after reunification and the deregulation of product and labour markets gave companies in sectors and enterprises in which trade union density was low and where there were few elected works councils (creating a representation gap) an opportunity to change strategy. They left the employers' associations or, in the case of newly founded companies, simply did not join one. The Hartz legislation of 2003 was aimed at expanding the low-wage sector. By reducing unemployment benefits – previously means-tested – for the long-term unemployed to the lower social benefit level, and by resetting the 'reasonableness' criteria, the Hartz reforms stepped up pressure on the unemployed to accept work with pay as much as 30 per cent below the going rate for their locality. Deregulation of temporary agency work and of so-called mini-jobs made it possible to replace employees on standard contracts with workers on precarious contracts.

Coverage by collective agreement fell to 62 per cent, which led to the emergence of a large low-wage sector. However, the existence of strong works councils in key industries prevented the complete collapse of industry-wide collective agreements in the private sector, as happened in the UK. In important parts of the economy, the old autonomous collective bargaining system is still functioning, while in others employers set wages unilaterally. Since the low-wage sector, through its outsourcing strategies, is also increasingly exerting a strong knock-on effect on those segments of the labour market that continue to be regulated by collective agreement, in 2006 trade unions in the manufacturing sector joined the service-sector unions in calling for the introduction of a minimum wage. The introduction, firstly of industry-wide minimum wages (2007) and then a statutory minimum wage (2015), marked the transition from an autonomous to a hybrid wage system with direct state interventions in the wage-setting process. The trade unions exerted considerable influence over the form taken by the statutory minimum wage that was agreed by the German Social Democratic Party (SPD) in the coalition talks at the end of 2013. As a consequence, the parties to collective bargaining are able to exert greater influence over the minimum wage than their counterparts in France or the UK, for example. The reference points for any proposed increases are to be the collectively agreed wage rises, so that collective bargaining takes precedence over political considerations in determining rises in the minimum wage. In the same vein, the unions' objective is to use the minimum wage as an *activating minimum wage* for strengthening free collective bargaining.

Belgium has a hybrid system with a combination of strong protective and high participative standards. The participative rights are based on rights of co-determination at establishment level and management of the unemployment insurance scheme, which is known as the 'Ghent system', after the Belgium model. In addition, the bargaining power of the Belgian trade unions is further strengthened by protective standards in the shape of a statutory minimum wage and a process for declaring collective agreements in most industries generally binding. The dual protection offered by this hybrid system results in a combination of high trade union density (50 per cent) and virtually universal coverage by collective agreement (96 per cent). In practice, the statutory minimum wage plays very little role, since the trade unions in most sectors are able to negotiate higher wages which, moreover, apply to all employees in an industry because the agreements are declared generally binding. As a result, the share of low-wage workers in Belgium is very low.

Until well into the 1970s, the UK was one of the countries with autonomous pay bargaining systems and had high trade union density and extensive coverage by collective agreement. However, there was no state support in the form of participative standards. Unlike in Germany, therefore, the unions had no legally safeguarded organisational base at establishment level. Further weakened by the major structural crisis in manufacturing industry, they had little in their armoury to counter the employers' associations' withdrawal from collective bargaining during the Thatcher years. The abolition in 1993 of the wages councils, which used to set minimum wages in several low-wage industries, shifted the balance of power in wage-setting further in favour of the employers. The sharp increase in the incidence of low pay and in-work benefits for low earners was the reason for the introduction of the statutory minimum wage in 1999, so that today the UK is one of the countries whose wage-setting systems are unsupported by statutory participative standards and in which the state grants only weak protective rights. However, the share of low earners has remained high because of this 'isolated minimum wage' (Grimshaw *et al.*,

2014). In the private sector, the strong negotiating parties who could have used the minimum wage as a starting point for agreeing higher wages simply did not exist. Instead, in some sectors, such as retailing, the minimum wage has actually exerted a downward pull on wages.

In France, on the other hand, the state intervenes very strongly in the wage-setting process. It not only sets a floor on pay through the statutory minimum wage but also declares virtually all collective agreements generally binding. Furthermore, the participation of trade unions and works councils has been strengthened, although the rights that have been granted are weaker than in Germany or Sweden. Unlike in Belgium, where the unions with their high membership rates are able to bring the employers' associations to the table without state intervention, the unions in France are weak, so that pay bargaining is usually triggered only when the state raises the minimum wage. Since the lowest collectively agreed rates in most industries are close to the statutory minimum wage (SMIC), the frequency of collective bargaining and increases in pay rates are determined largely by increases in the minimum wage. In November 2011, for example, the lowest pay grade in 86 per cent of all collective agreements was at the level of the minimum wage or slightly above (>105 per cent of the SMIC) and in 9.2 per cent of collective agreements it was actually lower than the SMIC. One month after the SMIC was raised, the share of collective agreements with pay rates below the minimum wage had risen to 49 per cent. This triggered a pay bargaining round in which most rates were again raised above the SMIC (DARES, 2012: 351). Thus, as a result of the increases in the lowest collectively agreed rates, the entire wage grids, with their percentage differences between the individual pay grades, are shifted upwards.

Since 2013 it has been possible, in the event of competitiveness problems, to negotiate changes to wages and working time at establishment level, although the minimum wage, statutory working-time regulations and industry-level collective agreements must not be undercut. At the same time, employees were for the first time granted the right to have a representative on the top-tier body (*conseil d'administration* or *conseil de surveillance*) of firms with at least 5,000 employees in France. While it is true that the state grants the unions rights to consultation, it has not strengthened the unions' organisational base by introducing the Ghent system, in contrast to the situation in neighbouring Belgium or in Sweden. Only a small number of employees are union members. Consequently, the French unions have little financial power and are unable adequately to support their representatives at company and establishment level. Thus the French unions, unlike their counterparts in Sweden, are very concerned – not without justification – that decentralised negotiations on derogation clauses in collective agreements or labour legislation would inevitably see them on the losing side.

These fears were further fuelled by the passing of a new French labour law in the summer of 2016, as we discuss in the next section.

The dismantling of protective and participative labour standards

The most bitterly disputed clause in the French labour legislation imposed by decree in July 2016 stipulates that a company agreement on working-time issues takes precedence over the relevant industry-level collective agreement, even if its provisions are less favourable for employees. The declared objective of abolishing the favourability principle is to create more room for manoeuvre for negotiations at company level in order that industry-wide regulations 'can be adapted as closely to possible to conditions at establishment level' (Assemblée Nationale, 2016: 9).

This new initiative in state support for the decentralisation of collective bargaining marks a paradigm shift. In the year 2000, when the legislation on the introduction of the 35-hour week in France was enacted, decentralisation was still intended to make it easier for the actors at establishment level to negotiate compromises on working-time organisation *within the framework* of the existing industry-level collective agreements. This *enabling state approach*, in which industry-level collective agreements continued to take precedence over agreements negotiated at lower levels, was reflected in a sharp increase in working-time negotiations at company level and a high satisfaction rate among employees with the outcomes (Lehndorff, 2014). The new legislation, on the other hand, adopts a *disabling* state approach. It is true that the new policy provides for a strengthening of participative standards in the shape of extended bargaining rights at company level. However, this explicit reversal of the standards hierarchy gives primacy to a bargaining level at which the power imbalance in favour of capital is usually at its strongest. This weakens the generalising effect of collective agreements just as much as a decline in coverage by collective agreement, but via a different route.

In principle, trade unions can counter strong pressure from employees or the state in favour of decentralised agreements that diverge from those concluded at industry level by massively strengthening their internal coordination and central monitoring of decentralised negotiations. This was the route, in conjunction with the reactivation of their membership base, that the two largest German trade unions went down with some success at the beginning of the 2000s (Haipeter and Lehndorff, 2014). The trade unions in Italy have to date also successfully resisted government pressure to negotiate similarly divergent company agreements (Cruces *et al.*, 2015; Leonardi 2017). In France, on the other hand, the competition between the various trade union confederations, whose membership base at company level remains weak, means it is unlikely that such courses of action will be adopted in the near future (Pernot, 2017).

Thus the core of the disabling state approach is to deprive the trade unions of the legally guaranteed 'institutional anchors' (Grimshaw and Lehndorff, 2010) that underpin their negotiating power in the collective bargaining system. Since the beginning of the persistent European economic crisis, this approach has been taken furthest in several countries in the so-called European 'periphery'.

Greece is the most prominent example of those countries whose labour markets have been deregulated in recent years at the behest of the so-called Troika (the European Commission, European Central Bank and the International Monetary Fund). In Greece's case, it was not only the speed and rigidity of this process that were remarkable, but also the scale of the attack on protective labour standards.

The Greek collective bargaining system, which since the beginning of the 1990s and following the economic and political upheavals of the previous decades had been shored up by the three main actors involved – the employers' associations, the trade unions and the state – was based essentially on just a few pillars (on what follows, see Karamessini, 2015; Schulten and Müller, 2015; Koukiadaki and Kokkinou, 2016). The most important were the periodic national general collective employment agreements, concluded between the employers' umbrella associations and the private-sector trade unions, which stipulated a minimum wage for all dependent employees as well as other minimum standards. These agreements were given legal power by the government, so that that the statutory minimum wage in Greece was in fact the result of a negotiating process involving the parties to collective bargaining. The second pillar comprised collective agreements for individual industries and occupational groups; these could be declared generally binding by the government, so that, until the crisis, collective bargaining coverage was estimated to be around 65 per cent. The hierarchy of standards was safeguarded by the favourability principle. Industry and company agreements – the latter being concluded only seldom – could only improve the conditions laid down in agreements negotiated at the higher level.

The underdevelopment of company-level bargaining reflects a typical characteristic of the constellation of powers on which the collective bargaining system was based. It is true that the multiplicity of company and occupational trade union organisations (trade union density was still 24 per cent in 2010) could bring their influence to bear in top-level negotiations – supported in disputes by general strikes and large demonstrations. However, besides the public service (in which there were no pay negotiations), this power base was founded primarily on the public utility companies, the banks and some individual industries. In an economy in which small companies predominated, therefore, the unions' bargaining power rested on a very small number of supports, which were safeguarded essentially by protective labour standards.

This one-sidedness made the system extremely fragile in a situation in which the protective standards were abrogated by diktat in the years from 2010 onwards. The following changes were of crucial significance for the collective bargaining system:

*   The statutory minimum wage was cut by 22 per cent (and by 32 per cent for the under-25s) and frozen. Moreover, it is no longer negotiated but fixed by statute (see Chapter 17).
*   Collective bargaining in the large public utility companies was stopped and pay throughout the public sector was cut by government decree.
*   Industry-level collective agreements were no longer declared generally binding and the favourability principle was abolished. Employers have the possibility of opting out of the national framework agreement and from industry-wide agreements, which now apply only to members of the employers' associations.
*   These last measures and the three-month limit on the residual validity of collective agreements that are not renewed are intended to encourage the negotiation of company agreements that are less favourable (to employees) than the industry agreements; such agreements can also be concluded with so-called 'associations of persons' (i.e. employee representatives without a trade union mandate).

These measures had an immediate and wide-ranging effect. Since 2012, not a single national framework agreement has been concluded. The number of sectoral and occupational agreements at national level sank from 65 in 2010 to 12 in 2015, while the number of company agreements concluded in 2012 shot up from the previous norm of around 200 to almost 1,000 (Koukiadaki and Kokkinou, 2016). As a result of this sweeping destruction of the collective bargaining system, real wages fell by about 24 per cent between 2010 and 2014 (Schulten and Müller, 2015).

The importance of declarations of general applicability and the favourability principle as protective anchors of last resort is made clear by comparison with Spain (on what follows, see Banyuls and Recio, 2015; Köhler and Calleja Jiménez, 2017; Schulten and Müller, 2015). National framework agreements and regional and sectoral collective agreements became established practice there from the 1990s onwards. Besides pay, they also regulated an ever-growing number of minimum labour standards and automatically applied to all employees in the relevant industry or region (*erga omnes* principle). This resulted in a traditionally high level of collective bargaining coverage of around 80 per cent of employees and a smaller share of low-wage workers than in Germany. In a similar way to their counterparts in Greece, the trade unions, operating in an economy made up primarily of small and medium-sized firms, concentrated their bargaining power on disputes over these multi-employer agreements and, if the disputes remained unresolved, used their power to mobilise workers to call general strikes. The same applied to occasional disputes over trilateral social pacts with the government.

Since these national, regional or industry agreements merely laid down minimum conditions with relatively low wage rates, more favourable agreements were agreed in many large companies. The *erga omnes* rule ensured that the favourability principle was upheld. In these circumstances, the favourability principle acted not only as a protective standard but also as an important participative standard, because it provided crucial support for the trade unions and interest representation bodies in medium-sized and larger companies and strengthened their bargaining power beyond the rights of co-determination on dismissal protection.

The deregulatory measures introduced in 2010 and, more especially, in 2012 resembled those introduced in Greece. Besides numerous radical changes, principally to dismissal protection, the following measures came into effect:

- the residual validity of collective agreements that are not renewed was reduced to one year;
- employers were given the possibility, under certain conditions, of opting out unilaterally from collective agreements; and
- the favourability principle was abolished for company agreements.

Thus the *erga omnes* principle, unlike the declarations of general applicability in Greece, was not abolished but punctured in order to set its erosion in motion. In some cases, the parties to collective bargaining tried to maintain the previous hierarchy of standards. Thus in some industry collective agreements the favourability principle was strengthened, and in one framework agreement the regional and industry actors were encouraged to conclude new collective agreements in order to prevent earlier agreements from expiring. The opt-out possibility is used primarily by larger companies, but to date to a much lesser extent than was initially assumed – in 2013, 160,000 employees were affected by opt-out agreements, compared with around 10.3 million employees in companies covered by collective agreements (see Ministerio de Empleo y Seguridad Social, 2017;

Fernández Rodríguez *et al.,* 2016), so that the expected drastic decline in collective bargaining coverage has not yet been observed.

Thus, unlike in Greece, the dismantling of protective and participative labour standards has not brought the edifice of the collective bargaining system tumbling down, but has significantly weakened its effectiveness, as is demonstrated by the evolution of collectively agreed wages and salaries. Agreed nominal wage increases at both industry and company level have declined massively, which has led to cuts in real wages since the beginning of deregulation (Eurofound, 2014, 2015).

This weakening of the collective bargaining system can also be observed in the narrowing of the range of topics addressed in collective bargaining (Fernández Rodríguez *et al.,* 2016). The main topic again today is pay, although the balance of power at both company and industry level is significantly less favourable for the trade unions than before the crisis.

The developments in Spain outlined above may well prove to be typical of the prospects for protective and participative labour standards in several European countries. As Schulten and Müller's (2015) comparative survey of changes in collective bargaining systems shows, the most widespread approach is not to destroy existing institutions completely but rather to weaken and hollow them out.

Conclusions

The state interventions in free collective bargaining systems outlined here demonstrate the urgency of Rubery's plea, cited in the introduction to this chapter, for a more highly regulated labour market based on a 'proactive state' and 'extended opportunities for workers and citizens to exercise voice'. A proactive state is important for collective bargaining systems because it can establish and uphold both protective and participative standards. The wage-setting systems described in the literature as 'autonomous' are actually not so autonomous at all. In reality, the 'shadow of the law' hangs over these autonomous negotiations. As an 'enabling state', the Swedish state has acted to compensate for the unions' structural inferiority by establishing strong participative labour standards. This makes it possible to delegate the negotiations to the social partners without the state having subsequently to intervene with corrective measures, such as minimum wages, because of high shares of low-wage workers. The counter-example is Greece where, at the behest of the 'institutions', the state was able in no time at all to rip out the few anchors that had kept the collective bargaining system in place over the previous 20 years. This underscores the importance of co-determination rights at establishment and company level which in several countries stabilise the collective bargaining systems by establishing statutory rights to participation. When such rights do not exist, on the other hand, and the bargaining power of employee representatives at company level is weak, the entire edifice of collective agreements stands on very shaky ground.

Another important observation is that protective and participative standards can mutually support each other, as the Belgian example demonstrates. Thus statutory rights to participation make it easier to set up employee representative bodies in the workplace and to organise members, which in turn improves the opportunities for free collective bargaining. In France, on the other hand, where participative labour standards and trade union bargaining power at company level are weak, decentralisation of the collective bargaining system combined with the abolition of the favourability principle may set in motion a vicious circle at all levels of the collective bargaining system. This sort of decentralisation encourages pay to evolve pro-cyclically (Schulten and van Gyes, 2015). It widens the wage spread between companies and industries and is inimical to efforts to reduce income inequality.

Thus efforts to combat social inequality should not rely solely on direct state intervention in the wage-setting process but should also seek to develop participative standards. However, these will not have any effect in practice unless they have substance and extend the options and resources available to employee representatives. In contrast, the purely formal participation of 'powerless' trade unions in social dialogue, which is standard practice at EU level and in many member states (Meardi, 2012), serves only to provide political legitimation for governments and has little to do with genuine participation. Sooner or later, however, the pendulum swings back against the state; the weaker the institutional backing for strong bargaining systems is, the more frequently employees require recourse to labour courts and other state institutions. The example of Spain shows that, as a result, 'the state is brought back into labour relations in a more direct manner but without the necessary capacity to support labour relations' (Fernández Rodríguez et al., 2016: 551). This also makes plain the political peril that the disabling state may conjure up – it undermines employees' trust in the state and democratic institutions.

Participative and protective labour standards arose out of social conflicts between capital and labour and reflect the balance of power at a particular point in time. However, this balance of power can change, such that the historic compromises are called into question (Pontusson, 2005). In virtually no other area can the balance of power shift as quickly as in the employment system, which is not without consequences for state action. While education and welfare systems, which are largely state-dominated, often exhibit considerable durability and path dependency, the same does not necessarily apply to

industrial relations. As a result of the deregulation of product and labour markets, free trade agreements, the privatisation of state activities, the transfer of
functions from highly unionised plants to unregulated segments of the national
or international labour market, economic crises and the rapid growth of new
service industries with lower trade union density, the balance of power has
shifted in recent decades in favour of employers, which can have significant
negative effects on job quality.

This change has often taken place gradually as the various influencing factors have steadily accumulated, causing labour standards to be eroded slowly.
The deregulation promoted by the economic governance framework of the
European Union (EU) has accelerated this process. Jill Rubery (2015: 16) draws
attention to this connection when she writes: 'the complexion of the state may
change or may be forced to change by international pressures.' However, this
is precisely what makes it so difficult to halt and reverse the prevailing trend in
Europe away from the enabling towards the disabling state. National institutions can rapidly be weakened or even destroyed under pressure from EU-wide
agreements, but it takes longer to build up new, enabling institutions and in
today's EU, with the priority now given to competitive regulations, this task is
more difficult than ever. With Rubery, we have concluded from our European
comparisons that 'more emphasis on positive integration policies is needed by
improving the capabilities of national actors to develop proactive policies and
create new regulatory institutions at the European level', but also that 'this focus
on the EU as a constraint on national actors does not and should not let national
actors off the hook. There is still scope for national actors to take bold action to
develop new and innovative institutional arrangements and indeed to promote
these ideas at the European level' (Bosch et al., 2009: 51).

We are grateful to Jill Rubery for the inspiration and insights she has given us
in our many years of collaboration and feel strengthened in our academic and, on
occasions, also political commitment to strive for an 'enabling state' in our own
country, which would greatly aid the process of 'multi-level institution building' in the EU and its member states.

Notes

1   Parts of this chapter are based on Bosch (2015).
2   'Instead of more flexible employment, policies are needed to extend and reinforce
    SER-type [Standard Employment Relationship] relationships, alongside new higher legal

minimum standards and mechanisms to reduce the penalties for not being on an SER-type contract' (Rubery, 2015: 15).

3   Sengenberger also identifies promotional standards, which increase the options open to individuals. They include family-friendly working times, employee rights to further training and the option to use certain wage components for specific purposes, such as old-age insurance.

References

Assemblée Nationale (2016), *Projet de loi, présenté par Mme Myriam El Khomry, ministre du travail, de l'emploi, de la formation professionnelle et du dialogue social* (Paris).

Banyuls, J. and Recio, A. (2015), 'A crisis within the crisis – Spain under the regime of a conservative neoliberalism', in Lehndorff, S. (ed.), *Divisive Integration: the Triumph of Failed Ideas in Europe – Revisited* (Brussels: European Trade Union Institute), pp. 39–68.

Bernaciak, M. (2014), Gumbrell-McCormick, R. and Hyman, R., *European Trade Unionism: from Crisis to Renewal?* (Brussels: European Trade Union Institute).

Bezzina, E. (2012), 'In 2010, 17% of employees in the EU were low-wage earners', *Eurostat Statistics in Focus*, 48/2012 (Luxembourg: Eurostat).

Bosch, G. (2015), 'Shrinking collective bargaining coverage, increasing income inequality: a comparison of five EU countries', *International Labour Review*, 154:1, 57–66.

Bosch, G., Lehndorff, S. and Rubery, J. (eds) (2009), *European Employment Models in Flux: A Comparison of Institutional Change in Nine European Countries* (Basingstoke: Palgrave Macmillan).

Bosch, G., Mayhew, K. and Gautié, J. (2010), 'Industrial relations, legal regulations, and wage setting', in Gautié, J. and Schmitt, J. (eds), *Low-Wage Work in the Wealthy World* (New York: Russell Sage), pp. 147–82.

Bosch, G. and Weinkopf, C. (2013), 'Wechselwirkungen zwischen Mindest-und Tariflöhnen', *WSI-Mitteilungen,* 66:6, 393–403.

Cruces, J., Álvarez, I., Trillo, F. and Leonardi, S. (2015), 'Impact of the euro crisis on wages and collective bargaining in southern Europe – a comparison of Italy, Portugal and Spain', in van Gyes, G. and Schulten, T. (eds), *Wage Bargaining under the New European Economic Governance* (Brussels: European Trade Union Institute), pp. 93–138.

DARES (2012), *Bilans et rapports – La Négociation Collective en 2011* (Ministère du Travail, de l'Emploi et de la Santé: Paris).

Dunlop, J. T. (1957), 'The task of contemporary wage theory', in Taylor, G. W. and Pierson, F. C. (eds), *New Concepts in Wage Determination* (New York, Toronto and London: McGraw-Hill), pp. 117–39.

Eldring, L. and Alsos, K. (2012), 'European minimum wage: a Nordic outlook', Report No. 16 (Oslo: Fafo).

ETUI (European Trade Union Institute) (2015), 'National industrial relations, Brussels', http://worker-participation.eu/National-Industrial-Relations, accessed 19 February 2015.

Eurofound (2014), *Developments in Collectively Agreed Pay 2013* (Dublin: European Foundation for the Improvement of Living and Working Conditions).

Eurofound (2015), *Developments in Collectively Agreed Pay 2014* (Dublin: European Foundation for the Improvement of Living and Working Conditions).

Fernández Rodríguez, C. J., Ibáñez Rojo, R. and Martínez Lucio, M., (2016), 'The reform of collective bargaining in the Spanish metal and chemicals sectors (2008–2015): the ironies and risks of de-regulating employment regulation', in Koukiadaki, A., Távora, I. and Martínez Lucio, M. (eds), *Joint Regulation and Labour Market Policy in Europe During the Crisis* (Brussels: European Trade Union Institute), pp. 499–554.

Grimshaw, D. (2010), 'United Kingdom: developing a progressive minimum wage in a liberal market economy', in Vaughan-Whitehead, D. (ed.), *The Minimum Wage Revisited in the Enlarged EU* (Cheltenham: Edward Elgar and Geneva: International Labour Organization), pp. 473–508.

Grimshaw, D., Bosch, G. and Rubery, J. (2014), 'Minimum wages and collective bargaining: what types of pay bargaining can foster positive pay equity outcomes?', *British Journal of Industrial Relations*, 52:3, 470–98.

Grimshaw, D. and Lehndorff, S. (2010), 'Anchors for job quality: sectoral systems of employment in the European context', *Work Organisation, Labour and Globalisation*, 4:1, 24–40.

Grimshaw, D. and Rubery, J. (2015), 'Neoliberalism 2.0: crisis and austerity in the UK', in Lehndorff, S. (ed.), *Divisive Integration: The triumph of failed ideas in Europe – Revisited* (Brussels: European Trade Union Institute), pp. 209–32.

Haipeter, T. and Lehndorff, S. (2014), 'Decentralisation of collective bargaining in Germany: Fragmentation, coordination and revitalization', *Economia & Lavoro*, 48:1, 45–64.

Hayter, S. and Weinberg, B. (2011), 'Mind the gap: collective bargaining and wage inequality', in Hayter, S. (ed.), *The Role of Collective Bargaining in the Global Economy: Negotiating for Social Justice* (Cheltenham), pp. 136–86.

Karamessini, M. (2015), 'Greece as an international test-case: economic adjustment through a Troika/state-induced depression and social catastrophe', in Lehndorff, S. (ed.), *Divisive Integration: The Triumph of Failed Ideas in Europe – Revisited* (Brussels: European Trade Union Institute), pp. 95–126.

Kjellberg, A. (2009), 'The Swedish Ghent system and trade unions under pressure', *Transfer* 15, 3:4, 481–504.

Köhler, H. D. and Calleja Jiménez, J. P. (2017), 'Spain: a peripheral economy and a vulnerable trade union movement', in Lehndorff, S., Dribbusch, H. and Schulten, T. (eds.), *Rough Waters – European Trade Unions in a Time of Crises* (Brussels: European Trade Union Institute), pp. 59–79.

Koukiadaki, A. and Kokkinou, C. (2016), 'Deconstructing the Greek system of industrial relations', *European Journal of Industrial Relations*, http://ejd.sagepub.com/content/early/2016/05/06/0143831X16643206.abstract.

Leonardi, S. (2017), Trade unions and collective bargaining in Italy during the crisis, in Lehndorff, S., Dribbusch, H. and Schulten, T. (eds.), *Rough Waters – European Trade Unions in a Time of Crises* (Brussels: European Trade Union Institute), pp. 81–105.

Lind, J. (2007), 'A Nordic saga? The Ghent system and trade unions', *International Journal of Employment Studies* 15:1, 49–68.

Meardi, G. (2012), *Social Failures of EU Enlargement* (Routledge: New York).

Ministerio de Empleo y Seguridad Social (2017), Estadística de convenios colectivos de trabajo, http://www.empleo.gob.es/estadisticas/cct/welcome.htm, accessed 10 March 2017.

Pernot, J. M. (2017), 'France's trade unions in the aftermath of the crisis', in Lehndorff, S., Dribbusch, H. and Schulten, T. (eds.), *Rough Waters – European Trade Unions in a Time of Crises* (Brussels: European Trade Union Institute), pp. 35–58.

Pontusson, J. (2005), 'Varieties and Commonalities of Capitalism', in Coates, D. (ed.), *Varieties of Capitalism, Varieties of Approaches* (Basingstoke: Palgrave Macmillan), pp. 163–88.

Rubery, J. (2005), 'The shaping of work and working time in the service sector: a 233 segmentation approach', in Bosch, G. and Lehndorff, S. (eds), *Working in the Service Sector: A Tale from Different Worlds* (London: Routledge), pp. 233–56.

Rubery, J. (2015), *Re-regulating for Inclusive Labour Markets*, Conditions of Work and Employment Series No. 65 (Geneva: International Labour Organization).

Salverda, W. and Mayhew, K. (2009), 'Capitalist economies and wage inequality', *Oxford Review of Economic Policy,* 25:1, 126–54.

Schulten, T. and Müller, T. (2015), 'European economic governance and its intervention in national wage development and collective bargaining', in Lehndorff, S. (ed.), *Divisive Integration: The Triumph of Failed Ideas in Europe – Revisited* (Brussels: European Trade Union Institute), pp. 331–64.

Schulten, T. and van Gyes, T. (2015), 'Concluding remarks: a transnational coordinated reconstruction of collective bargaining as a precondition for inclusive growth in Europe', in van Gyes, G. and Schulten, T. (eds), *Wage Bargaining Under the New European Economic Governance* (Brussels: European Trade Union Institute), pp. 401–12.

Sengenberger, W. (1994), 'Protection – participation – promotion: the systemic nature and effects of labour standards', in Sengenberger, W. and Campbell, D. (eds), *Creating Economic Opportunities: The Role of Labour Standards in Industrial Restructuring* (Geneva: International Labour Organization), pp. 45–60.

Visser, J. (2016), *Database on Institutional Characteristics of Trade Unions, Wage Setting, State Intervention and Social Pacts (ICTWSS) in 51 countries between 1960 and 2014* (Amsterdam: Amsterdam Institute for Advanced Labour Studies (AIAS)), http://uva-aias.net/en/ictwss.

3

The persistence of, and challenges to, societal effects in the context of global competition

Phil Almond

Introduction

The notion of the 'societal effect', as posited by the Laboratoire d'Economie et de Sociologie du Travail (LEST) school (Maurice *et al.*, 1986), has long represented a bulwark against universalist thinking within research into labour markets, the wider structuration of the wage-employment relationship and organisation studies.

The specific methodological commitments of the LEST school itself (see the appendices to Maurice *et al.*, 1986) are perhaps more honoured in the breach than in the observance. However, the underpinning idea of the importance of integrating 'the comparison and analysis of the genesis and dynamics of institutional forms, social rules, policies and cultures' (Michon, 1992: 223) into an analysis of economic systems has inspired a broad comparative literature on the organisation of capitalism (Hall and Soskice, 2001; Lane, 1989; Whitley, 1992, 1999). This broader literature is sometimes referred to as 'societal institutionalism' (Djelic and Quack, 2003). When applied to labour market organisation, this stresses the idea that labour supply and demand are the result not of the application of abstract economic norms, but of mutually interlocking spheres of social structuring of the opportunities and constraints facing work organisation and workers (see Rubery, 1992).

Essentially, societal institutionalism argues that capitalism is embedded at a national–societal level in mutually reinforcing and interlocking 'spheres' of political economy, in ways which create national 'logics' of employment relations, labour market construction and production organisation which combine to create a certain degree of internal coherence. As we will reflect on below, in contemporary societal institutionalist work there are different degrees of insistence on, or questioning of, the national closure of such logics, and implicitly on the long-controversial concept of 'coherence', and how far this implies functionality (Maurice and Sorge, 2000; Rubery, 1992). However, this embeddedness, or process of institutionalised social construction, is a necessary feature of the complex socio-economic relations involved in the reproduction of capitalism within specific political-geographical spaces, rather than being only a feature of those societies which depart more obviously from liberal norms of the employment relationship. Thus 'the notion of juxtaposing a labour market structured by institutions and a deregulated labour market structured by market forces is invalid. If explicit labour market regulations are dismantled then the labour market will be exposed to the influences of firm-specific employment policies on the one hand and the institutions of social reproduction on the other, with no regulatory systems or norms to restrict the extent of inequality or segmentation' (Rubery, 1992: 258).

Methodologically, societal institutionalism was originally developed in conscious opposition to approaches, often based in forms of contingency theory, which try to draw relations between variables in all national environments, 'posing the existence of a rationality above and beyond national specifics and cultural particularities' (Maurice, 1979: 43). Maurice was referring to research using contingencies drawn from organisational theory (Lammers and Hickson, 1979), such as markets, technology and size. However, it is also the case that a fairly large volume of cross-sectional international research, often based on statistical comparisons of a large number of countries, uses indicators of more macro-level economic, social and political characteristics.

The debate between formal contingency approaches and internationally comparative methods no longer has the prominence it once did (see the various contributions to Lammers and Hickson, 1979). In practice, however, a very considerable volume of international research follows the precepts of comparing standard variables, divorced from their socio-political-cultural contexts, in making statements about differences in outcomes at national level. These 'thin' forms of comparison are favoured by the political economy of research, in particular through the frequent need for research to cover large numbers of countries due to funder requirements, and the incentives to make positivistic claims about the relations between variables across as large a number of countries as possible.

Societal institutionalism rejects such cross-sectional analysis, at least as the sole form of comparative research. Instead it argues that analysis of labour market construction, or of organisational decision-making, must be predicated on an understanding of how the dependent variable(s) of interest are socially constructed through the interplay of a large range of forces, or societal 'spheres', which interact together in mutually co-constitutive ways. For the original LEST research of Maurice and colleagues, a comparison of internal labour markets in industrial firms in France and Germany required an analysis of the mutual co-constitution of the educational and vocational training system, the nature of business organisation, and the structure of employer–worker struggle in the industrial relations sphere. For societal analysis, it is essential to analyse how these 'spheres' are constructed in different societies, and how they relate to each other; the best research in this tradition goes beyond positing institutional logics and attempts to understand the socialised rationality of actors (see the methodological appendix to Maurice *et al.*, 1986).

Rubery's work provides an illustration of how such a methodology might proceed, which is worth quoting at length:

> According to the LEST school, it is in fact crucial to understand the articulation of social and economic organisation within a given society and not seek to find universal patterns between societies through cross-sectional analysis. Apparently similar forms of economic or social organisation may in fact serve very different functions within different societies. To take part-time employment as an example, before it can be determined what role part-time work plays in absorbing surplus labour in recessions…, it is necessary to undertake a detailed analysis of, amongst other factors, the share of the informal economy, the overall participation rates, the measured level of unemployment, the family division of labour and hours of work for full-timers, and the role of part-time work in the productive system. In short the relative importance of the role of part-time work in disguising unemployment cannot be simply read off from a comparison of the shares of part-time work between societies. (Rubery, 1992: 247)

Societal institutionalist literature outside the original LEST school, and other comparative frameworks strongly influenced by the LEST principles of comparison, is often interested in different 'spheres' and 'interlockages'. Indeed, societal institutionalist research needs to be wary of concretising the explanatory factors that it investigates too strictly, as 'deep' comparativism can only achieve its objectives to the extent that the researcher is confident of having understood the relevant interdependencies and interconnections between all the different spheres of social space which shape his/her particular area of interest. These are likely to change if the research focus changes, and may also vary themselves across societies. Thus while the spheres elucidated by the LEST school and other societal institutionalists are helpful as a guide, for a given concrete piece of research the relevant 'spheres' and their 'interlockages' can only really be discovered inductively, and may emerge in a relatively ad hoc way in the research process. For example, in our own comparative research on the involvement of social actors in the attraction and retention of foreign direct investment (FDI), the structuring of territorial politics, and the channelling of populist as opposed to mainstream politics, emerged as key co-constitutive variables (Almond *et al.*, 2017). Thus, we would argue that the precise labelling of spheres is less important than retaining the core idea of a system of interlocking societal spheres structuring economic organisation (or for labour market analysis more specifically, labour supply and demand).

Challenges for societal institutionalist analysis

Sympathetic critics of societal institutionalism have tended to focus on the somewhat functionalist approach of the LEST school – exacerbated, we would argue, in some subsequent work influenced by it, particularly the *varieties of capitalism* approach (see Almond and Gonzalez, 2006) – and consequent difficulties in developing 'a dynamic analysis of change in societal organisation, as change usually arises out of conflict and tension and not out of harmony and complementarity' (Rubery, 1992: 248). Somewhat relatedly, sympathisers and critics alike have questioned the merits of defending specifically *national-societal* embeddedness, in the context of international integration over the last 30 years.

Part of the problem in analysing change arises if the notions of 'coherence' and societal 'logics' are taken to mean that it is necessary to boil societal effects down into underpinning guiding forces of national capitalisms. This is a frequent but in our view non-necessary component of societal institutionalist research – it should be possible to trace the mutual interactions of conflicts and power struggles in different spheres of society, and identify the logics these interactions embody, without positing that these interlockages provide path dependencies that are necessarily 'coherent' in the sense of being functional (see Rubery, 1994 on the UK productive system). Indeed, the recent trend towards a more actor-centred institutionalism analysing the role of actors in changing institutions (e.g. Streeck and Thelen, 2005) is strongly affected by societal institutionalism, at the same time as questioning the national stability of societal systems as regulatory forces under neoliberal globalisation.

Equally, it is clearly the case that any sort of 'coherence' of national-societal systems is predicated on some sort of coherence with the demands of international political economy and globalising capitalism. To be practically adequate, comparative analysis needs both to take systematic account of the selective 'efficiency' of societies as informed by processes of international integration (Rubery, 1992; Wilkinson, 1983), and to recognise that these processes imply that institutional embeddedness is not exclusively at the national level. This means taking into more systematic account sectoral and sub-national variations (Rubery, 1992: 248), as well as supranational or transnational structuration.

The remainder of this chapter revisits some of these challenges, in the context of the transnationalisation of productive capital, and the dynamics of regime competition that have ensued at national and more local levels. We argue that it is important to retain an emphasis on the mutual interdependencies shaping the social construction of labour markets, while giving greater emphasis to the ways that, within 'variegated' neoliberal capitalism (Peck and Theodore, 2007), the dynamics of competitiveness both depend on, but also challenge, relatively coherent 'societal' fixes as to the nature of socio-productive systems.

International competition and societal effects

At one level, specific factors causing increased international competition for production can readily be identified: the more systematic incorporation of large parts of the Global South into global circuits of capital; trade liberalisation at continental and transnational levels; the financialisation of the firm; and the variety of ways in which technology and product market liberalisation have enabled markets to be serviced remotely and enabled more accurate surveillance of the international operations of multinational firms.

Notwithstanding current nationalist-populist challenges, these factors are related to a broad shift in the emphases of national governments, from the protection and development of national productive capitalisms to securing positions in international contests for mobile investment (Jessop, 2004). Countries – but also cities, subnational regions and, to an extent, supranational trade blocs – engage in competition to attract private-sector investment. More broadly, policy decisions are inflected by efforts to develop or maintain international or global 'competitiveness' (Pedersen, 2010), influenced not only by flows of capital but also by the active agency of transnational regulators. In other words, the contemporary international organisation of production and the nature of state regulation are intricately intertwined; the state, at regional, national and supranational levels, has been and remains a constitutive actor in enabling and reproducing patterns of international competition, through active processes of re-regulation, both of product markets and of factors of production, including labour (Cerny, 1997; Jessop, 2013).

Where does this leave societal-level analysis? One stock answer to the challenges of globalisation for societal institutionalists has been to posit some form of comparative institutional advantage, such that the nature of coordination used in a national economy will present it with certain advantages in specific types of production (Sorge, 1991). Thus Germany and the other densely institutionalised economies labelled by varieties of capitalism analysts as 'coordinated market economies' have advantages in sectors where progress is built upon incremental improvements in engineering, requiring collaborative relationships between employers and highly competent, adaptable employees, aided by patient capital. But despite the continued popularity of the varieties of capitalism argument as a device for labelling national economies, Hall and Soskice's (2001) vision of globalisation leading to a relatively benign process of nations building upon their path-dependent institutionalised strengths seems over-optimistic, given the extent to which liberalising pressures have been felt even in the core 'coordinated market economies' such as Germany (Holst, 2013), and the broader difficulties faced in persuading individual firms to tolerate 'constraints', even if their effects are acknowledged to be beneficial at an aggregate, national level (Marsden, 2015). In other words, the globalisation of capital makes free-riding by firms very much easier in weakening any notion of solidarity within national capitalisms. The locational flexibility of important fractions of productive capital is a key factor here.

Multinationals, regime shopping, resource shopping and societal effects

It is important to take explicit account of the fact that multinational companies (MNCs) can, to greater or lesser extents, choose where to locate. 'Regime-shopping' (Streeck, 1991) has many different aspects, including notably fiscal and labour regulation. Following societal institutionalism, we would argue that favourable forms of societal-institutional embeddedness (e.g. skills institutions with favourable outputs and so on) as well as the local-national availability of particular forms of extra-firm coordination (e.g. access to innovation networks, relations with local firms and so on) are one set of forces structuring MNC choices about location.

If different societal-institutional complexes create possibilities for competitive advantage in specific fields of activity, then a certain degree of self-selection is likely to take place as to which types of foreign direct investor have significant presence in which types of national business system. If this argument holds, then how MNCs behave in terms of their interactions with host-domestic institutions, and the degree of compatibility between the supply of, and demand for, specific forms of institutional resources, are likely to operate substantially differently between different types of national economy. Thus, in this case, regime shopping by MNCs may reinforce national and local institutional complementarities and contribute to divergence between business systems in different locations, as represented in Hall and Soskice's (2001) discussion of globalisation as a relatively benign force, at least for coordinated and liberal market economies.

Alternatively, if international market and political pressures on societies to follow uniform means of competing for productive investment are strong enough to disturb fundamentally the socio-economic foundations of host institutions, then patterns of firm coordination within MNCs may move back more within the hierarchy of the global firm itself, and its dependent supplier networks. Given evidence of the important role of the state and of socio-historically contingent institutions in promoting innovation (Crouch, 2005), such a development would be unlikely to have positive consequences even if our only interest were in the promotion of exportable innovation. Such a vision would also have negative implications for visions of MNCs as leading local economic development in ways that produce positive-sum games with localised productive systems, as positive spillover effects from MNCs to host economies would be more limited.

In seeking the reality between these alternate binary positions, it is important also to disaggregate the MNC itself (Dörrenbächer and Geppert, 2011). To a societal institutionalist, societal systems provide the resources allowing firms to compete, and do so in different ways in different types of business systems. For an MNC which has choices about location, each host business system is to some extent a 'supplier of embeddedness', operating in competition with systems elsewhere. However, to managers of a particular subsidiary unit, the specific host business system is the only one available. This may mean that managerial interest in attempts to create productive links in host economies differs between different levels of the international firm – local managers may have powerful incentives to find ways of collaborating with other local actors to achieve productivity, financial or other targets, even if corporate actors have little interest. Where regime competition is particularly intense, as, for example, in the automobile industry, the places that are successful in attracting new investment often benefit from tight networks between the local/national state, development agencies and labour market institutional actors (Hudson, 2003). In such cases, regime competition and insecurity of future investment may lead to greater, rather than lesser, degrees of associational/network 'embeddedness' with these non-firm actors, at the same time as co-opting local institutions to the vagaries of international competition.

These processes of ongoing competition for productive investment have been extensively researched by a literature on global production networks (GPNs) (see Coe and Yeung, 2015), which gives analytical priority to how lead firms coordinate international production through relations with a wide range of actors. These include dependent firms, the state at various geographical levels, education, training and research infrastructures, and a wide range of associational actors, including employers' associations and trade unions. It therefore attempts to locate an analysis of the roles of such actors within geographically and organisationally 'fragmented' (Herrigel and Zeitlin, 2010), yet still actively coordinated, international networks of the production and exploitation of value.

Importantly, for GPN scholars, the strategies regional actors must adopt to develop favourable positions in global production networks go beyond the more established notions of 'comparative institutional advantage' often found in the comparative capitalisms literature. In other words, while comparative institutionalists often posit relatively 'static' forms of comparative advantage, work on global production networks sees the relationship between regions and firms as a more dynamic relationship of 'coupling' (Coe et al., 2004). This core concept implies that there is, or needs to be, a continual process of adaptation of 'host' human and other resources to the constantly evolving needs of firms within global production networks. These processes of adaptation are not limited to occasional institutional reforms; rather, they refer to continual, mutually adaptive, relations between international firms and geographically embedded state and other governance actors.

In arguing for an explicit consideration of how regional actors activate networks in order to respond to the demands of international competition, the GPN literature builds upon, and extends, earlier arguments within regional studies and economic geography that the global fragmentation of production was likely to cause the local network embeddedness of the subsidiary operations of MNCs to increase (e.g. Morgan, 1997). Routine branch plants, serving national markets and operating to well-established corporate production methods, could often function with limited interactions with local business system actors. However, where lead firms develop the capacity to make fine-grained decisions about the geographical and organisational location of their activities, subsidiary units increasingly compete to exercise functions, or 'mandates', on an international basis (Birkinshaw, 2013), which may be global or at the level of the supranational 'region'. Units which are unsuccessful in these contests are increasingly marginalised, and threatened in cases where access to markets no longer requires the existence of local/national 'branches'.

Clearly, the fact that much productive investment is mobile makes it much more difficult for regional governments, businesses, employees and trade unions to reach long-term relationships with inward investors. However, this marked shift in the balance of power does not mean that the role of host institutions has been reduced to a simple avoidance of 'constraints'. Rather, host institutions have been repurposed to at least some extent, as the attraction and retention of the investment and jobs associated with the high value-added components of global production networks require that regional and national actors seek, through the agency of their business system actors, to provide embedded resources.

Societal institutionalism and multinational companies

Although research in the coordination of MNC subsidiaries often argues that international firms need to develop local (network) embeddedness (e.g. Andersson et al., 2002) this works shows, for the most part, very limited interest in the wider social contexts which underpin the extent and type of network relations which an MNC might pursue. It therefore largely ignores the structures of incentives and constraints which shape the ability and willingness of MNCs and of local network actors to participate in the relations of trust and mutual obligation which it focuses on. If it is true that 'a unit's most important resource is the web of specific relationships in which the subsidiary is embedded' (Andersson and Forsgren, 1996: 487), then it is vital, particularly for comparative and policy-oriented research, to take much more serious account of an array of research which indicates that national business and innovation systems differ from each other in non-trivial ways, even between countries of comparable wealth and development (Lundvall, 2010), and that sophisticated MNCs are capable of taking these differences into account when deciding where to locate different types of activities (Cantwell and Iammarino, 2000). It is here that societal institutionalist research can make a key contribution.

The societal institutionalist view has frequently been deployed in the human resource management and organisational studies literatures in order to investigate the multiple embeddedness of MNCs in different national structures for the coordination of capitalism (Bélanger et al., 2013; Dörrenbächer and Geppert, 2011). There is a substantial literature on how MNC capabilities and behaviours are affected by elements of the socio-economic structure of their countries of origin – whether MNCs 'attempt to take with them and apply their own, nationally idiosyncratic, repertoire of HRM [human resource management] practices to their subsidiaries in foreign countries' (Gooderham et al., 2006: 1507). Equally, there is a wide range of research examining the influences of societal effects on the management of MNC host units (Belizón et al. 2013; Parry et al., 2008; Saka-Helmout and Geppert, 2011;).

Host societal embeddedness is sometimes viewed as causing constraints; societal effects, whether in the form of concrete institutions or more diffuse artefacts of culture or ideology, may impede MNCs in attempts to achieve commonalities of organisational policies across their international operations (e.g. Myloni *et al.*, 2004). However, while these may be constraints from the perspective of corporate HQ managers, they may present opportunities for sub-sidiary-level managers, who may derive power resources from their ability to interpret local host environments and the limitations and possibilities these raise for corporate action. Possessing this institutional understanding, and being able to apply it in the context of the MNC, is likely to complement the potential rela-tional advantages of host managers being embedded in the host environment. As argued above, however, and particularly given regime competition, host-country institutions do not only provide MNCs with constraints (indeed, if they did, there would be much less FDI), but rather more focus should be placed on both (relatively) static comparative institutional advantage and more dynamic patterns of relational or network embeddedness in MNCs' interactions with host societies.

Thus while societal institutionalist literature on MNCs has predominantly concentrated on firms' internal management structures and processes, it also argues that firms' embeddedness in national institutions is likely to have implica-tions for how they coordinate relations with external actors (Morgan, 2001). The ability of subsidiary-level actors to network usefully in their host environ-ments cannot be assumed. Neither is it simply a question of good management. Rather, the capacity to establish embedded patterns of relations is shaped by the nature of local and national institutions (Kristensen and Zeitlin, 2005): what host economy actors may contribute to the capacity of the MNC unit to com-pete internationally, and how national and local patterns of relations of trust and authority operate, both between different firms and, more broadly, between firms, labour, the state and civil society organisations.

Logically, firms are more likely voluntarily to engage in external relations, and therefore have a more active effect on the performativity of local institu-tions, the more there are actors within the host context with whom there is demonstrable value-added in coordinating. These may include, for example, supplier and other related firms who have the capacity to engage with MNCs in relational contracting, or institutional actors, such as labour market system actors capable of providing, or co-producing, local human resource advantages. Such relations, perhaps particularly those with institutional actors, are more likely to operate successfully where host institutions empower actors to engage in localised innovation (Maskell and Malmberg, 1999). This includes insti-tutional innovation, or what has sometimes been termed 'experimentation', where social actors develop the capacities and capabilities necessary to allow interactions on a flexible basis without threatening the stability of the overall institutional architecture (Morgan and Kristensen, 2006).

The capacity of firm and non-firm actors to engage in long-term coordi-nation is, of course, a core concern of societal institutionalism. A simplistic interpretation of work in this tradition tends to argue that non-market, long-term, trust-based relations are of more importance in 'coordinated market economies' such as Germany and Japan, as opposed to the market and hierarchy-centred creation and exploitation of resources in more liberal economies (Hall and Soskice, 2001). However, there is obvious evidence of relational coordination in liberal economies; one need only think of well-known clusters of activity such as Silicon Valley, or life sciences around Cambridge, UK, to see examples of firms in such economies behaving in decidedly 'coordinated', or at least net-worked, ways (Crouch, 2005). Such cases may be exceptions to the national rule, explained by local or sectoral specificities, or by the importance of state institutions in embedding activities in strategically important sectors. However, they nonetheless point to the need for a granular analysis of how national social structure shapes patterns of firm coordination.

Equally, and importantly in so far as a discussion on societal institutionalism is concerned, the institutionalised patterns of transactions said to favour high-trust patterns of 'relational embeddedness' in countries such as Germany and Japan were developed historically with domestic firms (and the core industrial labour force) as key stakeholders, not foreign MNCs. There is insufficient systemic empirical evidence as to the extent to which foreign MNCs voluntarily engage in such forms of embeddedness in the most 'coordinated market' economies. Theoretically, though, it may well be possible for inward investors to obtain at least some of the institutionalised advantages such countries are often argued to present – such as high-skilled, adaptable workforces – through free-riding. There are certainly some signs of this in economies with intermediate levels of coordination (Almond et al., 2014).

Finally, any comparative analysis in this area needs to get a much clearer picture of what happens when host institutions are seen as inadequate. If slotting into existing host-economy patterns of coordination is inadequate for the needs of the MNC, then at least two possibilities would seem to be available. On the one hand, foreign MNC units might develop fewer voluntary active links with network actors in the domestic economy, and rely to a greater extent on their own internal global networks and hierarchies, alongside their market power in standard contractual relations. Alternatively, they may choose to engage in vari-ous forms of institution-building, taking the business of creating frameworks for the development of external coordination with local firms, civil society actors and governments into their own hands.

In summary, we would expect patterns of relations to differ across the various sorts of host political economies. But the picture is almost certainly more compli-cated than simply positing that the volume of external network linkages is greater in one 'variety of capitalism' than another. Tracing the nature of such potential cross-national differences, and their interactions with standard contingencies such as sector, technology and so on, is likely to require an analysis built on the thick description of relational networks, and what they mean to the actors concerned.

On the whole, where the international management literature explores relations between MNC units and host economies, it tends implicitly to concentrate on involvement in innovation networks and relations with local firms that are assumed to have the potential to result in positive-sum games. Yet it is frequently the case that subsidiary units engage with local/national institutions or networks for more defensive or tactical reasons. For example, firms which would prefer not to have relations with institutions representing collective labour may be required to do so in some host environments. Equally, access into some markets requires joint ventures with domestic firms, which the MNC might not have chosen freely. Further, host states or localities frequently tie subsidies and other forms of state support to the establishment of links with local firms, universities or other actors. While the latter arrangements may be voluntary, they nonetheless represent the host state shaping the 'market' for 'embeddedness'.

Some of these arrangements may well eventually create outcomes which the MNC unit is able to turn to its advantage, and indeed doing so is a key skill in subsidiary management. This does not alter the fact that their original impetus, from an MNC perspective, is either tactical or defensive. Unless it results in some form of perceived local advantage, 'involuntary' relations are particularly liable to being opposed by MNCs; this is therefore one of the areas in which MNCs are particularly likely to challenge elements of established institutionalised societal systems.

Global, national and local effects

As observed above, early societal institutionalism, itself embedded in the relatively solid societal arrangements of 1970s/1980s France and (West) Germany, was over-confident in stressing that the national society (and national sovereign state) was *the* container of societal effects. It is clear, though, that contemporary societal institutionalism cannot depend solely on a vision of relatively contained national systems, given that their integrity has been increasingly challenged by transnational influences, usually of a neoliberalising nature. This can very clearly be seen in the productive sphere, not just through the international firm per se, but more broadly by the reconfiguration of productive capitalism into global production networks. Equally, it is very clear that financial systems are strongly interdependent, and also that regulatory national sovereignty is conditional, as has been amply demonstrated in the course of the crisis in Southern Europe.

At the same time, when investigating how global productive networks inter-act with host societies, it is clear that many demonstrable 'societal' effects which influence the nature of MNCs' relations with host economies and societies are relatively local in scope. It is also not a coincidence that globalisation has increas-ingly gone hand in hand with questioning of the national sovereign state from 'below'. In some of these cases, it is probably relatively uncontroversial to say that 'subnational' societal effects are strong enough that specific places merit, for some comparative purposes, somewhat separate treatment. Quebec, in some respects, may not appear to have a very 'Canadian' variant of capitalist govern-ance, for example (Almond *et al.*, 2014).

Additionally, it has sometimes been argued that the shifts in the functions of economic governance actors associated with a focus on international com-petitiveness have been, or should be, accompanied by shifts in the levels of governance. The nation state, in other words, becomes increasingly 'leaky' as a 'container of governance' (Brenner *et al.*, 2003). Its coordinating capacities are fragmented, with some capacity transferred upwards (e.g. supranational or transnational institutions providing competition rules) and some downwards (with subnational regions or localities charged with developing flexible infra-structure, and tailoring to local economic and social needs). Influential ideas on industrial policy, not least of which is the current EU institutionalisation of 'smart specialisation' through Regional Innovation Strategies (RIS3) (see European Commission, 2014), provide examples of this; regional governments are charged with identifying their potential competitive strengths, and how these might be operationalised, in association with producer and user stakeholders.

Clearly, if nothing else, the political situation of the UK at the time of writing should alert us to the danger of teleology with such claims. The balance between geographical levels of governance, and thus the resources available to state and other governance actors at subnational levels, remains heavily contingent on national systems of political and economic governance, which themselves differ for deeply societally embedded reasons. Nonetheless, societal institutionalist research must be able to accommodate various effective geographical levels of the 'societal' construction of capitalism if it is to be practically adequate in the contemporary world.

Conclusions

Societal institutionalist researchers act under an assumption – whether explicit or otherwise – that *economic activity is always embedded in something* (inter alia, a system of property rights, rules about corporate governance and financing, rules and less formal norms about the appropriate patterns of interaction between firms, social understandings about the rights and responsibilities of workers and so on). It is important to be clear that this is ultimately an ontological position. In other words, the assumption of embeddedness is not refuted by empirical findings that fail to show national effects in specific cases, or indeed, by 'deregulation' (Almond and Rubery, 2000). This means that a societal institutionalist can either test for the effects of specific institutions at specific geographical levels, or, alternatively, can attempt to understand the social and institutional foundations of actor choices, whether or not these lie primarily in national-level institutional arrangements. Because of this, as the frameworks governing economic activity have become progressively 'de-nationalised' as a result of broader changes in global political economy (Gilpin, 2011), societal institutionalists increasingly seek influences on patterns of the coordination of MNCs that may form at multiple transnational, sectoral and subnational levels (Morgan, 2007; Meyer and Nguyen, 2005; Djelic and Quack, 2010), as well as the more traditional national level.

But moving the analysis to different geographical levels does not resolve the more basic tension within societal institutionalism as to whether embeddedness itself is an assumption – which would mean that we could perform institutionalist analysis on the underpinnings of even relatively pure market forms of exchange (e.g. Biggart and Beamish, 2003) – or an alternative reading – which refers to embeddedness as meaning the social arrangements that have historically attempted to make capitalism, and market exchange, coherent with the stabilisation of society (Polanyi, 1944). Such arrangements are geographically variable, as the varieties of capitalism literature reflects. For example, Hall and Soskice's binary model posits that US and German styles of capitalism are roughly equally successful economically, but that the social compromises that shape them are different, with distinct distributional consequences. Equally, they are historically variable; institutionalised systems for the governance of capitalism are the crystallisation of contests of power between social actors, and liable to be subject to change when they no longer fulfil their economic or social roles, as judged by powerful contemporary actors (Streeck and Thelen, 2005).

Corporate globalisation, while clearly not the sole driving factor, has played a significant role in making the establishment and maintenance of coherent national business systems more difficult. MNCs, as is well known, 'shop' between regulatory and fiscal regimes with some alacrity, both when making location choices and in ongoing negotiations with host-country social and political actors (Kristensen and Rocha, 2012). There is also a known problem of 'cherry picking' (Geppert and Matten, 2006), where firms seek to drink from the well of positive outputs of national business systems – such as highly educated workforces – while seeking to abstain from contributing to the other components of these systems (e.g. welfare states, employment relations regimes) that have been central to the construction of these advantages. Additionally, MNCs are, collectively and often individually, powerful actors, with de facto and sometimes de jure negotiating power over the nature of many of the social compromises on which liberal and social democratic variants of capitalism are built, at least in so far as how these arrangements apply to them. In this context, it is important that a comparative institutionalist approach to transnational capitalism also interrogates societal embeddedness in its original Polanyian sense of the overall coherence of the means of organising the economy within society (Polanyi, 1944). Societal institutionalist research, if pursued in a geographically open and actor-sensitive manner, can make a key contribution to this endeavour by accessing the relations between societal spheres and their interlockages.

References

Almond, P., Gonzalez, M.C., Lavelle, J. and Murray, G. (2017), 'The local in the global: Regions, employment systems and multinationals', *Industrial Relations Journal* (forthcoming).

Almond, P., Gonzalez, M.C., Gunnigle, P., Lavelle, J, Luque, D., Monaghan, S. and Murray, G. (2014), 'Multinationals and regional economies: embedding the regime shoppers', *Transfer*, 20:2, 237–53.

Almond, P. and Rubery, J. (2000), 'Deregulation and societal systems', *Advances in Organization Studies*, 4, 277–94.

Andersson, U. and Forsgren, M. (1996), 'Subsidiary embeddedness and control in the multinational corporation', *International Business Review*, 5:5, 487–508.

Andersson, U. and Forsgren, M. (2002), 'In search of centre of excellence: Network embeddedness and subsidiary roles in multinational corporations', *Management International Review*, 40:4, 329–50.

Andersson, U., Forsgren, M. and Holm, U. (2002), 'The strategic impact of external networks: subsidiary performance and competence development in the multinational corporation', *Strategic Management Journal*, 23:11, 979–96.

Bélanger, J., Lévesque, C., Jalette, P. and Murray, G. (2013), 'Discretion in employment relations policy among foreign-controlled multinationals in Canada', *Human Relations*, 66:3, 307–32.

Belizón, M.J., Gunnigle, P. and Morley, M. (2013), 'Determinants of central control and subsidiary autonomy in HRM: the case of foreign-owned multinational companies in Spain', *Human Resource Management Journal*, 23:3, 262–78.

Biggart, N. W. and Beamish, T. D. (2013), 'The economic sociology of conventions: habit, custom, practice, and routine in market order', *Annual Review of Sociology*, 29, 443–64.

Birkinshaw, J. (2013), 'How multinational subsidiary mandates are gained and lost', *Journal of International Business Studies*, 27:3, 467–95.

Brenner, N., Jessop, B., Jones, M. and MacLeod, G. (2003), 'Introduction: state space in question', in Brenner, N., Jessop, B., Jones, M. and MacLeod, G. (eds), *State Space: A Reader* (Oxford: Blackwell), pp. 1–26.

Cantwell, J. and Iammarino, S. (2000), 'Multinational corporations and the location of technological innovation in the UK regions', *Regional Studies*, 34:4, 317–32.

Cerny, P. (1997), 'Paradoxes of the competition state: the dynamics of political globalization' *Government and Opposition*, 32:2, 251–274.

Coe, N., and Yeung, H. (2015), *Global Production Networks: Theorizing Economic Development in an Interconnected World* (Oxford: Oxford University Press).

Coe, N., Hess, M. and Yeung, H. (2004), '"Globalizing" regional development: a global production networks perspective', *Transactions of the Institute of British Geographers*, 29:3, 468–84.

Crouch, C. (2005), *Capitalist Diversity and Change* (Oxford University Press: Oxford).

Djelic, M. L. and Quack, S. (2003), *Globalization and Institutions. Redefining the Rules of the Economic Game* (Aldershot: Elgar).

Djelic, M. L. and Quack, S. (eds) (2010), *Transnational Communities: Shaping Global Economic Governance* (Cambridge: Cambridge University Press).

Dörrenbächer, C. and Geppert, M. (eds) (2011), *Politics and Power in the Multinational Corporation: The Role of Institutions, Interests and Identities* (Cambridge: Cambridge University Press).

European Commission (2014), *National/Regional Innovation Strategies for Smart Specialisation (RIS3)* (Brussels: European Commission).

Geppert, M. and Matten, D. (2006), 'Institutional influences on manufacturing organization in multinational corporations: The 'cherrypicking' approach', *Organization Studies*, 27, 491–515.

Gertler, M.S. (2010), 'Rules of the game: the place of institutions in regional economic change', *Regional Studies*, 44:1, 1–15.

Gilpin, R. (2011), *Global Political Economy: Understanding the International Economic Order* (Princeton: Princeton University Press).

Gooderham, P., Nordhaug, O. and Ringdal, K. (2006), 'National embeddedness and calculative human resource management in US subsidiaries in Europe and Australia', *Human Relations*, 59:11, 1491–513.

Hall, P. and Soskice, D. (eds) (2001), *Varieties of Capitalism* (Oxford: Oxford University Press).

Herrigel G. and Zeitlin, J. (2010), 'Interfirm relations in global manufacturing: disintegrated production and its globalisation', in Morgan, G., Campbell, J., Crouch, C., Kristensen, P. H., Pedersen, O. and Whitley, R. (eds), *The Oxford Handbook of Comparative Institutional Analysis* (Oxford: Oxford University Press), pp. 527–61.

Holst, H. (2013), 'Commodifying institutions: vertical disintegration and institutional change in German labour relations', *Work Employment and Society*, 28:1, 3–20.

Hudson, R. (2003), 'European integration and new forms of uneven development', *European Urban and Regional Studies*, 10:1, 49–67.

Jessop, B. (2004), *Towards a Schumpetarian Workfare State? Preliminary Remarks on Post-Fordist Political Economy* (Lancaster: University of Lancaster, originally 1993).

Jessop, B. (2013), 'Revisiting the regulation approach: Critical reflections on the contradictions, dilemmas, fixes and crisis dynamics of growth regimes', *Capital and Class*, 37:1, 5–24.

Kristensen, P. H., and Rocha, R. S. (2012), 'New roles for the trade unions five lines of action for carving out a new governance regime', *Politics and Society*, 40:3, 453–79.

Kristensen, P. H. and Zeitlin, J. (2005), *Local Players in Global Games* (Oxford: Oxford University Press).

Lammers, C. and Hickson, D. (1979), *Organisations Alike and Unlike* (London: Routledge).

Lane, C. (1989), *Management and Labour in Europe* (Aldershot: Elgar).

Lundvall, B. Å. (ed.) (2010), *National Systems of Innovation: Toward a Theory of Innovation and Interactive Learning*, Vol. 2 (London: Anthem Press).

Marsden, D. (2015), 'The future of the German Industrial Relations Model', *Journal for Labour Market Research*, 48:2, 169–87.

Maskell, P. and Malmberg, A. (1999), 'The competitiveness of firms and regions "Ubiquitification" and the importance of localized learning', *European Urban and Regional Studies*, 6:1, 9–25.

Maurice, M. (1979), 'For a study of the societal effect: universality and specificity in organisational research', in Lammers, C and Hickson, D. (eds), *Organisations Alike and Unlike* (London: Routledge).

Maurice, M. and Sorge, A. (eds) (2000), *Embedding Organizations: Societal Analysis of Actors, Organizations and Socio-economic Context*, Vol. 4 (Amsterdam: John Benjamins Publishing Company).

Maurice, M., Sellier, F., and Silvestre, J. J. (1986), *The Social Foundations of Industrial Power: A Comparison of France and Germany* (Cambridge, MA: MIT Press).

Meyer, K. E., and Nguyen, H. V. (2005), 'Foreign investment strategies and sub-national institutions in emerging markets: Evidence from Vietnam', *Journal of Management Studies*, 42:1, 63–93.

Michon, F. (1992), 'The institutional forms of work and employment: towards the construction of an international historical and comparative approach', in Castro, A., Méhaut, P., and Rubery, J. (eds), *International Integration and Labour Market Organisation* (London, Academic Press).

Morgan, G. (2001), 'Transnational communities and business systems', *Global Networks*, 1:1, 113–30.

Morgan, G. (2007), 'National business systems research: Progress and prospects', *Scandinavian Journal of Management*, 23:2, 127–45.

Morgan, G. and Kristensen, P. H. (2006), 'The contested space of multinationals: varieties of institutionalism, varieties of capitalism', *Human Relations*, 59:11, 1467–90.

Morgan, K. (1997), 'The Regional Animateur: taking stock of the Welsh Development Agency', *Regional and Federal Studies*, 7:2, 70–94.

Myloni, B., Harzing, A. and Mirza, H. (2004), 'Host country specific factors and the transfer of human resource management practices in multinational companies', *International Journal of Manpower*, 25:6, 518–34.

Parry, E., Dickmann, M. and Morley, M. (2008), 'North American MNCs and their HR policies in liberal and coordinated market economies', *The International Journal of Human Resource Management*, 19:11, 2024–40.

Peck, J. and Theodore, N. (2007), 'Variegated capitalism', *Progress in human geography*, 31:6, 731–772.

Polanyi, K. (1944), *The Great Transformation: The Social and Political Origins of Our Time* (Boston: Beacon Press).

Pedersen, O. (2010), 'Institutional competitiveness: How nations came to compete', in Morgan, G. Campbell, J., Crouch, C., Kristensen, P., Pedersen, O. and Whitley, R. (eds), *The Oxford Handbook of Comparative Institutional Analysis* (Oxford: Oxford University Press).

Rubery, J. (1992), 'Production systems, international integration and the single European market', in Castro, A., Méhaut, P., and Rubery, J. (eds), *International Integration and Labour Market Organisation* (London: Academic Press).

Rubery, J. (1994), 'The British production regime: a societal-specific system?', *Economy and Society*, 23:3, 335–54.

Saka-Helmout, A. and Geppert, M. (2011), 'Different forms of agency and institutional influences within multinational enterprises', *Management International Review*, 51:5, 567–92.

Sorge, A. (1991), 'Strategic fit and the societal effect: interpreting cross-national comparisons of technology, organization and human resources', *Organization Studies*, 12:2, 161–90.

Streeck, W. (1991), 'More uncertainties: German unions facing 1992', *Industrial Relations*, 30:3, 317–49.

Streeck, W. and Thelen, K.A. (2005), *Beyond Continuity: Institutional Change in Advanced Political Economies* (Oxford: Oxford University Press).

Whitley, R. (ed.) (1992), *European Business Systems: Firms and Markets in their National Contexts* (London: Sage).

Whitley, R. (1999), *Divergent Capitalisms: The Social Structuring and Change of Business Systems* (Oxford: Oxford University Press).

Wilkinson, F. (1983), 'Productive systems', *Cambridge Journal of Economics*, 7:3/4, 413–29.

4

The networked organisation: implications for jobs and inequality

Rosemary Batt and Eileen Appelbaum

Introduction

The vertical integration of production into large hierarchical firms was a dominant organisational form during the twentieth century. Since the 1980s, however, firms have increasingly decentralised production to networks of sub-contractors. Organisational boundaries have become blurred, work processes have been fragmented, and new forms of inter-firm contracting and outsourcing of work have grown. The greater use of business strategies that re-allocate workers across networked organisations has important implications for employment relations and for wages, job quality and inequality.[1]

More than a decade ago, in a series of important essays written with colleagues, Jill Rubery drew attention to the blurring of firm boundaries and the fragmenting of work in the UK. Rubery was already a leading scholar of labour market flexibility and the rise of temporary and contingent jobs in Europe. In the research on the fragmentation of work, she moved beyond that narrower focus on the rise of precarious employment to examine developments at the firm and organisational level. She was among the first to bring workers into academic studies of the rise of networked production – arguing not only that new forms of *organising production across firms* spill over into *the organisation of work within firms*, but that the outcomes for firms, suppliers, workers, customers and relations of power in inter-firm networks depend importantly on variation in the institutional context within and across countries.

Building on her extensive work on labour market segmentation, Rubery also emphasised that employers as a whole do not have a unified set of interests.

As she and her colleagues wrote in *Fragmenting Work: Blurring Organizational Boundaries and Disordering Hierarchies*:

> The situating of employing organisations in a web of inter-organisational relations provides a framework through which we can understand the development of employment relations in the context of the restructuring of capital–capital relations. The twin tensions between cooperation and conflict underpin both capital–capital and capital–labour relations. These tensions and opposing tendencies need to be considered conjointly rather than separately. ... we need to recognize that inter-firm relations rely on elements of cooperation, competition, and dominance. (Rubery *et al.*, 2005: 87)

With colleagues, she went on to argue:

> A second step is to bring work back into the analysis. ... It enables us to introduce such questions as: Does the network form represent a new concentration of power among employers better able to avoid or oppose the collective demands of labor? Do networks promote new divisions and new inequalities among workers? (Grimshaw *et al.*, 2005: 40)

These remain key questions today in the analysis of networked forms of production. Where is value created and how and where is it extracted? Does outsourcing deliver on promises of increased efficiency and, if so, do workers share in productivity gains? How are workers allocated among different organisations in an inter-firm network? How does this affect the quality of jobs, wage growth, wage inequality and the power of collective forms of representation?

In this chapter we examine the original contributions Rubery and her colleagues have made to our understanding of the effects of the rise in outsourcing and production networks on work and workers. While the outcomes for workers continue to receive far less attention than warranted, some important new case-study and empirical research address these issues. We conclude with a discussion of directions for future research.

Blurring boundaries and the employment relation

Research on the networked organisation emerged in the 1980s and 1990s, with attention paid primarily to describing the phenomenon, why it was emerging in the context of heightened competition and the enabling features of digital technologies, and whether it led to superior firm performance. Few scholars paid attention to the implications of these structural changes for work and employ-ment relations. At the forefront of new scholarship investigating these issues, Rubery and her colleagues published a series of qualitative case studies and a co-edited book in the early to mid-2000s (Marchington *et al.*, 2005). They did not assume any particular outcome for workers, but rather drew on their qualitative research to build an inventory of ways in which the rise of networked forms of production affects the quality of jobs and the nature of employment relations. This approach allowed them to expand on the institutional conditions under which networked forms may lead to better or worse outcomes for workers.

A common thread in this ambitious undertaking is the multiple ways in which boundaries between organisations have become blurred as firms increasingly contract out and fragment work. Rubery and her colleagues were among the first to recognise that existing scholarship – which examined changes in the organisation of production and changes in the employment relation in isola-tion from each other – missed the main point: changes in the organisation of production and the extent of outsourcing both shape and are shaped by changes in the employment relation (Grimshaw and Rubery, 2005). They were at the forefront in recognising that changes in *the organisation of production across firms* spill over into changes in *the organisation of work within firms,* with implications for human resource (HR) management and the quality of jobs (Rubery *et al.*, 2002). They demonstrated that combining analyses of the disintegration of production processes and of the fragmentation of the employment relation allows for a more complete understanding of both.

Explaining the rise and fall of the vertically integrated firm

To understand the changes now underway, it is helpful to step back and briefly review why vertically integrated and hierarchical forms of organisation emerged during the twentieth century and replaced the price mechanism as a primary form of coordinating production.

Businesses choose whether to perform certain functions in-house or to con-tract with other firms for those inputs when producing goods and services for final demand. The transactions cost framework (Coase, 1937; Williamson, 1975, 1985) favoured by mainstream economists explains the make or buy deci-sion on the basis of relative *transaction* costs. Firms and markets, Coase argued, are alternative ways to organise transactions, coordinate production and allocate labour and other resources. Markets rely on the price mechanism to do this, which is efficient when transactions are straightforward, non-repetitive and do not require specific investments in assets in order to carry them out. Where these conditions are not met – where outcomes are uncertain, interactions are

repeated and transaction-specific investments are required – vertically integrated firms are more efficient than markets for coordinating production. In
this view, large, vertically integrated firms that retained production activities
in-house emerged in the twentieth century to minimise firms' transaction costs.
In particular, firms internalised the employment relation when the costs of
bureaucratic monitoring and control of workers were less than the costs of
specifying and enforcing external contracts with vendors or suppliers.

Alternative explanations for the emergence of hierarchical organisations also
focus on the internalisation of the employment relationship. Political economists
view hierarchy as a governance mechanism for managing the inherently antago-
nistic interests of employers and workers in the production process (Marglin,
1974). Employers are able to exercise authority over workers to achieve labour
flexibility and cooperation in productive activities. In return, workers gain the
economic security provided by regular work and wages.

A third approach, favoured by Rubery, notes the importance of labour
market segmentation theory (Jacoby, 1984; Osterman, 1984; Rubery, 1978)
and rejects the simple capital–labour struggle story that underlies the political economy rationale for hierarchical organisation as overly deterministic
(see Chapter 1). Rather than a pre-determined identity of interests among all
employers, this approach views the internalised employment relation as emerging out of competitive struggles among capitalists for market share and among
workers for jobs that offer economic and employment security – as well as the
struggles between employers and employees within firms. Capital–capital as
well as capital–labour relations are important for understanding how production is organised. The internalisation of the employment relationship, according
to this line of argument, is not an outcome imposed on workers by employers
unified by their common interests. Rather, 'the historical internalization of
employment is interpreted through the process of identity and interest formation' (Marchington et al., 2005: 11).

In the 1980s, large hierarchical firms began to lose their comparative organisational advantage in the face of technological innovation, heightened competition, market deregulation and the 'shareholder value revolution'. Flexible
manufacturing technologies, for example, undermined mass production by
allowing factories to produce a greater variety of goods in small batches, enabling
decentralised production in flexibly specialised firms (Piore and Sabel, 1984).
Japanese lean production, characterised by lead firms controlling manufacturing processes in a complex web of supplier firms (Dore, 1986), achieved higher
levels of innovation, lower time-to-market for new products and higher quality and efficiency than mass production models (Jaikumar, 1986; MacDuffie,
1995). The rising influence of institutional investors and shareholders also put

pressure on firms to reduce costs and headcount and dismantle the corporation by selling off assets or less profitable business units and returning cash to shareholders (Appelbaum and Batt, 2014; Batt and Appelbaum, 2013). And finance and management scholars urged firms to respond by focusing on their 'core competencies' or 'what they do best', and outsourcing the rest (Kogut and Zander, 1992; Lepak and Snell, 1999; Prahalad and Hamel, 1990). The core competency model has diffused widely across many industries and countries.

Our understanding of the extent of outsourcing within and across countries – and the number of workers affected by this process – is seriously inadequate given that national data collection continues to be based on traditional definitions of firms and industries. Nonetheless, extensive field-based and industry-specific research has documented the powerful restructuring of supply chains – particularly in manufacturing – since the 1980s. Our most advanced understanding is found in the literature on global production networks (Dicken, 1992) or global commodity chains (Bair, 2009; Gereffi and Koreniewicz, 1994); but here, the poor outcomes for workers are often attributed to the location of jobs in low-wage countries with poor labour standards. Much less attention has focused on how and why workers in advanced countries are affected by *domestic* outsourcing, and here is where Jill Rubery's research has made a lasting contribution.

The emergence and outcomes of networked forms of production

Rubery's critique of the mainstream literature on the networked firm offers several insights. Firstly, she argues that beyond tangible benefits, such as greater efficiency or profitability, the network form is important for many intangible benefits it provides. These include the capability to exploit new knowledge, preferential access to financing, organisational learning through access to technical capabilities, sharing of tacit knowledge and development of a shared understanding of rapidly changing markets. The extent to which networked organisations can obtain these intangible benefits depends importantly on how labour is managed across the network (Marchington et al., 2005). Empirical studies of the links between technological change, organisational structure and knowledge creation support this view (Grimshaw et al., 2000; Hagedoorn and Duysters, 2002; Miozzo and Grimshaw, 2005; Saxenian, 1996).

Closely related to this argument is Rubery's conceptualisation of skill. Skill is not a set of objectively measured technical competencies, which can be distinguished according to the value they contribute to firm profitability, as argued by core competency theorists. Rather, skills are defined and determined via social and political processes. Equating skill with technical competence means that tacit skills and social capital – two dimensions of skill that are critical to the success of networked organisations – are overlooked. She disputes the assumption that a clear divide exists between jobs that require cooperation and commitment (or those with high technical skills) and those that do not. Thus attempts to separate out strategic from non-strategic jobs on the basis of a narrow technical definition of skill are likely to fail (Rubery et al., 2004; Ward et al., 2001). Similarly, there is no neat division of inter-firm networks into 'relational' (where employment relations are internalised to the network and investments in human capital are shared) or 'transactional' (where employment is externalised to the market) (Rubery and Grimshaw, 2001).

Networked forms of production also 'complexify' the capital–labour relationship, according to Rubery. Her early insights into capital–capital as well as capital–labour conflicts, developed in her work on labour market segmentation, carry over to her analysis of inter-firm relationships. Both sets of relationships shape the extent to which firms internalise or externalise (outsource) labour. Moreover, organisations in inter-firm networks need to gain the cooperation both of other firms across the network and of workers within their firm. Conflicting employer–employee interests persist, but within a framework of inter-organisational relations that provide new opportunities for cooperation and division between firms in addition to the opportunities for conflict and mutual benefit generated by the employment relationship. Thus it is an empirical question whether the shift from vertically integrated firms to boundary-less organisations, and related changes in the organisation of work, are positive or negative, and for whom (Rubery, 2007).

Rubery also emphasises the importance of asymmetrical power relations among these firms, which more often than not create pressures for less collaboration. This view contrasts with the conventional view that firms in a network necessarily provide complementary as opposed to competing inputs (Miles and Snow, 1986). Her argument is that the rents generated in the production process may be distributed unevenly among the organisations in the production network, with more powerful organisations positioned to extract a disproportionate share. More powerful organisations may then share those rents with their workforce in order to harness workers' cooperation in producing goods and services. Unequal power relations among network members may enable some organisations (e.g. primary or client firms) to impose performance goals on weaker network members (e.g. force cost reductions onto subcontractors). Weaker firms in a network may operate on narrow margins and rely on the externalisation of labour in order to lower labour costs, with negative outcomes for workers limited only by social and political institutions, such as employment laws and the strength of unions. Thus Rubery avoids drawing generic principles about outcomes for workers as these are contingent on power relations within the network as well as on the institutional landscape – unions, trade associations, government legislation (Grimshaw et al., 2005). Her analysis leaves open the possibility of positive outcomes and a role for political intervention.

In Rubery's theoretical framework, three dimensions of institutional context – trust, power asymmetries and institutional embeddedness – play a central role in determining the conditions under which networked organisations may lead to better or worse outcomes for stakeholders. Firstly, networks may be distinguished between those that rely primarily on the market mechanism and legal contracts ('arm's length' relations) versus those that rely on relations of trust and reputation (relational contracting) (Adler, 2001; Sako, 1992). The latter require greater interdependence among members of a network and are underpinned by 'goodwill trust' and a 'moral commitment' to maintain the relationship. Secondly, power asymmetries between capital and capital – between primary and contractor firms, for example – may undermine the mutual sharing of benefits. Contractor firms may find themselves facing a powerful rationale for externalising labour in order to reduce costs. This may lead to differentiated outcomes for workers in lead and subcontractor firms. Thirdly, networks are embedded in national institutional landscapes, which may in some cases encourage trust and limit the exercise of power within production networks – for example, if national law mandates the extension of collective bargaining agreements to all parties in an industry (Grimshaw and Miozzo, 2006). In countries such as the USA and the UK, where institutional arrangements that undergird moral contracts are weak, it is the stronger organisations that are likely to exercise power over the weaker ones in the network. This may be a second-best way to organise production, but it is likely to be preferred in situations where the cost of conflict is preferable to the costs and risks of contracts secured by trust.

Thus Rubery and her colleagues argue that because relations of trust, power and risk are so important in shaping production networks, efficiency is a second-order concern for understanding the dynamics of changing organisational forms. Their analysis breaks new ground in theorising about the nature of employment contracts and the quality of jobs – by analysing how networked forms, within and across industries, lead to new types of labour market segmentation and inequality among workers.

What have we learned since the Great Recession?

As Rubery and her colleagues developed their research programme on the implications of the networked firm for management and employment relations in the 2000s, interest in this question was emerging among other scholars – prompted by growing evidence of stagnant wages, the decline in the quality of jobs and rising inequality in advanced economies. The financial crisis and recession in 2008, and the subsequent austerity regime in Europe, exacerbated these problems by increasing incentives for public entities and private enterprises alike to cut labour costs by outsourcing and restructuring. These events made more salient the need for empirical research to identify the impact of these strategies on workers and unions.

As we noted above, Rubery and colleagues argued that the relative outcomes for workers are an empirical question, contingent on the power relations among capitalists in the supply chain and between capital and labour, and on the points of institutional leverage available to the parties involved. Existing empirical research, unfortunately, presents a sobering landscape in the context of an overall shift in power to capital and the weakening of unions in recent decades. In the European Union (EU) specifically, the ability of elites to advance a programme of market liberalisation and privatisation of public services has increased dramatically.

Most empirical research in both the USA and Europe suggests that the rise of the networked firm and outsourcing of production has led to a deterioration in the jobs and pay of workers and to a growth in wage inequality. The European research appears to be more advanced than its US counterpart (Bernhardt *et al.*, 2015), but the findings are quite consistent. The negative effects of outsourcing are particularly noteworthy for low-wage workers, but also for public sector workers and middle-income groups. At the same time, the comparative institutional research to which Rubery has prominently contributed also shows the ways in which negative outcomes can be moderated or reversed – depending on a range of national and local institutional factors, public policies and the particular strategies of actors.

At a general level, a handful of studies using national government statistical data provide persuasive evidence linking outsourcing to lower pay and pay inequality for working people. A recent US study using national government data attributes a large portion of the rise in earnings inequality since the 1970s to increased dispersion in earnings across establishments – consistent with a story of increased sorting of workers into higher- and lower-paying establishments (Barth *et al.*, 2014). Similarly, recent US research has shown that increased occupational concentration of workers in establishments accounts for a large share of the growth in wage inequality (Handwerker, 2015; Handwerker and Spletzer, 2015). This would suggest that firms have found it useful to increase the specialised division of labour – segmenting labour markets based on occupational expertise or 'core competencies' and the sorting of workers by skill level or skill type into higher and lower paid firms and establishments. If firms focus on their 'core competencies' – for example, engineering, IT services or value-added manufacturing – they may shift ancillary work to firms specialising in HR services, cleaning services, food services, logistics and the like. Consistent with this story, Davis and Cobb (2010) examined the size distribution of firms in a large-scale multi-country study and found that the lower the proportion of workers in large firms, the higher the wage inequality.

Two studies of low-wage workers in ancillary services provide a more detailed examination of how outsourcing leads to lower pay and pay inequality. In a critical study that links longitudinal employer and employee data in Germany, Goldschmidt and Schmieder (2015) documented a dramatic growth in domestic outsourcing of ancillary services (janitors, security guards, food service workers) since the early 1990s. They found that wages for these groups fell on average by 10–15 per cent when these workers moved from in-house firms to outsourced contractors and that they remained permanently lower. Wages of temp agency cleaning workers fell by 26 per cent. More generally, they showed that the outsourcing of cleaning, security and logistics services alone accounted for roughly 10 per cent of the increase in German wage inequality since the 1980s. Similarly, a US study using national government data found an outsourcing wage penalty of 4 to 7 per cent for janitors and 8 to 24 per cent for guards (Dube and Kaplan, 2010). The similarity of these results in the context of remarkably different national labour laws and industrial relations systems suggests that this type of restructuring may be a source of rising within-country inequality in many countries.

These studies are suggestive of broad-based patterns linking outsourcing to lower pay, although they do not provide the kind of nuanced detail to identify potential causal mechanisms or variation across institutional settings and actor strategies – the hallmark of Rubery's approach. Other qualitative and mixed methods research follows more in this latter tradition. This stream of research also generally finds negative outcomes for workers in outsourced operations, although variation in the magnitude of the effects on job quality depends on institutional and other external factors. The case-based research in Europe is considerably more advanced than in North America, perhaps because outsourcing has been more publicly salient – as in the privatisation of public services or outsourcing of work in highly unionised settings where deep institutional legacies are challenged and unions have waged public and media campaigns.

Call centres were an early focus of attention in part because they were a new phenomenon that used new technologies to industrialise service work in a dramatically new way. But early research did not distinguish between in-house and outsourced centres, viewing them equally as a new form of Taylorisation and degradation of work; rather, it focused on the threat of job loss owing to offshoring. Later research, however, clearly showed that within advanced countries, outsourced centres had consistently lower job quality and pay. A 20-country study based on field research and identical establishment-level surveys, for example, showed systematic differences between union in-house, non-union in-house and outsourced operations, with the latter scoring the lowest on virtually all dimensions of job quality – including substantially lower pay, benefits, training and discretion at work – and the highest on the use of electronic monitoring and part-time and contingent work. These conditions also led to higher quit rates (Batt, Holman and Holtgrewe, 2009; Doellgast *et al.*, 2009). The average wage penalty for outsourced establishments was 10.8 per cent in the USA and Canada, but 14.6 per cent in major European countries (Batt and Nohara, 2009) – higher in Europe because employers shifted work not only from in-house to outsourced centres, but from *union* in-house to *non-union* outsourced centres. These findings are consistent with the theoretical predictions that outsourcing leads to new forms of labour market segmentation and inequality for workers performing similar tasks in the same industry.

Other sector-specific research has focused on construction and transportation services, where the accelerated use of subcontracting has also led to a decline in wages and working conditions in both Europe and the US. While construction work has always relied on a network of contractors, market liberalisation in Europe and deregulation in the USA have undermined union power and facilitated the emergence of new non-union competitors. In Europe, this has taken the form of transnational contractors hiring migrant workers within the EU ('posted workers') to work on shipbuilding and construction sites for lower wages (Lillie, 2012). In the USA, subcontracting to non-union firms in residential construction and to owner-operators in trucking was the key strategy to undermine union power in those industries, leading in turn to the proliferation of low-wage, non-union jobs (Belzer, 1994; Milkman, 2008).

Some research has also addressed the impact of outsourcing in manufacturing. In the European auto industry, for example, the major players adopted three strategies that have led to two-tier wage and employment conditions (Doellgast and Greer, 2007): the establishment of separate subsidiaries with second-tier union contracts; the greater outsourcing of parts production; and the use of contractors to staff on-site activities – including those for ancillary services such as logistics, cleaning, food service and maintenance, as well as temporary staffing agencies to fill core jobs in assembly and parts production. Consistent with this grounded research, econometric studies of German manufacturing have found that while the wages in primary manufacturing firms have not fallen, their labour costs have – supporting the idea that they have shifted some work to lower-wage contractors to reduce overall labour costs (Dustmann *et al.*, 2014).

Other research demonstrates that workers in outsourced operations face far worse health and safety conditions or higher violations of basic labour standards and labour and employment laws (Weil, 2014). Compared to primary firms, contractor firms have shown substantially higher injury rates or safety hazards in the US context (Boden, Spieler and Wagner, 2016), and specifically in the US petrochemical industry (Rebitzer, 1995), mining (Muzaffar et al., 2013), trucking (Belzer, 1994) and among staffing agency workers in a variety of occupations (Foley et al., 2014; Morris, 1999). Franchising is another fast-growing form of contracting out; and recent US research shows that establishments owned by franchisees have a 24 per cent higher probability of non-compliance with wage and hour laws than those owned by franchisors (the primary firm) – attributable to differences in the profit models and cost pressures that each type of establishment faces (Ji and Weil, 2015).

Research on the outcomes of outsourcing for knowledge and professional workers is less developed, and the evidence is more mixed. In theory, if outsourcing creates a more specialised division of labour across firms, then workers with specialised occupational skills (or higher human capital) should have substantial bargaining power and be able to extract rents, for example, in engineering, IT or consulting firms. A specialised division of labour should also allow these firms to compete on the basis of differentiated or 'value-added' services, facilitating their revenue growth that in theory may be shared with workers. Moreover, workers should benefit from knowledge-sharing and promotion opportunities. One study, for example, found that dieticians and food service managers had better job promotion opportunities if they worked for a contract food service company than if they were a direct-hire employee of an individual school or hospital (Erickcek et al., 2003). By contrast, research on the unbundling of corporate functions (law, accounting, HR functions, shared services) provides no clear evidence regarding the quality of jobs in outsourced high-skilled occupations (Sako et al., 2013).

In Europe, a particularly important stream of research has examined the restructuring of public sector service provision in response to government pressure to reduce costs, as well as strategies of the EU to create integrated markets for services across member states. New Public Management strategies have included a blurring of boundaries between the public and the private sectors via public–private partnerships or the use of market-based incentives, as well as complete outsourcing of traditionally public sector work to private sector vendors that are increasingly trans-European providers. This trend accelerated as the EU and member countries adopted widespread austerity policies from 2012 on. Two large-scale research projects investigating the impact of public service outsourcing (WORKS and PIQUE)[2] provide substantial evidence that it has led to the deterioration in pay, benefits and a range of working conditions – including longer or flexible work hours, understaffing and work intensification, and job insecurity – across a wide swathe of different types of services and different countries (Flecker and Hermann, 2011; Flecker and Meil, 2010; Hermann and Flecker, 2012; Vrangbæk et al., 2013). Case studies showing specific sectoral dynamics also document lower wages, employment contracts or work intensification in health care (Greer et al., 2013), adult social care (Grimshaw et al., 2015; Rubery and Urwin, 2011) and municipal services (Mori, 2015).

More importantly, Rubery and her colleagues have been at the forefront of documenting the ways in which public sector outsourcing and privatisation exacerbates gender inequality as women have historically dominated public sector jobs and have been the hardest hit by austerity measures designed to outsource public sector services (Rubery and Karamessini, 2013). After two decades of proactive gender policy and economic progress for women in Europe, the austerity turn has undermined many of those gains (Rubery, 2015). The intersection between outsourcing and European migration patterns is also noteworthy in current research, as the fragmentation of work across organisational boundaries places disproportionate risks on migrant workers who are least able to organise or who may or may not be incorporated into union strategic campaigns (Danaj and Sippola, 2015; Haidinger, 2015).

In the context of these broad-brush trends, however, the comparative institutionalist research tradition that Rubery and her colleagues have fostered does offer theory and evidence for the effectiveness of political and strategic action (see Chapters 1 and 3). The devil is in the detail, as research illustrates how national and local institutions and activist strategies have shaped the magnitude of outsourcing's effects. Unions and social movement organisations have used different points of institutional leverage to moderate the negative impact of outsourcing or to resist it all together. Doellgast's (2012) careful comparison of the dynamics of outsourcing in German and US telecommunications demonstrates, for example, the specific mechanisms through which union power and co-determination rights were used to limit the unilateral power of managers and the extent and conditions of outsourcing in Germany. And Doellgast and colleagues' (2016) follow-on study of telecommunications call centres in 10 countries found that while outsourcing produced wage inequality between in-house and outsourced or externalised groups of workers, the magnitude of the effect depended importantly on how national institutions shaped the cost structures faced by employers as well as the sources of bargaining power that unions could call upon (Doellgast et al., 2016).

Rubery and colleagues' recent work on local government outsourcing illustrates how public sector sourcing decisions are complex and varied – depending on the extent to which the public and private sectors differ in terms of pay levels, union coverage and opposition, collective bargaining provisions, labour market protections, the level of the minimum wage and differences in the legal status of public and private sector workers (Grimshaw *et al.*, 2015). As a result, public sector outsourcing calculations are complex, with outcomes shaped by political contestation, which varies markedly across national and local institutional contexts. This variety – and new strategies for organising and solidarity across organisational boundaries and supply chains – is illustrated in a series of recent case studies of resistance to public and private sector outsourcing across Europe (Danaj and Sippola, 2015; Doellgast *et al.*, 2017; Drahokoupil, 2015; Haidinger, 2015).

Conclusions: Implications for research and policy

Recent scholarship has advanced our understanding of how and why organisational restructuring and outsourcing has occurred in advanced economies and what the general implications are for working people. But there is much to be done. Accurate data on the prevalence and growth of outsourcing appears to be weak in both Europe and North America, as government statistical agencies typically do not collect data based on contractor status, and researchers have often relied on industry or trade association surveys or consulting reports instead. Nationally representative data linking contractor status to wages and employment conditions are also rarely available. Thus, at a general level, we do not know how much organisational restructuring and outsourcing have occurred and the extent to which they have contributed to stagnant wages and wage inequality in advanced economies – information that is needed to inform public policy debates.

In the meantime, however, researchers can and should pursue the kind of grounded, industry- or occupation-specific studies that can inform public policy. These studies may be undertaken from the perspective of the contracting industry (autos, hotels, health care) but also from the angle of contractor industries (third-party logistics companies, professional and business services). Industry studies can capitalise on a rich combination of sources – including government and administrative data, media analysis, company and union archival data, interviews with industry actors and on-site observation – which taken together can advance our understanding of the complex causal mechanisms linking firm organisational strategies to better or worse employment outcomes for working people (Bernhardt *et al.*, 2015).

Industry studies of this kind are also important because the dynamics of outsourcing and the different forms that networked organisations take vary according to the institutional legacies and market dynamics of specific sectors. Plotting complex network ties is also a first step to examine a relatively unexplored topic – highlighted in Rubery's theoretical perspective – that is, the importance of asymmetrical power relations between and among primary and contractor firms. Strategic analysis of power relations is critical to identify the points of leverage for negotiating better outcomes for workers across supply chains, to pinpoint opportunities for public policy reform and to begin to construct models of new inter-organisational industrial relations systems to represent workers' rights.

Research on the differential effects of outsourcing on distinct demographic and occupational groups is also undeveloped. There have been some important studies of public sector restructuring and its unequal gender effects, as well as case studies of migrant or posted workers. And some studies of organisational restructuring have highlighted outcomes for certain occupations and demographic groups. But we lack deep empirical investigations at the intersection of organisational restructuring on the one hand, and race, gender and ethnicity on the other.

In addition, as we have noted, emerging research has identified some promising forms of collective action via coalitions of labour, community, consumer and other constituencies in both the USA and Europe. Unions in some cases have moved beyond only protecting their core members to embrace a broader advocacy agenda for the rights of migrants and other 'peripheral' workers. But a central question for future research is whether these promising examples can diffuse more broadly – or get to scale. Which mobilisation strategies or policy reforms are the most effective in securing minimum job and income security as the employer of record and location of work continually shift? Broad-based campaigns, such as minimum- and living-wage campaigns, are particularly effective as they disproportionately affect low-wage workers – often working for subcontractors or franchised operations. In the USA, the 'fight for fifteen' is an example of a broad grassroots movement to raise the minimum wage to $15 an hour that rapidly and unexpectedly moved into the mainstream, with many states and localities now raising their minimums to at least $10 per hour and some to $15. But that still does not deal with challenges of ensuring workers' rights when existing employment laws continue to assume that the employment relationship is between a single employer and employee.

The challenge, as Rubery and her colleagues point out, is to rethink employment policy to respond to the growing importance of networked forms of organisation and fragmented work. As organisational boundaries have become blurred, assigning responsibility for poor job quality, poor customer service, inefficient use of resources or poor economic performance becomes ambiguous. Employment law and labour market policy that assumes a single employer may mean that no one is accountable or that legal liability falls on less powerful and less well-resourced organisations. The most vulnerable workers are the most at risk from the fragmentation of work. But the lack of regulation may also be detrimental to the interests of employers and production networks, as unfettered competition may undermine the collaboration and coordination among capitalists necessary for innovation and growth. A better balance of power among stakeholders in production networks, achieved through government policy and legislation and new forms of worker representation, can improve outcomes for workers, citizens and national economies more generally. Meeting this challenge will require another type of collaboration – among researchers, practitioners and policy-makers.

Notes

1   This chapter benefited greatly from the joint work of Bernhardt and colleagues (2015).
2   WORKS (Work Organisation and Restructuring in the Knowledge Society) Project – Changes in Work (www.worksproject.be); PIQUE (Privatisation of public services and the impact on quality, employment and productivity) Project (http://www.pique.at).

References

Adler, P. (2001), 'Market, hierarchy and trust: the market economy and the future of capitalism', *Organization Science*, 12:2, 214–34.
Appelbaum, E., and Batt, R. (2014), *Private Equity at Work: When Wall Street Manages Main Street*. (New York: Russell Sage Foundation).
Bair, J. (ed.) (2009), *Frontiers of Commodity Chain Research* (Stanford: Stanford University Press).
Barth, E., Bryson, A., Davis, J. C. and Freeman, R. (2014), 'It's where you work: increases in earnings dispersion across establishments and individuals in the US', Working Paper 20447, National Bureau of Economic Research, September 2014.
Batt, R., and Appelbaum, E. (2013), *The Impact of Financialization on Management and Employment Outcomes*, Working Paper No. 13-191 (Kalamazoo, MI: UpJohn Institute).
Batt, R., Holman, D. and Holtgrewe, U. (2009), 'The globalization of service work: comparative institutional perspectives on call centers', *Introduction to a Special Issue of Industrial and Labor Relations Review*, 62:4, 453–88.

Batt, R. and Nohara, H. (2009), 'How institutions and business strategies affect wages: a cross national study of call centers, *Industrial and Labor Relations Review*, 62:4, 533–52.

Belzer, M. (1994), 'The motor carrier industry: truckers and teamsters under siege', in Voos, P. (ed.), *Contemporary Collective Bargaining in the Private Sector* (Madison, WI: Industrial Relations Research Association), pp. 259–302.

Bernhardt, A., Batt, R., Houseman, S. and Appelbaum, E. (2015), 'Domestic outsourcing in the U.S.: a research agenda to assess trends and effects on job quality', Department of Labor Conference Paper on the Future of Work. 10 December 2015. https://www.dol. gov/asp/evaluation/completed-studies/Future_of_work_research_agenda_to_assess_ trends_and_effects_on_job_quality.pdf.

Boden, L., Spieler, E. and Wagner, G. (2016), 'The changing structure of work: implications for workplace health and safety in the US', Paper prepared for the Future of Work Symposium, US Department of Labour.

Coase, R. H. (1937), 'The Nature of the Firm', *Economica,* 4:16, 386–405.

Davis, G. and J. A. (2010), 'Corporations and economic inequality around the world: the paradox of hierarchy', *Research in Organizational Behavior*, 30, 35–53.

Danaj, S. and Sippola, M. (2015), 'Organizing posted workers in the construction sector', in Drahokoupil, J. (ed.), *The Outsourcing Challenge: Organizing Workers across Fragmented Production Chains* (Brussels: European Trade Union Institute), pp. 217–36.

Dicken, P. (1992), *Global Shift: The Internationalization of Economic Activity* (New York: Guilford Press).

Doellgast, V. (2012), *Disintegrating Democracy at Work: Labor Unions and the Future of Good Jobs in the Service Economy* (Ithaca, NY: Cornell University Press).

Doellgast, V. and Greer, I. (2007), 'Vertical disintegration and the disorganization of German industrial relations', *British Journal of Industrial Relations,* 45:1, 55–76.

Doellgast, V., Holtgrewe, U. and Deery, S. (2009), 'The effects of national institutions and collective bargaining arrangements on job quality in front-line service workplaces', *Industrial and Labor Relations Review*, 64:4, 489–509.

Doellgast, V., Lillie, N. and Pulignano, V. (eds) (2017), *Reconstructing Solidarity: Labour Unions, Precarious Work, and the Politics of Institutional Change in Europe* (Oxford: Oxford University Press).

Doellgast, V., Sarmiento-Mirwaldt, K. and Benassi, C. (2016), 'Institutions, cost structures, and the politics of externalization', *Industrial and Labor Relations Review*, 69:3, 523–50.

Dore, R. (1986), *Flexible Rigidities: Industrial Policy and Structural Adjustment in the Japanese Economy, 1970–1980* (Stanford: Stanford University Press).

Drahokoupil, J. (ed.) (2015), 'The outsourcing challenge: organizing workers across fragmented production chains' (Brussels: European Trade Union Institute). www.etui.org/ Publications2/Books/The-outsourcing-challenge-organizing-workers-across-fragmen ted-production-networks.

Dube, A. and Kaplan, E. (2010), 'Does outsourcing reduce wages in the low-wage service occupations? Evidence from janitors and guards', *Industrial and Labor Relations Review*, 63:2, 287–306.

Dustmann, C., Fitzenberger, B., Schönberg, U. and Spitz-Oener, A. (2014), 'From sick man of Europe to economic superstar: Germany's resurgent economy', *Journal of Economic Perspectives*, 28:1, 167–88.

Erickcek, G., Houseman, S. and Kalleberg, A. L. (2003), 'The effects of temporary services and contracting out on low-skilled workers: evidence from auto suppliers, hospitals, and public schools', in Appelbaum, E., Bernhardt, A. and Murnane, R. J. (eds), *Low-Wage America: How Employers Are Reshaping Opportunity in the Workplace* (New York: Russell Sage Foundation), pp. 368–403.

Flecker, J. and Hermann, C. (2011), 'The liberalization of public services, company reactions and consequences for employment and working conditions', *Economic and Industrial Democracy*, 32:3, 523–44.

Flecker J. and Meil, P. (2010), 'Organisational restructuring and emerging service value chains: implications for work and employment', *Work, Employment and Society*, 24:4, 680–98.

Foley, M., Ruser, J., Shor, G., Shuford, H. and Sygnatur, E. (2014), 'Contingent workers: workers' compensation data analysis strategies and limitations', *American Journal of Industrial Medicine*, 57:7, 764–75.

Gereffi, G. and Koreniewicz, M. (eds) (1994), *Commodity Chains and Global Capitalism* (Westport, CT: Greenwood Press).

Goldschmidt, D. and Schmieder, J. F. (2015), *The Rise of Domestic Outsourcing and the Evolution of the German Wage Structure*, IZA (Institute of the Study of Labour) Discussion Paper No. 9194 (Bonn: Institute for the Study of Labor), http://ftp.iza.org/dp9194.pdf.

Greer, I., Schulten, T. and Böhlke, N. (2013), How does market making affect industrial relations? Evidence from eight German hospitals', *British Journal of Industrial Relations*, 51:2, 215–39.

Grimshaw, D., Cooke, E. L., Grugulis, I. and Vincent, S. (2000), 'New technology and changing organizational forms: implications for managerial control and skills', *New Technology, Work and Employment (Special Issue: The Future of Work)*, 17:3, 186–203.

Grimshaw, D., and Miozzo, M. (2006), 'Institutional effects on the market for IT outsourcing: analysing clients, suppliers and staff transfer in Germany and the UK', *Organization Studies*, 27: 9, 1229–60.

Grimshaw, D. and Rubery, J. (2005), 'Intercapital relations and the network organization: redefining the work and employment nexus', *Cambridge Journal of Economics*, 29:6, 1027–90.

Grimshaw, D., Rubery, J., Anxo, D., Bacache-Beauvallet, M., Neumann, L. and Weinkopf, C. (2015), 'Outsourcing of public services in Europe and segmentation effects: the influence of labour market factors', *European Journal of Industrial Relations*, 21:4, 295–313.

Grimshaw, D., Rubery, J. and Ugarte, S. M. (2015), 'Does better quality contracting improve pay and HR practices? Evidence from for-profit and voluntary sector providers of adult care services in England', *Journal of Industrial Relations*, 57:4, 502–25.

Grimshaw, D., Willmott, H. and Rubery, J. (2005), 'Interorganizational networks: trust, power, and the employment relationship', in Marchington, M., Grimshaw, D., Rubery, J. and Willmott, H. (eds), *Fragmenting Work: Blurring Organizational Boundaries and Disordering Hierarchies* (Oxford: Oxford University Press).

Hagedoorn, J. and Duysters, G. (2002), 'External sources of innovation capabilities: the preference for strategic alliances or mergers and acquisition', *Journal of Management Studies,* 39:2, 67–88.

Haidinger, B. (2015), 'Organizing fragmented workers in parcel delivery', in Drahokoupil, J. (ed.), *The Outsourcing Challenge: Organizing Workers across Fragmented Production Chains* (Brussels: European Trade Union Institute), pp. 199–216.

Hermann C. and Flecker, J. (eds) (2012), *Privatization of Public Services: Impacts for Employment, Working Conditions, and Service Quality in Europe* (New York, Routledge).

Handwerker, E. (2015), 'Increased concentration of occupations, outsourcing, and growing wage inequality in the United States', BLS Working Paper, February 2015 (Washington, DC: Bureau of Labor Statistics), http://www.iza.org/conference_files/inequality_2015/handwerker_e20486.pdf

Handwerker, E. and Spletzer, J. (2015), *The Concentration of Occupations and the Role of Establishments in Wage Inequality*, IZA (Institute of the Study of Labour) Discussion Paper No. 9294 (Bonn: Institute for the Study of Labor).

Jacoby, S. M. (1984), 'The development of internal labor markets in American manufacturing firms', in P. Osterman, P. (ed.), *Internal Labor Markets* (Cambridge, MA: MIT Press).

Jaikumar, R. (1986), 'Postindustrial manufacturing', *Harvard Business Review,* 64:6, 69–76.

Ji, M. and Weil, W. (2015), 'The impact of franchising on labor standards compliance', *Industrial and Labor Relations Review,* 68:5, 977–1006.

Kogut, B. and Zander, U. (1992), 'Knowledge of the firm, combinative capabilities, and the replication of technology', *Organization Science,* 3:3, 383–97.

Lepak, D. P. and Snell, S. A. (1999), 'The human resource architecture: toward a theory of human capital allocation and development', *Academy of Management Review,* 24:1, 31–48.

Lillie, N. (2012), 'Subcontracting, posted migrants and labour market segmentation in Finland', *British Journal of Industrial Relations,* 50:1, 148–67.

MacDuffie, J. P. (1995), 'Human resource bundles and manufacturing performance: organizational logic and flexible production systems in the world auto industry', *Industrial and Labor Relations Review,* 48:2, 197–201.

Marchington, M., Grimshaw, D., Rubery, J. and Willmott, H. (2005), *Fragmenting Work: Blurring Organizational Boundaries and Disordering Hierarchies* (Oxford: Oxford University Press).

Marglin, S. (1974), 'What do bosses do?', in Gorz, A. (ed.), *The Division of Labour: The Labour Process and Class Struggle in Modern Capitalism* (Brighton: Harvester Press).

Miles, R. E. and Snow, C. (1986), 'Fit, failure and the hall of fame', *California Management Review,* XXVI, 10–28.

Milkman, R. (2008), 'Putting wages back into competition: deunionization and degradation in place-bound industries', in Bernhardt, A., Boushey, H., Dresser, L. and Tilly, L. (eds), *The Gloves-Off Economy*, Annual Research Volume, Labor and Employment Relations Association (Champaign: University of Illinois Press), pp. 65–90.

Miozzo, M. and Grimshaw, D. (2005), 'Modularity and innovation in knowledge intensive business services: IT outsourcing in Germany and the UK', *Research Policy*, 34: 9, 1419–39.

Mori, A. (2015), 'Outsourcing public services: local government in Italy, England and Denmark', in Drahokoupil, J. (ed.), *The Outsourcing Challenge: Organizing Workers across Fragmented Production Chains* (Brussels: European Trade Union Institute), pp. 137–56.

Morris, J. A. (1999), 'Injury experience of temporary workers in a manufacturing setting: factors that increase vulnerability', *Workplace Health and Safety*, 47:10, 470.

Muzaffar, S., Cummings, G., Hobbs, K., Allison, P. and Kreiss, K. (2013), 'Factors associated with fatal mining injuries among contractors and operators', *Journal of Occupational and Environmental Medicine*, 55:11, 1337–44.

Osterman, P. (ed.) (1984), *Internal Labor Markets* (Cambridge, MA: MIT Press).

Piore, M. and Sabel, C. (1984), *The Second Industrial Divide: Possibilities for Prosperity* (New York: Basic Books).

Prahalad, C. K., and Hamel, G. (1990), 'The core competence of the corporation', in Zack, M. H. (ed.), *Knowledge and Strategy* (Cambridge: Routledge), pp. 41–60.

Rebitzer, J. B. (1995), 'Job safety and contract workers in the petrochemical industry,' *Industrial Relations*, 34:1, 40–57.

Rubery, J. (1978), 'Structured labour markets, worker organization, and low pay', *Cambridge Journal of Economics*, 2:1, 17–37.

Rubery, J. (2007), 'Developing segmentation theory: a thirty year perspective', *Économies et Sociétés*, 28:6, 941–64.

Rubery, J. (2015), 'Austerity and the future for gender equality in Europe', *Industrial and Labor Relations Review*, 68:4, 715–41.

Rubery, J. and Grimshaw, D. (2001), 'ICTs and employment: the problem of job quality', *International Labour Review*, 140:2, 165–92.

Rubery, J. and Karamessini, M. (eds) (2013), *Women and Austerity: The Economic Crisis and the Future for Gender Equality* (Abingdon: Routledge).

Rubery, J., Carroll, M., Cooke, F. L., Grugulis, I., and Earnshaw, J. (2004), 'Human resource management and the permeable organization: the case of the multi-client call centre', *Journal of Management Studies*, 41:7, 1199–222.

Rubery, J., Earnshaw, J. and Marchington, M. (2005), 'Blurring the boundaries to the employment relationship: from single to multi-employer relationships', in Marchington, M., Grimshaw, D., Rubery, J. and Willmott, H. (eds), *Fragmenting Work: Blurring Organizational Boundaries and Disordering Hierarchies* (Oxford: Oxford University Press), pp. 63–88.

Rubery, J., Marchington, M., Cooke, R. L. and Vincent, S. (2002), 'Changing occupational forms and the employment relationship', *Journal of Management Studies*, 39:5, 645–72.

Rubery, J. and Urwin, P. (2011), 'Bringing the employer back in: why social care needs a standard employment relationship', *Human Resource Management Journal*, 21:2, 122–37.

Sako, M. (1992), *Price, Quality and Trust: Inter-Firm Relations in Britain and Japan*, Cambridge Studies in Management (Cambridge: Cambridge University Press).

Sako, M., Chondrakis, G. and Paul Vaaler, P. (2013), 'How do firms make-and-buy? The case of legal services sourcing by Fortune 500 companies?' Oxford University Working Paper (Oxford: Novak Druce Centre for Professional Firms).

Saxenian, A. L. (1996), *Regional Advantage* (Cambridge, MA: Harvard University Press).

Vrangbæk K., Petersen, O.H. and Hjelmar. U. (2013), 'Is contracting out good or bad for employees? a review of international experience', *Review of Public Personnel Administration,* 20:10, 1–21.

Ward, K., Grimshaw, D., Rubery, J. and Beynon, H. (2001), 'Dilemmas in the management of temporary work agency staff', *Human Resource Management Journal,* 11:4, 3–21.

Weil, D. (2014), *The Fissured Workplace* (Cambridge, MA: Harvard University Press).

Williamson, O. (1975), *Markets and Hierarchies: Analysis and Antitrust Implications* (New York: Free Press).

Williamson, O. (1985), *The Economic Institutions of Capitalism* (New York: Free Press).

5

The challenges for fair voice in liberal market economies

Mick Marchington and Tony Dundon

Introduction

The notion of fair voice sits centre stage in arguments about the relative importance of employee, organisational and societal goals because it connects directly with questions of managerial prerogative and social legitimacy. This creates tensions which are particularly apparent in liberal market economies (LMEs) – such as the UK, Australia, Ireland and New Zealand – where the law plays a relatively limited role in structuring workplace practice. In the case of the UK, following the decision to leave the EU in June 2016, it is uncertain whether the rhetoric and reality of fair voice will move further away from the EU social model. The notion of 'fair voice' is difficult to define because it does not relate to any one *specific* form of voice but can be seen through a variety of mechanisms, whether formal or informal, direct or representative. While some forms of representative participation might be seen as getting closer to achieving fair voice owing to the involvement of independent and effective trade unions, other forms of voice such as informal or individual channels may engage and involve workers in decisions and so achieve a degree of perceived fairness. An evaluation of 'fair voice' depends on who is asked, and when, about their level of participation. We return to this issue throughout the chapter.

This chapter draws upon the long-standing and distinctive academic contribution of Professor Jill Rubery by posing multiple challenges to the idea of 'fair' voice. This relates to her work in areas such as disorganised organisational hierarchies, feminisation, formal and informal labour market segmentation, flexibility and liberal market economic regimes. It reviews the notion of fair voice via a discussion of three key challenges. Firstly, it challenges simplistic definitions which treat fair voice as a uni-dimensional concept by showing how formal/informal and direct/representative practices operate beyond and within organisations in LMEs. These include European Works Councils (EWCs), partnership agreements, joint consultative committees (JCCs), problem-solving groups and informal interactions between line managers and staff, many of which operate alongside each other in large organisations. Also, the terms are elastic and debatable, subject to different interpretations by the principal actors: governments, employers and their organisations, trade unions, professional associations, HR and line managers, and employees. Secondly, it challenges the notion that employers have complete freedom to decide how to deliver fair voice. At an institutional level, so-called 'hard' national and transnational level forces shape voice through legislation (e.g. information and consultation or EWCs). Voice is also shaped by 'soft' forces – for example, by the Advisory Conciliation and Arbitration Service (Acas) or the Involvement and Participation Association (IPA) in the UK. At the intermediary level, lead bodies for employers and trade unions, professional associations, specialist bodies promoting partnership, management consultants and 'movements' such as Engage for Success have also captured space to promote specific forms of voice (Marchington, 2015a). Thirdly, it explores challenges to fair voice at the organisational level where formal practices can be undermined by managerial preferences for informal voice which is difficult to sustain. Moreover, contracting-out, agency work and multi-employer partnerships make it difficult to identify the employer at many workplaces, further fragmenting efforts to achieve fair voice (Marchington et al., 2005).

Challenges of definition: meanings and interpretations of fair voice

The range of terms used to describe employee voice makes it a highly debatable concept. For many managers, 'information-sharing' or 'communications' are regarded as normal and legitimate, symbolising fair expectation. However, for trade union officials, and even government policy advisors, labels such as 'participation', 'consultation' and 'bargaining' constitute voice systems. Much depends on context: size of the employer, labour and product markets, occupational mix, different management styles, inter-organisational relationships and whether or not the labour force is unionised. The choice of which practices to adopt is shaped by the degree of power and influence exercised by different actors. Negotiation, for example, implies mangers agree to relinquish some of their prerogative when they negotiate and make agreements with union officials representing the interests of workers. Employee involvement, on the other hand, may seek ideas but the final decision remains with management. Given these different interpretations and approaches, we define employee voice broadly, following Boxall and Purcell (2011: 162), as incorporating a range of mechanisms 'which enable, and at times empower employees, directly and indirectly, to contribute to decision-making'.

Further meanings arise when considering employee voice in international terms. For instance, in many European countries, statutory rights suggest a more equal or fairer system for employees to have a say on matters that affect them, such as via EWCs. In other liberal market countries however, such as the USA or Australia, there is limited emphasis on statutory provisions for fair voice, so much depends on managerial prerogative, union bargaining power or the role of other institutional actors. But things also vary between European countries and voice can be tailored to fit national customs and cultures. In the UK and Ireland, for instance, the content of the European Directive for Employee Information and Consultation (the ICE Directive) has been transposed with minimal regulatory power and enforcement (Hall *et al.*, 2013). While the European ICE Directive explicitly called for indirect forms of employee voice with elected representatives, the transposed UK and Irish regulations allow for direct and individual channels of communication and information-sharing (Dobbins *et al.,* 2016).

The meanings of voice can further differ depending on the presence or absence of a trade union. It is common for non-unionised companies to use the terms 'empowerment' and 'communications', even when they utilise representative forums such as EWCs (Ackers *et al.,* 2004). In Britain, the Workplace Employment Relations Study (WERS) surveys indicate that the majority of managers generally prefer to consult with workers in more direct than indirect ways: only 10 per cent of all workplaces use a combination of both representative and direct forms of voice, while 37 per cent of establishments use neither of these methods (van Wanrooy *et al.*, 2013: 66).

There are two underlying philosophical perspectives that can help conceptualise fairness in relation to voice. First is the idea of political citizenship where fairness relates to ideas derived from societal democracy. Hyman (2015: 12) has observed that one cannot justify the notion of a 'free citizen in the public sphere but a slave in the workplace'. Rights and access to voice as a citizen of a democratic country, say in political elections or referenda, do not end inside the factory or workplace. In this context, fair voice is seen as a fundamental human right and the principle of having an input on decision-making at workplace level is as legitimate as voting in political elections. A second perspective assesses how fair voice relates to economic efficiency ideas. The argument here is that allowing workers and/or their representatives to contribute to management decisions may encourage higher levels of commitment and ultimately better performance (Marchington *et al.*, 2016). Some forms of voice, such as partnership, draw upon both approaches, but 'patrimonial capitalism' (Piketty, 2013) allows managerial decision-making to take place beyond independent scrutiny, thus providing a further challenge to the concept fair voice.

One way of addressing the challenge is to specify voice with informed precision, using a fourfold schema including the 'degree', 'level', 'scope' and 'form' of the mechanisms used in practice (Wilkinson *et al.*, 2013). *Degree* is central to ideas of fair voice, as it captures the extent to which employees have a genuine or influential say about organisational matters that concern them (Marchington *et al.*, 2016). A stronger degree occurs when employees, either directly or indirectly, can influence decisions traditionally reserved for management. By contrast, a diluted degree of fair voice is evident when employees have little or no say, perhaps merely being informed by management of their decisions. Second is the *level* at which voice occurs, covering a small work unit, department, division or company but this is based on judgements about the appropriate level to make decisions. For example, asking all employees for a detailed input about new corporate investment plans would be too far-removed from employees' day-to-day matters, though it would offer an opportunity for fair voice if workers representatives were involved via EWCs or JCCs. Likewise, deciding to restructure a team or department without any input from front-line managers or employees would be unfair for those most likely to be affected by the decision. Third is the *scope* of voice, which relates to the issues on which workers or their representatives are involved. Scope can range from relatively minor work task issues to more substantive employment conditions outcomes; for example, involvement in procedures to ensure equal pay or promotion criteria may signal wide scope and potentially fairer voice opportunities (Rubery and Fagan, 1995; Rubery, 2015a).

There are three main *forms* of voice. First is *representative* voice, where employee voice is indirect and heard through formal bodies such as trade unions, JCCs, negotiating committees and employee forums. This category is typically high in degree and wide in scope, providing opportunities for employee representatives to discuss issues with managers, or where collective bargaining exists to negotiate terms and conditions of employment. Second is *direct* voice, where individual employees receive information and have a say through mechanisms including team briefing or problem-solving groups, suggestion schemes, engagement surveys or social media platforms, which have all become more widespread in LMEs (Marchington, 2015a). Direct voice may be fair or not, depending on the scope and depth of a particular mechanism. For example, Rubery and Fagan (1995) recognised the issue of gender blindness in employment relations systems, including voice and participation, pointing out that many sections of the labour force can be marginalised or silenced. At the same time, however, individualised direct channels may offer new avenues for voice as front-line managers are allowed to provide opportunities for team members to offer ideas (Cox *et al.*, 2009). Third is *informal* voice, which has been seen as either a substitute for or a supplement to formal voice mechanisms (Marchington and Suter, 2013). It includes ad hoc interactions between front-line managers and employees, typically sharing information and ideas through conversations. Research across LMEs indicates that informal voice is important not just in small firms, where formal mechanisms are less prevalent, but also in larger organisations (Marchington, 2015b). Informal dialogue may be an important lubricant to fair voice as communications are seen as friendly and regular, adding to a broader engagement culture where processes are often regarded as more important than formal structures (Schaufeli, 2014). However, as Purcell (2014: 251) notes, much of the engagement literature ignores the strong-established connections between voice and fairness, justice and trust, preferring to focus primarily on organisational performance.

This demonstrates voice is more complex than a straightforward continuum from no involvement (information) to extensive workforce involvement (control). The extent to which voice practices are perceived as fair depends on the degree to which they are embedded, the ways in which they overlap, the scope of topics covered and the level at which voice decisions are taken. However, there are also challenges from beyond the workplace in how hard and soft regulatory and intermediary forces shape fair voice.

Challenges for fair voice from beyond organisations: hard, soft and intermediary forces

The role of 'hard' institutional forces in shaping voice at organisational level

Most of the literature examines voice at the organisational level. To varying degrees, factors of interest tend to include product and labour markets, organisation size, culture, management choice, and union or non-union structure (Marchington, 2007). Unfortunately, as Rubery (2015b) notes, these studies tend to ignore how regulatory institutions can shape voice practices for more inclusive labour markets. Furthermore, Rubery and Grimshaw (2003) point out that these institutions in different countries can constrain and reconfigure employer choice about employment policy and practice. As such, the perceived fairness of voice can be facilitated or undermined in LMEs by the application of employment laws or by national business systems operating within a country. In short, institutional structures and systems do matter.

In comparison with coordinated market economies (CMEs), 'hard' institutional forces have a lesser role in shaping mandated voice rights in the UK, Australia, New Zealand, Ireland and the USA. Dundon and colleagues (2014: 9) report that at a transnational EU policy level, lobbying from employers and employer bodies, such as the US Chambers of Commerce, has been successful in influencing employee information regulations *before* wider and formal public consultations. In particular, employers were able to persuade policy agencies to support information obligations via direct voice rather than wider collective representative bargaining channels for ICE. At national levels the situation was similar to the minimalist rights to fair voice found at the transnational – European Union (EU) – level. In Ireland, for example, the harder EU regulations for voice were transposed with a conscious 'light-touch' impact on employer obligations (Dobbins *et al.*, 2016). In the UK, laws that support employees to receive information and be consulted by their employer were perceived by Taylor and colleagues (2009) to constitute little more than 'an umbrella full of holes', broadly compatible with other concerns about the future of the UK's tradition of liberal collectivist forms of employment regulation (Grimshaw and Rubery, 2012).

However, light-touch regulation does not imply totally unfettered free choice for employers (Edwards *et al.*, 2007). In the UK, worker participation was shaped partly by public policy for representative voice which reflected government views on best practice partnership (Ackers, 2010: 69). In Ireland, voluntary rather than statutory partnership was endorsed by government policy with evidenced gains for workers and unions (Geary, 2008). Moreover, legislation on ICE and EWCs means some employers in LMEs are bound by statutory laws that mandate certain forms of voice. Both Hall and Purcell (2012) and Marchington (2015a) found that where large employers in the UK had used JCCs and/or partnership forums for some time, they were quite comfortable with these arrangements and open to EWCs if they had locations in several EU countries. In Australia, too, the Federal Court has powers to fine employers for failing to consult workers properly. However, when institutional support is withdrawn or seen as partial, incentives to maintain existing forms of voice can dissipate if government and employer support is lukewarm (Roche and Teague, 2014).

Consequently, minimalist 'hard' institutional forces have a limited impact on managerial choice, which raises questions about the extent of fair voice for employees across LME regimes. Any specific impact on direct and informal voice is likely to be minimal because these forms of engagement are not included in legislation, but 'hard' institutions can shape representative voice, particularly EWCs and some ICE forums, *if* the organisations concerned fall within the remit of statutory laws. The limited impact of fair voice can further be reinforced by national business systems which promote flexible labour markets and privilege choice, informality and light-touch regulation. As such, while 'hard' institutional forces can influence the *take-up* of representative voice they cannot shape the fairness of the *processes* accompanying it, and thus in themselves may not be able to address the challenges to fair voice. The impact of ICE in the UK and Ireland showed that 'hard' institutional forces were treated in 'a reluctant and half-hearted manner' by employers, who – while implementing voice forums within their own businesses – traditionally favour the primacy of flexibility and choice within a voluntarist employment relations regime (Hall *et al.*, 2013).

The role of 'soft' institutional forces in shaping voice at organisational level

Given the limited direct impact of 'hard' institutional laws mandating worker voice in LMEs, perhaps 'softer' institutional forces designed to improve voice, employee well-being and organisational performance by supporting partner-ship, engagement and workplace cooperation stand a better chance of being adopted because they are better aligned with the voluntarist traditions in these countries. These take two broad forms:

(1) Specific 'soft' institutional initiatives funded by government, designed to embed workplace partnership, have been tried in the UK, Ireland, Australia and New Zealand since the mid-1990s. These can be regarded as 'soft' because they do not compel employers to implement specific voice mechanisms but rather persuade them to adopt the principles of mutuality (Stuart *et al.*, 2011). Consequently, this type of voice is assumed, in the LME context, to have more chance of being implemented at organisation level because it is seen as less rigid by senior managers and employers. However, it is susceptible to collapse, espe-cially when economic conditions deteriorate and/or political power struggles in government change priorities because they are not enshrined in law.

(2) Longer-standing government and other semi-autonomous organisational schemes that may help lubricate fairer voice on a voluntary basis continue to figure prominently in LMEs. Examples include Acas in the UK and the Workplace Relations Commission (WRC) in Ireland,[1] both of which publish codes of practice and information sheets, as well as run seminars for practition-ers which can be seen to promote fairer systems for voice. For example, Stuart and colleagues (2011) demonstrate how Acas officials played a key role in help-ing to support partnership and workplace cooperation. Moreover, because they

build trusting networks with practitioners over time, their ideas for voice have a greater chance of acceptance. As with Rights Commissioners in Ireland and Fair Work Commissioners in Australia, officials and advisors are recognised as 'impartial, objective and independent' which adds legitimacy to their role and influence – unlike private consultancy firms which are typically hired by management and openly biased towards employer views (Stuart *et al.*, 2011: 3802).

'Soft' institutional forces have shaped representative and direct voice at organisational level in Australia and New Zealand because managers and unions were willing recipients of the advice offered. The scope of voluntary support also seemed to allow a degree of flexibility which appealed to employers. However, as many voice initiatives were relatively short-lived, the longevity of fairness for employees or impact across the whole economy remained in some doubt (Marchington, 2015b). Similarly, in Ireland, many workplace partnerships were endorsed as exemplar best-practice models by the state institution, the National Centre for Partnership and Performance (NCPP). In these cases, however, as economic uncertainty increased, cooperative forms of engagement faltered despite the good intentions among managers, employees and unions (Dobbins and Dundon, 2016). Several factors exposed the limitations of softer institutions supporting representative voice. For example, local managers had difficulty sustaining collaborative initiatives and fulfilling employee expectations for fair voice, often owing to external economic pressures that were beyond their control and that of the supportive state institutions. In addition, senior managers at multinational HQs used their influence to constrain local managerial discretion for partnership arrangements. While some semi-autonomous state institutions provided a lubricant for voice by maintaining networks of trust between employers and trade unions and helped to mediate issues and tensions, in others the impact on employers was less significant and the longevity of fair voice constrained owing to external economic and political pressures.

The role of intermediary forces in shaping voice at organisational level

Given that LMEs traditionally have highly deregulated systems for employee voice, it is surprising to find so little interest in the role of intermediary forces which operate between government and employers, independent of both. As Edwards and colleagues (2002: 6) note, 'there remains a large gap (the missing middle) between public policy and what happens on the ground, and the opportunity to narrow it should be grasped'. These 'intermediary forces' include employers' organisations, professional associations and other bodies with a specialist interest in voice and engagement.

Many employers' organisations provide advice and support to promote voice that may not otherwise exist among their members. Both the Confederation for British Industry (CBI) in the UK and the Irish Business and Employers' Confederation (IBEC) support voluntary voice practices, particularly direct and informal voice, and many members have EWCs or other forms of representative voice. The Chartered Institute of Personnel and Development (CIPD) has had a strong interest in voice for many years, funding research, running an annual UK conference, advising members about the potential impact of EU legislation as well as contributing to the Employee Engagement Task Force and the IPA Council. The CIPD believes a flexible approach which fits with organisational needs is most appropriate, including representative voice where trade unions or staff associations exist. These ideas are disseminated to HR specialists via national and local presentations, research reports from CIPD-funded projects (e.g., Alfes *et al.*, 2010; Dundon *et al.*, 2004) and its monthly magazine. The CIPD Ireland branch also held a research conference on employee engagement (Hickland, 2011). While the potential for the CIPD to shape voice practices is potentially sizeable, it is hard to be precise about its contribution because ideas are diffused through a range of different channels. In addition, the IPA has had a specific interest in employee voice for many years, including its role in promoting partnership and representative participation.

Not all intermediary bodies have a 'permanent' presence but they can still influence the implementation of voice. A good example here is Engage for Success in the UK, which has received support from government to make employee engagement more visible (see also MacLeod and Clarke, 2009). It is funded by members, either by seconding staff or providing technical expertise, though whether it will remain a key part of the voice agenda or merely be the latest fad and fashion in management thought is contested (Guest, 2014). Marchington's (2015a, b) research demonstrated that in some UK and Irish organisations, employee engagement went way beyond surveys to include training opportunities for all staff, organisational change programmes and, in relation to fair and independent voice, employee champions drawn from the workforce to sit on key committees. For example, one large, highly unionised firm had set up a system of workplace teams which had autonomy to identify work improvements within the context of a strong representative voice structure. Engage for Success encourages organisations to create dedicated programmes by drawing upon ideas from across the network but adapting them to suit their own organisation context.

While intermediary forces can shape representative voice, they are more likely to influence direct and informal voice; the latter in particular fits well with the discourse of flexibility and voluntarism associated with LMEs. Before moving to the next section, two points need to be reiterated. Firstly, in LMEs with light-touch regulation all forms of voice are susceptible to break down if they have not been well-embedded with other organisational HR practices; if they become susceptible to economic or political change factors; or if they are perceived as unfair by employees or unions (Dobbins and Gunnigle, 2009). Such fragility is likely to be even more prevalent for informal voice (Marchington, 2015b). Intermediary forces are potentially unstable because they are not enshrined in law but rely on flexible business systems and neoliberal political ideologies. Secondly, fair (and successful) voice initiatives tend to be copied by other organisations, either directly or via consultants, and thus spread more widely. Accordingly, the process of transfer is not solely one-way from intermediary level to organisations but also takes place internally, particularly among foreign-owned multinational corporations (MNCs) (Lavelle *et al.*, 2010).

It appears that 'hard' and 'soft' institutional and 'intermediary' forces are active across LMEs, though their role varies between countries, as Table 5.1 shows. This draws on research by Marchington (2015b) and Dobbins and Dundon (2016) to show that 'hard' regulations shape patterns of representative voice more than they do direct forms. Intermediary institutional forces are important for representative voice in different economic regimes (Rubery and Grimshaw, 2003), though the impact is confined to the organisations actively involved in such initiatives and institutional arrangements. The contribution of intermediary forces to fair voice is harder to evaluate given their primary target on direct and informal voice, both of which can lack underpinning independent, formal structures.

Challenges for fair voice at the organisational level

Front-line managers and informal voice

While some would argue that fair voice is only achievable through independent trade unions representing their members through high-level committees such as EWCs, it could be argued that these are not sufficient on their own to embed voice effectively at workplace level (Wilkinson *et al.*, 2013). Indeed, for many years unions have not been good at including the voices of women and ethnic minorities, although recent strategies have been designed to correct the gender representation gap with specific committees to input union decision-making (Kirton, 2015). Fair voice might well rely on a mix of practices at different levels, including the opportunity for workers to raise issues directly with their

Table 5.1   External forces shaping voice policy and practice

Forces shaping voice	Components of forces shaping voice	Forms of voice shaped by forces
'Hard' institutional forces	Legal regulation via EU laws and directives in UK and Ireland, and federal Court in Australia National business system in each country supports voluntary light-touch regulations for voice	Representative voice at organisations covered by these regulations Direct and informal voice plus employee engagement
'Soft' institutional forces	Government-funded initiatives Semi-autonomous government activities	Representative and direct voice, typically limited to those actively involved in initiative All forms of voice to some extent, but especially direct and informal voice
Intermediary forces	Employers organisations (and trade union federations) Professional associations Organisations specialising in voice and engagement	Some representative forms of voice, but more the promotion of direct, flexible and informal voice Direct and informal voice but also representative voice if already exists Direct and informal voice, employee engagement and some representative voice

front-line manager at any time. Because blockages can occur within managerial and union hierarchies, informal voice may fill some of these gaps.

Evidence suggests that workers like informal voice as it gives them a chance to engage directly with front-line managers. Some find it easier to communicate with their front-line managers on a one-to-one basis because they are nervous about speaking in large groups (Marchington and Suter, 2013). Informal dialogue may provide a conduit to fairer voice from the perspective of employees because this allows workers to hear about new developments and provides them with an opportunity to discuss matters immediately at a level which is directly relevant. As Purcell and Georgiadis (2007: 197) note, 'employers who want to gain the maximum value from voice systems would do well to note that all the evidence points to the need for direct face-to-face exchange with employees at their work stations and in groups'. Similarly, in organisations with formal non-union employee representation (NER) committees, some employees found their immediate supervisor more responsive to their needs and tended to raise concerns with line managers rather than utilising formal NER channels (Cullinane *et al.*, 2014). Dundon *et al.* (1999: 262) found that informal communications at workplace level helped ameliorate some of the harsher working conditions felt by employees in small firms; in particular, informal voice facilitated friendly relations among co-workers and gave garage mechanics work satisfaction because they could discuss technical challenges and speak directly with customers. Informal voice can also be attractive to front-line managers because research indicates that informal chats account for the vast majority of what they learn about employee feelings, and it also gives them the chance to discuss issues directly with workers and offers some choice about whether or not to accept or modify employee ideas for improvement (Marchington and Suter, 2013). However, as we have already suggested, informal interactions alone are unlikely to achieve fair voice without clear underpinning from formal practices and a strongly stated commitment from senior managers that workers' ideas and contributions are vitally important.

Accessing fair voice across organisational boundaries

The way in which employee voice practices operate across organisational boundaries at multi-employer workplaces raises even greater challenges for fair voice because authority, power and trust can be further undermined by added layers of subcontracting and multiple contracts. Several Manchester-based research projects (e.g. Grimshaw *et al.,* 2010; Marchington *et al.*, 2005; Rubery and Urwin, 2011) provide evidence that workers employed across organisational boundaries enjoy less voice than their in-house colleagues at the same workplace. In short, 'non-citizen' workers in these contexts experience a double whammy. They suffer not just from the usual hazards that arise from being the weaker party to a traditional employment contract, but also from the additional risks of having their work governed by commercial contracts over which they have no influence and whose systems offer them little or no opportunity for voice.

This is especially problematic for workers employed for relatively short periods of time at a particular site, such as agency supply teachers (Hebson *et al.*, 2003). In such situations, agency workers can move between establishments regularly, consequently feeling little identification with or involvement in issues at the host organisation. Missing out on vital pieces of information limits the opportunity to contribute to discussions about work organisation, with or without unions having an active presence. Accordingly, fair voice can be found wanting when the proportion of contracted workers is small since they can easily be overlooked or regarded as not important enough to be included in communications available to employees at the host organisation. Moreover, if there is resentment to 'external' (agency) workers, perhaps because they are employed on lower rates of pay or are felt to have taken jobs from 'internal' workers, their chances of being included in formal and informal voice are also reduced (Marchington *et al.*, 2005). Moreover, agency and subcontract workers based at a host organisation can also miss out on more formal opportunities to participate – such as in-house suggestion schemes or JCCs – because they are not actually 'employees' and managers may be reluctant to share confidential data with people who are seen as peripheral or regarded as having little commitment to the host employer.

A slightly different scenario occurs at large, multi-employer sites – such as airports or hospitals – where people are employed by many different organisations on a range of employment contracts, even though they are all aiming to provide an integrated and holistic service for customers (Grimshaw *et al.*, 2010; Rubery *et al.*, 2003). At the same time, each organisation has competing priorities, a multiplicity of different management styles and occupational mixes which result in the emergence of representative, direct and informal voice practices that lack integration, consistency and alignment. The case-study research tradition has been particularly insightful in unpacking the tensions and ambiguities of fairness, voice and employment equity issues.

Although mechanisms of representative and union participation have declined over recent decades in LME regimes such as the UK (van Wanrooy *et al.*, 2013), the implementation of statutory information and consultation arrangements has had a mixed response. At one level, the idea of regulatory support reinvigorated interest in representative voice at the workplace, while at another trade unions have largely vacated the regulatory space for voice, perhaps seeing European-style employee information rights as a back-door form of non-union voice (Hall *et al.*, 2013). While EWCs, JCCs and some NERs offer employees some say in matters that affect them and their work, the barriers for those on the periphery of the employment relationship – agency and outsourced workers, and those working in public–private partnerships – can result in a lower level of access to these voice institutions than for those working for the dominant employer in these relationships. Worse still, in the case of statutory works councils, flexible workers have no legal recourse to collective representation. Similarly, in terms of outcome, in the case of JCCs or other voluntarist NER forums in the UK and elsewhere, agency workers can be proactively excluded by managers as well as core employees.

Conclusions

As we noted in the introduction, this chapter is part of a celebration and recognition of the academic career of Professor Jill Rubery. Many of her contributions – often in conjunction with other long-standing Manchester researchers such as Goodman, Marchington and Grimshaw – have instigated and extended key debates about labour market regulations and institutions that shape voice and other aspects of employment relations. Ackers (2010) analyses the way in which these research trajectories shaped numerous investigations into labour markets over the last 30 years. Rubery, in different ways, discredited the populism of a new right political agenda of free market managerialism while questioning materialist traditions of economic Marxism as a source of realistic social change amidst restructured labour markets, blurred organisational boundaries and flexible and feminised employment patterns (Marchington et al., 2005; Rubery, 2015b). A body of research brought centre stage the voices of many of those who had become marginalised and disenfranchised from access to fair voice (e.g. low-paid workers, women, agency and outsourced workers, those in precarious jobs, and part-time and casualised contract employees). This work has added an important gendered and, more recently, intersectional focus to the study and analysis of fairness surrounding employment issues, particularly pay, working hours and skill, but also voice and representation in comparative context (Hebson and Rubery, 2017).

We acknowledge it is difficult to define, develop and sustain fair voice. Regulation, such as the Organisation for Economic Co-operation and Development's 2012 objective to promote 'better regulation' (OCED, 2012), is usually advanced as one way to ensure fairness, but the future prognosis for more or better regulation seems unlikely in LMEs. Opportunities for fair voice do exist but there are also multiple challenges to its development and sustainability in LMEs, particularly the waves of light-touch regulation minimising deeper forms of voice. A contemporary pragmatic challenge for fair voice, at least among large UK and UK-based MNCs, is what to do post-Brexit. One response might be an extension of individualism alongside light-touch regulation as part of a continued neoliberal system. A consequence of this might be further individualisation and flexibility for voice shaped by managerial prerogative, without the checks and balances of a European social model for fairer voice. However, the agency influence of employers, unions and other soft institutions may reconfigure the agenda for fair voice to some extent in a post-Brexit world. For example, managers may opt to support the institutional arrangements for representative voice such as JCCs and EWCs, particularly if these 'fit' with the organisation's business objectives. This might provide the opportunity for employers to embed the importance of fairness, justice and best-practice efficiency by signalling to employees and stakeholders the value of voice as a fundamental right and a major contributor to employee well-being.

In celebrating Rubery's career, this chapter has posed multiple challenges to the promotion of fair voice in LMEs within the context of global labour market restructuring. As we mention, the very concept of fairness is of course debatable. Important insights to such debates have been advanced from both the 'case-study' research tradition and the use of 'comparative international analysis' used by Rubery (and others) in teasing out the complexities of work and the sources of power, equality and inequality in employment systems (see Beynon et al., 2002; Karamessini and Rubery, 2013; Marchington et al., 2005). Whether voice is seen as fair or not is shaped to a significant degree by forces at different levels: hard and soft regulations, intermediary market institutions, fragmented organisational structures and informal workplace relationships. These forces all play a role in undermining or blurring the impact of formal systems of fair voice within employing organisations, particularly for those workers on the periphery of the labour market. Our contention is that fair voice is a legitimate and valuable goal, irrespective of measures of performance, although without harder regulations for worker rights, the achievement of fairness may remain fuzzy and elusive, particularly in a more uncertain post-Brexit world.

Note

1   The WRC was formed in 2016 from previous state agencies, including the former Labour Relations Commission (LRC), Rights Commissioners and Equality Authority.

References

Ackers, P. (2010), 'An industrial relations perspective on employee participation', in Wilkinson, A., Gollan, P., Marchington, M., and Lewin, D. (eds), *The Oxford Handbook of Participation in Organisations* (Oxford: Oxford University Press).

Ackers, P., Marchington, M., Wilkinson, A. and Dundon, T. (2004), 'Partnership and voice, with or without trade unions: changing UK management approaches to organisational participation', in Stuart, M. and Martinez Lucio, M. (eds), *Partnership and Modernisation in Employment Relations* (London: Routledge).

Alfes, K., Truss, C., Soane, E., Rees, C. and Gatenby, M. (2010), *Creating an Engaged Workforce: Findings from the Kingston Employee Engagement Consortium Project* (London: CIPD).

Beynon, H., Grimshaw, D., Rubery, J. and Ward, K. (2002), *Managing Employment Change: The New Realities of Work* (Oxford: Oxford University Press).

Boxall, P. and Purcell, J. (2011), *Strategy and Human Resource Management*, 3e (London: Palgrave).

Cox, A., Marchington, M. and Suter, J. (2009), 'Employee involvement and participation: developing the concept of institutional embeddedness', *International Journal of Human Resource Management*, 20:10, 2150–68.

Cullinane, N., Donaghey, J., Dundon, T., Dobbins, T. and Hickland, E. (2014), 'Regulating for mutual gains: non-union employee representation and the Information & Consultation Directive', *International Journal of Human Resource Management*, 25:6, 810–28.

Dobbins, T. and Dundon, T. (2016), 'The chimera of sustainable labour-management partnership', *British Journal of Management*. doi: 10.1111/1467-8551.12128

Dobbins T. and Gunnigle P. (2009), 'Can voluntary workplace partnership deliver sustainable mutual gains?', *British Journal of Industrial Relations,* 47:3, 546–70.

Dobbins, T., Dundon, T., Cullinane, C., Hickland, E. and Donaghey, J. (2016), 'Employment regulation, game theory, and the lacuna in employee participation in liberal economies', *International Labour Review*. doi: 10.1111/j.1564-913X.2015.00053.x

Dundon, T., Grugulis, I. and Wilkinson, A. (1999), 'Looking out of the Black-Hole: non-union relations in an SME', *Employee Relations*, 22:3, 251–66.

Dundon, T., Wilkinson, A., Marchington, M. and Ackers, P. (2004), 'The meaning and purpose of employee voice', *International Journal of Human Resource Management*, 15:6, 1149–70.

Dundon, T., Dobbins, T., Cullinane, N., Hickland, E. and Donaghey, J. (2014), 'Employer occupation of regulatory space of the Information and Consultation (I&C) Directive in liberal market economies', *Work Employment and Society*, 28:1, 1–19.

Edwards, P., Gilman, M., Ram, M. and Arrowsmith, J. (2002), 'Public policy, the performance of firms, and the "Missing Middle": the case of employment regulations and a role for business networks', *Policy Studies*, 23:1, 5–20.

Edwards, T., Collings, T. and Ferner, A. (2007), Conceptual approaches to the transfer of employment practise in multinational companies: an integrated approach', *Human Resource Management Journal*, 17:3, 201–17.

Geary, J. (2008), 'Do unions benefit from working in partnership with employers? Evidence from Ireland'. *Industrial Relations,* 47:4, 530–68.

Guest, D. (2014), 'Employee engagement: fashionable fad or long-term fixture?', in Truss, C., Delbridge, R., Alfes, K., Shantzm A. and Soane, E. (eds), *Employee Engagement: Theory and Practice* (Abingdon: Routledge).

Grimshaw, D. and Rubery, J. (2012), 'The end of the UK's liberal collectivist social model? The implications of the coalition government's policy during the austerity crisis', *Cambridge Journal of Economics*, 36:1, 105–26.

Grimshaw, D., Rubery, J., and Marchington, M. (2010), 'Managing people across hospital networks in the UK: multiple employers and the shaping of HRM', *Human Resource Management Journal*, 20:4, 407–23.

Hall, M., Hutchinson, S., Purcell, J., Terry, M. and Parker, J. (2013), 'Promoting effective consultation? Assessing the impact of the ICE Regulations', *British Journal of Industrial Relations*, 51:2, 355–81.

Hall, M. and Purcell, J. (2012), *Consultation at work: Regulation and practice* (Oxford: Oxford University Press).

Hebson, G., Grimshaw, D. and Marchington, M. (2003), 'PPPs and the changing public sector ethos: case study evidence from the health and local authority sectors', *Work, Employment and Society*, 7:3, 483–503.

Hebson, G. and Rubery, J. (2017), 'Employment relations and gender equality', in Wilkinson, A., Dundon, T., Donaghey, J. and Covin, A. (eds), *Routledge Companion of Employment Relations* (Abingdon: Routledge).

Hickland, E. (2011), 'Retail Co – employee voice and engagement: case study evidence & reflections', Paper presented to Chartered Institute of Personnel and Development Research Symposium on '*Employee Voice and Engagement: Establishing the Link and Exploring the Evidence of Policy and Practice in Ireland*', Galway, November.

Hyman, R. (2015), 'The very idea of democracy at work', *Transfer: European Review of Labour and Research*, 22:1, 11–24.

Karamessini, M. and Rubery, J. (eds) (2013), *Women and Austerity: The Economic Crisis and the Future for Gender Equality* (Abingdon: Routledge).

Kirton, G. (2015), 'The Coalition of labor union women: still a space of social creativity and a force for social change', *Labor Studies Journal*, 40:2, 129–48.

Lavelle, J., Gunnigle, P. and McDonnell, A. (2010), 'Patterning employee voice in multinational companies', *Human Relations*, 63:3, 395–418.

MacLeod, D. and Clarke, N. (2009), *Engaging for Success: Enhancing Performance through Employee Engagement* (London: Department for Business, Innovation and Skills).

Marchington, M. (2007), 'Employee voice systems', in Boxall, P., Purcell, J. and Wright, P. (eds.), *The Oxford Handbook of Human Resource Management* (Oxford: Oxford University Press).

Marchington, M. (2015a), 'The role of institutions and intermediary bodies in shaping patterns of employee involvement and participation (EIP) in Anglo-American countries', *International Journal of Human Resource Management*, 26:20, 2594–616.

Marchington, M. (2015b), 'Analysing the forces shaping employee involvement and participation (EIP) at organisation level in liberal market economies (LMEs)', *Human Resource Management Journal*, 25:1, 1–18.

Marchington, M., Grimshaw, D., Rubery, J. and Willmott, H. (eds) (2005), *Fragmenting Work: Blurring Boundaries and Disordering Hierarchies* (Oxford: Oxford University Press).

Marchington, M. and Suter, J. (2013), 'Where informality really matters: patterns of employee involvement and participation in a non-union firm', *Industrial Relations*, 52:S1, 284–313.

Marchington, M., Wilkinson, A., Donnelly, R. and Kynighou, A. (2016), *Human Resource Management at Work*, 6e (London: Chartered Institute of Personnel and Development).

OECD (Organisation for Economic Co-operation and Development) (2012), *Better Regulation in Europe – the EU 15 project*, http://www.oecd.org/gov/regulatory-policy/betterregulationineurope-theeu15project.htm, accessed 18 April 2016.

Piketty, T. (2013), *Capital in the Twenty First Century* (Cambridge, MA: Harvard University Press).

Purcell, J. (2014), 'Disengaging from engagement', *Human Resource Management Journal*, 24:3, 241–54.

Purcell, J. and Georgiadis, N. (2007), 'Why should employers bother with worker voice?', in Freeman, R., Boxall, P. and Haynes, P. (eds), *What Workers say; Employee Voice in the Anglo-American Workplace* (Ithaca, NY: Cornell University Press).

Roche, W. and Teague, P. (2014), 'Successful but unappealing: fifteen years of workplace partnership in Ireland', *International Journal of Human Resource Management*, 25:6, 781–94.

Rubery, J. (2015a), 'Austerity and the future for gender equality in Europe', *Industrial and Labor Relations Review*, 68:4 715–41.

Rubery, J. (2015b), *Re-regulating for inclusive labour markets*, ILO Working Papers: Conditions of Work and Employment Series No. 65 (Geneva: International Labour Organization).

Rubery, J., Cooke, F., Earnshaw, J. and Marchington, M. (2003), 'Inter-organisational relations and employment in a multi-employer environment', *British Journal of Industrial Relations*, 41:2, 1100–222.

Rubery, J. and Fagan, C. (1995), 'Comparative industrial relations research: towards reversing the gender bias', *British Journal of Industrial Relations*, 33:2, 209–36.

Rubery, J. and Grimshaw, D. (2003), *The Organisation of Employment: An International Perspective* (London: Palgrave).

Rubery, J., and Urwin, P. (2011), 'Bringing the employer back in: Why social care needs a standard employment relationship', *Human Resource Management Journal*, 21:2, 122–37.

Schaufeli, W. (2014), 'What is engagement?' in Truss, K., Delbridge, R., Alfes, K., Shantz, A. and Soane, E. (eds), *Employee Engagement: Theory and Practice* (Abingdon: Routledge).

Stuart, M., Martinez-Lucio, M. and Robinson, A. (2011), '"Soft regulation" and the modernisation of employment relations under the British Labour government (1997–2010); partnership, workplace facilitation and trade union change', *International Journal of Human Resource Management*, 22:18, 3794–812.

Taylor, P., Baldry, C., Danford, A. and Stewart, P. (2009), 'An umbrella full of holes? Corporate restructuring, redundancy and the effectiveness of the ICE Regulations', *Relations Industrielle*, 60:1, 27–49.

Van Wanrooy, B., Bewley, H., Bryson, A., Forth, J., Freeth, S., Stokes, L. and Wood, S. (2013), *Employment Relations in the Shadow of Recession* (Basingstoke: Palgrave Macmillan).

Wilkinson, A., Dundon, T. and Marchington, M. (2013), 'Employee involvement and voice' in Bach, S., and Edwards, M. (eds), *Managing Human Resources* (Chichester: John Wiley).

6

Working-time flexibility: diversification and the rise of fragmented time systems

Iain Campbell

Despite a lack of consensus concerning its meaning and measurement, labour market flexibility has been central to employment research and policy for at least three decades. Much of the impetus for its persistence comes from the stubborn push by neoliberal policy-makers, under the banner of flexibility, for deeper market liberalisation and the elimination of labour market rigidities. Even after the disarray and shock of the Global Financial Crisis, increased flexibility, now wedded with austerity politics, continues as a fundamental goal of public policy in most countries.

Employment protection and wages feature prominently in ongoing debates on labour market flexibility, but working time is also conspicuous. At the same time, working time is perhaps the most puzzling aspect of the flexibility debate. The organisation of working time is at the centre of employer strategies of competition and proposals for further labour market deregulation, but it also figures in employee demands for improved job quality and decent work. At the level of practice, an array of changes, often labelled 'flexible working-time arrangements', has emerged in many industrialised societies, signalling a significant diversification of working-time patterns for the workforce (Lee, 2004; Lee *et al.*, 2007; Messenger, 2004). In some cases, the new working-time arrangements represent increased insecurity and precariousness for employees, while in other cases they are welcomed and actively pursued by employees. Further complicating the task of understanding this phenomenon is the cross-national variation in both the extent and the content of diversification, which reveals the significance of societal systems in mediating the outcomes of change and contestation (Berg *et al.*, 2014; Rubery, 2005a; Rubery and Grimshaw, 2003).

This chapter explores the theme of working-time flexibility,[1] seeking to disentangle the meanings of the term, to develop a useful conceptual framework and to identify patterns of change. It concentrates on description of change rather than analysis of its causes and consequences. The chapter draws on reflection by numerous scholars, but it is particularly indebted to the rich vein of research from a labour market segmentation perspective (see Chapter 1), as it has been revised and reformulated in order to overcome the weaknesses of dualistic versions (Rubery, 2005a).

The first section, 'What is working-time flexibility?', examines how flexible working-time arrangements fit within the context of the traditional regulatory system, before outlining a conceptual framework that can be used for differentiating the varied forms of flexible working-time arrangements. The second section, 'Patterns of change', scans contemporary patterns of change in industrialised societies, focusing on evidence of diversification in working-time arrangements. The third section, 'Fragmented time systems', underlines the significance of the concept of 'fragmented time systems' for pursuing an analysis of one important set of working-time changes. The conclusion summarises the central arguments.

What is working-time flexibility?

Working time is time spent engaged in activities of paid work. For employees, working time can be further defined as time spent at the disposal of an employer, who plays the major part in organising working time into 'working-time arrangements', that is, specific schedules or rosters, for individuals or groups. Working time can be distinguished from non-work time, which is devoted to other activities, including tasks of personal care (such as eating, sleeping and grooming), tasks of unpaid household labour (such as cooking, cleaning, physical care of children and shopping) and what is often loosely called free time or leisure time (Bittman, 2016: 529). More broadly, working time can be juxtaposed to workers' own time or their (personal) life, as in formulations that refer to the challenges of work–life integration or balance (Fagan et al., 2012).

Although the concept of working time is straightforward, it is difficult to find a plausible definition of *flexible* working time. As with all calls for flexibility, the notion of working-time flexibility derives most of its immediate appeal from an implicit contrast with its antonym – rigidity or inflexibility (Campbell, 1993). Despite constant invocation by policy-makers of the term 'flexibility', scholars have had little success in moving much beyond this rather empty metaphor. For the purposes of this chapter, however, it is not necessary to settle on a definition.

Flexible working-time is understood here, not so much as a cohesive set of practices, amenable to tight definition, but rather as a zone for exploration.

The regulatory system and flexible working-time arrangements

In order to analyse flexible working-time arrangements it is useful to situate them in relation to *the regulatory system for standardised working hours*, which was established via collective bargaining and statutory regulation and which reached out to cover the majority of the waged workforce in most industrialised countries by the middle of the twentieth century (Bosch 2004, 2006). Like the broader Standard Employment Relation (SER) with which it is linked, this regulatory system fulfils several functions, including service to firms and the broader economy, but its central aim is protection of employees, in line with a principle of de-commodification (Bosch, 2004: 632–3).[2] Though under challenge, this regulatory system remains an important force in most industrialised societies.

The regulatory system for standardised working hours comprises two main components: (1) a working-time standard – a standard working-time arrangement; and (2) provisions for deviation from the standard. A common misconception holds that flexible working-time arrangements inevitably involve a rupture in a regulatory system for standardised working hours. It is true that practices such as part-time work, evening and night work, and weekend work fall outside the *traditional working-time standard*, which can be summarily defined in terms of continuing ('permanent') full-time employment of approximately 40 hours per week, distributed in equal daily segments over the daytime hours from Monday to Friday and joined with paid annual and public holiday entitlements equivalent to several weeks per year (see Berg *et al.*, 2014: 807–8). But this does not mean that such flexible working-time arrangements necessarily fall outside the regulatory system as a whole.

Even at the height of the dominance of the traditional working-time standard, the regulatory system always incorporated elements of working-time flexibility. For example, the regulatory system has always incorporated rules that allow *employers* to adjust ('flexibilise') standard working-time arrangements. For example, rules for shift work and overtime allow organisational needs – for example, for continuous production in manufacturing, in emergency services, for safety and maintenance work, or to improve capital utilisation in capital-intensive industries – to be met. In this case, however, the rules enforce a compromise so that employees continue to be protected – for example, by imposing limits and requiring that the deviations from the standard should be compensated, planned, subject to agreement, safe and equitable.

At the same time, the system always provided for elements of flexibility to suit individual *employee* needs. Recent examples include flexitime systems, which allow scope for workers to vary start and finish times according to individual choice or external constraints (as long as a set number of hours are worked and core periods are covered) and individual 'right to request' legislation, which allows employees to request variations to their work arrangements (Fagan *et al.*, 2014). But the key historical example is paid leave arrangements, including annual leave, public holidays and sick leave, extended more recently into an array of family-related leave entitlements such as maternity, paternity, parental and other carers' leave entitlements. Paid leave arrangements are significant in that they not only help to preserve health and well-being but also, more positively, allow employees to pursue personal needs (which may of course also be social needs associated with families and communities) without incurring substantial penalties as a result of absence from paid work or failure to be available to the employer. Such arrangements bridge paid work and personal life and support employees' capacities to reduce the conflict between the two. Though often overlooked in narrow definitions of working-time arrangements in terms of weekly schedules, such paid (and unpaid) leave arrangements have been integral elements of the system from the start, signalling recognition of employees as individual human beings with lives outside of the workplace. They represent a crucial step away from the highly commodified forms of work such as casual work or 'day labour', characteristic of the late nineteenth century, where employees were simply suppliers of labour-time in return for hourly or daily wages and were dependent on employers on a recurrent day-to-day basis for offers of work and pay (Bosch, 2006: 44–5).

A broad understanding of the regulatory system of standardised working hours allows us to see how it functions to protect workers' own time (Hinrichs, 1991: 37–8). In effect, the system establishes and defends a series of important temporal boundaries. Most obvious is the basic distinction between work time and non-work time, which in turn overlaps with another boundary between 'social' and 'unsocial' hours. Also important is a boundary between paid time and non-paid time. The notion of paid time is extended beyond time at the workplace through entitlements to periods of paid leave and training time, while conversely rules such as those on the definition of work time ensure that workers are not obliged to commit parts of their own time, either at the workplace or elsewhere, as unpaid time to the employer. Similarly, rules requiring agreement and adequate notice for changes to schedules help to consolidate rosters that are regular and predictable, thereby protecting workers' time from the sudden incursion of work demands. And rules about the use of labour time support the health and safety of employees and defend against escalation of work demands through intensification or extension of working hours.

In short, from the point of view of individual employees, the regulatory system of standardised working hours has always been enabling as well as constraining. It helps to protect and expand a realm of individual choice and helps employees to achieve a measure of time autonomy (Lee and McCann, 2006: 78; McCann, 2007). Because the system incorporates – in addition to the standard – provisions for flexibility to suit employer and employee needs, it would be inaccurate to label it as 'rigid' and to argue that it is the antithesis of *all* flexible working-time arrangements. On the contrary, the system readily incorporates at least some flexible working-time arrangements.

It remains true that the traditional working-time standard at the heart of the system was framed in terms of full-time working hours and a model of the male breadwinner, female carer household. It was connected to a wider set of societal institutions, which constituted a Fordist model of employment (Rubery, 2005b). Because the standard functioned as a regulatory pivot and guided access to entitlements, not only in employment but also in social protection, it had exclusionary effects that disadvantaged workers whose employment fell outside the standard, including, in particular, women workers who picked up part-time schedules in order to respond to demands of caring for children (Vosko 2011). Many of these effects continue to be felt. Nevertheless, the answer is to adapt and modernise, not abandon, the regulatory system. As Bosch suggests, the central challenge is to modernise the traditional working-time standard, distinguishing the form (full-time employment) from the substance (de-commodification) and pushing towards a new, flexible SER which would continue to serve firms and the society as a whole but would accommodate a more diverse workforce and more diverse patterns of participation in paid work. Revision in this direction, already underway in many countries, would build on the elements of flexibility for employees that are already in the system, extending these through initiatives such as new systems of paid leave in order to facilitate labour market transitions, good-quality part-time employment and new flexi-time systems (Bosch, 2004; 2006: 57–62; see also Fagan *et al.*, 2014; Schmid, 2008).

The policy challenge here also extends to the broad swath of casualised work arrangements that have sprung up as 'new' forms of flexibility at the edges or even outside the regulatory system. McCann (2014) aptly argues that a modernised version of the SER can be the crucial starting point and prompt for designing new regulation in areas with highly casualised working-time patterns such as domestic work (see also, McCann and Murray, 2014). In this perspective, revising and extending the SER would figure as one element in a comprehensive reform agenda aimed at re-regulating for inclusive labour markets (Rubery, 2015).

Differentiating flexible working-time arrangements

Flexible working-time arrangements occur in varied forms, which have distinct and often contrasting implications for employees, households, firms, communities and the society as a whole (see Fagan et al., 2012: 6–7). It is vital to differentiate among these forms if we are to make sense of patterns of change in the current period. The concept of 'flexibility' is not in itself adequate for this task; instead, it is necessary to develop a more robust analytical framework.

An analytical framework can start with the basic division between duration (the number of usual working hours) and position (the distribution of usual working hours over the day or week).[3] From the point of view of the traditional working-time standard, flexible working-time arrangements involve deviation: (1) in terms of *duration* (i.e. short hours below the full-time standard or long hours well above the standard); and/or (2) in terms of *position* (i.e. schedules that involve evening and night work or weekend work). Each of these two basic dimensions can in turn be divided according to the degree of variability. Is the duration and/or the position of the particular working-time arrangement fixed or does it vary in some way?

The discussion so far allows a basic differentiation of contemporary working-time arrangements. But the task of differentiation needs to go further. Working-time arrangements, whether standard or flexible, differ in their impact according to the degree of worker control (discretion, autonomy) over the varied features of the working-time arrangement. With respect to the theme of flexibility, the pertinent question is always: flexibility for whom? The answer generally comes down to either the employer (the organisation) or the individual employee, and the most common way of denoting the division is in terms of 'employer-oriented flexibility' or 'employee-oriented flexibility' (Campbell, 1993; Chung and Tijdens, 2012; Heron and Charlesworth, 2012).[4] This distinction can be applied across all features of flexible working-time arrangements. It is most clearly needed in connection with arrangements that involve variation, either in duration or in position, but the distinction is also salient when the discussion turns to rosters based on relatively fixed short or long hours and relatively fixed schedules situated outside standard hours.

The distinction between employer-oriented and employee-oriented flexibility is essential to any plausible account of working-time flexibility, but it should not be seen as a chasm separating two entirely distinct phenomena. It is best seen in terms of a spectrum, with opportunities for an overlap of interests located in the middle. For example, working-time accounts (time banking) can – if properly designed – be a mechanism that offers increased internal flexibility for employers while also enhancing flexibility for employees (Fagan, 2004: 125–9; Messenger, 2004: 181–3). Similarly, it can be noted that employer interests are not transparent; the strict pursuit of short-term interests in employer-oriented flexibility is not necessarily in the long-term interests of firms. Moreover, in practice even opposed interests may interact and lead to negotiated compromise rather than an open clash, as in the case of the shift-work and overtime systems incorporated into the system of standardised working hours. Similarly, contextual factors can modify the extent and form of flexibility pursued by both parties. For example, employers may soften their demands and accommodate the interests of employees in flexibility if they are dealing with a tight labour market and with groups of skilled workers who need to be retained and motivated. Conversely, lower-skilled employees may tolerate high levels of working-time insecurity associated with employer-oriented schedules if they judge that they have few alternatives (poor labour market conditions, restricted access to social security, limited availability of childcare, limited rights in the employment contract) to improve their situation or if they feel that they are at least partly compensated for their insecurity by premium rates of pay.

Patterns of change

The framework sketched out above can assist in describing and analysing contemporary working-time trends, especially flexible working-time arrangements. A useful starting point is the national level, reflecting the influence of national systems of employment and social protection and allowing us to draw on relatively rich sources of data on working-time arrangements at national (and cross-national) level.

Description of working-time trends at the national level is often couched in terms of *diversification*, that is, the emergence of multiple flexible working-time arrangements in conjunction with the traditional standard (Lee *et al.*, 2007).[5] Drawing on the above discussion, we can distinguish three ideal typical patterns at national level:

1) a pattern of little diversification, in which the traditional standard remains dominant;
2) a pattern of moderate to strong diversification, in which the traditional standard shrinks in its reach and is now supplemented by new flexible working-time arrangements that are embedded in the system of standardised working hours; and
3) a pattern of strong diversification, in which the traditional standard shrinks in its reach and is now supplemented by a proliferation of new flexible

working-time arrangements that are largely, if not entirely, disconnected from a system of standardised working hours.

Both latter ideal types involve diversification, but they differ in terms of whether employees in flexible working-time arrangements are integrated into a regulatory system oriented to worker protection.

The last ideal type appears as the most problematic, rarely embracing working-time changes in favour of employees but instead centring on changes that are employer-oriented and that threaten increased precariousness for employees. It is useful to note here that disconnection from the system of protective regulation is generally associated with regulatory gaps or 'protective gaps' (Grimshaw et al., 2016), which provide opportunities for employers to avoid, either partially or totally, the conventional protections available to employees. Such gaps offer 'exit options' for employers (Jährling and Méhaut, 2013). They include gaps that are associated with the absence of key protective regulations (e.g. maxima for daily or weekly working hours) or gaps owing to ineffective enforcement, but more commonly they are associated with exemptions, exclusions, high thresholds and lengthy service requirements, which affect both employment regulation and the institutions of social protection (Grimshaw et al., 2016). Patterns of long work hours, for example, tend to spread most vigorously when, as in Australia, employers can use gaps that exempt them from an obligation to pay for overtime (Campbell, 2008: 137–9). Regulatory gaps may be either long-standing or only recently introduced as a result of policy changes. They may lead directly to easily recognised flexible working-time arrangements or they may unfold in a more covert way, through a weakening of the standard working-time arrangement. One special type of gap is located on the boundary between employee and non-employee status, where artificial arrangements or outsourcing and long chains of subcontracting can lead to employees being falsely classified as non-employees and thereby excluded from most protections provided through employment regulation.

Matching advanced industrialised societies against the ideal types is difficult. Societies may show a leaning to one or another ideal type but they rarely fall neatly into just one type. As a liberal market economy, Australia, for example, would seem to approximate fairly closely to the third ideal type, as a result of shrinkage in the reach of the standard, weakening of the substance of the standard and proliferation of poor-quality working-time arrangements, including long hours based on unpaid overtime and varied forms of casualised part-time schedules. These flexible working-time arrangements are largely disconnected from the regulatory system, emerging within regulatory gaps that are partly inherited from the past and partly created in the course of labour market deregulation since the late 1980s (Campbell, 2008). Employers continue to push for further dismantling of the working-time entitlements embodied in modern awards, such as minimum shift payments, access to annual leave and penalty rates for work in non-social hours (Heron and Charlesworth, 2012). Nevertheless, even in the Australian case, it is possible to observe changes that reinforce the system, such as improvements in paid leave arrangements, including the introduction in 2011 of a comprehensive system of paid parental leave (Pocock et al., 2013). Moreover, it is also possible to detect elements of the second ideal type, consistent with the notion of a move towards a flexible SER. An individual 'right to request' flexible work is now enshrined in the National Employment Standards (Pocock et al., 2013) and similar principles underpin the provisions in many awards that allow some employees to request a conversion from casual to permanent status. Unfortunately, both new measures have failed to fulfil the promise of increased temporal autonomy for employees. They remain limited in scope and impact, running into difficulties because employees tend to be reluctant to put forward a request because they are worried about employer reprisals and do not see a change as feasible in their workplace (Skinner et al., 2016).

A further difficulty in assessing the reach of the ideal types stems from the deficiencies of standard labour force data in identifying and differentiating new flexible working-time arrangements. National data sets are strong in measuring aspects such as working-time duration, but they generally lack the ability to distinguish arrangements that are employee-oriented from arrangements that are better suited to employer needs. Some advances have been made, generally in association with investigations of job quality and using special data sets that offer more detail on job content, including issues of control, such as the regular European Working Conditions surveys (Fagan and Vermeylen, 2016; Green et al., 2013; Piasna, 2015). Data on employee preferences concerning working-time duration, position and regularity are relevant and can in principle make a contribution. But responses to simple, closed-ended questions on preferences are by no means transparent, given that preferences are formed (and re-formed) in a social context: firstly, the context of the life course (Anxo et al., 2006) and the household (Anxo, 2004), but also more generally in the context of institutions of social welfare and gender norms. An Australian study of stated preferences among employees engaged in long hours of unpaid overtime found, in subsequent qualitative interviews, that the answers to preference questions were unstable and that employees who declared that they were content with their long hours were often ambivalent, judging that long hours were unavoidable components of the job or of a professional ethic (Campbell and van Wanrooy, 2013).

The challenge of differentiating flexible working-time arrangements is sharpest in the case of the multiple forms of part-time work (Messenger and Ray,

2015). Fortunately, this is also where thinking is most advanced and policy initiatives are most developed – for example, not only at national level but also through the International Labour Organization (ILO) Part-Time Work Convention (No. 175) and the EU Directive on part-time work. Research has long noted the division between marginalised and integrated part-time work (O'Reilly and Fagan, 1998) and discussion of the latter is developed in the subsequent literature on good-quality part-time employment, which proposes criteria for differentiating good quality from poor quality (Fagan *et al.*, 2014; Lyonette *et al.*, 2016). However, it remains difficult to use the criteria with national labour force data, except through relatively crude indicators, such as the incidence of marginal part-time hours and employee preferences for longer hours (i.e. time-related underemployment) (Lee *et al.*, 2007: 55–60; but cf. Piasna, 2015).

Despite all difficulties, it is possible to make a rough aggregate judgement of working-time trends at national level. Substantial cross-national variation exists (Berg *et al.*, 2014; Rubery *et al.*, 1998). It would be wrong to exaggerate the move away from the system of standardised working hours; in most industrialised countries the standard working-time arrangement remains influential. Similarly, in many countries at least some changes, especially around good-quality part-time work, indicate evolution of the system along the lines of the second ideal type and a move towards a 'flexible SER'. Nevertheless, the problematic third ideal type is clearly significant, and indeed several countries, especially the liberal market economies, seem to approximate to this ideal type. Trends towards flexible working-time arrangements that are disconnected from the system and are the product of employer needs are widespread. For example, in addition to evidence of moves towards good-quality part-time work, evidence exists for a proliferation of poor-quality, casualised part-time work arrangements that are closely associated with employer needs and offer little to workers (Lee *et al.*, 2007).

Fragmented time systems

The spread of flexible working-time arrangements that are disconnected from the regulatory system and that are associated with high risks of precariousness for employees is a major challenge for research and policy. To understand these practices, it is helpful to dig beneath national level data sets. One valuable contribution stems from case-study research in the UK, initially in organisations across a range of sectors in the early 2000s (Beynon *et al.*, 2002; Marchington *et al.*, 2005; Rubery *et al.*, 2005; Rubery *et al.*, 2006), subsequently supplemented by further research in organisations in other sectors such as domiciliary care (Rubery *et al.*, 2015; see also Grimshaw *et al.*, 2016).

The research builds on a powerful analytical framework, linked to a segmentation perspective. It follows the principle of a multi-level analysis, in which the agency of the employer (the organisation) is brought to the fore, but within a context that pays attention to the influence of structural forces associated with the national institutional framework, segmentation processes on the demand side and the supply side, and internal organisational pressures. The research pursues a comparison across different sectoral and regional locations in the UK, paying attention inter alia to the differential impact of tertiarisation and new information and communication technologies.

The research centres on working-time flexibility as a site of transformation. It points to a multiplicity of changes, made up largely, though not exclusively, of employer-oriented forms of working-time flexibility. The authors identify two main 'modes of flexibility' (Rubery et al., 2005; Rubery et al. 2006). In both cases the employer interest is in reducing unit labour costs, in particular through altering the wage/effort bargain and soliciting greater effort, but differences arise according to the type of worker. Drawing on Supiot (2001), Rubery and colleagues (2006: 135–41) suggest that among high-skilled employees the trend is towards results-based systems, in place of time-based systems, in which working time is extended and intensified through indirect pressures such as lean staffing, heavy workloads and new reward systems.

For lower-skilled, low-wage employees, on the other hand, employment contracts remain time-based but working hours are increasingly broken down and reduced. The principle here is careful scheduling in order to match hours to uneven patterns of demand, marked by core staffing for troughs in demand but then 'fragmented and variable' scheduling for other employees to match the peaks (Rubery et al., 2006: 139–41). Such scheduling in turn implies careful monitoring, often facilitated by new technologies, both of demand patterns and of the time taken for the tasks involved in meeting demand. The resulting fragmented time systems or arrangements are defined as 'when employers use strict work scheduling to focus paid work hours at [periods of] high demand ... and do not reward or recognise work-related time between periods of high or direct customer demand' (Rubery et al., 2015: 754). The system can be used for conventional operations during daytime hours on weekdays, but its full potential emerges when used, with flat hourly rates of pay, for longer operating and opening hours, where it appears as a radical alternative to traditional overtime and shift-work systems. As the definition suggests, the employer aims to achieve cost savings in the first place by avoiding payment for idle time, as in conventional strategies of intensification designed to fill in the 'pores' in the working day. The logic of cost savings readily extends, however, to all types of paid time that do not appear as time that is immediately productive for the employer. Thus it targets several features of protective regulation such as rest periods, which can be avoided by careful scheduling of the length of shifts, and it also extends to standard arrangements for holiday leave, training and transport time. Though still vulnerable to conflicts and contradictions, the new time organisation allows risk to be shifted away from the employer towards the employee and his/her family or perhaps towards the state.

The UK case-study analysis resonates strongly. The concepts offer a rich research agenda for examining working-time trends in many industrialised socie-ties. In particular, the notion of fragmented time systems is helpful for describing trends towards casualised working-time arrangements and for connecting them to employer labour-use strategies in a wide range of industries. To underline the relevance of the analysis, it is useful to draw out three points, which link up with the earlier reflections on flexible working-time arrangements.

Firstly, schedules under fragmented time systems can be diverse. Shifts may be long or short, though they are more likely to be short, and – depending on operating or opening hours – they may be distributed across any time of the day and week, including split shifts in the one day. The shifts may be fixed or variable, with variation often implying an on-call element that plays havoc with employees' lives outside of work. In short, flexibility in this case can involve employer control of duration and/or position and, in both cases, it can further entail employer control of variation; commonly it involves an unwelcome com-bination of *all* elements. The content of the schedules is partly dependent on the pattern of demand to which the hours are matched, thereby allowing the risks associated with fluctuating demand to be shifted onto the employee. But it should be noted that the system generates pressures towards variable schedules even when demand is relatively predictable and relatively fixed schedules would be possible in principle. As a result of short, fragmented shifts with flat-rate pay-ments, scheduling is often a site of intense inequalities. Because it may be more difficult to fill less attractive shifts and, even when they are filled, such shifts may be disproportionately affected by absenteeism, the system often requires extra temporal availability to cover all potential gaps. The problem can be solved by adding layers to the workforce and using different employment contracts and sources of recruitment such as temporary agencies. Another common approach is to design temporal availability into the employment contract or the job for the majority of employees, for example by ensuring that they have fewer hours than they want and are therefore willing to be available to pick up extra shifts – what has been called 'passive flexibility' (Lehndorff and Voss-Dahm, 2005).

Secondly, reduction and fragmentation of working time in contemporary societies depend on the existence of regulatory gaps in employee protection.

If we set aside the issue of non-compliance, then opportunities for employers are greatest when they can use particular types of employment that are equipped with reduced employment rights, including, especially, reduced rights to working-time security. Several options exist in the UK, but a central place in the debate is taken by *zero-hours contracts* (ZHCs), defined as 'contracts or arrangements under which an employer agrees to pay for work done but makes no commitment to provide set hours of work' (Adams and Deakin, 2014: 1). ZHCs appear as an extreme form of on-call work, allowing extensive and unpredictable variation in both the duration and the position of working time. They are associated with fragmented time systems in domiciliary care (Rubery *et al.*, 2015), but are also influential in other sectors such as cleaning services, hospitality and even education. Scholars warn that the concept has no clear legal status and embraces a variety of practices that exist at the edges of protection, indeed at the edges of employee status (Rubery and Grimshaw, 2016). In all their forms, zero-hours arrangements come equipped with a shortfall of employment rights, but evidence points to pervasive uncertainty among both employers and employees about the extent of the shortfall, indicating that in practice these arrangements act as important covers for employer avoidance of rights, whether deliberate or inadvertent (Rubery and Grimshaw, 2014).

Thirdly, fragmented time systems imply a significant restructuring of temporal boundaries for employees. The difficulties extend beyond the perforation of the boundary between standard and non-standard (community) time and beyond the difficulties associated with intensification of work time. One further change concerns the redrawing of the boundary between paid time and unpaid time, so that only hours of direct (and intense) labour are regarded as deserving of remuneration by the employer. This reverses one of the central achievements of the regulatory system for standardised working hours, and reinstates a fundamental feature of the highly commodified casual ways of working in the nineteenth century. Also important is the implication of the on-call principle of availability, whether this is an explicit obligation in a contract or a more informal understanding between employee and employer. Availability involves time spent waiting for work and can itself be seen as a form of working time, albeit unpaid. Expectations of availability represent a major incursion of working time into personal life (Rubery *et al.*, 2005).

Conclusions

This chapter examines the important theme of working-time flexibility. It draws on recent work from a segmentation perspective, including the work of Jill

Rubery and her colleagues, in order to throw more light on this pivotal and puzzling arena of change and contestation.

The chapter situates flexible working-time arrangements in relation to the regulatory system of standardised working hours. It outlines a conceptual framework that can help to describe the varied types of flexible working-time arrangements and to analyse their implications. It sketches out three ideal typical patterns of diversification. It underlines the significance of the notion of 'fragmented time systems' for an understanding of the spread of highly casualised working-time arrangements. Though first formulated in the UK context, this concept has broad relevance to organisations and industry sectors in many other industrialised societies. It is associated with new forms of scheduling, often with a strong bias to employer-led variation, new forms of employment such as zero-hours arrangements and a major restructuring of temporal boundaries.

Notes

1   I prefer to use the term 'working-time flexibility' rather than 'temporal flexibility'. The latter is effectively a synonym, but it often appears in typologies at firm level, where it is identified with 'internal numerical flexibility', defined as practices where the number of working hours is adjusted in line with business needs, but the number of workers remains unchanged (Messenger, 2004: 152). As a result, temporal flexibility tends to be associated just with forms of employer-oriented flexibility and risks missing other forms that are more employee-oriented (see the section 'What is working-time flexibility?').

2   Bosch underlines the significance of working-time regulation when he points out that the three main buffers against the market that are linked to (partial) de-commodification for employees are: (1) the welfare state; (2) provisions in the employment contract for employment security, support in case of accident and illness, and support for retirement; and (3) rules about the use of labour time within employment such as maximum hours, rest periods and holiday leave (Bosch, 2006: 44–5; see also Rubery and Grimshaw, 2016: 242–3).

3   Duration (or time) and position (or timing) are the basic dimensions of working time. A third dimension is variously described as 'tempo', 'intensity' or the 'degree to which working time is utilised' (Noon and Blyton, 1997: 56). Tempo is indeed important in how work time is structured and experienced, and increased tempo (intensification') has become an important theme in the discussion of contemporary changes at the workplace. But tempo is best seen as a contingent outcome of processes such as supervision and should not be equated with duration and position as necessary aspects of *working-time arrangements*.

4   Other parallel formulations speak of 'employer-driven' versus 'employee-driven' flexibility or 'employer-led' versus 'employee-led' flexibility.

5   Other terms include de-standardisation (Carré, 2016). 'Fragmentation' is sometimes used in this, as in several other contexts, but it is best reserved for the time systems discussed in the section 'Fragmented time systems'. Another alternative is 'individualisation', but this is misleading unless we distinguish genuine forms of individualisation from the often-spurious claims of individualisation associated with market processes (McCann, 2007).

References

Adams, Z. and Deakin, S. (2014), *Re-regulating Zero Hours Contracts* (London: Institute of Employment Rights).

Anxo, D. (2004), 'Working time patterns among industrialized countries: a household perspective' in Messenger, J. (ed), *Working Time and Workers' Preferences in Industrialized Countries: Finding the Balance* (London: Routledge), pp. 60–107.

Anxo, D., Boulin, J. Y. and Fagan, C. (2006), 'Decent working time in a life-course perspective', in Boulin, J. Y., Lallement, M., Messenger, J. and Michon, F. (eds), *Decent Working Time: New Trends, New Issues* (Geneva: International Labour Organization), pp. 93–122.

Berg, P., Bosch, G. and Charest, J. (2014), 'Working-time configurations: a framework for analyzing diversity across countries', *Industrial and Labor Relations Review*, 67:3, 805–37.

Beynon, H., Grimshaw, D., Rubery, J. and Ward, K. (2002), *Managing Employment Change: The New Realities of Work* (Oxford: Oxford University Press).

Bittman, M. (2016), 'Working time', in Edgell, S., Gottfried, H. and Granter, S. (eds), *The Sage Handbook of the Sociology of Work and Employment* (London: Sage), pp. 520–40.

Bosch, G. (2004), 'Towards a new standard employment relationship in Western Europe', *British Journal of Industrial Relations*, 42:4, 617–36.

Bosch, G. (2006), 'Working time and the standard employment relationship', in Boulin, J. Y., Lallement, M., Messenger, J. and Michon, F. (eds), *Decent Working Time: New Trends, New Issues* (Geneva: International Labour Organization), pp. 41–64.

Campbell, I. (1993), 'Labour market flexibility in Australia: enhancing management prerogative?' *Labour and Industry*, 5:3, 1–32.

Campbell, I. (2008), 'Australia: institutional changes and workforce fragmentation', in Lee, S. and Eyraud, F. (eds), *Globalization, Flexibilization and Working Conditions in Asia and the Pacific* (London: Chandos), pp. 115–52.

Campbell, I. and van Wanrooy, B. (2013), 'Long working hours and working-time preferences: between desirability and feasibility', *Human Relations*, 66:8, 1131–55.

Carré, F. (2016), 'Destandardization: Qualitative and quantitative', in Edgell, S., Gottfried, H. and Granter, S. (eds), *The Sage Handbook of the Sociology of Work and Employment* (London: Sage), 385–406.

Chung, H. and Tijdens, K. (2012), 'Working time flexibility components and working time regimes in Europe: using company-level data across 21 countries', *International Journal of Human Resource Management*, 24:7, 1418–34.

Fagan, C. (2004), 'Gender and working time in industrialised countries', in Messenger, J. (ed.), *Working Time and Workers' Preferences in Industrialized Countries: Finding the Balance* (London: Routledge), pp. 108–46.

Fagan, C., Lyonette, C., Smith, M. and Salaña-Tejeda, A. (2012), *The Influence of Working Time Arrangements on Work-Life Integration or 'Balance': A Review of the International Evidence*, Conditions of Work and Employment Series No. 32 (Geneva: International Labour Organization).

Fagan, C., Norman, H., Smith, M. and González Menéndez, M. (2014), *In Search of Good Quality Part-Time Employment*, Conditions of Work and Employment Series No. 65 (Geneva: International Labour Organization).

Fagan, C. and Vermeylen, G. (2016), 'Working time trends and work-life balance in Europe since the onset of the Great Recession', in Lewis, S., Anderson, D., Lyonette, C., Payne, N. and Wood, S. (eds), *Work-Life Balance in Times of Austerity and Beyond: Meeting the Needs of Employees, Organizations and Social Justice* (London: Routledge).

Green, F., Mostafa, T., Parent-Thirion, A., Vermeylen, G., van Houten, G., Biletta, I. and Lyly-Yrjanainen, M. (2013), 'Is job quality becoming more unequal?' *Industrial and Labor Relations Review*, 66:4, 753–84.

Grimshaw, D., Johnson, M., Keizer, A. and Rubery, J. (2016), *Reducing Precarious Work through Social Dialogue: The Case of the UK* (European Work and Employment Research Centre: University of Manchester).

Heron, A. and Charlesworth, S. (2012), 'Working time and managing care under Labor: whose flexibility?' *Australian Bulletin of Labour*, 38:3, 214–33.

Hinrichs, K. (1991), 'Working-time development in West Germany: departure to a new stage', in Hinrichs, K., Roche, W. and Sirianni, C. (eds), *Working Time in Transition: The Political Economy of Working Hours in Industrial Nations* (Philadelphia: Temple University Press), pp. 27–59.

Jährling, K. and Méhaut, P. (2013), '"Varieties of institutional avoidance": employers' strategies in low-waged service sector occupations in France and Germany', *Socio-economic Review*, 11:4, 687–710.

Lee, S. (2004), 'Working-hour gaps: trends and issues', in Messenger, J. (ed.), *Working Time and Workers' Preferences in Industrialized Countries: Finding the Balance* (London: Routledge), pp. 29–59.

Lee, S. and McCann, D. (2006), 'Working time capability: towards realizing individual choice', in Boulin, J. Y., Lallement, M., Messenger, J. and Michon, F. (eds), *Decent Working Time: New Trends, New Issues* (Geneva: International Labour Organization), pp. 65–91.

Lee, S., McCann, D. and Messenger, J. (2007), *Working Time Around the World: Trends in Working Hours, Laws and Policies in a Global Comparative Perspective* (Geneva: Routledge and International Labour Organization).

Lehndorff, S. and Voss-Dahm, D. (2005), 'The delegation of uncertainty: flexibility and the role of the market in service work', in Bosch, G. and Lehndorff, S. (eds), *Working in the Service Sector: A Tale from Different Worlds* (London: Routledge), pp. 289–315.

Lyonette, C., Baldauf, B. and Behle, H. (2016), 'An exploration of quality part-time working in Europe, with a focus on the UK case', in Connerley, M. and Wu, J. (eds), *Handbook on Well-Being of Working Women* (Dordrecht: Springer), pp. 489–502.

McCann, D. (2007), 'Temporal autonomy and the protective individualisation of working-time law: The case of overtime work', *Labour and Industry*, 17:3, 29–43.

McCann, D. (2014), 'Equality through precarious work regulation: lessons from the domestic work debates in defence of the standard employment relationship', *International Journal of Law in Context* 10:4, 507–21.

McCann, D. and Murray, J. (2014), 'Prompting formalisation through labour market regulation: a "framed flexibility" model for domestic work', *Industrial Law Journal*, 43:3, 319–48.

Marchington, M., Grimshaw, D., Rubery, J. and Willmott, H. (eds) (2005), *Fragmenting Work: Blurring Boundaries and Disordering Hierarchies* (Oxford: Oxford University Press).

Messenger, J. (2004), 'Working time at the enterprise level: business objectives, firms' practices and workers' preferences', in Messenger, J. (ed.), *Working Time and Workers' Preferences in Industrialized Countries: Finding the Balance* (London: Routledge), pp. 147–94.

Messenger, J. and Ray, N. (2015), 'The "deconstruction" of part-time work', in Berg, J. (ed.), *Labour Markets, Institutions and Inequality: Building Just Societies in the 21st Century* (London: Edward Elgar), pp. 184–206.

Noon, M. and Blyton, P. (1997), *The Realities of Work* (London: Macmillan).

O'Reilly, J. and Fagan, C. (eds) (1998), *Part-time Prospects: An International Comparison of Part-time Work in Europe, North America and the Pacific Rim* (London: Routledge).

Piasna, A. (2015), '"Thou shalt work hard": Fragmented working hours and work intensification across the EU', *Forum Socjologiczne*, SI 1, 77–89.

Pocock, B., Charlesworth, S. and Chapman, J. (2013), 'Work-family and work-life pressures in Australia: advancing gender equality in "good times"', *International Journal of Sociology and Social Policy*, 33:9/10, 594–612.

Rubery, J. (2005a), 'The shaping of work and working time in the service sector: a segmentation approach', in Bosch, G. and Lehndorff, S. (eds), *Working in the Service Sector: A Tale from Different Worlds* (London: Routledge), pp. 201–88.

Rubery, J. (2005b), 'Labor markets and flexibility', in Ackroyd, S., Batt, R., Thompson, P. and Tolbert, P. (eds), *The Oxford Handbook of Work and Organization* (Oxford: Oxford University Press), pp. 31–51.

Rubery, J. (2015), *Re-regulating for Inclusive Labour Markets*, Conditions of Work and Employment Series No. 65 (Geneva: International Labour Organization).

Rubery, J. and Grimshaw, D. (2003), *The Organization of Employment: An International Perspective* (London: Macmillan).

Rubery, J. and Grimshaw, D. (2014), 'New forms of employment – zero hours contracts in the UK', unpublished report for Eurofound (Dublin: Eurofound).

Rubery, J., Grimshaw, D., Hebson, G. and Ugarte. S. (2015), '"It's all about time": time as contested terrain in the management and experience of domiciliary care work in England', *Human Resource Management*, 54:4, 753–72.

Rubery, J. and Grimshaw, D. (2016), 'Precarious work and the commodification of the employment relationship: the case of zero hours in the UK and mini-jobs in Germany', in Bäcker, G., Lehndorff, S. and Weinkopf, C. (eds), *Den Arbeitsmarkt verstehen, um ihn zu gestalten. Festschrift für Gerhard Bosch* (Wiesbaden: Springer), pp. 241–54.

Rubery, J., Smith, M. and Fagan, C. (1998), 'National working-time regimes and equal opportunities', *Feminist Economics,* 4:1, 71–101.

Rubery, J., Ward, K. and Grimshaw, D. (2006), 'Time, work and pay: understanding the new relationships', in Boulin, J. Y., Lallement, M., Messenger, J. and Michon, F. (eds), *Decent Working Time: New Trends, New Issues* (Geneva: International Labour Organization), pp. 123–51.

Rubery, J., Ward, K., Grimshaw, D. and Beynon, H. (2005), 'Working time, industrial relations and the employment relationship', *Time and Society,* 154:1, 89–111.

Schmid, G. (2008), *Full Employment in Europe: Managing Labour Market Transitions and Risks* (Cheltenham: Edward Elgar).

Skinner, N., Cathcart, A. and Pocock. B. (2016), 'To ask or not to ask? Investigating workers' flexibility requests and the phenomenon of discontented non-requesters', *Labour and Industry,* 26:2, 103–19.

Supiot, A. (2001), *Beyond Employment: Changes in Work and the Future of Labour Law in Europe* (Oxford: Oxford University Press).

Vosko, L. (2011), 'Precarious employment and the problem of SER-Centrism in regulating for decent work', in Lee, S. and McCann, D. (eds), *Regulating for Decent Work: New Directions in Labour Market Regulation* (London: Palgrave Macmillan and International Labour Organization), pp. 58–90.

Part II

International evidence:
precarious employment and gender
inequality

7

Labour segmentation and precariousness in Spain: theories and evidence

Josep Banyuls and Albert Recio

Introduction

Spain is a country with strongly marked contrasts in the labour market. Since the economic crisis of the 1970s until today it is the European country that has experienced the greatest fluctuations in the volume of employment. During periods of recession, unemployment rates have been among the highest worldwide, but conversely, during recovery periods, employment growth has been very intense. It is also the European labour market with the greatest use of temporary employment. As a result of these conditions, many significant labour reforms have been implemented and, consequently, the Spanish economy can in some ways be considered as a laboratory of their impact.[1] It is because of this that the debate on the functioning of the labour market in general, and on segmentation in particular, has been especially intense in Spain during these years.

The segmentation approach arrived in Spain, as in many other places, from the hands of heterodox economists (in a broad sense) and it had a strong echo among labour sociologists. In the early 1980s, neoclassical economists in academia and leading economic think tanks (particularly the Spanish Central Bank and the research services of large banks) ignored this approach. Those were times when the official debate revolved around the rigidity of labour markets and the economy. In Europe, the discussion was about Eurosclerosis (Krugman and Wells, 2006), which portrayed Europe's poor performance compared with the USA in terms of its 'generous' unemployment protection systems and strong trade union bargaining power. In Spain, owing to the absence of these aspects at the beginning of democracy, rigidity was attributed to the persistence of laws and practices inherited from the Franco regime. The situation changed in 1987 when, for the first time, the Labour Force Survey published information on the level of temporary employment and estimated the temporary employment rate at 17.7 per cent. Suddenly, Spain had gone from being a country with rigid employment to being one of the most advanced countries in terms of the use of flexible forms of employment.

The official explanation of unemployment had necessarily to be revised, and with this change, the concept of segmentation (in its most simplistic version of duality) eventually became the reference point for new discussions. As we shall see, the interpretation of segmentation by neoclassical economists is completely different from the heterodox view developed by Jill Rubery (Rubery, 1978; Rubery, 1992; Rubery and Wilkinson, 1994) and other members of the International Working Party on Labour Market Segmentation (IWPLMS) (Wilkinson, 1981; see Chapter 1). This approach suggested alternative lines of analysis based on a more wide-ranging analysis of segmentation and an appreciation of the influences of national models of employment (Bosch, Lehndorff and Rubery, 2009). For the conventional approach, at least for the mainstream neoclassical economists, markets work reasonably well in terms of competitive balance, and employment problems are essentially caused by the interference of extra-market institutions that generate inadequate incentives and create discrimination and inefficiency. Therefore, the main recipe against unemployment is to carry out structural reforms of labour market institutions, which lead to some extent to a competitive behaviour of unemployment itself.

For heterodox economists, unemployment is a macroeconomic problem generated by the normal functioning of capitalism, labour market segmentation is in part a product of company policies, and the specific problems of each country cannot be interpreted only as a result of their local institutions but also in terms of their interaction and positioning in the global economy (e.g. Recio, 1994; Rubery, 2007; Wilkinson, 1981). Drawing on the key ideas developed by Rubery about labour market segmentation, this chapter discusses how this debate has materialised in Spain, and how the empirical evidence vindicates the heterodox approach. Spain is a particularly interesting case to consider these different points of view due to its high unemployment rate and the huge amount of reforms that have taken place in the labour market's regulatory framework. We begin by addressing the main lines of argument of the neoclassical approach to explain labour market problems in Spain. We then offer an alternative perspective rooted in the structural and historical characteristics of the Spanish National Employment Model based on a broad set of empirical evidence. The chapter closes with some brief conclusions.

The conventional approach 'discovers' segmentation

In the economic crisis of the 1970s, Spain experienced a high rate of unemployment and, for the first time, there was a theoretical debate about its causes. The explanation offered from the neoclassical economics perspective was articulated around the idea that unemployment originated in problems of labour market rigidity caused by the existing institutional framework (Bentolila and Jimeno, 2003; Malo de Molina, 1983). The rigidity stemmed from the persistence of many labour norms inherited from the Franco period, as well as from the concessions made to trade unions during the political transition (Dolado *et al.*, 2002). Reviewing the debates of those years, the arguments used to explain unemployment were articulated around five issues:

1) *Labour market rigidity* associated with difficulties for businesses to make quantitative adjustments of their workforce, thereby impairing the speed of response to economic shocks. This rigidity materialised in difficulties in flexible hiring, in dismissal and in limits on work organisation;

2) *Wage rigidity and excessively high wages* as a result of Spain's collective bargaining model (involving bargaining at the sector level, not company level) and the existence of minimum wages set by collective agreement at levels higher than the statutory national minimum wage, as well as social contributions;

3) *Malfunctioning of labour intermediation* (that is, inefficient active labour market policies) and problems of availability of sufficiently skilled workforce;

4) *Overly generous unemployment subsidies* that discouraged the search and acceptance of job vacancies by unemployed people and maintained real wages at too high a level; and

5) *Supply-side shocks.* Although the origin of shocks was changing, the argument ultimately relied always on the idea that the collective bargaining model prevented the fall of real wages against shocks. The main causes of shocks that were identified were a rising active population (without a corresponding reduction in wages), falling total factor productivity (again without lower wages), rising interest rates (in the context of the 1970s crisis) and production costs out of balance with wages that did not diminish sufficiently to sustain the stimulus to investment.

These five explanations were not attributed equal importance. Factors such as labour rigidity, the collective bargaining model, which generated wage rigidity, and social subsidies (overly generous) were highlighted as having a greater responsibility in generating high unemployment rates, as well as some personal characteristics (lack of training), which discouraged the acceptance of positions and kept wages high. Yet the two central arguments that were raised at that time and that persist today from the conventional perspective were, and still are, the problem of quantitative rigidity and the low flexibility of wages (Andrés et al., 2010; FEDEA, 2012). Unemployment benefits have been gradually losing importance as a cause of unemployment, given the evidence of their low coverage.

Hence, arguments were gradually closing in around the two aforementioned aspects, quantitative rigidity and wage rigidity, and continue to this day. The economic policy proposals derived from these approaches have always presented themselves, both in the crisis of the 1970s and today, as the inevitable course of action, as the only way out of the various crises experienced by the Spanish economy. Underpinning them there is always a blind belief that businesses fail to create employment because the labour market cannot afford it. The problem, it is claimed, is not in the characteristics of the production structure, nor in the demand of goods or the management strategies. It is in regulation – a regulation that allows wages to be excessively high (above productivity) and forces businesses to experience great difficulties in the quantitative adjustment of the workforce (Dolado and Jimeno, 1997).

This explanation faced an important test when, in 1984, labour legislation was reformed and the use of temporary contracts without requiring a justification was legalised. In 1987, the Labour Force Survey included, for the first time, information about the kinds of labour contracts, and temporality was placed over 17 per cent, a much higher value than the usual rate in Europe. In subsequent years, the percentage share continued to grow as numbers in total employment also increased until it reached an average rate of around 33 per cent, right up to the 2008 crisis. In terms of ease of temporary hiring and of employment sensitivity regarding economic activity, employment in Spain was shown to be very flexible, and labour market rigidity became a difficult argument to sustain as an explanation of continued high rates of unemployment (Figure 7.1). Neither could excessive unemployment benefits be sustained as an argument, given that during the 1980s, the percentage of unemployed people who received subsidies was placed at around 25 per cent.

By the early 1990s, it was clear that the neoclassical economics explanation was in need of repair. It was at that moment when the defenders of rigidity as the cause of unemployment 'discovered' the idea of labour market segmentation, in its most radical version of dualism, but limiting its causes to the stylised impact of labour market regulations. In this reformulated approach, dualism in labour markets emerged simply from the adaptation of businesses

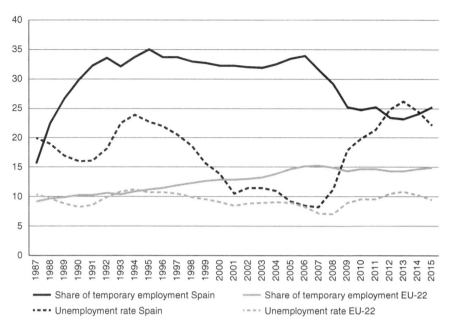

40

35

30

25

20

15

10

5

0

1987 1988 1989 1990 1991 1992 1993 1994 1995 1996 1997 1998 1999 2000 2001 2002 2003 2004 2005 2006 2007 2008 2009 2010 2011 2012 2013 2014 2015

— Share of temporary employment Spain   — Share of temporary employment EU-22

∙ ∙ ∙ ∙ Unemployment rate Spain   ∙ ∙ ∙ ∙ Unemployment rate EU-22

Figure 7.1 Temporary and unemployment rate (%) in Spain, 1987–2015

Source: OECD.stat.

to a rigid institutional market (Bentolila and Dolado, 1994). The introduction of flexibility stemming from the labour contract with the 1984 reform had been a reform 'on the margin', it was claimed, because employment protections for workers with permanent contracts remained untouched. In this way, businesses faced the dilemma of making permanent contracts with a high cost of dismissal or temporary contracts at no cost.[2] The majority of businesses opted for the second option and this accounted for the growth of temporary employment. Permanent employees saw their bargaining position strengthened, because now they not only enjoyed the protection of the law, but they also had the protective cushion of temporary employees. When businesses faced a drop in demand, the adjustment would be applied exclusively or mainly to the temporary workers.

The next step of the argument relied on the idea that unions represented solely permanent workers and, therefore, they could push for foolish wage increases, or resist downward adjustments, because if these increases generated workforce adjustments they would be applied to temporary workers rather than their members. The Spanish labour market behaved as a dual market with *insiders* protected by the law and by trade unions and *outsiders* outside protections and subject to market forces. This implied not only a high segmentation in terms of employment and wages, but also important macroeconomic effects (Jimeno and Ortega, 2003: 107). On the one hand, there was an inflationary pressure, derived from collective bargaining, which only took into account stable employment. On the other, businesses' preference for hiring temporary employees affected the training of human capital and favoured specialisation in low-productivity activities.[3] Overall, these studies represent an adaptation to the Spanish case of the initial neoclassical economics analysis of Lindbeck and Snower (1988, 2001), which sought to incorporate some of the ideas of Piore's dualism (1980).

However, unlike Piore's work, the revised studies of Spanish neoclassical economists implied a shift in the causes of labour segmentation. Instead of highlighting the demand factors and the business strategies at the origin of segmentation in response to both the problems generated by the control of the workforce and the functioning of the diverse product markets, they point to labour regulations and unions as the main causes of segmentation. This argument ignores that segmentation is visible in countries such as the USA, with high labour deregulation and a low union presence. It also has an enormous political burden, since it tries to make permanent adult workers, and the unions that represent them, responsible for the dualisation of the labour market, shifting from a capital–labour conflict to a conflict between workers.

This analysis has been used to justify the 1994 labour reform, launched as a response to the 1991–94 economic crisis, as well as the following reforms of 1997, 2002, 2010 and 2012, which cut severance payments and made the procedures for dismissal easier. Despite these series of reforms, the argument has been persistent. The discourse is promoted by influential organisms of economic opinion (particularly Fundación de Estudios de Economía Aplicada (FEDEA), the research service of the Spanish Central Bank, and that of the Banco Bilbao Vizcaya Argentaria (BBVA)) and by mainstream economists from the Universities who have always considered these labour reforms insufficient. The current policy recommendation for eliminating segmentation is to introduce a single contract with a dismissal compensation growing proportionally to the number of years worked.[4] This is an idea for which they have gathered important international support, especially from the Organisation for Economic Co-operation and Development (OECD) and International Monetary Fund (IMF). However, it is not clear whether this measure would change the massive use of short-term employment in an economy with a high degree of seasonality in key sectors (especially in those depending on tourism). What would be achieved, however, would be the disappearance of the statistical indicator of the percentage of temporary employment, which shows the poor quality of employment in Spain.

The contradictions of the conventional view

The conventional view reduces labour market segmentation to a mere response of businesses to the institutional framework (in the case of Spain, to the contractual arrangements) and as such ignores the main achievements of institutionalist labour economics. From an institutionalist approach, developed for decades as an alternative to the mainstream economic orthodox thinking, segmentation is a result of business policies oriented to resolve the complexity of conflicts and problems faced by companies, both in the management of labour activity and in the product market, and not just a simple problem of regulation.

As noted by Rubery (1992, 2007), the segmentation approach places the employment practices of businesses and their determining factors at the centre of the analysis in order to explain employment conditions and labour inequalities. The role of the employer is therefore central in accounting for the level and characteristics of employment, and is a key factor in shaping the dynamics of employment structure. Therefore, from this perspective, and in contrast with the conventional approach, the core factors that shape labour market dynamics are on the side of demand. This contrasts with the neoclassical economics approach to which individual decisions in human capital investment, job search and wage demands are reflective of, and somehow account for, labour demand.

Another notable aspect of the segmentation approach is that segmentation is present both within an economy and between economies, with different forms and manifestations. The determining factors change over time and are specific in each case, so that in practice we find a wide variety of situations, without any tendencies toward 'natural' convergence of employment models, neither within a society nor between societies (Bosch, Lehndorff and Rubery, 2009). A good example is the case of the European Union, in which the various processes of integration (monetary, trade and so on) have not resulted in a convergence of labour market patterns. In this dynamic, key importance is attributed to institutions and strategies of social actors. Both are crucial in shaping the diversity of labour market structures.

Obviously, the focus of orthodox economics does not consider all these aspects. The analytical reductionism that it applies in the case of Spain leads it to explain segmentation in the exclusive terms of permanent and temporary contracts, overlooking aspects of the real functioning of the labour market which in other approaches are relevant. A quick review of key aspects of the Spanish labour market that are easily detectable empirically raises clear questions for the conventional explanation, as follows.

- The choice of an explanatory variable of labour inequalities – for example, the type of contract – suggests significant results in terms of labour duality. For instance, in terms of wages, people with permanent contracts have higher wages than temporary workers. But the same result can be achieved by choosing a different explanatory variable. One can, for example, build a dualist explanation of the Spanish labour market based on the gender variable and construct a plausible theory of a dual market in terms of gender. Age (and seniority) could also be suggested. However, these forms of differentiation are not explainable in the terms of the proposed model.

- Disaggregation by sector shows substantial diversity in the use of temporary employment and the strategies that explain their use. For instance, in the sector where use of temporary employment is highest – construction – its use corresponds in part to the functioning of professional markets where skilled workers change employers fairly frequently while maintaining a certain professional career. However, in hospitality, another sector with a high temporary rate, this is instead due to the seasonality of tourism.

- A detailed analysis of the evolution of the relationship between temporary and fixed-term employment offers paradoxical results that contradict the conventional model. In the 1991–94 crisis, the adjustment was higher among permanent employment contracts than temporary contracts because it was basically an industrial crisis and, in many businesses, insiders did not have any ability to 'unleash' adjustments on temporary workers (Alba and Alonso, 1997). Conversely, the period of expansion prior to the 2008 crisis shows a fall in temporality rates in most sectors. This was due largely to collective bargaining where in many cases unions decided to moderate wage demands in exchange for transforming temporary employment into stable employment (contrary to the behavioural assumptions of insider–outsider models). There is no evidence that there was strong growth of wages in this expansive period as suggested by the orthodox theory. The increase in temporary employment in this period was primarily due to the explosive growth of employment in construction and the strong growth of temporary employment in the public sector.

- The huge adjustment of temporary employment in the first phase of the 2008 crisis is explained by its rapid impact in the construction sector. As the crisis has progressed, job destruction has also impacted many permanent jobs (Banyuls and Recio, 2015).

- The various reforms that have delivered lower costs and easier dismissal procedures have not altered employers' preference for temporary employment (Toharia, 2005; Toharia, 2011). As we explain in the next section, temporary employment is a resource that is part of a larger and more complex raft of labour management practices, which aim to minimise labour costs and contribute to a dismantling of Spain's industrial relations model.

An alternative view of segmentation: new and old dynamics

Although rather discreet, labour market segmentation theory had already entered the debate on the Spanish labour market long before the analysis was reformulated into crude dualistic terms. A mandatory starting point is the contribution of Lluis Fina and Luis Toharia in the 1980s (Fina *et al.*, 1989; Fina and Toharia, 1987), which addressed the causes of unemployment during that period. For them, the analysis of the Spanish labour market could not be separated from the analysis of the characteristics and dynamics of the production structure and business policies. The depth of the crisis and the rise in unemployment during the 1980s was largely the result of opening up the Spanish economy to internationalisation, with massive job losses in outdated and over-sized industries. After the sharp rise in unemployment in those years, its continuity over time is largely explained by a truncated process of modernisation. On the one hand, parts of the traditional sectors (agriculture, retail, some small industrial activities) with high levels of informal employment were modernised and yet Spanish businesses at the time lacked the capabilities and structures to generate stable, decent quality, formal jobs. On the other hand, the public sector was insufficiently developed, although its growth during the 1980s played an important role in the consolidation of an educated middle class.

The Spanish labour market has always been strongly segmented (Recio, 1999). Leaving aside the public sector, with its specific labour system, a central difference exists between big business and the huge mass of small and medium-sized enterprises (SMEs). In the former, internal labour markets were developed, while in most SMEs a system of highly personalised labour relations prevailed. The collective bargaining system implemented in 1959 reflected this duality with the combination of enterprise agreements, particularly in the large firms, and sectoral agreements, in which the working conditions of SMEs were established and where union presence was practically non-existent. This resulted in a significant wage differentiation. In addition to this, sectors with a high level of seasonal employment (tourism, agriculture) or temporary employment (construction) have for many years exerted a strong weight in the production structure, and other areas of the economy have generated important and persistent spaces for the informal economy where the work is mostly performed by women (e.g. domestic service, clothing industry, some industrial activities, small assemblies and so on). All of this accounts partially for the high level of temporary employment showed by the Labour Forces Survey (LFS) in 1987 that questioned the alleged rigidity of the Spanish labour market. Rather than a dual market, we have faced for many years a series of interacting labour segments that offered varying degrees of labour protection, remuneration and rights. At the peak are situated the major energy and finance companies (along with some of the large, successful industrial companies) and at the base small businesses and sectors characterised by high labour turnover.

The transformations that took place in subsequent years have only strengthened this differentiation due to both the effect of the legislative changes that have facilitated the deregulation of working conditions and the substantial organisational changes adopted by large companies. In these processes we can detect two parallel dynamics: firstly, the expansion and remodelling of secondary markets; and secondly, changes in the conditions in which domestic markets operate towards greater individualisation of working conditions and increased flexibility.

The extension and complexity of secondary markets: temporality and outsourcing

Changes in regulation have fuelled the growth of employment precariousness, but it is a considerably more complex process than suggested by conventional analysis which simply states that the high volatility of temporary employment is caused by an excessive protection of permanent employment. In the previous section we have already noted some of these aspects, such as the high concentration of temporary employment by sectors, which is partly owing to the different degree of variability in demand. But there are other issues to be considered. The use of temporary and part-time employment is due in many cases to a business strategy to minimise labour costs, and to consider such contracts as an adjustment mechanism. For instance, a fall during the summer of employment in the education sector is a recurring fact, caused by the massive use of discontinuous fixed-term contracts in the sector. However, such contracts are also a clear control mechanism, since employers can reward appropriate worker behaviour with a succession of temporary contracts.

The extension of part-time employment is also due in large part to this time management logic in all those activities where activity peaks predominate on certain days or hours, as is the case in retail, hospitality, leisure activities and care services for the elderly, among others (Recio et al., 2015). The minimisation of working time has become part of the dominant model of personnel management (O'Reilly and Fagan, 1998; Sandor, 2009), especially as the commodification of service activities has demonstrated the importance of time constraints in many activities (Rubery *et al.*, 2015). The extension of temporal flexibility is one of the forces which promotes the extension of short-term employment and the spasmodic use of the workforce as an adjustment variable. Some studies show, in addition, that temporary and part-time contracts are also a mechanism to intensify work effort (Moreno *et al.*, 2014; Pinilla, 2004).

These contractual forms are often presented as an employment form that favours the reconciliation of work and home life and as a pathway for women's entry into the labour market. However, their expansion is concentrated in the services most affected by irregular and unstable working-time patterns and characterised by very low levels of wage income. Often it is not only the problem of too few hours of work and little income, but also too few hours during anti-social and undesirable times or even, which is probably worse, at varying schedules at the employer's demand (particularly in retail and hospitality).

We should also take into account the intense immigration experienced in Spain during the last phase of economic growth. This fuelled a segment of secondary, unregulated and informal employment, which is totally beyond the control of unions or public bodies (Recio *et al.*, 2006). Elderly care is probably the sector where this type of employment is most expressive, although the presence of migrant workers employed in such conditions is also important in agriculture, construction and hospitality.

The other motor of change is the outsourcing of productive activities, which has notably progressed, although it is governed by different organisational patterns in each sector. Compared to the model of the large, vertically integrated companies, today most large companies are characterised by organising production around a huge national and international network of suppliers and auxiliary companies that perform substantial functions in the production process (Alonso and Fernández, 2012; Grimshaw and Rubery, 2007; Harrison, 1997; see also Chapter 4 in this volume).

This transformation has occurred following different routes. A general trend has involved business strategies to outsource those activities considered ancillary or secondary (e.g. cleaning, maintenance, catering, security, logistics, assembly) to companies that specialise in these tasks (Aguiar, 2001). A second trend has involved the unbundling of the production process and subcontracting a wide range of activities to outside companies (this can be seen in sectors such as the automotive or the civil construction sector) (Banyuls and Lorente, 2010; Recio, 2007). A third trend has taken place in sectors where, paradoxically, there has been a growing concentration and centralisation of activities at all stages of the production process – especially those activities concerning retail and design – while other phases are outsourced to companies over which strict control is exercised in all that affects the production cycle (quality, delivery deadlines and so on); we witness this pattern most notably in the food and textile industries (Castillo, 2005a). The fourth trend highlights the process of privatisation and the outsourcing of public services, generated by policies designed to dismantle monopolies and, it is claimed, to generate greater productive efficiency among private enterprises (Recio Cáceres, 2014). These four processes converge in a way that has favoured the configuration of large enterprise networks with a smaller labour core, but with a capacity to influence the employment relations and productive activities of a far wider production space. In many cases, the networks of production replicate themselves with an ever-growing number of tiers of contracting generating production chains that can result in activities carried out under conditions of informality (Castillo, 2005b).

The conventional argument that justifies this reorientation is that of efficiency and flexibility. Greater efficiency is explained by the advantage of labour division and specialised knowledge. Flexibility regards the consideration that we are facing increasingly volatile markets, rendering the traditional stock-adjustment model undesirable. Smaller-sized, less-integrated companies would have a greater ability to respond to this variability, through the reconfiguration of their own production network and, in turn, each one of these specialised companies could reconfigure its activity by placing themselves in other parallel networks. However, there is evidence that calls these arguments into question. On the one hand, it is found that large business groups end up being established in the field of ancillary services offering a very extensive range of activities, which contradicts the argument of the effectiveness of specialisation. On the other, neither does the flexibility of the overall production network seem clear as a mechanism of adaptation to the economic changes. For instance, in a sector highly disaggregated, such as construction, the current crisis has exposed the inability of the sector's production network to adapt to demand sinks or to move to other activities. At any rate, what is interesting is to observe what the impacts of these policies are on working life. Here we illustrate three issues.

In the first place, outsourcing is almost always a path to reduce wage costs, given that in most cases, external companies operate in labour frameworks where wage conditions are inferior. This becomes evident in the case of ancillary activities where in several countries in which studies were undertaken collective agreements provide for lower wages or are absent altogether (Dube and Kaplan, 2010; Havard, Rorive and Sobezck, 2009; Prieto et al., 2011; Lethbridges, 2012). There are many reasons that account for this: the greater difficulties of union organisation related to the fact that employees in these sectors are often isolated spatially; the competitive pressures that these companies hold before their customers, which lead them to exert downward pressures on labour conditions; and the social valuation of these jobs where outsourced can often be conflated with meanings about 'low-skilled', 'simple' and unimportant activities, which have a damaging impact on these workers' bargaining capacity.

But this same situation can be seen in the subcontracting of activities of other kinds. In some cases, outsourcing allows subcontractor companies to operate in collective agreements more appropriate to their own interests or even to differentiate the collective agreements of each of their plants (Castillo, 2013). For instance, in the motor industry one supplier firm can have different collective agreements depending on the area in the country in which it is located (using territorial collective agreements) or the specific product manufactured (using sector agreements) (Banyuls and Lorente, 2010). In other cases, as in the construction sector, the enormous fragmentation of the production process, and constraints on the use of time in each one of the different teams, opens the way for a low ability to control labour conditions and leads in many cases to the breach of certain labour conditions (Bosch and Philips, 2003; Recio, 2007).

In the second place, the chains of production have been found in certain situations to generate greater control over labour. Workers in subcontractor companies are likely to be subject to a double hierarchy: that of their employer and that of the client organisation to which they are contracted. As the detailed case studies in Rubery's work with her Manchester colleagues show, this may involve the sharing of workspace with client managers, or strict controls by the client over product and service quality, or direct client influence over staff deployment and discipline (Marchington *et al.,* 2005). This has an impact on labour process issues such as work rhythms, control of safety conditions and other issues (Castillo, 2005a).

This 'double' direction effectively shifts part of the conflict at the heart of the employment relationship to an external actor, which is outside the negotiating frame of subcontracted worker and employer and sets the interface with customer demands (Moreno *et al.*, 2014). A particular and especially interesting case is represented by the use of temporary work agencies, because in this case the worker is completely under customer orders. In Spain, working conditions depend on the collective agreement that prevails in the company where one works. The temporary work agency only has secondary control over their labour activity – most importantly, to 'reward' workers with new contracts in case of good behaviour. And yet regarding job security and bargaining for workers' labour conditions, agencies are relatively helpless. When, after a strong trade union mobilisation, a legal reform required the equalisation of the wages of agency employees with employees in the client organisations, the market response was the creation of new service companies. These companies assumed the labour activity of a part of the production process, had their own collective agreement (or were cooperatives) and favoured wage discrimination in the sense that bargained wages are usually lower than those formerly paid by temporary work agencies. Moreover, in some cases this new organisational form results in the appearance of 'false' self-employed workers who are tied to the service company through individual negotiation and do not enjoy the protections enshrined in labour law.[5]

In the third place, subcontracting opens up a process of continuous pressure on working conditions, since it frames the necessity of adaptation in seemingly 'objective' terms whereby the subcontractor must adjust working conditions in order to avoid losing the contract; in other words, it shifts the blame outside the sphere of union influence. It is a kind of pressure that has similarities with that affecting employees of core companies, especially those operating internationally, which practice a similar strategy of fragmentation of units (plants) that must compete among themselves (Banyuls and Haipeter, 2008; Korczynski, 2004). The automotive sector is illustrative; it has combined internal flexibility with increased subcontracting (inside and outside the plants) focused around enhanced production specialisation and reduced labour costs (Banyuls and Lorente, 2010). At upper levels, activities with higher added value are carried out and as the pyramid descends, pressure for cost reduction is more intense. In the lower rungs, activities with less added value are carried out by a less-qualified workforce subject to worse working conditions. Greater labour instability, more deregulated labour relations and more intense work are elements that have facilitated cost reduction. Ultimately, the uncertainty to which the matrix company is subject shifts to the ancillary company and, in turn, to its workers. Different studies (Banyuls and Haipeter, 2008; Recio et al., 1991; Martínez and Pérez, 2000) show that the use of subcontracting, network structures with the purpose of increasing production flexibility leads to increased labour flexibility across the entire network and a worsening of employment conditions.

The transformation of stable jobs

Increased use of outsourcing and continued high reliance on temporary employment contracts have not left intact the conditions faced by workers with permanent contracts of employment. Considering all permanent workers as a homogeneous collective is a mistake since it loses sight of the substantial differences that can be detected according to the size and type of organisation. The most important changes have occurred in large companies, since in small firms there remains a more personalised and informal management system. A great variety of labour management practices have been introduced in recent years, aimed at transforming employment conditions and increasing the individualisation of employment conditions under the stated goal of the flexibilisation of labour conditions (Pérez de Guzman and Prieto, 2015). Permanent jobs today are, in many cases, rather different from those 20 years ago, something that has also been strengthened by the generational renewal of staff.

Among the new management practices, the introduction of time flexibility measures and of new remuneration systems oriented to the individualisation of labour relations stand out powerfully. Although these processes have been in great part introduced through collective bargaining, in practice they have allowed companies an important degree of freedom in labour management and they have favoured increased wage differentiation. In some large companies, two-tier wage scales have come to be introduced for incumbent and newly recruited workers and, although this is illegal, in practice it has resulted in the gradual reduction of salaries for new employees. In some sectors, such as finance, the use of individual incentives is so widespread that it is customary to perform unpaid overtime to meet performance targets for the salary bonus. As for professional markets, traditional recruitment policies have been replaced by more competitive processes in which some applicants end up being excluded or relegated to precarious underemployment (Oliva et al., 2012).

Analyses of collective bargaining show that all these policies have resulted in a sustained pattern of wage moderation (Gutiérrez Calderón, 2011; Sanabria, 2013). In addition, unions have prioritised job creation and reduction of precarious employment rather than real wage gains and within corporations different units and plants have increasingly had to compete via cost concessions to maintain employment and investment from the centre. The 2012 labour reform, by introducing mechanisms that break the collective bargaining model, opened new potentialities for employer policy and practice. The legislation grants privileged status to the company agreement and therefore provides new ways for companies to detach themselves from the conditions collectively agreed at sector and regional levels. This offers new opportunities to the myriad small and medium-sized businesses with scarce union representation for introducing labour conditions à la carte, and of generally increasing wage inequality and differences in labour conditions. While it is still early to assess the net impact of this reform, preliminary analyses provide a fairly clear result – that the deregulation far from generating greater equity in the labour market has resulted in wage cuts in precisely those sectors that already had the lowest wages (Lago, 2015).

Conclusions

The interpretation of labour market segmentation solely in terms of duality has turned into the key reference point of the main international organisations for employment policy and of the academic world. It promises both a powerful analytical model (underpinned by neoclassical economics rigour) and clear recommendations for policy. It suggests that reduced precariousness and visible inequalities in the labour market are achieved by eliminating the excessive protections enjoyed by core segments of the workforce. In one sense, these models extend to the labour market the simplistic assumption that perfectly competitive markets lead to the maximisation of collective welfare. In the case of Spain, a country affected by high shares of people in temporary employment and unemployment, this model has become a persistent axis of the public debate.

In our analysis of this debate, this chapter has identified the shortcomings of this approach and raised doubts about the stylised temporary–permanent duality of the Spanish employment model. Detailed scrutiny of the Spanish labour market reveals enormous diversity of working conditions, and not just a proliferation of non-standard jobs, in a way that is far more complex than the portrait presented by the orthodox approach. Employees with stable contracts in outsourced sectors experience labour conditions similar to those of temporary employees. Even temporary employment itself has a different meaning, depending on the context in which it has emerged. There are significant differences for stable employment and what it means by type of business, productive network position or productive sector. These differences have implications for wages, careers, working conditions and working hours. Also, internal labour markets have been weakened but differences persist between companies. Diversity is also present in temporary employment and in the secondary market, both characterized by a remarkable diversification of situations. For example, some professional markets facilitate mobility, while other spheres of the economy are characterised by perfectly bounded secondary markets – such as youth employment in fast-food chains and the textile industry and related informal spaces where immigration policy plays a crucial role. Analyses using cluster methods (Prieto *et al.*, 2011) or working life data (Miguelez and Lopez Roldan, 2014) show that we face an increasing picture of social diversification and a continuum of increasing inequalities, far away from a stylised dual market model.

The analytical question is not only to determine the character of labour market segments, in Spain and elsewhere, but also to understand their dynamics. Contributions from comparative labour market segmentation theory explaining the changing patterns of national employment models (Bosch *et al.*, 2009) are far more useful in explaining contemporary labour market transformations than the orthodox economics approach. The Spanish case shows clearly that labour market trends cannot be understood as the mere result of a handful of labour regulations. Therefore, we consider the institutionalist approach of segmentation more appropriate for analysis, since it shows the plurality of factors involved in shaping labour markets, and crucially the importance of business strategies in shaping labour segments. At a general level of analysis, the situation of labour market segmentation reflects the nature of Spain's production system, its positioning in the world economy, and the productive and social options of Spanish elites. These options have for many decades generated a societal lock-in around low wages and precarious labour conditions rather than promoting a high-skill production model in technology and quality production. To a great extent, deregulation policies do nothing but help to maintain this model.

We end with a response to the current policy proposal in Spain for a single employment contract as a means to eliminate duality. The orthodox approach needs to recognise that, firstly, various labour reforms to cut protections for permanent employment have not generated the desired change and, secondly, the early effects of the 2012 reform seem to go in the opposite direction by in fact worsening labour conditions of so-called 'outsiders'. This is a predictable outcome based on a reading of the labour market segmentation approach associated with Rubery's work and members of the IWPLMS: in deregulated labour markets, where individual entrepreneurs have greater power, greater differentiation of labour conditions occurs. Imagining a world with inclusive development that generates better labour conditions for everybody requires a radical rethinking of interventions from a global perspective that encompass macroeconomic, institutional and organisational change.

Notes

1   Since 1984 until the present, more than 50 labour reforms have been implemented in Spain. The major reforms, judged by the significance of their change, took place in 1984, 1992, 1994, 2002, 2010 and 2012.
2   From 1984 to 2001 fixed-term contracts were without economic compensation. In 1997, a labour market reform placed some limits on the length of the fixed-term contracts. In 2001, the government established a small dismissal cost for this type of contract: 8 days' pay per year of tenure. In 2010, this compensation was increased in some cases to 12 days' pay per year of tenure.
3   This connects with another one of the reform proposals that was implemented during these years: the necessity of reducing wages and of making them flexible, with a change in the collective bargaining model. The proposed line is that there must be a shift

towards a negotiation model that is decentralised, individualised and at the company level, not the sectorial level.

4   This proposes that a single employment contract should replace the several types that currently exist. The objective is also to reduce the costs and simplify the process of dismissal. Currently, individual dismissals of permanent employees can be legally justified by economic or similar reasons and in this case the compensation is 20 days' pay per year of tenure (with a ceiling of 12 months' pay). The single contract proposes to remove the need to justify dismissals and that the value of the compensation would be incremental according to tenure.

5   Temporary work agencies pay their employees the same wage as those of employees directly employed by the customer firm. 'The "new service companies" are subcontracted to carry out a part of the production process and pay wages according to their own collective agreement. The most extreme case is the extensive use of "cooperatives", in slaughterhouses and in construction, where employees become "self-employed" and do not have labour rights' (Allepuz, 2000).

References

Aguiar, L. M. (2001), 'Doing cleaning work 'scientifically': the reorganization of work in the contract building cleaning industry', *Economic and Industrial Democracy*, 22, 239–69.

Alba, A. and Alonso, C. (1997), 'Tipo de contrato y empleo en el ciclo económico 1987–1996', *Papeles de Economía Española*, 72, 231–49

Allepuz, R. (2000), *Incidència sectorial i territorial en l'estructura del mercat de treball: el cas dels escorxadors i la industria càrnia a la província de Lleida* (PhD Thesis, Universitat de Lleida).

Alonso, L.E. and Fernández, C.J. (eds) (2012), *La financiarización de las relaciones salariales* (Madrid: Catarata).

Andrés, J., Boscá, J. E., Doménech, R., Ferri, J. (2010), 'Creación de empleo en España: ¿Cambio en el modelo productivo, reforma del mercado de trabajo o ambos?', *Papeles de Economía Española*, 124, 28–45.

Banyuls, J. and Haipeter, T. (2008), 'Labour on the defensive? The global reorganisation of the value chain and industrial relations in the European motor industry', in Caputo, P. and Della Corte, E. (eds), *The Labour Impact of Globalisation in the Automotive Industry* (Roma: Fondazione Giacomo Brodolini), pp. 17–59.

Banyuls, J. and Lorente, R. (2010), 'La industria del automóvil en España: globalización y gestión laboral', *Revista de Economía Crítica*, 9, 32–52.

Banyuls, J. and Recio, A. (2015), 'Gestión empresarial y dinámica laboral en España', *Ekonomiaz*, 87, 182–205.

Bentolila, S and Dolado, J. (1984), 'Labour flexibility and wages: lessons from Spain', *Economic Policy*, 31:86, 53–99.

Bentolila, S. and Jimeno, J. F. (2003), *Spanish Unemployment: The End of the Wild Ride?*, CESifo Working Paper Series No. 940, https://papers.ssrn.com/sol3/papers.cfm?abstract_id=413841.

Bosch G., Lendorff S. and Rubery J. (eds) (2009), *European Employment Models in Flux: A Comparison of Institutional Change in Nine European Countries* (New York: Palgrave Macmillan).

Bosch, G. and Philips, P. (2003), *Building Chaos: An International Comparison of Deregulation in the Construction Industry* (London and New York: Routledge).

Castillo, J. J. (2005a), *El trabajo recobrado. Una evaluación del trabajo realmente existente en España* (Madrid and Buenos Aires: Miño y Dávila Editores).

Castillo, J. J. (2005b), 'Contra los estragos de la subcontratación: trabajo decente', *Sociología del trabajo*, 54, 3–38.

Castillo, J. J. (2013), 'Nuevas tendencias de organización en las relaciones laborales en la crisis: trabajar en cliente y trabajar en proyecto', *Anuario de Relaciones Laborales de España*, 4, 54–66.

Dolado, J. J. and Jimeno, J. F. (1997), 'The causes of Spain unemployment: a VAR approach', *European Economic Review,* 41:97, 1281–307.

Dolado, J., García Serrano, C. and Jimeno, J. F. (2002), 'Drawing lessons from the boom of temporary Jobs in Spain', *Economic Journal,* 112, 270–95.

Dube, A. and Kaplan, E. (2010), 'Does outsourcing reduce wages in the low-wage service occupations? Evidence from janitors and guards', *Industrial and Labor Relations Review,* 63:2, 287–306.

FEDEA (Fundación de Estudios de Economía Aplicada) (2012), *Diez principios fundamentales para una reforma laboral eficaz y justa*, http://fedea.net/10-principios/10_principios_fund amentales.pdf

Fina, Ll. and Toharia, L. (1987), *Las causas del paro en España: Un punto de vista estructural* (Madrid: Fundación Instituto de Estudios Sociales Avanzados).

Fina, Ll., Meixide, A. and Toharia, L. (1989), 'Regulating the labor market amid an economic and political crisis. Spain 1975–1986', in Rosemberg, S. (ed.), *The State and the Labor Market* (New York: Plenum Press), pp. 107–26.

Grimshaw, D. and Rubery, J. (2005), 'Intercapitalist relations and the network organisation: redefining the work and the employment nexus', *Cambridge Journal of Economics*, 29:6, 1027–51.

Gutierrez Calderón, C. (2011), *Competitividad y costes laborales*, Estudios de la Fundación, No. 49 (Madrid: Fundación Primero de Mayo).

Harrison, B. (1997), *Lean and Mean: The Changing Landscape of Corporate Power in the Age of Flexibility* (New York: Guilford Press).

Havard, C., Rorive, B. and Sobczak, A. (2009), 'Client, employer and employee: mapping a complex triangulation', *European Journal of Industrial Relations*, 15:3, 257–76.

Jimeno, J. F. and Ortega, A. C. (2003), 'Veinticinco años de mercado de trabajo en España', *Economía Industrial*, 349/350, 103–10.

Korczynski, M. (2004), 'Back-office service work: Bureaucracy challenged?', *Work, Employment and Society*, 18:1, 97–114.

Krugman, P. and Wells, R. (2006), *Macroeconomics* (New York and Basingstoke: Worth Publishers).

Lago, M. (2015), *Análisis gráfico de la devaluación salarial y la gran recesión* (Madrid: Fundación Primero de Mayo).

Lethbridge, J. (2012), 'Empty Promises. The impact of outsourcing on the delivery of NHS services', report commissioned by UNISON, http://www.psiru.org/sites/default/files/2012-04-H%20UNISONEmptyPromisesOutsourcing_0.pdf, accessed 15 March 2017.

Lindbeck, A. and Snower, D. J. (1988), *The Insider-Outsider Theory of Employment and Unemployment* (Cambridge, MA: MIT Press).

Lindbeck, A. and Snower, D. J. (2001), 'Insiders versus outsiders', *Journal of Economic Perspectives*, 15:1, 165–88.

Malo de Molina, J.L. (1983), 'El impacto del cambio institucional en el mercado de trabajo durante la crisis', *Papeles de Economía Española*, 15, 239–57.

Marchington, M., Grimshaw, D. and Rubery, J. (2005), *Fragmenting Work Blurring Organizational Boundaries and Disordering Hierarchies* (Oxford: Oxford University Press).

Mártinez, A. and Pérez, M. (2000), 'Organización para la producción flexible: el caso de la industria auxiliar de automoción en Aragón', *Economía Industrial*, 332, 61–72.

Miguelez, F. and Lopez-Roldan, P. (2014), *Crisis, empleo e inmigración en España: un análisis basado en las trayectorias laborales* (Barcelona: Universidad Autónoma de Barcelona).

Moreno, S., Godino, A. and Recio, A. (2014), 'Servicios externalizados y condiciones laborales. De la competencia de precios a la presión sobre el tiempo de trabajo', *Sociología del Trabajo*, 81, 50–67.

Oliva, J., Iso, A. and Feliú, R. (2012), 'Trabajo fluido y ciudad desigual. Los patios traseros de las economías creativas y del conocimiento', *Sociología del Trabajo*, 75, 53–72.

O'Reilly, J. and Fagan, C. (1998), *Part-Time Prospects: An International Comparison in Part-Time Work in Europe, North America and the Pacific Rim* (London: Routledge).

Pérez de Guzmán, S. and Prieto, C. (2015), 'Políticas empresariales de mano de obra y configuración social del empleo en España: una aproximación desde los trabajos de investigación sociológica', *Revista Internacional de Sociología*, 73:2, http://revintsociologia.revistas.csic.es/index.php/revintsociologia/article/view/623/676)

Pinilla, J. (2004), 'Intensificación del esfuerzo de trabajo en España', *Cuadernos de Relaciones Laborales*, 22:2, 117–35.

Piore, M. (1980), 'Dualism as a response to flux and uncertainty', in Piore, M. and Berger, S. (eds), *Dualism and Discontinuity in Industrial Societies* (Cambridge: Cambridge University Press), pp. 23–54.

Prieto, C., Arnal, M., Caprile, M. and Potrony, J. (2011), *La calidad del empleo en España: Una aproximación teórica y empírica* (Madrid: Ministerio de Trabajo e Inmigración).

Recio Cáceres, C. (2014), *El empleo en el sector de atención a las personas en España* (PhD thesis, Universitat Autònoma de Barcelona).

Recio, A. (1994), 'Flexibilidad laboral y desempleo en España (reflexiones al filo de la reforma laboral)', *Cuadernos de Relaciones Laborales*, 5, 57–74.

Recio, A. (1999), 'La segmentación del mercado laboral en España', in Miguélez, F. and Prieto, C. (eds), *Las relaciones de empleo en España* (Madrid: Siglo XXI), pp. 125–50.

Recio, A. (2007), 'Construction sector: what model of regulation is moving towards?', Annual Conference of International Working Party on Labour Market Segmentation and Dinamo project (Aix-en-Provence: Laboratoire d'Economie et de Sociologie du Travail).

Recio, A. (2015), 'Política Económica y Empleo', in Miguelez, F. (ed.), *Diagnostico socio-económicodelaspolíticasdeempleo2012–2014*(Barcelona: Universitat Autonoma de Barcelona), https://ddd.uab.cat/pub/llibres/2015/142865/diasocecopol_a2015_resumexecutiu. pdf, accessed 5 May 2017.

Recio, A., Moreno, S. and Godino, A. (2015), 'Out of sight: dimensions of working time in gendered occupations', in Holtgrewe, U., Ramioul, M. and Kirov, V. (eds), *Hard Times in New Jobs* (London: Palgrave Macmillan), pp. 189–207.

Recio, A., Banyuls, J., Cano, E. and Miguélez, F. (2006), 'Migraciones y mercado laboral', *Revista de Economía Mundial,* 14, 171–93.

Recio, A., Miguelez, F. and Alós, R. (1991), *Descentralización productiva y cambio técnico en la industria auxiliar de automoción* (Barcelona: Ceres).

Rubery, J. (1978), 'Structured labour markets, worker organization and low pay', *Cambridge Journal of Economics*, 2:1, 17–37.

Rubery, J. (1992), 'Productive systems, international integration and the single European market', in Castro, A., Méhaut, P. and Rubery, J. (eds), *International Integration and Labour Market Organisation* (London: Academic Press) pp. 244–61.

Rubery, J. (2007), 'Developing segmentation theory: a thirty years perspective', *Economies et sociétés*, 41:6, 941–64.

Rubery, J., Wilkinson, F. (eds) (1994), *Employer Strategy and the Labour Market* (Oxford: Oxford University Press).

Rubery, J., Grimshaw, D., Hebson, G. and Ugarte, S. (2015), '"It's all about time": time as contested terrain in the management and experience of domiciliary care work in England', *Human Resource Management*, 54:5, 753–72.

Sanabria, A. (2013), 'Algunos apuntes en torno al mito de la competitividad en España', www.1mayo.ccoo.es, accessed 15 March 2017.

Sandor, E. (2009), *Part-time work in Europe* (Dublin: Eurofound).

Toharia, L. (2011), 'El debate sobre las reformas necesarias para la economía española: el mercado de trabajo', *Gaceta Sindical*, 17, 201–36.

Toharia, L. (ed.) (2005), *El problema de la temporalidad en España: un diagnóstico* (Madrid: Ministerio de Trabajo y Asuntos Sociales).

Wilkinson, F. (1981), *The Dynamics of Labour Market Segmentation* (London: Academic Press).

8

Subsidiary employment in Italy: can commodification of labour be self-limiting?

Francesca Bettio and Alberto Mazzon

Introduction

In May 2015, the President of Italy's National Social Security Agency (INPS) presaged that vouchers – the Italian version of the pre-financed French *Chèque emploi service* (*CES*) – threatened to become the 'new frontier of precarious employment' in the country (La Repubblica, 2015).[1] This warning was prompted by information that the number of recipients of vouchers had increased from less than 25,000 in 2008 to nearly 1 million in 2014.

The alarm sounded by the INPS President would appear to add further substance to concerns about rising 'commodification' of the labour relationship which are being increasingly voiced in scholarly circles in Europe and elsewhere. Here we understand growing commodification as a process whereby labour (power) is increasingly treated as a 'spot' commodity, hired when, and for exactly as long as, production requires, with few or no strings attached in terms of social security, severance pay and sick pay. The need to ensure sufficient earnings to enable the 're-production' of labour power – as Marx would put it – and to nurture labour by means of education, training and good health are thus shifted progressively onto the worker or the state.[2]

Commodification of labour thus understood follows from the progressive demise of the standard employment relationship. Jill Rubery is an authoritative voice in the literature opposing this demise (Rubery and Grimshaw, 2016; Rubery *et al.*, 2015). She and her co-authors argue that commodification is being driven by increasing flexibility and precariousness of employment, compounded by fragmented time practices such as those prevailing in the elderly care services in the UK. Breman and van der Linden (2014) bring an even more sombre perspective to the debate with the claim that commoditised labour power is the general rule in the history of market economies, with the standard employment relationship actually representing an historical exception that may have run its course.

It is tempting to see the growth of vouchers in Italy as one of the clearest cases of rampant commodification in Europe. Unlike mini-jobs in Germany, Italian vouchers are not labour contracts (Pala, 2014). Presently, they can be bought at a tobacconist's shop (as well as other selling points, including online) and can be used to buy multiple hours of services. Unlike pre-financed *CES* in France, they can be used across practically all sectors, types of firm and type of 'worker' (with very few exceptions).[3] The current gross value is 10 euros, 7.5 of which accrue to the worker net of income taxes, while the remaining 2.5 go partly towards financing an insurance against occupational hazards and partly to a 'special' (state) pension fund. They do not, however, entitle the worker to sick pay, holiday pay, maternity or parental leave, unemployment benefits or severance pay.

Despite such premises, the story of Italian vouchers is reassuring in some important respects. Although since 2008 their growth exploded, the available evidence suggests that they have been used to replace more 'structured' employment forms, but not as frequently as was initially feared. On the contrary, they may have helped some occasional and seasonal labour to surface from the underground economy.[4] This is no reason for complacency, however, because the story of Italian vouchers is still in the making, since the number of workers depending solely on vouchers for their income is very small but growing, and because, importantly, evidence is still scant. However, the current situation raises questions about what may prevent even stronger forms of commoditised labour exchanges from becoming pervasive, and what may relegate such exchanges to niche labour markets while contributing to regularising 'pin money' employment.[5]

The following discussion recounts the specific Italian experience but concludes by raising more general questions about commodification. The section titled 'How vouchers work in Italy' sets out the current legal framework for vouchers in the country; it also discusses how they evolved through successive statutory revisions along a trajectory that started with a French-style *cheques service* scheme and ended with what may be viewed as an idiosyncratic version of German-style mini-jobs. The next section, 'Exponential growth: who is involved and how?', factually documents this trajectory, focusing in particular on the characteristics of the workers involved and of the employment opportunities being offered. The last section, 'What do Italian vouchers teach us about commodification? Questions in search of answers', asks whether and how the spread of such forms of commodification that may otherwise look rampant may actually be contained by in-built 'stabilisers' as well as effective regulation.

The account of the growth of the Italian payment-by-voucher system which we provide below intersects with the scholarly work of Rubery in at least two respects. As noted, the main intersection is with her research on the consequences of the demise of the standard employment contract. An additional intersection concerns the shape such a demise can take, especially in feminised areas such as care work. Rubery and her co-authors coined the term 'fragmented time practices' (see also Chapter 6) to group different forms of de-commodification within the care sector. Towards the end of the chapter we explore similarities and differences with the Italian-style use of vouchers within elderly care.

How vouchers work in Italy

The text of the Italian law refers to vouchers as '*lavoro accessorio*', literally 'subsidiary employment'. When first introduced in 2003, as part of one of the milestone reforms of the national labour market (the so-called 'Legge Biagi'), subsidiary employment competed with a host of other newly introduced contractual arrangements, and was consequently assigned distinctive goals. As a means of payment, vouchers were limited to *casual* and *ancillary* activities 'performed by individuals at risk of social exclusion, not participating in the labour market or about to leave it'.[6] They were intended to provide a viable alternative to informal employment for a set of activities often confined to the shadow economy, while favouring the inclusion of peripheral and marginalised workers (Ministero del Lavoro e delle Politiche Sociali, 2016). The activities in question ranged from housework and care work to private tuition, small-scale gardening and cleaning, natural disaster management and the organisation of occasional events – from conferences to athletic contests. Eligible workers included the long-term unemployed, housewives and retirees, as well as non-EU migrants with a regular residency permit. Hours of work were limited to 30 per month and earnings to 3,000 euros per year.

On most counts, the inspiration clearly came from the French *CES* instituted in 1993, but two closely related differences are worth noting. The French scheme did not set a fixed per-hour value, whereas in Italy each voucher was intended to equate to an hour's work. Its initial price was set at 7.5 euros gross, 5.8 of which accrued to the worker net of tax and social security while the remainder was divided between a small fee for operating costs and employer's contributions to a special pension fund, as well as to the abovementioned national, occupational hazard insurance scheme.[7]

Hence, social security costs were (and remain) much lower than for any other type of contract in Italy. So too were benefits, since voucher recipients could not and still cannot claim any benefits other than insurance payments in case of work-related accidents, and a very small pension income. By contrast, in France social security benefits were (and remain) comparable to other types of employment with the difference that contributions were heavily subsidised while providing full benefits (in proportion to earnings). Also, the (variable) value of *CES* was intended to factor in holiday pay, sick pay and so on. From the start, therefore, Italian law set vouchers as something clearly apart from anything like a standard labour contract.

A second difference is that, unlike in France, the Italian scheme did not take off immediately. In 1998, five years after actual enforcement, the monthly figure for average hours worked under the ES schemes was over 8 million in France. This compares with slightly over 100,000 in Italy five years after enforcement (2008) even though the total population of the two countries was of a roughly comparable magnitude in the respective years.[8] As we document in the section 'What do Italian vouchers teach us about commodification? Questions in search of answers', the main reason for poor results in Italy is that the scheme was and remains relatively unpopular with households.

In the attempt to remedy a shaky start, the scheme was repeatedly revised. The most consequential changes were enforced at different dates between 2008 and 2015, which actually had the effect of turning the vouchers into minimum-protection, German-style, mini-jobs anchored at a set wage. Firstly, the range of admissible activities was expanded until eventually encompassing the whole economy, with a few specific exceptions within agriculture (INPS, 2016b). Secondly, eligible workers no longer need to belong to groups on the margins of the labour market but comprise almost everybody, including full-time employees or self-employed workers wishing to supplement their earnings. Employers can be families, entrepreneurs, professionals, non-profit organisations and even public authorities. Thirdly, the price per voucher was eventually set at the current value of 10 euros and total earnings were capped higher: each worker can now cash vouchers for up to 2,000 euros, net, per year from the same employer and for up to 7,000 euros, net, per year from all employers (Natali, 2016). The selling of vouchers was also made easier, for example by adding tobacconists to the list of authorised sellers. As a result, about two-thirds of all vouchers in 2015 were sold by tobacconists (INPS, 2016d: figure1). Employers can also purchase vouchers via the website of the National Social Security Institute (or at its local offices), in most banks and in post offices.

To gauge similarities and differences between vouchers and mini-jobs recall that the latter are also permitted across sectors and according to individual employment status. Like the Italian vouchers, moreover, they are not incompatible with other sources of income, including wages, unemployment benefits and pensions. Also, with the introduction of a statutory national minimum wage in Germany (which was actually prompted by fears of wage exploitation of mini-jobbers), a large share of mini-jobbers is currently likely to be paid 8.5 euros gross per hour (the minimum wage rate until December 2016; see also Chapter 2), which may actually be lower in purchasing power parity than the 7.5 euros per hour in Italy, net of taxes and any contributions. Annual earnings are capped at 5,400 euros per year for German mini-jobbers compared to 7,000 for Italian voucher recipients, although the former may actually receive extra compensation for in-work-related expenses which are not taxed and are not counted towards the earnings ceiling (Mazzon, 2013).

Differences are also worth noting. Mini-jobs are proper labour contracts that grant mini-jobbers the status of employed individuals, whereas vouchers do not. From the very start, the text of the Italian law clearly stated that being in receipt of vouchers does not affect the employment status of the recipient. As a result, German mini-jobbers enjoy the same labour rights as regular workers. Employers pay full contributions at a 30per cent, a flat rate which slightly exceeds the average rate. Employees are generally expected to pay contributions only towards their pension, with the possibility for some to be exempted, in which case they also forfeit future pension income (Federal Ministry of Labour and Social Affairs, 2014).

With regard to pension entitlements, however, practical differences between mini-jobs and vouchers are likely to be slim: both voucher recipients and mini-jobbers are likely to be entitled to pensions well below the poverty line should they rely only on this source of income during their working life. For example, the Federal Ministry of Labour and Social Affairs estimated that each additional year as a mini-jobber adds 3.11 euros to one's monthly pension amount, thus requiring 37 years to be entitled to 116 euros in Germany! (Mazzon, 2013:6). In Italy, social security contributions are set aside in a special pension scheme called *Gestione separata*. Each year a so-called *minimale* is set, corresponding to the minimum amount of money that a worker must pay into the scheme for her or him to be credited one full year of contributions. If a worker pays less than the *minimale* he or she will be credited only a fraction of a full year (INPS, 2016a). Given the current limitations on annual earnings, a worker who relies solely on vouchers cannot reach the *minimale* even at the maximum level of earnings. To clarify this point with numbers, in 2015, a worker on vouchers receiving 7,000 euros (the earnings ceiling) would have paid 1,213 euros into the pension scheme. With a *minimale* of 3,653.78 euros, he or she would have been credited four months of contributions. However, very few workers earn up to 7,000 euros; with approximately 64 vouchers per worker cashed per year the average worker would pay just 83 euros into the scheme, corresponding to less than a month of contributions.

Exponential growth: who is involved and how?

Was the transformation of the voucher system from *a CES*-style provision to mini-jobs-of-a-kind successful? The short answer is yes if success means that vouchers have become much more popular. We already noted that growth was exponential between 2008 and 2015, as measured by the number of vouchers sold and the persons (recipients) involved. If we qualify a recipient as all those who cashed at least one voucher in the reference year, their number grew from almost 25,000 in 2008 to almost 1.4 million in 2015 (Figure 8.1). During the same period, the number of vouchers actually cashed grew from less than half a million in 2008 to more than 115 million in 2015 (Figure 8.2). The use of vouchers did spread across sectors, some more than others, but households remain peripherally involved. In 2015, the number of employers doubled with respect to 2013, exceeding 473,000 units. As shown in Figure 8.3, about two-thirds of them are firms operating in the secondary or tertiary sector, with the largest shares accruing to tourism and manufacturing. Only 15 per cent

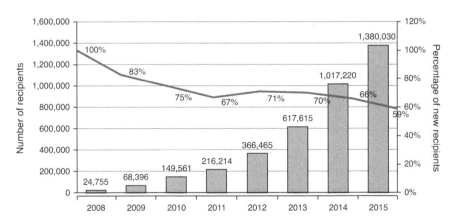

Figure 8.1   Number of recipients and percentage of new recipients per year: 2008–15

Source: INPS (2016d).

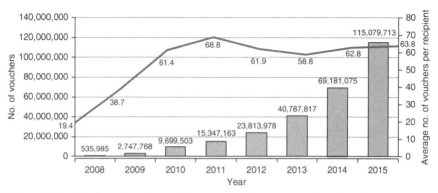

Figure 8.2 Number of vouchers sold per year and average number of vouchers per recipient per year, 2008–15

Note: Vouchers cashed are less than vouchers sold which explains possible discrepancies between Figures 8.1 and 8.2.

Source: INPS (2016d).

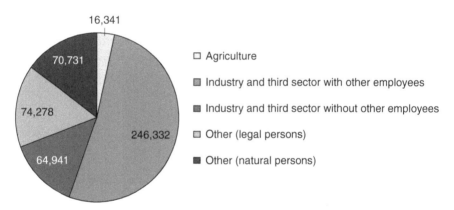

Figure 8.3 Number of employers by sector, 2015

Source: INPS (2016d).

of all employers are families, while employers operating in agriculture account for less than 4 per cent.[9] With more than 400,000 employers each year, many of them are bound to have used only a limited number of vouchers. The 2015 average of 3.5 recipient per employer actually obscures the fact that only 3 per cent of them hire more than five workers over the course of one year, with each of whom receiving at least 70 vouchers (Bombelli *et al.*, 2016: table 10).

Unsurprisingly, the share of women cashing vouchers has grown in parallel with the number of vouchers, reaching 52 per cent in 2015 against a female representation of 42 per cent across the rest of the employed population. Hence women are over-represented among those who work for vouchers, but the imbalance 'in favour' of women is still contained in comparison with recipients of the French *CES* or German mini-jobbers. However, the final judgement should be suspended in view of the ongoing upward trend in feminisation in Italy. The share of very young recipients has also grown in Italy alongside the volume of vouchers, with the average age on a downward trend, a small incidence of recipients older than 60 and one in every three recipients below 25 years of age in 2015.

With demographic indicators evolving rapidly, it is still too early to conclude that vouchers will enhance the segmentation of the Italian Labour market by further shifting the risks of precariousness onto women and young people. But we cannot rule out such risks. As with migrant labour, available data only separate out non-EU migrants from EU recipients (including nationals) and show that the former are not over-represented. Again, however, over-representation among voucher recipients cannot be ruled out for migrants from EU countries, as we simply do not have enough information.

Overall, the demographics of voucher recipients are not (yet) particularly informative about the role this scheme is playing in the labour market. Indicators of turnover, earnings and displacement effects are more telling. The main facts are as follows.

Turnover of recipients is and remains high despite a downwards trend. Year after year, new entrants (or re-entrants) were and remain the majority of voucher recipients. The percentage of voucher recipients not having performed subsidiary work in the previous year followed a decreasing trend since 2008, but stayed well above 50 per cent since 2008 (Figure 8.1). This may simply reflect the fact that we have witnessed fast growth in the number of recipients in recent years. But, again, we cannot rule out the possibility that for most recipients, employment by means of vouchers will continue to represent a largely temporary condition lasting less than one year.

The average number of vouchers per recipient is low. Despite the pace of growth in the number of vouchers, the average number of voucher per worker per year was roughly stable around 60units in the last five years or so (Figure 8.2). This suggests that most work spells on vouchers tend to be short, sometimes even just a few hours in the whole year.

Average earnings per recipient are low. Earnings per recipient are also low, consistent with the previous finding on vouchers per head. In 2015, annual average earnings ranged from 554 euros for the youngest recipients to 700 for the oldest

Table 8.1 Annual earnings by age of voucher recipients

Age	Number of recipients	%	Average annual earnings per recipient (€)
<25	431,613	31.0	554
26–59	849,968	61.0	660
60–65	57,483	4.1	762
>65	53,842	3.9	700

Source: Ministero del Lavoro e delle Politiche Sociali (2016: 5).

(Table 8.1), exhibiting the familiar concavity of most age-earnings profiles. If, moreover, we look at the distribution of average earnings across age groups the tail is thicker on the left-hand side. In 2015 more than three-fifths of all recipients totalled less than 500 euros each and more than one in seven recipients cashed less than five vouchers in the whole year (Bombelli *et al.*, 2016: 4)

The striking findings in this respect is that the earning ceiling of 7,000 euros, net, per year is set about ten times higher than actual, average figures. To gauge the anomaly of these figures compare them with earnings for mini-jobbers in Germany. In 2014, the number of German mini-jobbers was slightly more than 7 million, 6,803,327 hired by firms, 267,478 by families; the former earned €282 per month (or the annual equivalent of more than three thousand euros), the latter €181 per month (Minijob Zentrale, 2015).

Vouchers are the sole source of income for only a minority of recipients. In the light of the preceding figures, it would be surprising if vouchers represented the only source of labour income for the majority of recipients. There are no clear official data in this respect, but Cicciomessere (2015: 4) cites Anastasia and colleagues (2015) to estimate that, if we exclude very young people who are still likely to be dependent on their family, the share of recipients for whom vouchers are the sole source of monetary income may be less than 25 per cent,[10] a large minority who cannot be ignored, but still a minority.

Displacement effects are contained. Italian trade unions often voiced concern that the deregulation of vouchers would encourage their use to replace existing, less-profitable contractual relations rather than encouraging shadow employment to emerge. It seems that this happened but 'only' affected some 10 per cent of recipients. The specific finding is that one in ten recipients of vouchers appear to have worked for the same employer in the previous six months, either as an employee or as an own account worker – one in eight if the period is restricted to the previous three months (Ministero del Lavoro e delle Politiche Sociali, 2016: 7). However, there is great variability across branches of activity, with what we may call the 'displacement rate' ranging from a maximum of 15 per cent for firms in the tourist sector to a minimum of 0.7 per cent for housework and carework (2016: 8).

If we take all this evidence together what does it suggest about the role of vouchers in the Italian labour market? With the due caveat that any inference is bound to be speculative against a background of limited information and ongoing change, the introduction of vouchers seems to have partially missed the purpose of the *CES* in France to bring into the regular market unpaid and grey work in the household sector. At the same time, the employment opportunities that have been created yield occasional, seasonal or marginal earnings, too small to fully qualify as mini-jobs, although on paper, similarities with mini-jobs are strong. Unsurprisingly, official assessment of the voucher scheme (Ministero del lavoro e delle Politiche Sociali, 2016) turns failure to create (or regularise) opportunities that may somehow qualify as 'jobs' – however mini – into success for the scheme, hinting that vouchers by and large create or regularise truly subsidiary employment, as they were originally intended to do.

What do Italian vouchers teach us about commodification? Questions in search of answers

The evidence illustrated in the previous section raises at least three interconnected questions which hark back to the issue of commodification we raised in the introduction to this chapter. The first question is why vouchers remained relatively unpopular with Italian households, unlike the French *CES* that had inspired them. The second question is why voucher earnings per recipient are so low, and, in particular, why they are much lower than for German mini-jobs despite the fact that Italian vouchers are less costly for Italian employers and subject to equivalent- or higher-earnings ceilings than in Germany. The final question follows partly from the preceding ones and asks why a commoditised, employer-friendly, simple-to-use, no-strings-attached labour transaction is eroding traditional labour relationships only to a limited extent.

In answer to the first question let us further substantiate the claim that vouchers are only moderately popular with Italian households. It is not possible to know from available data exactly how much demand from households is contributing to the spread of vouchers, but we can venture an estimate of only about 6 per cent of all vouchers sold in 2015, based on data from Bombelli and colleagues (2016).[11]

The reasons are not entirely clear, but 'wrong' pricing could be one of them, as occurred in Austria (Farvaque, 2013). To shed some light on the issue, consider the two main alternatives to vouchers, namely hiring on the black market on the one hand and, on the other, hiring on the legal market using the contract for domestic and care workers (*'collaboratori famigliari'*). For the sake of argument, consider two polar cases from the point of view of the continuity of the relationship: on the one hand, demand is for services expected to be occasional or rather temporary; on the other hand, demand is for services with a long or indefinite horizon. In both cases demand is for a limited number of hours, say five per week.

Let us focus now on demand for occasional services and suppose the hourly rate for domestic and care workers is 8 euros on the black market, the most convenient alternative to vouchers.[12] For the worker the alternative of pocketing 7.5 euros with a voucher would not be especially attractive given that pension benefits attached to vouchers are very small and uncertain. The additional benefit for her or him would be insurance against work-related injuries, but this risk is likely to be perceived as rather low in the domestic work sector. The household buying the voucher, on the other hand, would need to pay an extra 2.5 euros per hour compared to the black-market rate in exchange for avoiding the risk of being sanctioned for irregular hiring. Taking this risk could be costly in some cases, for example if the worker is injured at the employer's premises; or if he or she commits a wrongdoing, in which case irregular employment makes it difficult for the employer to seek justice. However, such possibilities are likely to be perceived as sufficiently remote, especially when the domestic worker has been engaged via networks of friends, catholic institutions and the like. Hence for occasional house-help or care work, informal hiring may still be a strong competitor of vouchers, at least in some regions of Italy.

Next, let us consider demand for housework/care services on a longer-term basis, retaining the previous assumption that hiring on the irregular market would cost 8 euros per hour. In this case, irregular employment might lose attractiveness for both sides of the transaction. For households employing irregular family helpers or carers the cumulative risk of being caught increases with the length of the relationship, and sanctions are severe. All the more so because workers can report employers for irregular hiring. Workers are often migrants from within or outside the EU, and both depend on a formal regular source of income in order to be eligible for residency and have full access to the National Health Service. At the going rate in the shadow economy, therefore, vouchers may compete effectively with irregular work. To be used on a large scale, however, vouchers also need to effectively compete with the special contract for domestic helpers (*'collaboratori famigliari'*). If a regular contract were drawn, the employee would need to pay 40 cents per hour in social contributions. Assuming that the gross contractual pay also amounts to 8 euros, the employee would receive 40 cents less which would leave her or him practically indifferent in monetary terms between a voucher and a regular contract (INPS, 2016c). And if her/his only source of labour income were those five hours per week he or she would have to pay no taxes. However, he or she may prefer the contract because it grants holidays, sick leave etc. as well as ensuring greater continuity.[13]

On her and his side, the employer would pay 1.57 cents in contributions, per hour, to hire on a regular contract, in addition to the gross salary of 8 euros for the employee (INPS, 2016c). He or she might find the voucher slightly more convenient in strictly monetary terms than the standard contract for domestic helpers (or carers) as the latter would also require granting employee holidays, sick leave and maternity leave in proportion to the weekly hours. However, direct gains in monetary terms are likely to be more than compensated by indirect transaction costs. These would arise from the fact that a regular contract strengthens trust and enhances collaboration between domestic workers and families: trust lowers the cost of security (household helpers generally have keys to the house or live with the family) and promotes collaboration from employees with positive effects on the quality of services that are supplied. The upshot is that for short-hours employment within a long-lasting relation the monetary incentive to replace existing contractual alternatives with vouchers may be too slim to always compensate for losses in the quality of services and in security risks.

In sum, if our back-of-the envelope calculations are roughly correct, the answer to the first question is that vouchers in Italy may not be 'cheap' enough to strongly compete with existing alternatives, be it irregular hiring or regular hiring on the existing contract for *collaboratori famigliari*.

The second question we raised is best answered with reference to the non-household sector. As we described above, average annual earnings per recipient are very low and the vast majority of recipients are far from reaching the ceiling of 7,000 euros per year. We see three possible reasons for this. The first is that most recipients do not rely on vouchers as the only source of income. The second is the fraudulent use of vouchers, especially for workers who declare no other source of labour income. The third is that vouchers are not attractive enough for anything qualifying as non-marginal employment. As we have already discussed the first reason, we now turn to the remaining two.

Fraudulent use of vouchers has been feared from the very introduction of the scheme. Until recently, in fact, no legal provision was in place to ensure that each voucher would be made to correspond to at least one hour of work. Hence firms might pay fewer vouchers than the hours they contract, or they might use vouchers to cover up irregular employment. For example, they could pay workers cash in hand as a rule and hold a minimum set of vouchers to be exhibited in the event of an inspection or when a worker injures herself or himself and needs insurance coverage. At the time of writing, there is little information as to whether this happens and to what extent. Cicciomessere (2015: 4) speculates that the segment of recipients at risk of fraudulent behaviour is likely to coincide with those relying on vouchers as the only source of income. However, information may be forthcoming soon since the Parliament recently approved amendments to existing regulations which ensure practically instant tracking of the vouchers' recipients including where, when and for how long they are expected to work.[14] If growth in the sale of vouchers halts or even reverses in the months ahead, then it will be indirect proof that fraudulent use was most likely widespread.

The final explanation, which is not necessarily in opposition to the previous two, is that there are insufficient net advantages to resort to vouchers when in non-marginal employment. This leads to the third question, namely, why a fairly commoditised labour exchange has not spread beyond a labour market niche (up to now).

In order to put the matter into context, let us first return to the current importance of vouchers within the Italian labour market. A telling indicator to this purpose is the number of full-time equivalent employment financed by vouchers. Assuming that one voucher actually corresponds to one hour's work and taking the average number of annual hours worked by full-timers as a reference, in Italy vouchers actually paid for the equivalent of around 65,000 full-time, year-round employment positions in 2015.[15]

Conclusions

Although it is still early days to take stock of the Italian experience, it may be worthwhile to ask why vouchers have filled only a small niche of the labour market and have not become more pervasive in the last eight years. Not only do average earnings per recipient amount to 'pin money', for both men and women, but also, as noted above, vouchers appear to have displaced pre-existing labour contracts only to a modest extent.

Legal restrictions provide a partial answer. For the employer to fill even a part-time job requiring 800 hours per year (about half of the average figure for full-timers) s/he would need to hire four different workers for each of them to stay within their annual ceiling (assuming the price of vouchers is 'right' for the job). That alone is likely to considerably raise transaction and organisational costs. For very short-term, temporary contracts, such costs can be much lower, thus increasing the risk of being replaced by vouchers. However, additional transaction costs may be relevant. By their nature, vouchers imply that the employment relationship can be terminated by the worker or the employer any day, nay, any hour. Given the asymmetry in bargaining power between the recipient and the employer it is more likely that termination is in the latter's hand. But whoever may be more at risk, such risk inevitably lowers trust and cooperation, implying additional transactions costs. The aforesaid costs may increase with the complexity of jobs, whether complexity is measured in terms of hard or soft skills.

The above example of care services illustrates the importance of soft skills; if you need to hire a carer for your elderly parents you will be willing to pay more to avoid the excessive turnover of carers, because learning individual idiosyncrasies takes time and emotional continuity is especially important in old age. Clearly the importance of such transaction costs is bound to vary in different market and institutional contexts. Compare, for example the use of vouchers for elderly care in Italy and fragmented time practices such as those reported by Rubery and colleagues (2015) for UK firms offering elderly care services. With respect to time management, Italian style vouchers may be likened to fragmented time practices. In the UK, the latter range from employers focusing paid hours primarily to high demand and sometimes limiting them to face-to-face engagements in in-person services, to failing to recognise and pay work-related time between demand peaks or between direct customer demand (Rubery *et al.*, 2015: passim). Rubery and her co-authors document a clear relationship between fragmented time practices and inferior quality of care services, as well as between fragmented time practices and employers' difficulty of recruiting and retaining staff. They argue that firms using fragmented time practices try putting in place Human Resources practices to counteract the shortcomings stemming from fragmented time management, but the shortcomings ultimately prevail because customers (the elderly clients) do not have enough voice and clout. However, this may be different in Italy where families retain a strong role either as direct employers or as intermediaries between the elderly and the service firms. Hence, the disadvantages of using vouchers to implement fragmented time management are likely to be weighed more heavily against the advantages in the Italian context.

Our answer to the third question is therefore that commodification entails costs as well as advantages to the employers and it is not a foregone conclusion that the latter more than compensate for the former. In fact, the experience of Italian vouchers suggests that we may need to carefully identify and evaluate such costs in different institutional contexts precisely in order to learn how to contain the worst effects of commodification. Within the confines of this chapter and the limitations of available data, we are unable to progress any further with this analysis for Italy. Hopefully, however, this does not detract from the significance of our endeavour and the wider implications of Italy's policy of subsidiary employment.

Notes

1   Our translation for *la nuova frontiera del precariato*, the term used by INPS President Tito
    Boeri in a public speech on 15 May 2015.
2   This understanding of commodification differs from those of institutionalists à la
    Putterman (1989) but, also from that of Marx. In the former case, commodification
    is simply the existence of a legal contract specifying the terms at which labour is sold.
    As with Marx's notion, the 'equilibrium' (long-run) price of labour power covers its
    cost of reproduction, that is, the market system (or employers) must take charge of
    reproducing labour power in the long run.
3   We use quotations marks for 'workers' to underscore the fact that receiving vouchers
    in exchange of labour service does not affect employment status in Italy.
4   Regularising shadow labour was perhaps the main goal assigned to vouchers when they
    were first introduced in Italy; unsurprisingly so, since the original inspiration came
    from French-style *CES*. In Belgium, too, French-style vouchers are officially hailed as
    a tool to fight shadow employment (see, for example, http://www.emploi.belgique.
    be/defaultTab.aspx?id=651).
5   Expectations that schemes such as vouchers would encourage what may be called
    'regularisation of employment at the margin' actually inspired support for the voucher
    system from the International Labour Office, which is very active in fighting employ-
    ment precariousness and the demise of the Standard Labour Contract (see, for exam-
    ple, ILO, 2013).
6   Act 276/2003, article 70. The text is available at http://www.normattiva.it/urires/
    N2Ls?urn:nir:stato:decreto.legislativo:2003–09–10;276@originale~art70
7   Employers wishing to pay workers more than the set hourly rate can use more than one
    voucher for an hour of work. However, while this is implicit in the text of the law, it
    is rarely discussed in the literature and is most likely infrequent in practice.
8   The French population totalled 60.2 million in 1998 compared to 58.8 million for
    Italy in 2008. According to the data reported by the European Monitoring Centre on
    Change (http://www.eurofound.europa.eu/observatories/emcc/case-studies/tackl
    ing-undeclared-work-in-europe/universal-service-employment-cheque-france: table
    1) a total of 101.0 million hours were worked under the *CES* scheme in 1998, that is,
    more than 8 million per month. In Italy, the total number of vouchers sold between
    August and December 2008 in Italy was 536,321 according to INPS data, that is, just
    over 107,000 per month, assuming that one voucher actually paid for one hour of work
    as the law prescribes (INPS, 2011: table 7.6).
9   The proportion of families is an estimate based on the assumptions that employers
    officially coded as natural persons (*persone fisiche*) largely coincide with families (see
    Figure 8.3).
10 According to data referring to the Veneto Region, a large industrial area accounting for
    about 14 per cent of all vouchers sold, 57 per cent of vouchers recipients are workers
    with a regular job, often a standard contract while 11 per cent are young people under 24

years of age who are likely to live with their parents. Only for the remaining 32 per cent are vouchers the only source of labour income. Reportedly, however, it was not possible to separately identify self-employed workers or pensioners cashing vouchers. Netting the latter out, Cicciomessere estimates the 'true' share of people for whom vouchers are the only source of labour income at 25 per cent (Cicciomessere, 2015: 4, 15).

11 Data on buyers of vouchers allow us to separate out *persone fisiche* (physical entities) from other 'legal entities'– organisations, firms, professionals regularly enrolled in a register and so on (see Figure 8.3). Assuming that all *persone fisiche* represent households, in 2015, 70,000 households (15 per cent of all buyers) bought little more than 5 million vouchers (6 per cent of the total) to engage 128,000 recipients (7.5 per cent of all recipients).

12 Note that 8 euro per hour is currently the black-market rate in the capital city of Rome.

13 Note that vouchers count towards minimum earnings to be eligible for renewal of a work permit, provided that they are not the only source of income.

14 The Act can be found at the website of the Italian Parliament, Senate of the Republic: http://www.senato.it/leg/17/BGT/Schede/docnonleg/32659.htm

15 According to Eurostat data, average hours worked in Italy per week by full-timers was 40 in 2015, when 25 million vouchers were sold in the country. Assuming 220 working days per year – as in the standard calculation of full-time equivalent employment – annual hours amounted to 1760. With more than 115 million vouchers sold in that year, full-time equivalent employment financed by vouchers amounts to 65,386 positions. In turn, 65,386 full-time equivalent workers correspond to about 0.3 per cent of the 23.3 million full-time equivalent employment units recorded for the last quarter of 2013 (ISTAT, 2014).

References

Bombelli, S., Anastasia, B. and Maschio, S. (2016), *Il lavoro accessorio 2008–2015 Profili delle aziende e dei lavoratori*. Available from: https://www.venetolavoro.it/documents/10180/1736717/ Voucher_16_5_2016.pdf, accessed 30 June 2016.

Breman, J. and van der Linden, M. (2014), 'Informalizing the economy: the return of the social question at a global level', *Development and Change*, 45:5, 920–40.

Cicciomessere, R. (2015), 'Il lavoro occasionale di tipo accessorio', *Italia Lavoro*, Roma, http://www.robertocicciomessere.eu/Lavoro_occasionale_accessorio[02].pdf, accessed 28 June 2016.

Farvaque, N. (2013), 'Developing personal and household services in the EU: a focus on housework activities', *Report for the DG Employment, Social Affairs and Social Inclusion* (ORSEU: Lille).

Federal Ministry of Labour and Social Affairs (2014), '450 Euro mini jobs/marginal employment', http://www.bmas.de/EN/Our-Topics/Social-Security/450-euro-mini-jobs-marginal-employment.html, accessed 8 July 2016.

ILO (International Labour Organization) (2013), 'Formalizing domestic work through the use of service vouchers – the particular case of France, Belgium and the canton of Geneva', (ILO Bureau for Workers Activity: Actrav), http://www.ilo.org/actrav/info/fs/WCMS_220717/lang--en/index.htm, accessed 22 June 2016.

INPS (Istituto Nazionale Previdenza Sociale) (2011), *Rapporto annuale 2011*, (INPS: Rome).

INPS (Istituto Nazionale Previdenza Sociale) (2016a), *Gestione separata legge 335/95: accredito contributivo* [*Gestione separata, act 335/95: pension contributions credited to workers*], http://www.inps.it/portale/default.aspx?iNodo=6288&bIntranet=true, accessed 4 July 2016.

INPS (Istituto Nazionale Previdenza Sociale) (2016b), *Le novità normative previste dal D.Lgs. n. 81 del 15 giugno 2015* [*The new provisions of act 81, 15 June 2015*], https://www.inps.it/portale/default.aspx?sID=0;5481;7978;&lastMenu=7978&iMenu=1, accessed 4 July 2016.

INPS (Istituto Nazionale Previdenza Sociale) (2016c), *Lavoratori domestici: contributi e agevolazioni fiscali* [*Domestic helpers: pension contributions and fiscal savings*], http://www.inps.it/portale/default.aspx?itemdir=5090, accessed 4 July 2016.

INPS (Istituto Nazionale Previdenza Sociale) (2016d), *Statistiche in breve – Lavoro accessorio* [*Figures on Subsidiary Employment*], http://www.inps.it/banchedatistatistiche/menu/voucher/focus.pdf, accessed 10 July 2016.

Istat (Istituto Nazionale di Statistica) (2014), 'Annuario statistico italiano', (Istat: Rome).

La Repubblica, (2015), 'Boeri: I voucher lavoro, la nuova frontiera del precariato' (2015), 24 May, http://www.repubblica.it/economia/2015/05/29/news/boeri_i_voucher_lavoro_la_nuova_frontiera_del_precariato_-115554918/, accessed 6 July 2016.

Mazzon, M. (2013), 'Minijob alla tedesca: facciamo un po' di chiarezza', *Bollettino Adapt,* 6 February, http://www.bollettinoadapt.it/minijob-alla-tedesca-meno-frottole-e-piu-chiarezza/, accessed 28 June 2016.

Ministero del Lavoro e delle Politiche Sociali (2016), *L'utilizzo dei voucher per le prestazioni di lavoro accessorio*, http://www.lavoro.gov.it/priorita/Documents/Report%20Voucher%20Lavoro%20Accessorio.pdf, accessed 5 July 2016.

Minijob Zentrale (2015), *Aktuelle Entwicklungen im Bereich der geringfügigen Beschäftigung*, https://www.minijob-zentrale.de/DE/02_fuer_journalisten/02_berichte_trendreporte/quartalsberichte/3_2016.pdf?__blob=publicationFile&v=1, accessed 26 June 2016.

Natali, A. I. (2016), 'Lavoro accessorio: condizioni e limiti operativi', *Diritto e Pratica del Lavoro,* 1/2016, January.

Pala, M. (2014), 'Criticità del lavoro accessorio (voucher) dopo la legge 99/2013', *Il Sole24Ore*,16 July, http://www.diritto24.ilsole24ore.com/art/dirittoLavoro/2014–07–16/critici ta-lavoro-accessorio-voucher-162618.php, accessed 5 July 2016.

Putterman, L. (1989), 'Commodification of labor follows commodification of the firm on a theorem of the New Institutional Economics', *Annals of Public and Cooperative Economics*, 60:2, 161–79.

Rubery, J. and Grimshaw, D. (2016), 'Precarious work and the commodification of the employment relationship: the case of zero hours in the UK and mini jobs in Germany', in Bäcker, G., Lehndorff, S. and Weinkopf, C. (eds), *Den Arbeitsmarkt verstehen, um ihn zu gestalten* (Wiesbaden: Springer Fachmedien), pp. 239–54.

Rubery, J., Grimshaw, D., Hebson, G. and Ugarte, S. M. (2015), '"It's all about time": time as contested terrain in the management and experience of domiciliary care work in England', *Human Resource Management*, 54:5, 753–72.

9

Job quality: conceptual and methodological challenges for comparative analysis

Agnieszka Piasna, Brendan Burchell, Kirsten Sehnbruch and Nurjk Agloni

Introduction

International development agencies such as the World Bank, the International Monetary Fund (IMF), the Organisation for Economic Co-operation and Development (OECD) and individual governments have traditionally been more concerned with the quantity of jobs – as measured by the rate of unemployment, or the rate of participation in the labour market – than the quality of available positions (Muñoz de Bustillo *et al.*, 2011; OECD, 2014; Sehnbruch, 2006). Much early psychological research on unemployment (e.g. Jahoda, 1982) tended to reinforce this simple model of a job being a good thing and unemployment a bad thing. But more recent research has taken a more nuanced approach, demonstrating that poor-quality jobs characterised, for instance, by high demands, low control over decision-making, high job insecurity or workplace bullying might have worse psychosocial effects on individuals than experiences of unemployment (Burchell, 1992; Butterworth *et al.*, 2011; Warr, 1987). One of Jill Rubery's most original and policy-orientated reports in recent years was Smith *et al.* (2013), in which she used, for the first time, the concept of job quality, in a holistic manner, to explore gender differences in working conditions. However, progress towards articulating job quality in public policy, in terms of not only overarching principles but also concrete actions, has been slow. One important impediment has been the conceptual confusion and the lack of a shared definition to inform both research and policy.

The variety of approaches led to multiple and relatively diffuse concepts developing in parallel, which limited their academic and political impact. The terminology used creates additional confusion; expressions such as 'quality of working life' (predominantly linked to the subjective evaluations of one's job), 'job quality' or 'quality of work' (often focusing on the job content and work environment) and, finally, 'quality of employment' (usually also including a broader overview of labour relations, policies, participation or equality in income and job distributions) are often used interchangeably and without clear definitions. This inconsistency reflects the complexity of the whole issue of quality of work. There are not only multiple facets of jobs that should be taken into account, but also multiple levels on which jobs can be analysed, ranging from a subjective evaluation of a particular working environment to broad labour market systems in which jobs are performed. Furthermore, the definition of job quality and the selection of facets of employment via which to measure it depend on the perspective adopted. The meaning attributed to job quality will be different depending on whether it is viewed from the standpoint of individual workers, families, employers or from a societal perspective.

The lack of conceptual clarity crept into institutional initiatives in this area, which are rare and have not seen much success either. The International Labour Organization (ILO) has attempted to define the quality of work through its concept 'Decent Work', which was officially launched in 1999. Among those institutions influenced by the ILO's approach, the European Union (EU) institutions – such as Eurofound (see, e.g., Green and Mostafa, 2012) – and some European governments stand out. Another example is an initiative that originated in 2000 as a series of seminars launched by the joint United Nations Economic Commission for Europe (UNECE)/ILO/Eurostat task force, which after 15 long years published a statistical framework for measuring the quality of employment (UNECE, 2015). The framework, however, was developed as a complex statistical toolbox rather than an indicator suitable for evaluating and guiding policy. Moreover, the OECD contributed to the debate with its work on measuring social progress and quality of life – largely following the Stiglitz, Sen and Fitoussi (2009) report – and, more recently, has also made a very useful proposal for measuring and assessing job quality in its 2014 Employment Outlook.

However, the overall impact that the concepts 'job quality' and 'decent work' have had on both research and public policy is extremely limited compared to the influence achieved, for example, by the Human Development Index (HDI) over a similar period (see discussion in Burchell et al., 2014 and Sehnbruch et al., 2015). The HDI, published by the United Nations Development Programme, is a summary measure of life expectancy, education and standard of living (measured by gross national income per capita), which has made a substantial contribution towards shifting the policy focus from economic growth to people and their capabilities.

This chapter explores the reasons for little effective progress in the conceptualisation and measurement of job quality (or related terms, such as precarious work) through considering the conceptual frameworks used as a basis for analysing job quality, the institutional context that encourages or impedes research and the availability of data. In what follows, the first section summarises methodological considerations of measurement, including the shortcomings in existing measures of the quality of employment and their potential for international comparison. We further consider the contribution that psychology has made to understanding job quality. We draw parallels with the way in which the Five-Factor Model of personality evolved and contributed to the inclusion of personality measures in large data sets. This example illustrates that consensus can and should be achieved in defining and measuring highly complex phenomena. Against this background, in the section titled 'A multi-level model for the measurement of job quality' we propose a conceptual framework that aims at a better articulation of job quality by positioning it within macro drivers such as employment protection legislation, welfare regimes and labour market segmentation. Much in the spirit of the societal system approach for comparative analysis (Bosch *et al.*, 2007; Bosch *et al.*, 2009; see Chapters 1 and 3), we demonstrate how jobs can be positioned within complex systems of labour market organisation that vary across countries, yet allow for a common evaluation of their quality. We develop a metaphor of 'jobs as vehicles' to clarify levels of analysis and to establish what job quality actually should be measuring. Finally, in the Conclusions, we argue that only in Europe, where comparable indicators from harmonised surveys have now become the norm and constitute extremely valuable data for analysts, has significant progress been made in conceptualising and measuring the quality of employment. We conclude that it is essential that this process of data collection and methodological consolidation be extended to other regions in the world where the quality of employment remains neglected.

Towards a framework for the measurement of job quality: methodological considerations

One of the first ways in which the academic literature approached the question of what constitutes a 'good job' was by focusing on non-pecuniary aspects of work and on workers' subjective perceptions of their jobs (Staines and Quinn, 1979; Yoshida and Torihara, 1977). Seashore (1974) and Land (1975) defined good jobs as those possessing attributes or consequences which are valued by the worker and are thus conducive to job satisfaction. Wnuk-Lipinski (1977) subsequently argued that job satisfaction is a vital component of quality of life and thus an end in itself. On the basis of the 'quality of life' perspective (Bauer, 1966), several criteria for assessing the quality of work were devised, encompassing both general measurements of job satisfaction and specific measurements of workers' contentment with an array of job facets (Kalleberg and Vaisey, 2005; Krueger *et al.*, 2002; Land, 1975; Staines and Quinn, 1979).

Over the years, a range of primarily psychological theories shifted the focus towards identifying a list of 'objective' job features linked to workers' well-being at work (Warr, 2007). For instance, a considerable amount of research on job quality conducted by occupational psychologists has focused on the deter-minants of subjective well-being and productivity at the level of task charac-teristics, such as variety, challenge, meaningful nature of the work performed, autonomy and teamwork (Hackman and Oldham, 1975). Karasek and Theorell (1990) focused on psychological stress and proposed a 'job-strain model' based on a balance between job control and demands. Nevertheless, no consensus has ever been reached on a way of organising a multitude of work dimensions into a coherent framework amenable to comparative research. The policy focus of most studies was firm-specific rather than comparative, aimed at achieving improvements in individual workplaces. In this section, we identify and discuss some of the key methodological and conceptual challenges faced by any attempt to define and measure job quality in comparative analysis.

Subjective and objective measurements

The development of a measurement of overall job quality based on subjective evaluation and job satisfaction proved problematic and was not without its crit-ics for, depending on workers' preferences and expectations, similar job char-acteristics may indeed be valued quite differently (Taylor, 1977). Davis (1977) argued, in a similar vein, that the widely differing and contradictory meanings attributed to job quality by different groups of workers are to blame for the lack of agreement on how to define the quality of work. Agassi (1982) argued convincingly that the measure of job satisfaction is the relationship between the quality of an employee's current job and the same employee's notions of what might reasonably be expected of a job. Insofar as expectations vary con-siderably between countries, it often turns out that a developed country may have lower aggregate job satisfaction than a developing one. Analysis based on the International Social Survey Programme, for example, shows that a broad range of countries show remarkably homogeneous indicators of job satisfaction (Muñoz de Bustillo *et al.*, 2011, figure 2.1: 10)

Adaptive preferences may also explain why some less-advantaged groups of workers (e.g. women) display higher satisfaction levels than others enjoying objectively better working conditions. More-advantaged workers might also expect more, in terms of personal satisfaction, from their jobs (see also Muñoz de Bustillo *et al.*, 2011), while those in less-favourable employment conditions may display a tendency to adapt to circumstances (Comin and Teschl, 2005; Nussbaum, 2000; Sen, 1999). While this is an interesting psychological phenomenon, it renders measurements of job satisfaction completely unsuitable for comparative research on job quality.

Furthermore, while indicators such as life expectancy and literacy can only really be improved by better health and education, there are, in principle, two ways to improve job satisfaction: either by changing employment conditions or by changing workers' perceptions of these conditions. Job satisfaction, in other words, can be increased either by improving jobs or by lowering employees' expectations. As the latter approach is likely to prove cheaper and easier than the former, job satisfaction measurements make poor policy levers.

It should be pointed out that there is considerable confusion with regard to the way in which the terms 'objective' and 'subjective' are applied, more generally, to debates concerning the quality of life and well-being and, more specifically, to job quality. 'Subjective' is usually taken to mean not only self-reported, but also pertaining to an attitude or psychological disposition towards an attribute – such as 'life satisfaction'. 'Objective' is taken to refer to the measurement of 'hard facts' (Veenhoven, 2002) such as weekly hours of work. Nevertheless, self-reporting is the method most frequently used and the basis of many survey items. Most would see self-report of objective measures (such as hours worked) as unproblematic, except for the fact that it may introduce some error and reporting bias, as respondents might misremember or exaggerate their hours of work. Self-reporting of subjective assessment (e.g. job satisfaction, work–life balance, perception of health and safety) is more problematic as it is shaped by adaptive preferences, societal norms and points of reference, which makes international comparisons particularly difficult. While in some cases such self-reported measurements of job quality can be compared with information from other sources – for instance, employees' perceptions of the safety of their jobs can be triangulated with national statistics on fatalities at work – many features of job quality can be realistically measured only by asking employees about their work. In assessing job quality we argue that there is a prima facie case that workers are experts on their own jobs, even if their reports are susceptible to bias and error.

However, we claim that a distinction that is more central to the development of job quality measurement is not whether we measure something by self-report or by other means, but rather whether we are interested in the reality and actual features of jobs, as opposed to individuals' attitudes, opinions or evaluations concerning their jobs, such as their job satisfaction. This is similar to the distinction made between the types of questions used to measure 'subjective phenomena', based on their purpose in Turner and Martin's (1984) seminal book on survey questions.

When we, as social scientists, ask questions of individuals we do so for very different reasons, even though the questions may appear similar both syntactically and semantically. Consider the two questions to be answered on Likert-type scales:

1) How often do you work with radioactive materials? All of the time ... Sometimes ... Never.
2) How often do immigrants make a positive contribution to the labour market in the UK? All of the time ... Sometimes ... Never.

The reasoning behind asking these two questions is very different. The first question is asked because we are interested in estimating how often radioactive material is handled in different jobs, and we can calculate means which (we hope) represent the level of use of radioactivity across different occupations, industries and countries. The second question is asked because we are interested, instead, in how people think – their attitudes, beliefs and values. We would not usually claim that responses to the question reflect the real contribution of immigrants; more likely we would use the results as an indication of attitudes towards immigrants, or immigration, or perhaps as an indicator of racism. This distinction between psychological measures of individual differences and survey items measuring the qualities of entities such as jobs is critical to understanding the nature of job-quality measurement. Drawing a parallel with the literature on well-being, we are measuring 'objective well-being', that is, we are interested in the job itself – that is, the features of work and the various dimensions of working conditions – as opposed to what the employee thinks about the job, even though we are usually relying on employees' own reports.

Psychologists are most often interested in measuring people's internal states (e.g. beliefs, attitudes, values, mental abilities), such that we expect each individual to score differently on a measure of, for example, attitude or personality or intelligence. In contrast, in the case of job quality, we aim to achieve a situation whereby, if the measures are well constructed and well devised, several individuals doing the same job will have very similar scores for the attributes of that job.

Empirical progress

Apart from the issues surrounding the lack of a theoretical framework, as well as the conceptual confusions, the literature on the measurement of the quality of employment has had to tackle yet another significant problem: successful measurements require reliable, and preferably also comparable, sources of data.

The availability of comparable data across European countries has thus generated a virtuous circle in which empirical evidence has expanded the theoretical understanding of labour markets, which in turn has increased the efforts invested in data gathering. In developing countries, however, where comparable data are not available, both empirical and theoretical analysis has stagnated. The patchy availability of data has led to a host of studies on one or two aspects of the quality of employment or that only look at a single country, while the number of studies that have attempted to develop a comprehensive framework taking account of multiple job characteristics is limited. It is hardly surprising then that policy-relevant, cross-country comparative analysis should have taken so long to emerge. Where such studies have been carried out, they tend to be limited to groups of EU member states.

A good illustration of the role of empirical data in conceptual progress is a recent outcome of co-operation between academic researchers and Eurofound, fuelled by a large-scale data set on working conditions in 34 European countries: the European Working Conditions Survey (EWCS). Eurofound has so far commissioned several reports to compare particular features of work and employment. However, it was not until the 2010 survey that a report was explicitly commissioned to undertake a comparative overview of general job quality between EU member states (Green and Mostafa, 2012).

The job quality index developed by Green and Mostafa (2012) draws on literature in the fields of psychology, sociology and economics. The model incorporates four dimensions of job quality: earnings, job prospects, working-time quality and the intrinsic quality of the job. Intrinsic job quality is further divided into four subscales: social environment, physical environment, skill and discretion, and work intensity. These scales consist of questions designed to produce a score to measure 'objective' features of respondents' jobs. Questions on job satisfaction (or satisfaction with specific aspects of a job, such as work–life balance) are not included. A particular employee might well express a desire to work evenings and weekends, but this is not the central issue; the point is that existing scientific evidence links these sorts of working pattern with stress, poor physical health and negative effects on partners and children. The job-quality indicator is constructed by assigning each respondent in the EWCS a score on each of its four main dimensions and four subdimensions, with higher scores indicating better job quality.

The public availability of the single data set from which the indices are derived allows researchers to embark on critical replications of the findings in an effort to refine and improve the model (e.g., for a gender critique, see Smith *et al.*, 2013). The success of this process is based on the simplicity and tractability achieved by a clear focus on the features of jobs as well as a synthetic indicator that is replicable across a broad range of countries.

It is precisely in the area of data gathering that the debate about the quality of employment can learn from other disciplines, in particular from the process through which psychologists developed the Five-Factor Model of Personality. It was developed to classify an endless set of personality traits, which could be combined in innumerable ways. In short, the discipline of psychology found a way to arrive at a consensus around the measurement through a synthetic indicator that is at least as complex and controversial as the quality of employment.

Lessons from the Five-Factor Model of personality

Reducing personality to the 'Big Five' broad dimensions defined as openness to experience, conscientiousness, extraversion, agreeableness and neuroticism, was in fact a largely data-driven process of building empirically based consensus that involved looking for patterns of association between hundreds or thousands of possible measures of personality traits. The journey from nearly 18,000 words describing personality found by Allport and Odbert (1936) in the Webster's dictionary, through 171 terms clustered into 35 and then 16 dimensions (Cattell, 1957), and then back and forth from more to less detailed lists of dimensions (Eysenck, 1991; Mershon and Gorsuch, 1988; Paunonen and Ashton, 2001), to the model with only five main personality dimensions (Costa and McCrae, 1992; Digman, 1997; Goldberg, 1993; Tupes and Christal, 1992) took several decades of academic research, driven by extensive collection of empirical data. The Big Five model is not without its critics, but it has probably come as close to achieving consensus as anything in psychology ever has. There are ongoing discussions, for instance, regarding the selection of survey items for measuring each dimension of personality (e.g. Gosling, Rentfrow, and Swann, 2003). Yet these are about details, not fundamentals; its success measured by the wide application in many fields is undeniable. The Big Five has been replicated by researchers worldwide and applied to a variety of different languages and cultures, including in Malaysia (Teh *et al.*, 2011), Turkey (Ozutku and Altindis, 2011), Iran (Erdle and Aghababaei, 2012;

Joshanloo and Afshari, 2011), Russia (Gindina *et al.*, 2011), China (Wang *et al.*, 2012) and Korea (Na and Marshall, 1999). Such is the widespread acceptance of the Big Five, it is now often included in large, general-purpose surveys, such as the British Household Panel Survey and the BBC's Lab UK project. This has made a major contribution to integrating psychological insights into interdisciplinary insights into sociological and economic analyses of individuals' working and family lives.

Achieving (near-) consensus within the discipline of psychology was clearly essential to the Big Five being adopted on such a wide scale. The field of job quality seems to be close to achieving a similar level of consensus. But there are most likely other features of the Big Five that are also essential in understanding why it has been used so widely, and perhaps the field of job quality can learn important lessons from the Big Five's success. For instance, not only has it been demonstrated that the Big Five can be measured with a high degree of validity and reliability, it can also be measured easily with just a small number of questionnaire items. While the feasibility of measuring job quality has also been demonstrated, more development work is needed to optimise the psychometric properties of the dimensions of job quality. In the literature on job quality, there has been little discussion of the most economical or 'short-form' way to measure it on a large scale.

Another prerequisite for such large-scale research is that one measurement tool is applicable to all individuals, whether 'normal' or 'abnormal'. If job-quality measures are to achieve anything like the ubiquity of the Big Five personality measures, this suggests that it is vital that one conceptual framework and one measurement tool are developed that can apply to all jobs, be they very good jobs or very bad jobs, or be they jobs in poor countries or rich countries. Such conceptual and methodological agreement was a major contributing factor to the success of the HDI: it applied to all countries, not just developing nations. The debate around the origins of the HDI emphasised from the beginning that public policies should involve planning at the global level to achieve international progress towards the narrowing of developmental gaps (Ul Haq, 1992). As a result, a composite statistic is calculated for each country to position it on a global map of development, recognising that better education, longer lives and more income are generally desirable in all contexts.

If recent publications are a guide of things to come, the success of the Five-Factor Model is such that it is starting to break into even bigger territories. Advances in big data and machine learning is seeing the emergence of a new literature based on social network sites (such as Facebook) where the Five-Factor Model of Personality test is administered and the test results, along with much other information that can be gleaned about users' online behaviour (or 'digital footprint'), can be analysed using tens or hundreds of thousands of cases, at very little cost to researchers (e.g. Youyou *et al.*, 2015). With many researchers predicting that advances in machine learning mean that 'Big Data' will become as important as academic and official surveys in the near future, this again demonstrates the importance of having measures that are amenable to large-scale survey administration.

A multi-level model for the measurement of job quality

One of the unresolved issues in the literature on the quality of employment involves deciding what types of information should be included in measures of job quality. In particular, those efforts that have attempted to cover a greater number of employment characteristics to reconcile different constituents of the policy-making community have failed to distinguish between different levels of analysis that are relevant to the labour market. At the simplest and most individualistic level, some models only consider the attitudes of individuals (e.g. their job satisfaction) and ignore details of the job itself or the context of the job. At the other extreme, some models are concerned more with the macro-level context of jobs, such as the level of legal protection of workers provided by the State, types of welfare systems that reduce the costs of job loss, and the economic conditions that account for the risk of job loss and unemployment. Such approaches that preclude operationalisation at the individual worker or the job level have further consequences. Some interesting issues, such as gender gaps in job quality and the relative quality of employment of migrants, cannot be addressed straightforwardly. Finally, some approaches mix up characteristics of individual workers, jobs themselves, the regulatory environment and the labour market as a whole.

The most extreme case of methodology that mixes up different levels of analysis is the ILO's 'decent work' approach. Some aspects of decent work are aimed at the individual worker (e.g. child labour and forced labour), some at the work environment (e.g. health and safety) and some at the aggregate level (e.g. social protection). The ILO's 'Country Profiles', which analyse decent work, look at almost every imaginable employment-related variable. This is not only conceptually confusing, but also makes international comparison impossible as very few countries have information on such a broad range of variables, while ranking countries becomes too cumbersome.

To overcome these difficulties and limitations we propose to identify clearly relevant levels of analysis for comparative job-quality research. Conditions of work and employment are embedded in, and shaped by, institutional arrangements and the social environment (Bosch *et al.* 2007; Bosch *et al.,* 2009). The outcomes will vary depending on not only the political and historical processes, the specialisation of countries or the macro-economic policy, but also the interactions between various rules and institutions. Such complexity prompted the development of various typologies (e.g. varieties of capitalism, welfare state regimes) to facilitate comparative analysis of social models. To allow for comparative analysis of job quality, we position jobs in the wider societal system (including the legal framework, welfare policy and structural features of the labour market), yet draw a line between the context in which a job is performed and the attributes of that job.

Different levels of job-quality analysis can be better understood and distinguished by using the metaphor of a vehicle for the quality of a job. For cars to be useful objects, they do not just need to be of good intrinsic quality (i.e. safe, comfortable and reliable); they also need to have good motorists, good roads, good services and be driven in a well-regulated setting. But if you ask somebody what constitutes a good car, it is unlikely that they would reply 'a qualified driver, comfortable seats, a powerful motor, safe roads and traffic laws that are complied with'. However, this is precisely what many methodologies measuring job quality have done. In what follows (see also Table 9.1), we discuss each level of analysis that applies to the labour market and, for clarity and illustrative purposes, draw a parallel with the car metaphor.

Workers (motorists)

In some measures of job quality much attention is paid to workers rather than jobs. This is manifest in two ways. The first issue pertains to the definition of workers and the conditions under which they are integrated into the labour market. Some people should not be working at all, such as young children or people forced to work against their will. The eradication of child and slave labour has been a priority for international development organisations such as the ILO. They are also quite correctly concerned about discrimination and segmentation in labour markets, which can exclude groups from jobs by virtue of their age, gender, sexual orientation or ethnic group. However, differentiation in employment terms and conditions not related to individual productivity is influenced by country-specific employment regimes, with their rules, institutions and employers' strategies (Rubery, 1978; 2007). This further complicates inclusion of worker characteristics in the evaluation of the quality of jobs.

Secondly, we might also be interested in workers' human capital, such as educational attainment, or their internal mental states, such as happiness or job satisfaction. However, from the perspective of our analytical framework, these dimensions should be considered as an important but distinct set of factors that impinge on labour market outcomes. This is particularly relevant from a policy perspective, as a focus on the characteristics of workers rather than jobs has been used to push for supply-side actions and policies (e.g. promotion of employability) instead of addressing challenges of poor-quality jobs.

Jobs (vehicles)

Vehicles are at the heart of understanding a transport system, in the same way that jobs are at the core of our job-quality model. However, note that we are not interested in what the motorists think of the car. They might think that a car is of a high quality for sentimental reasons, or because of limited knowledge of alternatives. Thus the role of a job-quality measure is to ascertain the true or objective quality of a job, just as a mechanic or vehicle tester evaluates a car, bringing their expert knowledge to the judgement. However, as discussed in the section 'Towards a framework for the measurement of job quality: methodological considerations', this metaphor is complicated by the fact that the most feasible way we have to measure job quality is usually through self-report of the job holder, and of course self-report is subject to bias. However, the important thing is to ask about 'objective' job features, such as the ergonomic and ambient features of the working environment, not about how satisfied the job holder is with these elements. We might expect some correlation between the quality of a job and the job satisfaction of the holder, insofar as adaptive preferences or differences in expectations would allow, but ontologically they are distinct.

Legal framework (traffic laws)

In the same way that road traffic needs to be policed to operate efficiently and safely, the quality of employment is dependent on the national legal framework. Therefore, a comprehensive model of quality of employment needs to take account of legislation such as employment protection legislation (EPL), laws against gender and racial discrimination in hiring, and health and safety protection. National legal systems can achieve the same ends by very different means, thus it is inherently complex to make quantitative comparisons between legal systems. Nevertheless, indices of labour market legislation have been created for this purpose and are used in debates on the importance or otherwise of EPL in creating efficient and fair labour markets (for a critique, see Rubery, 2011). Furthermore, without inspection and enforcement, labour market legislation is likely to be ineffectual. Thus the accessibility of legal redress to employees is also important. In some countries, the courts are the main enforcers of legislation; in others, enforcement might be carried out by trade unions or factory inspectors.

Welfare policy (road traffic safety)

With a traffic system, accidents will happen from time to time and systems are needed to minimise the damage, such as crash barriers and ambulances. The same is true of employment: when employees lose their jobs they need to be assisted in times of unemployment to give them an income that at least partially substitutes their lost wages. When they retire, they need a pension. Many countries operate active labour market policies to assist employees in getting back into work through mentoring and training. Some employees will also need welfare policies to help them retain jobs, such as parents of young children needing childcare provision to remain in work. In addition, welfare policies can be used to support low-income earners through such mechanisms as minimum wage-setting or earned income tax credits, and affordable childcare subsidised by the state can assist individuals and families through the life cycle. Yet the state is only one source of support; nuclear and extended families are more often providers rather than recipients of welfare and social provision (see House and Kahn, 1985).

Structural features of the labour market (roads)

In the same way that cars need roads to operate usefully and avoid traffic congestion and gridlock, we can situate jobs in the context of the supply and demand in a labour market through measures such as the rates of unemployment and participation rate and the pattern of job vacancies. Without the dynamic systems to generate continuously and allocate jobs, whole segments of the population can be excluded from access to good-quality jobs, or from the labour market altogether. Industrial organisation and labour market composition can impact the career structures of individuals, thus influencing access to good or bad jobs across the life course and according to fluctuations of the economy. The distribution of, and access to, good-quality jobs is crucial in describing the conditions of labour markets; this does not, however, affect the evaluation of certain features of jobs. A well-paid, secure job in a safe environment and without long or unsocial hours can be assessed positively irrespective of the wider socio-economic structure in which it is performed.

Table 9.1 Model for the measurement of job quality

Levels of analysis	Examples
Workers	Age, child labour, forced labour, gender, sexual orientation, ethnic origin, level of education
Jobs	Health and safety features, ergonomic and ambient features of the work environment, accident rates, employment contract, job security, autonomy, working hours, work intensity, adequate and fair remuneration
Legal framework	Right to unionisation, EPL, anti-discrimination legislation, equal opportunity legislation
Welfare policy	Pensions, unemployment and health insurance, family policies, active labour market policies
Structural features of the labour market	Unemployment and participation rates, transition rates between labour market statuses or employment contracts, vacancy rates, macroeconomic environment, efficient hiring mechanisms

The model sketched above and illustrated by drawing parallels between the labour market and a transport system, introduces a much-needed conceptual clarity to the debate about job quality and its measurement. By distinguishing a job from its holder and from a wider environment in which it is performed, including labour market policies, social provision and structural factors, we can arrive at a more focused study object. This way we can arrive at an indicator, or a concise set of indicators, that overcomes the difficulty of quantifying the contribution of a certain job to wider societal goals of equality, freedom and development.

Starting with the 'vehicle' or 'car' level of analysis and ignoring the other levels of analysis (motorists, roads and so on) has several clear advantages. Firstly, it is simpler – and once the analysis has been carried out adequately at that level, then other levels of analysis can be added, such as the welfare state and legal regulation of labour markets. Secondly, at this level of analysis, any groups can be compared, such as men and women or indigenous and migrant workers, whether locally, regionally or nationally. Thirdly, to analyse labour markets at this level requires only one type of data, easily collected by surveys of employees, making international comparisons relatively straightforward.

Like all metaphors, this model has its limitations. One shortcoming is that it treats the employee (or 'motorist') in a completely individualistic way, whereas, in reality, they are embedded within a context of a family and a community.

One could add the family as passengers in the car, but that might be pushing the metaphor too far! The important point is that, as the OECD's (2011) report emphasises, most aspects of job quality have direct implications for the family of the worker. For instance, if the worker has economic dependants, their freedom from poverty also depends on the income from the job, and their security and ability to plan for their future depends upon the worker's job security and prospects. But the most obvious way in which the job affects the quality of family life is through work–life balance, which becomes more difficult to achieve for low-quality jobs, for instance those involving unsocial and irregular hours or with little job security (Lyonette and Clark, 2009). And, as Giele (1996) points out, the relationship between employment and family is complex and contested, with the employer also benefiting from the support given to the employee by the family. A similar point could be made for the worker's community (Kamerade, 2009).

Another complicating factor for analysing job quality is where one person holds two jobs – typically one with a regular schedule of hours and the other non-standard hours, for instance evenings or a zero-hours contract (see Dunifon *et al.*, 2013). This emphasises the point that we need to be conceptually clear in the distinction between the motorist and the vehicle they are driving at that point in time.

Conclusions

This chapter has considered the challenges in conceptualisation and measurement of job quality in comparative analysis. Firstly, we considered the confusions that abound around how we measure job quality, the terms *subjective, objective* and *self-report*, and quality from whose perspective. Secondly, we examined how different levels of measurement in schemes of job quality, both academic and institutional, have been mixed together and we use the metaphor of cars, drivers and roads to clarify this confusion. We draw parallels with the Big Five personality scheme to show how the measurement of personality takes a long time to achieve consensus and conceptual clarity but, once this is achieved, it becomes feasible to include it in large surveys which facilitate progress and impact.

The review of academic research in this field is revealing. When little internationally comparable micro-level data in Europe existed, most research was single-firm or single-country focused. This limited the scope for conceptual progress in defining key and universal elements of job quality and thus no internationally relevant indicators of job quality were established at that time. This situation changed dramatically in Europe when large-scale data-sets were made available, such as the EWCS, the European Social Survey and the European Labour Force Survey. Starting with the standardisation of various labour force surveys in the EU member states, there followed several initiatives that provided rich and dynamic data sources for researchers to explore ideas and test theories about labour markets. These data sets not only facilitate statistical comparisons of national labour markets, but they also provide a fertile environment for theoretical developments in the understanding of the drivers of job quality.

In this respect, the Five-Factor model for measuring personality provides some important lessons. There are two important steps that make this such an effective model: the decision of what to measure, and then how to measure it. In this chapter, we argue that the project of the measurement of job quality faltered at the first hurdle, as there was conceptual confusion over what to measure, spanning micro- and macroeconomic variables, demographic variables and attitudinal variables (including job satisfaction). As we argue here, this complexity can be dealt with by clearly focusing on the job as a unit of analysis. Then, the development of universally applicable measures with good reliability and validity can follow, focusing on asking incumbents about specific features of their jobs.

Thus we argue that measurement development with solid empirical basis is key in the process of building the conceptual and methodological agreement. What is needed is availability of comparable cross-national data and conceptual clarity in defining the study object and setting boundaries as to what job quality is and what it is not.

Only with advances on these two fronts can we anticipate the attention to the improvement of people's working lives that could parallel the attention that the HDI directed towards human development. This, together with an openness to international comparisons, can create fertile grounds for the exchange and dialogue between research on job quality and evidence-based public policy.

References

Agassi, J. B. (1982), *Comparing the Work Attitudes of Men and Women* (Aldershot: Gower).

Allport, G. W. and Odbert, H. S. (1936), 'Trait-names: a psycho-lexical study', *Psychological Monographs*, 47:1, i–171.

Bauer, R. A. (eds) (1966), *Social Indicators* (Cambridge, MA: MIT Press).

Bosch, G., Lehndorff, S. and Rubery, J. (2009) 'European employment models in flux: Pressures for change and prospects for survival and revitalization', in Bosch, G., Lehndorff, S. and Rubery, J. (eds), *European Employment Models in Flux: A Comparison of Institutional Change in Nine European countries* (Basingstoke: Palgrave Macmillan) pp. 1–56.

Bosch, G., Rubery, J. and Lehndorff, S. (2007), 'European employment models under pressure to change', *International Labour Review*, 146: 3–4, 253–77.

Burchell, B. (1992), 'Towards a social psychology of the labour market: or why we need to understand the labour market before we can understand unemployment', *Journal of Occupational and Organisational Psychology*, 65, 345–54.

Burchell, B., Sehnbruch, K., Piasna, A. and Agloni, N. (2014), 'The quality of employment and decent work: definitions, methodology and ongoing debates', *Cambridge Journal of Economics*, 38:2, 459–77.

Butterworth, P., Leach, L. S., Strazdins, L., Olesen, S. C., Rodgers, B. and Broom, D. H. (2011), 'The psychosocial quality of work determines whether employment has benefits for mental health', *Occupational and Environmental Medicine*, 68:11, 806–12.

Cattell, R. B. (1957), *Personality and motivation structure and measurement* (World Book Co.).

Comin F. and Teschl, M. (2005), 'Adaptive preferences and capabilities: Some preliminary conceptual explorations', *Review of Social Economy*, 63:2, 229–47.

Costa Jr, P. T. and McCrae, R. R. (1992), 'Four ways five factors are basic', *Personality and Individual differences*, 13:6, 653–65.

Davis, L. E. (1977), 'Enhancing the quality of working life', *International Labour Review*, 116:1, 53.

Digman, J. M. (1997), 'Higher-order factors of the Big Five', *Journal of personality and social psychology*, 73:6, 1246–56.

Dunifon, R., Kalil, A., Crosby, D. A., Su, J. H. and Deleire, T. (2013), 'Measuring maternal nonstandard work in survey data', *Journal of Marriage and Family*, 75, 523–32.

Erdle, S. and Aghababaei, N. (2012), 'Evidence for the general factor of personality (GFP) in the Big Five from 600 Iranians', *Personality and Individual Differences*, 53: 3, 359–61.

Eysenck, H. J. (1991), *Manual of the Eysenck Personality Scales (EPS Adult)* (London: Hodder and Stoughton).

Giele, J. Z. (1996), 'Decline of the family: Conservative, liberal, and feminist views', in Popenoe, D. Elshtain, J. B. and Blankenhorn, D. (eds), *Promises to Keep: Decline and Renewal of Marriage in America* (Lanham, MD: Rowman & Littlefield), pp. 271–90.

Gindina, E., Nizamova, E., Lobaskova, M. and Barsky, P. (2011), 'Genetic and environmental influences on individual differences in "Big Five" personality traits in adolescent and young adult Russian twins', *Behavior Genetics*, 41:6, 909–10.

Goldberg, L. R. (1993), 'The structure of phenotypic personality traits', *American Psychologist*, 48:1, 26–34.

Gosling, S. D., Rentfrow, P. J. and Swann Jr, W. B. (2003), 'A very brief measure of the Big-Five personality domains', *Journal of Research in personality*, 37:6, 504–28.

Green, F. and Mostafa, T. (2012), *Trends in Job Quality in Europe*, Eurofound report (Luxembourg: Publication Office of the European Union).

Hackman, J. R. and Oldham, G. R. (1975), 'Development of the Job Diagnostic Survey', *Journal of Applied Psychology*, 60:2, 159–70.

House, J. S. and Kahn, R. L. (1985), 'Measures and concepts of social support', in Cohen, S. and Syme, S. L. (eds), *Social Support and Health* (Orlando, FL: Academic Press), pp. 83–108.

ILO (International Labour Organization) (1999), 'Decent Work. Report of the Director General', Report I-AI, International Labour Conference, 87th Meeting, Geneva, June.

Jahoda, M. (1982), *Employment and Unemployment: A Social-Psychological Analysis*, Vol. 1 (Cambridge: Cambridge University Press).

Joshanloo, M. and Afshari, S. (2011), 'Big five personality traits and self-esteem as predictors of life satisfaction in Iranian Muslim University students', *Journal of Happiness Studies*, 12:1, 105–13.

Kalleberg, A. L. and Vaisey, S. (2005), 'Pathways to a good job', *British Journal of Industrial Relations*, 43:3, 431–54.

Kamerāde, D. (2009), 'Part-time work and involvement in voluntary associations in Britain', *Sociological Research Online*, 14:5, 2.

Karasek, R. and Theorell, T. (1990), *Healthy work* (New York: Basic Books).

Krueger, P., Brazil, K., Lohfeld, L., Edward, H. G., Lewis, D. and Tjam, E. (2002), 'Organization specific predictors of job satisfaction', *BMC Health Services Research*, 2:1, 6.

Land, K. (1975), 'The role of quality of employment indicators in general social reporting systems', *American Behavioral Scientist*, 18:3, 304–32.

Lyonette, C. and Clark, M. (2009), *Unsocial Hours: Unsocial Families? Working Time and Family Wellbeing* (Cambridge: Relationship Foundation).

Mershon, B. and Gorsuch, R. L. (1988), 'Number of factors in the personality sphere: Does increase in factors increase predictability of real-life criteria?', *Journal of Personality and Social Psychology*, 55:4, 675.

Muñoz de Bustillo, R., Fernández, U., Macías, E., Antón, J. and Esteve, F. (2011), *Measuring More Than Money* (Cheltenham: Edward Elgar).

Na, W. and Marshall, R. (1999), 'Validation of the "Big Five" personality traits in Korea: a comparative approach', *Journal of International Consumer Marketing*, 12:1, 5–19.

Nussbaum, M. (2000), *Women and Human Development: The Capabilities Approach* (Cambridge: Cambridge University Press).

OECD (Organisation for Economic Co-operation and Development) (2011), *Doing better for families* (Paris: OECD).

OECD (Organisation for Economic Co-operation and Development) (2014), *Employment Outlook* (Paris: OECD).

Ozutku, H. and Altindis, S. (2011), 'Big five personality factors and other elements in understanding work stress of Turkish health care professionals', *African Journal of Business Management*, 5:26, 10462–73.

Paunonen, S. V. and Ashton, M. C. (2001), 'Big five factors and facets and the prediction of behavior', *Journal of personality and social psychology*, 81:3, 524–39.

Rubery, J. (1978), 'Structured labour markets, worker organisation and low pay', *Cambridge Journal of Economics*, 2:1, 17–36.

Rubery, J. (2007), 'Developing segmentation theory: a thirty year perspective', *Économies et Sociétés*, 28:6, 941–64.

Rubery, J. (2011), 'Reconstruction amid deconstruction: or why we need more of the social in European social models', *Work, Employment & Society*, 25:4, 658–74.

Seashore, S. E. (1974), 'Job satisfaction as an indicator of the quality of employment', *Social Indicators Research*, 1:2, 135–68.

Sehnbruch, K. (2006), *The Chilean Labour Market: A Key to Understanding Latin American Labour Markets* (Basingstoke and New York: Palgrave Macmillan).

Sehnbruch, K., Burchell, B., Agloni, N. and Piasna, A., (2015), 'Human development and decent work: why some concepts succeed and others fail to make an impact', *Development and Change*, 46:2, 197–224.

Sen, A. (1999), *Speech in the 87th ILO Meeting* (Geneva: International Labour Conference).

Smith, M., Piasna, A., Burchell, B., Rubery, J., Rafferty, A., Rose, J. and Carter, L. (2013), 'Women, men and working conditions in Europe', Eurofound report (Luxembourg: Publication Office of the European Union).

Staines, G. L. and Quinn, R. P. (1979), 'American workers evaluate the quality of their jobs', *Monthly Labor Review*, 102:1, 3–11.

Stiglitz, J., Sen, A. and Fitoussi, J. P. (2009), 'Report of the commission on the measurement of economic performance and social progress', Commission on the Measurement of Economic Performance and Social Progress.

Taylor, J.C. (1977), 'Job satisfaction and quality of working life', *Journal of Occupational Psychology*, 50:4, 243–52.

Teh, P. L., Yong, C. C., Chong, C. W. and Yew, S. Y. (2011), 'Do the Big Five Personality Factors affect knowledge sharing behaviour? A study of Malaysian universities. *Malaysian Journal of Library and Information Science*, 16:1, 47–62.

Tupes, E. C. and Christal, R. E. (1992), 'Recurrent personality factors based on trait ratings', *Journal of personality*, 60:2, 225–51.

Turner, C. F. and Martin, E. (eds) (1984), *Surveying Subjective Phenomena*, Vol. 1. (New York: Russell Sage).

Ul Haq, M. (1992), *Human Development in a Changing World* (Occasional Papers: United Nations Development Programme).

UNECE (United Nations Economic Commission for Europe) (2015), *Handbook for Measuring Quality of Employment, A Statistical Framework*, UNECE Expert Group on Measuring Quality of Employment (ECE/CES/2015/4/Add.2/Rev.1).

Veenhoven, R. (2002), 'Why social policy needs subjective indicators', *Social Indicators Research*, 58:1–3, 33–46.

Wang, J. L., Jackson, L. A., Zhang, D. J. and Su, Z. Q. (2012), 'The relationships among the Big Five Personality factors, self-esteem, narcissism, and sensation-seeking to Chinese University students' uses of social networking sites (SNSs)', *Computers in Human Behavior*, 28:6, 2313–19.

Warr, P. (1987), *Work, Unemployment and Mental Health* (Oxford: Clarendon Press).

Warr, P. (2007), *Work, Happiness, and Unhappiness* (New York: Routledge).

Wnuk-Lipinski, E. (1977), 'Job satisfaction and the quality of working life', *International Labour Review*, 115:1, 53–64.

Yoshida, K. and Torihara, M. (1977), 'Redesigning jobs for a better quality of working life', *International Labour Review*, 116:2, 139–52.

Youyou, W., Kosinski, M. and Stillwell, D. (2015), 'Computer-based personality judgments are more accurate than those made by humans', *Proceedings of the National Academy of Sciences*, 112:4, 1036–40.

10

Working longer and harder? A critical assessment of work effort in Britain in comparison to Europe

Alan Felstead and Francis Green

Introduction

Among the many outcomes of the Global Financial Crisis, which ravaged employment across Europe from the end of 2008, health problems surrounding work are gradually coming to be properly comprehended as a significant component of the costs of the economic stagnation. In the UK, which is the focus of this chapter, the number of working days lost between 2009 and 2013 owing to work-related stress increased by 24 per cent and the number lost because of serious mental illness doubled (Davies, 2014). Meanwhile, we know that work-related well-being fell significantly between 2006 and 2012 according to multiple measures (Green *et al.*, 2016). Long working hours and work intensification are frequently cited in media reports as the main causes behind the work-related stress epidemic. There is substantive evidence for the detrimental effects of long working hours on various aspects of health, especially in cases where workers are not able to exercise much choice or control over those hours (Bassanini and Caroli, 2014; Kivimaki *et al.*, 2015; Lee and Lee, 2016). Indeed, the European Directive on Working Time (which places regulatory limits on working more than 48 hours per week) derives in part from the principle that excessive work hours are a public health issue. There is also evidence that more intensive work is associated with lower work-related well-being (Green, 2008; Green *et al.*, 2016).

Yet the supposed linkage between deteriorating health and greater work effort is based on a prior assumption that British workers are working longer and harder than their predecessors. Furthermore, it is often suggested that British workers are exceptional in that they work longer than workers in Europe and beyond. The aim of this chapter is to subject these assumptions to empirical scrutiny.

Typically, long hours and work intensity are both referred to as work effort. The section which follows, therefore, delineates the conceptual differences between extensive and intensive work effort, with the former referring to the amount of time spent at work and the latter referring to the intensity of effort expended during those working hours (Green, 2001). The section proceeds to outline how these two aspects of work effort can be captured using survey instruments. The chapter then outlines the international data sources and surveys used to put the British results in a comparative context as well as outlining the surveys which allow us to track trends over time. The two substantive empirical sections which follow present the results for these two aspects of work effort.

The chapter concludes by rejecting the suggestion that workers in Britain work longer hours than those working elsewhere in Europe and beyond. However, the evidence is that while on average this suggestion is a myth, it does hold for one group of workers: male employees who work full-time. On the other hand, the evidence shows that workers in Britain work harder than other Europeans, that work intensity has risen in recent times and that women working full-time have experienced some of the largest rises since 2006. This provides further evidence of the persistence of gender inequalities which have been the subject of much research over many years (Rubery, 2015; Rubery and Fagan, 1995; see Chapter 1). The section also considers how the chapter's findings might help us to understand better patterns in work-related well-being and the sluggishness of productivity in Britain in recent times.

Concepts and measures

Although used in common parlance, the notion of 'work effort' has two distinct conceptual meanings. It is important therefore that this chapter clarifies both these meanings and outlines how they are measured.

We start, however, by clarifying three concepts – performance, efficiency and skill – which are sometimes mistakenly conflated in the popular discourse with work effort. Performance refers to the extent to which an individual carries out their contractual work tasks and so is synonymous with individual productivity (i.e. the quantity of outputs produced in a given time period). Performance is a function of the capabilities individuals have in carrying out the tasks involved and the speed with which those tasks are carried out – that is, the skills of the person and the effort they devote to the work process. These two aspects are substitutes and need not always go hand in hand (Green, 2006).

An individual's performance is 'efficient' if it could not be improved without an increase in skill and/or an increase in work intensity. A rise in performance triggered by an increase in work intensity does not signify an increase in efficiency since it comes about by increasing an input into the production process. The process of 'productivity bargaining' – common in the 1960s – recognised that increasing productivity often entailed costs for workers and hence trade unions only agreed to changes intended to improve quantitative efficiency in return for an increase in pay and/or other benefits (Gordon, 1976). Misunderstanding this fundamental, if simple, point is the source of one of the most frequent mistakes made in public discourse, with some commentators equating productivity gains with efficiency gains. Similarly, some organisations are structured and managed more efficiently than others. This occurs where an organisation's output could be increased without altering either the skills of workers or the intensity of the work carried out – sometimes characterised as working smarter but not harder.

Work effort, then, comprises the length of time spent carrying out work and the intensity of the effort expended during that time. We refer to the former as extensive work effort which can be relatively easily calibrated by counting the number of hours spent at work by day, week, month or year. Time conscious-ness and discipline are long-standing institutionalised features of the capitalist workplace which swept away pre-capitalist conceptions of time based on the seasons and the rhythms of nature, such as harvesting, lambing and the like. The factory system, on the other hand, was based on time discipline. Workers were expected to be on time and stay until the end of their shift. They were also expected to turn up every day without fail. Infringements resulted in loss of wages or of the job itself. This was further embedded by the spread of the school system, with its emphasis on punctuality and the regulation of activities by bells and whistles (Thompson, 1967). The measurement of time was crucial and the widespread use of clocks, watches and other timepieces made this relatively easy to achieve. Data sources, too, which measure the average number of hours spent at work, have a long history stretching back well into the nineteenth century. These allow us to chart change in the UK and set current levels of working time in an international context (see Table 10.1 and Figure 10.1). In this chapter and elsewhere (e.g., Green, 2001; 2006) we refer to this as extensive work effort.

Intensive work effort, on the other hand, is more difficult to calibrate, since it entails a mix of physical, mental and emotional demands at work, each of which are difficult to measure. Moreover, intensive work effort is inversely linked to the porosity of the working day – that is, paid periods of on-the-job inactivity between tasks during which the body or mind is at rest. It is also well-known that there is gradation of effort expended in completing a task as effort levels cannot be at the absolute maximum all of the time. These factors make some types of measurement impossible. Direct measures of intensive work effort are, for example, impossible in most practical circumstances as it would require minute-by-minute on-the-job tracking. Nevertheless, measuring relative intensive effort levels is achievable by taking a multi-dimensional approach. Indicators can be derived from workers' self-reports of effort levels since it is they, rather than managers or work measurement experts, who are best placed to know how intensively they work. In the words of Guest (1990: 306), 'if we want to know whether workers are working hard, we should ask them'. It is best to ask multiple questions focusing on different aspects of work intensity. To provide a robust evidence base requires worker surveys which use carefully worded questions, repeated over several years and administered on large samples of workers. Thankfully, we now have a series of such sources and evidence on which to draw (see the next section: 'Data sources').

In this chapter, we present data on three ways of measuring intensive work effort, all of which focus on objective indicators as reported by worker respondents. Crucially, none are related to personal circumstances and instead focus on the job – the requirement to work hard and the various conditions under which work is carried out. So, as a summary measure of work intensity, we use responses given to the question: 'please tell me how much you agree or disagree with the statement: my job requires that I work very hard.' If they strongly agree, we define the job as involving 'hard work'. Respondents to several of the surveys reported here are also asked to indicate how often they work at very high speeds. The response scales used vary a little between survey series, but importantly not within, thereby allowing over time or inter-country comparisons to be made. If respondents say that they work at very high speeds for three-quarters or more of the time (or all, or almost all, of the time), we classify them as occupying 'high-speed' jobs. If they report working to 'tight deadlines' for a similar amount of time we refer to these as 'tight deadline' jobs. The focus of all three measures is on the requirements of the job for intensive work effort. This is distinguished from 'discretionary' work effort, which focuses on the willingness to, or admission of, working unpaid overtime and/or working more intensively than required.

Data sources

To make European comparisons we draw on several survey series and data sources. They have in common that they are all focused on gathering data from the point of view of workers themselves, rather than relying on management respondents or work measurement experts. For European data on hours of work, we use the European Union Labour Force Survey (EULFS). The survey comprises a list of common questions, uses a common coding framework for the replies received and adopts agreed definitions. From this, the UK can be positioned and ranked according to working hours. Furthermore, different categories of worker can be delineated and a gender breakdown of the results presented.[1]

Data on working hours are also assembled by the OECD. This approach draws together sources such as the EULFS and other data sets – such as those outlined below – into metadata sets which are accessible online. This chapter uses this evidence in order to place the UK working hours in a much wider international context.

To examine UK trends, we use the Annual Survey of Hours and Earnings (ASHE) which, as the name suggests, has a special focus on hours of work. It is based on a 1 per cent sample of employees on the Inland Revenue Pay As You Earn (PAYE) register for February (approximately 187,000 employees in 2015). While this is still the main basis of ASHE, this sample is supplemented by two additional samples. One is drawn from the Inland Revenue PAYE register in April – to cover employees that have either moved into the job market or changed jobs between the time of selection and the survey date. A second is taken from the Inter-Departmental Business Register for businesses registered for VAT but not registered for PAYE – to cover businesses that do not have employees above the PAYE threshold. Once employees are selected, the ASHE questionnaires are sent to employers who supply the requested information on the employee's age, gender, occupation, earnings and hours of work (Bird, 2004). The evidence taken from ASHE over several years allows us to track recent changes in the length of the average working week. These results can also be placed in a wider historical context using Office for National Statistics (ONS) data stretching back to the late nineteenth century.

We use a similar mixture of data sources to compare levels of intensive work effort across countries and to plot change in Britain over time. For the former, we draw on data from two sources – the European Social Survey (ESS) and the European Working Conditions Survey (EWCS). The ESS is an academically driven social survey designed to chart and explain the interaction between Europe's changing institutions and the attitudes, beliefs and behaviour patterns of its diverse populations. The 2014 survey was the seventh in the series and covers over 20 nations. A 120-item module on 'Work, Family and Well-Being' was included in the second (2004) and fifth (2010) in the series (Gallie, 2013). This included data on the intensity of work.

Our second source of European data is the EWCS. The quality of work has been a focal point of this survey since its inception in 1991. Furthermore, its content has been expanded considerably since then – from 20 questions in 1991 to well over 100 in the sixth survey carried out in 2015. Its geographical coverage has also extended as new member states have been admitted to the EU. The 2015 EWCS was the largest. It included all 28 member states, the five EU candidate countries (Albania, the former Yugoslav Republic of Macedonia, Montenegro, Serbia and Turkey), as well as Switzerland and Norway, making a total of 35 countries and involving more than 43,000 workers (Eurofound, 2015, 2012; Smith et al., 2007). We extract data from the 2015 survey on the frequency of working to tight deadlines and at high speed. This is used to rank the UK against EU members in terms of levels of work intensity.

Finally, we draw on the Skills and Employment Survey (SES) series to provide insights into the prevalence, pattern and trends in intensive work effort over time in Britain. The 2012 survey was the sixth in a series of nationally representative sample surveys of individuals in employment aged 20–60 years old (although the 2006 and 2012 surveys additionally sampled those aged 61–65). The numbers of respondents were: 4,047 in the 1986 survey; 3,855 in 1992; 2,467 in 1997; 4,470 in 2001; 7,787 in 2006; and 3,200 in 2012. For each survey, weights were computed to take into account the differential probabilities of sample selection, the over-sampling of certain areas and some small response-rate variations between groups (defined by sex, age and occupation). All the analyses that follow use these weights (Felstead et al., 2015). Similarly, all the findings reported here make use of appropriate survey weights where available.

Extensive work effort

In public discourse, it is commonly assumed that British workers work excessively long hours, making their comparative levels of extensive work effort high by international standards. This assumption is often repeated. Since 1990, for example, there have been 1,423 references in English-language news outlets to this supposed fact.[2] However, the evidence is not quite as straightforward. In fact, average usual working hours per week in the UK in 2015 was 37.1, putting the UK below the EU28 country average and ranking the UK 22nd out of 28 countries.

Occasionally, news items nuance their claims by substituting the phrase 'some of the longest hours in Europe' (329 references). But only rarely do these claims refer specifically to those classified as full-time employees, or more precisely to male full-time employees. When they do, these claims can be supported by robust empirical evidence – male full-time employees work almost three hours

Table 10.1   Usual weekly hours of work in the UK and Europe, 2015

Category of worker	European 28 country average working hours	UK average working hours	UK rank (out of 28)
All workers	37.1	36.7	22
Male	40.1	41.0	7
Female	33.6	31.5	25
All full-time workers	41.4	42.9	3
Male full-time workers	42.4	44.2	2
Female full-time workers	40.0	40.6	10
All part-time workers	20.2	19.4	22
Male part-time workers	19.1	18.8	21
Female part-time workers	20.5	19.6	21
All full-time employees	40.3	42.4	1
Male full-time employees	41.0	43.7	1
Female full-time employees	39.3	40.4	7
All full-time self-employed	47.5	46.0	18
Male full-time self-employed	48.5	46.7	18
Female full-time self-employed	44.9	43.4	21

Source: Data downloaded from European Union Labour Force Survey data explorer found on: www. epp.eurostat.ec.europa.eu/portal/page/portal/statistics/themes

a week more than their counterparts elsewhere in Europe (see Table 10.1). The validity of the claim was stronger in the early 1990s, when those in Britain worked longer and the EU was smaller. Yet the assertion is incorrect if applied to the self-employed where typical weekly working hours for both men and women are in the bottom third of EU countries. By misrepresenting the high ranking of male full-time employees' hours as applying to the whole British workforce, the discourse about 'Britons' working the longest hours is not only sexist but also factually incorrect.

Academic writers make this mistake far less frequently. In fact, when they consider Britain's hours relative to elsewhere in Europe, they generally get it right. For example, it is useful to note men's long working hours when considering their role in family life and work–life balance as well as in identifying the difficulties of constructing meaningful part-time jobs given the long working hours of male full-time employees (Cousins and Tang, 2004; Lyonette and Crompton, 2011; Rubery and Grimshaw, 2015; Warren and Lyonette, 2015). Occasional attempts by academics and rare tries in the press have been made to defuse the popular myth about working hours for all using some hard facts, but with apparently little impact (e.g., Bonney, 2005; Green, 2008).

Most myths endure, but why this particular one lasts is unclear. One possibility is the pull of nationalism; being top or bottom of a country rank is like winning a competition. Working more hours is variously supposed to make British workers seem more hard-working, yet perhaps less happy and maybe less efficient. Nationalist self-deprecation vies in British culture with nationalist aggrandisement, each wanting to make British workers somehow special. The myth's survival is helped by its kernel of truth when filtered by the category of male full-time employees. At the same time, it provides a ready-made context for countless 'human interest' features related to the putative effects of long working hours, including deleterious stories about sexual appetite (too low), office sex (too much), marital infidelity, alcoholism, insomnia and obesity. A typical attribution is: 'Brits work the longest hours in Europe. It's only natural to want to let their hair down.'[3] As for explanation, Britain's supposedly long hours are sometimes claimed, without evidential support, to be associated with its opt-out from the EU Working Time Directive which restricts working hours to 48 per week.

Placed in an even wider international context, these claims of relatively high levels of extensive work effort in the UK also appear well wide of the mark. Data assembled by the Organisation for Economic Co-operation and Development (OECD) for 2014, for example, shows the wide range in the annual average number of hours worked by those in paid work. According to this evidence, the UK annual average of 1,677 hours is below the OECD average of 1,770 and well short of the extensive levels of work effort expended in Mexico, Costa Rica and Korea where the annual averages are around 500 hours higher (see Figure 10.1).

Furthermore, the average number of hours worked has been declining over the centuries (despite some periods of stability) and has continued to fall in recent times. In 1870, annual hours worked per person stood at 2,984. By 1913, this was down to 2,624 and continued moving downwards, reaching 1,489 in 1998. The decline in annual hours can also be seen in the reduced length of the average working week. For example, the average weekly hours of a manual worker fell from 53 hours in 1943 to 43.5 in 1987 (Lindsay, 2003). This pattern has continued. According to ASHE full-time employees – despite working the longest hours in Europe (cf. Table 10.1) – have seen their hours of work excluding overtime fall from 40.0 in 1997 to 39.1 in 2015. This decrease is most notable for men, while women's hours have remained stable. For men, there was a sharp dip between 2008 and 2009, from 40.7 to 40.1, and since then they have remained largely stable, not returning to the levels seen prior to the 2008–09 recession (see Figure 10.2). It should also be noted that official,

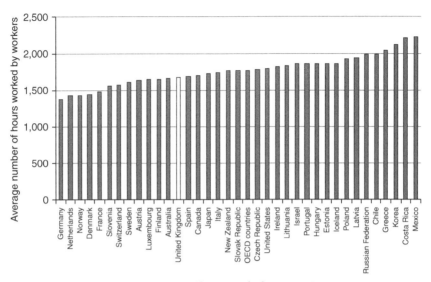

Figure 10.1   Annual average number of hours worked, OECD, 2014

Notes: The data presented refer to paid workers regardless of whether they are employees or self-employed.

Source: Data extracted from OECD. Stat, https://stats.oecd.org/.

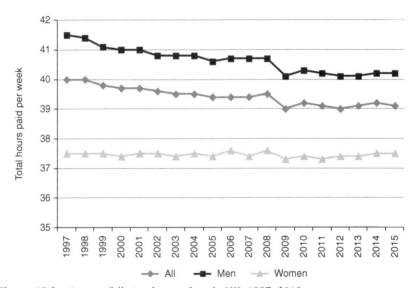

Figure 10.2   Average full-time hours of work, UK, 1997–2015

Notes: The data presented are for full-time employees working 30 hours or more and includes overtime.

Source: ONS, 2015: figure 20.

employer-reported, data often hide the extent to which people are working longer hours than they are explicitly paid for, sometimes while at home (see Felstead *et al.*, 2005). While this practice is widespread, especially among managerial and professional occupations, a similar picture of falling working hours since the mid-1990s can also be found in the Labour Force Survey data (also a trusted source of labour market information), where hours – including those that are unpaid – are reported by workers as opposed to their employers.

In short, extensive work effort in Britain has been on a long downward path since the late nineteenth century and has continued unabated over recent decades. Working time has therefore been falling not rising. International comparisons also suggest that working hours in Britain are on average shorter and not longer than elsewhere in the world despite newspaper reports proclaiming the contrary.

Intensive work effort

As previously argued, measuring the level of intensive work effort is difficult since there is no agreed yardstick to measure the degree of effort put into each hour of paid work. We must rely on proxies instead. One of these is to ask workers how strongly they agree or disagree with the statement that 'my job requires that I work very hard'. How this is felt will vary from job to job. Working very hard could be: coping with relentless pressure, multitasking, being required to concentrate for long spells, doing an emotionally draining job and/or remaining alert at all times. Respondents across Europe to ESS 2010 were asked to summarise the level of intensive work effort they were expected to expend using a five-point agree–disagree scale. This comparison suggests that UK jobs are among the most intensive in the EU. Over a third of UK workers (36 per cent) strongly agreed their jobs required them to work very hard – 15 percentage points above the EU28 average and far exceeding the 13–14 per cent recorded for Denmark and Sweden (see Figure 10.3). Respondents to the survey were also asked whether they agreed or disagreed with the statement that: 'I never seem to have enough time to get everything done in my job.' While this may also pick up organisational inefficiencies discussed above, it is telling that the UK comes second highest and well above the EU28 average on this measure too.

Estimates of the time spent working to tight deadlines and at very high speed (denoted as tight deadlines and high speed for short) offer further insights into the pattern of intensive work effort. They focus on two particular features of the labour process – its speed and the squeezing of more effort out of the available time – which feed into overall assessments of the pressure to work very hard. On the tight deadline measure, the UK tops the rankings with almost two out

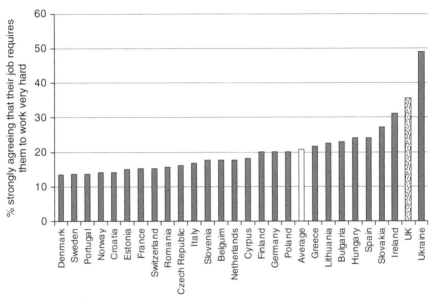

Figure 10.3   Intensive work effort – requirement to work very hard, Europe, 2010

Source: Authors' calculations from the European Social Survey 2010.

of five workers (39 per cent) reporting working to tight deadlines all or almost all of the time (see Figure 10.4). This compares to the EU28 average of around one in four.[4]

By contrast, the pressure to work 'at high speed' picks up a different aspect of work intensity, and such pressure in the UK is around the European average. About a quarter of workers (23 per cent) in the UK in 2015 reported working at very high speed all or almost all of the time. This puts the UK neither at the top with countries such as Cyprus, Romania, Greece and Spain, where well over 30 per cent were in high-speed jobs, nor at the bottom with Bulgaria and Latvia, where barely one in ten worked in such pressurised jobs (see Figure 10.5).

These international comparisons of the intensive effort requirements of jobs should be interpreted with the caveat that worker reports can be influenced by cultural expectations and by the nuances of language. It remains possible, therefore, that some international differences reflect the different interpretations of the questions and response scales, rather than real differences in effort requirements. The fact that multiple measures have been deployed goes only some way towards mitigating this reservation about our conclusions. When looking at how patterns of intensive work effort have changed over time within Britain, however, the caveat is further diminished; even though it remains possible that interpretations of intensive work might change over time, if multiple measures

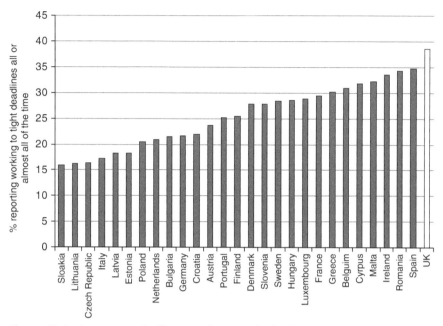

Figure 10.4 Intensive work effort – working to tight deadlines, Europe, 2015

Source: Data extracted from the European Working Conditions Survey 2015 data visualisation tool on: http://eurofound.europa.eu/surveys/data-visualisation/sixth-european-working-conditions-survey-2015

are indicating change in the same direction we can have considerable confidence that they are capturing genuine change.

To track these changes over time, we use four data points in the SES spanning two decades, from 1992 to 2012, to update the earlier analysis of intensive effort change given in Green (2006). This is complemented by data collected by other series such as the Workplace Employment Relations Survey (WERS), although over a much shorter time horizon. The evidence from SES is that jobs requiring hard work rose by over nine percentage points between 1992 and 1997, but remained around that figure in 2001 and 2006. However, from 2006 to 2012 hard work rose by around three percentage points – a resumption of work intensification after a decade of little change (see Figure 10.6). Both upward movements in work intensity – in the mid to late 1990s and then once again more recently – followed recessions and therefore provide some circumstantial support, though not proof, for the argument that employers use recessions to ratchet up effort levels. The most recent increase in work intensity is corroborated by comparing the answers given by employees to WERS in 2004 with those given to WERS in 2010. There was a sizeable seven percentage point rise in the proportion who

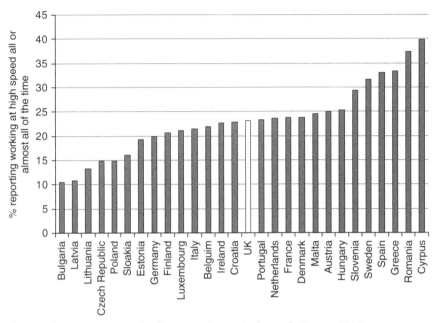

Figure 10.5   Intensive work effort – working to high speed, Europe, 2015

Source: Data extracted from the European Working Conditions Survey 2015 data visualisation tool on: http://eurofound.europa.eu/surveys/data-visualisation/sixth-european-working-conditions-survey-2015

strongly agreed that their job required that they work very hard. Furthermore, when asked if they had experienced any of a list of specified changes 'as a result of the most recent recession [in 2008–09]' while at their current workplace, 28 per cent reported an increase in workload. This was the second highest reported recession-induced experience (van Wanrooy *et al.*, 2014: 8, 40).

This pattern is reflected in the time respondents estimated that they worked at very high speeds. In 1992 around a quarter (23 per cent) said they worked at very high speeds three-quarters or more of the time. By 2001 the proportion had risen to 38 per cent and by 2012 it stood at 40 per cent. Similarly, the upward movement in intensive work effort is reflected in the rising proportion of respondents who reported that they worked under the pressure of tight deadlines. These tight deadline jobs rose from 52 per cent in 2001 to 55 per cent in 2006 and 58 per cent in 2012.

We can also use the data to examine which labour market segments have suffered most or least as a result of the intensification process. Such an analysis reveals that the pressure to work very hard has grown fastest among women

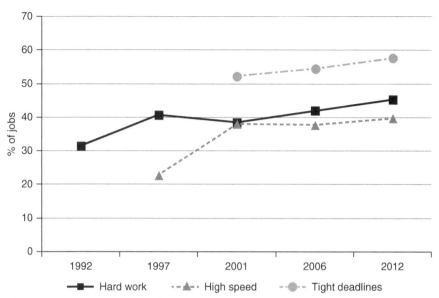

Figure 10.6   Intensive work effort in Britain, 1992–2012

Source: Felstead *et al.*, 2013b: figure 2.

in general and those who work full-time in particular. This gender difference echoes previous findings for the USA (Gorman and Kmec, 2007). In 1992 the gender gap was around two percentage points but by 2012 it had grown to eight points. Women working full-time appear to have suffered most, with 48 per cent of such jobs in 1997 requiring high effort levels rising to 57 per cent in 2012. This substantial expansion compares to a three-percentage-point rise for male full-timers and a two-point rise for female part-time workers over the same period. Moreover, female full-timers have experienced some of the largest rises in work intensity since 2006 (see Table 10.2).

From 1992 to 2012 required work intensity rose faster in the public sector than in the private sector. In 1992 around three in ten of all workers strongly agreed that their jobs required them to work very hard. However, by 2012 the proportion had risen to over half (55 per cent) of the public sector and around two-fifths (40 per cent) of the private sector. Within the public sector it was in the health industry where work intensification was especially sharp between 2006 and 2012 (see also Blackaby *et al.*, 2015). This is possibly reflection of the extension of 'new public management' into the public sector in the 2000s, followed by the austerity measures since 2010 which disproportionately affect women workers (Rubery and Rafferty, 2013). Thus nursing and medical professionals have seen their jobs change dramatically and have prompted junior doctors to take

Table 10.2   Percentage of jobs requiring hard work, 1992–2012

	1992	1997	2001	2006	2012
All	31.5	40.7	38.5	42.0	45.3
Gender					
Men	30.5	38.8	36.6	39.2	41.6
Women	32.6	43.1	40.7	45.2	49.6
Working time					
Women full-timers	NA	48.0	47.0	50.1	57.1
Women part-timers	NA	36.1	31.4	37.5	38.7
Sector					
Public sector industries	36.1	45.6	44.9	49.0	55.8
Private sector industries	29.7	38.9	35.9	38.8	40.7

Notes: To produce a consistent indicator of sector we define those working in public administration, education and health as 'public sector industries' and those working elsewhere as 'private sector industries'.

Source: Authors' calculations from the Skills and Employment Survey 1992–2012 updating Felstead *et al.*, 2013b: table 1.

industrial action in response (Menghji *et al.*, 2015). Parts of the private sector also experienced rapid rises in work effort over this period. The proportion of jobs requiring hard work in the construction industry, for example, rose by eleven percentage points, putting it on a par with education and health.

The requirement to work hard becomes stronger the higher the qualification level of worker. So, in 2012, a half of those with a degree or equivalent qualification strongly agreed that their job required them to work very hard. This is in contrast to those with no qualifications where around a third (35 per cent) of workers made similar claims. This difference has not changed over the last two decades, reflecting an enduring and widespread correlation between skill level and intensive work effort.

There is also evidence that the ratcheting up of work intensity has continued. A subset of those who took part in SES 2012 were re-interviewed in 2014. The evidence from this study suggests that, even over a relatively short time period, there was a tendency for jobs to become more intense. Increased use of computers and teamworking appeared to be driving the upward movement with both enhancing the level of surveillance possible by employers and/or fellow workers (Felstead *et al.*, 2016).

Conclusions

Comparing job quality over time and between countries is difficult due to the scarcity of data. The studies which do exist tend to focus on particular aspects of job quality where data are available. Working time is one such theme. Reductions in working time designed to share out declining volumes of employment and dampen the rise in unemployment following the 2008–09 recession sparked further interest in this feature of job quality. This labour market response received government backing in the case of Germany, and to a lesser extent France, but happened without it in the case of the UK (Bosch, 2010; Felstead, 2011; Kümmerling and Lehndorff, 2014). Yet even in the context of reductions in working time, newspaper commentaries continue to proclaim that workers in Britain work very long hours compared to those working elsewhere in Europe (e.g., *Daily Mirror*, 8 February 2014; *The Guardian*, 18 May 2010; *Daily Mail*, 25 February 2009; *The Sunday Times*, 10 June 2007). The aim of this chapter has been to subject this claim, as well as the associated one that work has become more intense, to robust empirical scrutiny. In conceptual terms the focus of the chapter is on two dimensions of work effort: its extensiveness and intensiveness.

The chapter makes four contributions to the debate. Firstly, it demonstrates that, on the whole, workers in Britain do not work the longest hours in Europe. However, the claim does apply to men who work full-time as employees, but not to all categories of worker. In fact, average hours of work for those who work part-time or are self-employed are below the EU28 average. When ranked this puts the UK in the bottom third of EU countries. Similarly, when compared against other OECD countries, UK working hours are below average and a long way short of countries whose working hours are much longer.

The chapter also puts data on the length of working hours in a much longer time horizon. It then becomes evident that the trajectory of travel for working hours has been downward since the late nineteenth century. This is our second contribution with recent evidence suggesting that these reductions have continued and may have accelerated somewhat with the preference for working-time adjustments rather than staffing cuts in response to the 2008–09 recession.

However, with respect to the intensity of work the data tell a different story, hence our third and fourth contributions to the debate. The third is that, when compared to other countries, the UK is towards the top of the European league table according to two out of three intensity indicators and about average for the third. The fourth and final contribution is that British workers are working harder, faster and to tighter deadlines than they did in the past. However, some have felt these pressures more than others. In particular, women workers and those working in the public sector have been hardest hit.

Based on the evidence concerning the detrimental health impacts of long and hard work, it can be inferred that the more intensive work effort in Britain may have contributed to at least some deteriorations in mental and physical health. According to Baumberg (2011, 2014), work intensification from the early 1990s can be linked to rises in incapacity benefit claims from then onwards, with those in poor health especially affected by work strain. More recent intensifications can only have exacerbated this tendency. Nevertheless, by contrast, the decline in working hours since the mid-1990s, including in the proportion of people working especially long hours, could have been expected to have led to an improvement in work-related health problems. Moreover, there are other, potentially equally important, sources of rising stress in the workplace, including the insecurities that grew after the Global Financial Crisis and the long-term decline in workplace autonomy. To illustrate, Green and colleagues (2016) found, using a decomposition analysis of the decline in work-related well-being between 2006 and 2012, that less than a fifth was attributable to changing intensive and extensive work effort.

Another negative conclusion can also be drawn, concerning the discourse on Britain's 'productivity puzzle'. Both the long-term lag of productivity in Britain behind similar economies in Europe and elsewhere, and the peculiar stagnation of labour productivity in Britain through the Global Financial Crisis are a source of concern and mystery occupying a large volume of researcher time (e.g. HM Treasury, 2015). Our findings – along with evidence that the skill levels of workers and their jobs in Britain have also increased (Felstead et al., 2013a) – can be of little help in resolving this puzzle. After all, the quality of labour inputs is improving, the skill demands of jobs have been increasing, the intensity of work is rising and hours in the long term have been falling. In these circumstances, one might have expected hourly productivity to be booming, notwithstanding the rising health costs and lost working days that have been reported. The solution to Britain's quest for greater productivity needs to be sought elsewhere, for example by raising aggregate demand and by remedying the lagging levels of investment and management skill, and not in a further intensification of work effort. Along with de Jong and colleagues (2016) we hold that employers' interest in combating the pressures of work stems not from altruism, but from a self-interested recognition that healthy employees are good for business performance.

Notes

1 While our preference is to report UK results, this is not always possible, with many surveys excluding Northern Ireland. Hence, some of the results apply to Britain and the UK; this is reflected in the text.

2 These figures are derived from a Nexis database search: https://nexis.com/. All English-language news sources were searched using the keywords 'Britain' or 'UK' and the phrase 'longest hours in Europe/the EU'. The search was restricted to items published between 1 January 1990 and 31 May 2016.

3 *The Sun*, 4 December 2006. Other references are less euphemistic; the Northern Ireland edition of the *News of the World* proclaimed, on 5 June 2011: 'Too much work and not enough play makes his penis feel very dull indeed and British men are particularly vulnerable since they work the longest hours in Europe.' The myth is not confined to the tabloids, as illustrated by features in *The Times* (28 June 2008), the *Independent on Sunday* (10 September 2006) and *The Guardian* (3 April 1998).

4 It should be noted that the Eurofound data visualisation tool which was used to download these data fails to provide an average; this is an estimate based on the pattern of results shown in Figure 10.4. The same applies to Figure 10.5.

References

Bassanini, A. and Caroli, E. (2014), *Is Work Bad for Health? The Role of Constraint vs Choice*, IZA (Institute of Labor Economics) Discussion Paper No. 7891.

Baumberg, B. (2011), 'The role of increasing job strain in deteriorating fitness-for-work and rising incapacity benefit receipt' (Ph.D. thesis, The London School of Economics and Political Science).

Baumberg, B. (2014), 'Fit-for-work – or work fit for disabled people? The role of changing job demands and control in incapacity claims', *Journal of Social Policy*, 43:2, 289–310.

Bird, D. (2004), 'Methodology for the 2004 Annual Survey of Hours and Earnings', *Labour Market Trends*, 112:11, 457–64.

Blackaby, D., Felstead, A., Jones, M., Makepeace, G., Murphy, P. and Vass, V. (2015), 'Is the public sector pay advantage explained by differences in job quality?', in Felstead, A., Gallie, D. and Green, F. (eds), *Unequal Britain at Work* (Oxford: Oxford University Press), pp. 147–66.

Bonney, N. (2005), 'Overworked Britons? Part-time work and work-life balance', *Work, Employment and Society*, 19:2, 391–401.

Bosch, G. (2010), 'Dismissing hours not workers: work-sharing in the economic crisis', in Heyes, J. and Rychly, L. (eds), *Labour Administration and the Economic Crisis: Challenges, Responses and Opportunities* (Geneva: International Labour Organization).

Cousins, C. R. and Tang, N. (2004), 'Working time and work and family conflict in the Netherlands, Sweden and the UK', *Work Employment and Society,* 18:3, 531–49.

Davies, S. C. (2014), *Annual Report of the Chief Medical Officer 2013, Public Mental Health Priorities: Investing in the Evidence* (London: Department of Health).

de Jong, T., Wiezer, N., de Weerd, M., Nielsen, K., Mattila-Holappa, P. and Mockałło, Z. (2016), 'The impact of restructuring on employee wellbeing: a systematic review of longitudinal studies', *Work and Stress*, 30:1, 91–114.

Eurofound (2012), *Trends in Job Quality in Europe* (Luxembourg: Publications Office of the European Union).

Eurofound (2015), *First Findings: Sixth European Working Conditions Survey* (Luxembourg: Publications Office of the European Union).

Felstead, A. (2011), 'Patterns of under-utilization in the Recession', *Skills in Focus* (Glasgow: Skills Development Scotland).

Felstead, A., Gallie, D. and Green, F. (eds) (2015), *Unequal Britain at Work* (Oxford: Oxford University Press).

Felstead, A., Gallie, D., Green, F. and Henseke, G. (2016), 'The determinants of skills use and work pressure: a longitudinal analysis', *Economic and Industrial Democracy*, http://eid.sagepub.com/content/early/2016/07/01/0143831X16656412.full.pdf+html, accessed 13 March 2017.

Felstead, A., Gallie, D., Green, F. and Inanc, H. (2013a), *Skills at Work in Britain: First Findings from the Skills and Employment Survey 2012* (London: Centre for Learning and Life Chances in Knowledge Economies and Societies: Institute of Education).

Felstead, A., Gallie, D., Green, F. and Inanc, H. (2013b), *Work Intensification in Britain: First Findings from the Skills and Employment Survey 2012* (London: Centre for Learning and Life Chances in Knowledge Economies and Societies: Institute of Education).

Felstead, A., Jewson, N. and Walters, S. (2005), *Changing Places of Work* (Basingstoke: Palgrave Macmillan).

Gallie, D. (ed.) (2013), *Economic Crisis, Quality of Work, and Social Integration* (Oxford: Oxford University Press).

Gordon, D. M. (1976), 'Capitalist efficiency and socialist efficiency', *Monthly Review*, 28:3, 19–39.

Gorman, E. H. and Kmec, J. A. (2007), 'We (have to) try harder: gender and required work effort in Britain and the United States', *Gender and Society*, 21:6, 829–56.

Green, F. (2001), '"It's been a hard day's night": the concentration and intensification of work in late twentieth-century Britain', *British Journal of Industrial Relations*, 39:1, 53–80.

Green, F. (2006), *Demanding Work: The Paradox of Job Quality in the Affluent Economy* (Princeton: Princeton University Press).

Green, F. (2008), 'Work effort and worker well-being in the age of affluence', in Cooper, C. and Burke, R. (eds), *The Long Work Hours Culture: Causes, Consequences and Choices* (Bradford: Emerald Group Publications).

Green, F., Felstead, A., Gallie, D. and Inanc, H. (2016), 'Job-related well-being through the Great Recession', *Journal of Happiness Studies*, 17:1, 389–411.

Guest, D.E. (1990), 'Have British workers been working harder in Thatcher's Britain? A re-consideration of the concept of effort', *British Journal of Industrial Relations*, 28:3, 293–312.

HM Treasury (2015), *Fixing the Foundations: Creating a More Prosperous Nation*, Cm 9098 (London: Her Majesty's Stationery Office).

Kivimaki, M., Virtanen, M., Ichiro Kawachi I., Nyberg, S. T., Alfredsson, L., Batty, G. D., Bjorner, J. B., Borritz, M., Brunner, E. J., Burr, H., Dragano, N., Ferrie, J. E., Fransson, E. I., Hamer, M., Heikkilä, K., Knutsson, A., Koskenvuo, M., Madsen, I. E. H., Nielsen, M. L., Nordin, M., Oksanen, T., Pejtersen, J. H., Pentti, J., Rugulies, R., Salo, P., Siegrist, J., Steptoe, A., Suominen, S., Theorell, T., Vahtera, J., Westerholm, P. J. M., Westerlund, H., Singh-Manoux, A., and Jokela, M. (2015), 'Long working hours, socio-economic status, and the risk of incident type 2 diabetes: a meta-analysis of published and unpublished data from 222 120 individuals', *Lancet Diabetes Endocrinol,* 3:1, 27–34.

Kümmerling, A. and Lehndorff, S. (2014), *The Use of Working Time-Related Crisis-Response Measures during the Great Recession*, Conditions of Work and Employment Series No. 44 (Geneva: International Labour Office).

Lee, J. and Lee, Y.K. (2016), 'Can working hour reduction save workers?' *Labour Economics,* 40, 25–36.

Lindsay, C. (2003), 'A century of labour market change: 1900 to 2000', *Labour Market Trends*, 111:3, 133–44.

Lyonette, C. and Crompton R. (2011), '"We both need to work": maternal employment, childcare and healthcare in Britain and the USA', *Work, Employment and Society,* 25:1, 34–50.

Menghji, S., Rajann, N. and Philpott, J. (2015), 'What does the junior contract mean for me, my patients and the NHS?', *Journal of the Royal Society of Medicine*, 108:12, 470–1.

ONS (Office for National Statistics) (2015), *Annual Survey of Hours and Earnings: 2015 Provisional Results* (Newport: ONS).

Rubery, J. (2015), 'Change at work: feminisation, flexibilisation, fragmentation and finan-cialisation', *Employee Relations,* 37:6, 633–44.

Rubery, J. and Fagan, C. (1995), 'Gender segregation in societal context', *Work, Employment and Society*, 9:2, 213–40.

Rubery, J. and Grimshaw, D. (2015), 'The 40-year pursuit of equal pay: a case of constantly moving goalposts', *Cambridge Journal of Economics*, 39:2, 319–43.

Rubery, J. and Rafferty, A. (2013), 'Gender, recession and austerity in the UK', in Karamessini, M. and Rubery, J. (eds), *Women and Austerity* (London: Routledge).

Smith, M., Burchell, B., Fagan, C. and O'Brien, C. (2007), 'Job quality in Europe', *Industrial Relations Journal*, 39:6, 586–603.

Thompson, E. P. (1967), 'Time, work-discipline, and industrial capitalism', *Past and Present*, 38, 56–97.

Van Wanrooy, B., Bewley, H., Bryson, A., Forth, J., Freeth, S., Stokes, L. and Wood, S. (2014), *The 2011 Workplace Employment Relations Survey: First Findings*, 4th edn (London: Department for Business Innovation and Skills).

Warren, T. and Lyonette, C. (2015), 'The quality of part-time work', in Felstead, A., Gallie, D. and Green, F. (eds), *Unequal Britain at Work* (Oxford: Oxford University Press), pp. 62–82.

11

Plague, patriarchy and 'girl power'

Jane Humphries

Introduction

The inspiration for this chapter comes from an earlier contribution, written with Jill Rubery in 1984, which surveyed theories of social reproduction and its relationship to the economy. We argued that the family, notwithstanding its extensive responsibilities for reproducing, training and socialising future workers, had not been established as an interesting, central and dynamic variable for economic analysis (Humphries and Rubery, 1984). Instead, across the whole spectrum of theoretical approaches, from the neoclassical to the Marxist/feminist, broadly similar methodologies dominated. These methodologies fell into two groups: (1) those which envisaged the family system as *absolutely autonomous*, that is, independent of the economy which therefore had to adapt and operate within its constraints; and (2) those which framed the relationship in *reductionist/functionalist* terms and so subsumed the family within the broader economic system. In the paper, we exposed flaws in both perspectives and demonstrated how several influential analyses failed to adhere to one methodology, but often flip-flopped incoherently between positions in order to explain social and economic change.

More constructively, we argued that what was needed was a theoretical approach which saw the organisation of social reproduction, taking place through the family, though in the modern era increasingly buttressed by educational, social and welfare services, as *relatively autonomous*. The system of social reproduction emerged as neither predetermined nor smoothly accommodating of economic changes; it must be understood as changing in response to economic development but itself subject to other powerful forces and in turn influencing economic trends. Essential to this relative autonomy was the identification of the borderlands between the spheres of production and social reproduction as terrain in which working people pushed back against the pressures of the economic system and sought space to improve their standard of living and exercise control over their own lives.

As a theoretical and position piece the paper has proved durable, providing insight into the co-evolution of economic structures and family life in both the past and the present. For gender scholars, it has proved valuable in understanding changes in the productive activities and family lives of women who mediate between the economy and social reproduction, their allocation of labour time often knitting together the ragged edges of the two spheres. Historically, it has proved particularly useful in analysing the pressures on family structures created by industrialisation, the transition to the so-called 'male breadwinner family structure' and more recently the time-poor, work-rich households of the twenty-first century. This chapter puts the ideas to work to explore another historical era which has been interpreted as emblematic both of the absolute autonomy of the family system and of its functionalist collapse into merely servicing the needs of the economy. The era is that of the demographic decimation caused by the Black Death. The elimination of up to 40 per cent of the labour force was a massive shock from which the economy took centuries to recover, not least because the plague made regular return visits, culling survivors of earlier bouts and ensuring that population was painfully slow to recover. The economic implications of this era have long fascinated historians and recently there has been particular interest in the impact on women's work, opportunities and family lives.

The post-Black Death era has been subject to both absolute autonomy and structuralist-functionalist interpretations, as we will see. It has also been identified as a historical watershed, setting in train the so called 'Little Divergence' whereby north-west Europe, defined loosely as a group of neighbouring economies clustered around the southern shores of the North Sea, Flanders, Brabant, Holland and England, embarked on slow but continuous and relatively reversal-free growth over many centuries, leaving behind an economically stagnant and prone-to-setbacks south and east, exemplified by the once-dominant Italy but including Spain and Portugal and the countries of eastern Europe (Broadberry et al., 2015). The relationship between the household and the economy and women's role within both is crucial to this new account of how the west got rich, and its study illustrates once again a persisting tension between absolute autonomy and structuralist-functionalist interpretations, neither of which provides a satisfactory frame. Seeing the era in terms of the relative autonomy of social reproduction provides a fresh lens on what are increasingly understood as pivotal developments in our history.

The chapter begins with a brief sketch of the ways in which classic theories of the family are dominated by the perception of industrialisation as the great divide. The pre-industrial era was falsely homogenised and seen as offering a natural and unchallenged fit between the economy and the household. Of course, historians were fully aware that neither medieval nor early modern society was as static as these theories suggested. The section titled 'The Black Death, the Golden Age and women's economic activities' focuses on a cataclysmic event which shattered the calm of the medieval world and had massive reverberations for both production and social reproduction: the Black Death. There is a large and growing literature on the post-Black Death era and specifically the ways in which demographic catastrophe affected women's economic position. The literature is seen to split into two strands with one captured by an absolutely autonomous interpretation of the reorganisation of economic and social reproduction and the other by a structuralist-functionalist account. In the section 'The Black Death, the north-west European marriage pattern and the "Little Divergence"' I show how the latter has been linked to influential readings of the '"Little Divergence"', providing a woman-centred interpretation of regional variations in long-run growth with north-west Europe, with England as the paradigm case, enjoying small but cumulative growth in advance of a stagnant south and east long before industrialisation. Recent research, including some of my own, is then used to trace how these interpretations suffer from an overly economistic theoretical frame and overlook the ways in which both the ruling elite and working people used the possibilities implicit in the shifting tectonic plates of production and reproduction to their own advantage. Women's roles were not cast in stone, but nor did they adapt smoothly to the evolving needs of the economy. Individuals and families sought to exploit new opportunities for their own advantage and to resist adaptations which they regarded with foreboding. They were not always successful, but their agency is at the heart of the case for the relative autonomy of social reproduction. Similarly, the state reacted to secure social control and protect the interests of the landed elite with unintended consequences for gender divisions, reinforcing the subordination of women and inhibiting their economic independence.

Theories of the family–economy interface

Structuralist-functionalist and evolutionary accounts of the household were essentially teleological, arguing back from a known present to a generally agreed-upon but imprecisely described and dated past. The historical development of the household unfolds as a process of differentiation (Parsons and Bales, 1965). A society undergoing economic change necessarily differentiates its household-based social structure. New institutions such as firms, schools, trade unions and the welfare state perform functions that had previously been undertaken in households. Of these, firms, the specialist units of production, were the most important. Differentiation drew a line between the household and economic activity. Kinship relations also undergo functional specialisation, becoming dominated by a system of small nuclear family units. The modern 'thin' family was adapted to the need for social and geographical mobility. The primary responsibility for household support came to rest on the male head, the 'breadwinner', whose 'job' linked the family to the economy from which it had become separated. The economic transition was accompanied by changes in ideas about decency and moral standards. The division of activities allowed values, such as selfishness and egotism, essential to the success of the modern economy to prevail in the marketplace while others, such as altruism and caring, could survive in the home, where they enabled breadwinners to be rejuvenated and children to be born, raised and socialised. In depicting the changes in the household as successful adaptations to the modern market economy, sociologists, historians and economists construed pre-industrial households as homogeneous, static and traditional.

Women played a role in these accounts, the pre-industrial household providing the space whereby they engaged in the subsistence production of food, clothing and shelter, as well as bearing and raising children and servicing the direct consumption needs of other family members. They could produce for the market but this was usually as part of a household production unit. With the industrial revolution subsistence opportunities shrivelled and work became limited to 'jobs' accessed via a labour market, organised by an employer and located in distinct and separate production sites. Once work required a continuous presence away from home, married women were left behind. Industrialisation represented the major challenge to the hitherto static fit between social reproduction and production, and it was this transition that dominated the theoretical accounts.

Not surprisingly, the depiction of the pre-industrial household and its relationship to the economy as static was consistent with an absolute autonomy interpretation of social reproduction. Gender history was home to a version of pre-industrial experience built around the ideas of patriarchal and biological continuities which were clearly visible in the social, legal and economic arrangements of medieval and early modern societies. Patriarchal continuities ruled in the household sphere but were not seen as problematic in the pre-industrial world of economic stasis. It was only with the appearance of capitalist production

processes, universal labour markets and modern manufacturing that social reproduction was transformed and alongside it women's roles in economy and society.

Both the absolute autonomy and stucturalist-functionalist models of the
household fell increasingly foul of growing empirical evidence, which suggested
that the relationship between industrialisation and the household was more
complex than implied. The idea of family history as fundamentally divided by
the era of industrialisation was increasingly challenged. Both long-run changes
and short-run variations in economic conditions shaped the organisation of social
reproduction. Many operated outside the time frame of the industrial revolution. For example, wage dependency, an important underlying cause of the high
frequency of small households in the English countryside, long preceded industrialisation, as did those small households. Surprising evidence demonstrated
that the English household was not only small and nuclear long before industrialisation but also remarkably homogeneous across time and space, with implications for England's precocious economic development to which we will return.

Consistent with the relatively autonomous thesis, the economy was not
alone in shaping and structuring households. There were other powerful forces.
Mortality grimly limited family size and shape and contributed to variation across
time and space. Cultural factors also mattered. Marriage became associated with
the formation of an independent household and contributed to the rarity with
which married children lived with parents. These cultural norms were not always
and everywhere functional for the smooth operation of the economy.

Moreover, polarising the history of the household into pre- and post-industrial
was increasingly out of synch with the revisionist view of the industrial revolution
as involving continuity as well as change. The vision of the medieval and early
modern economies as placing no new demands on the sphere of social reproduction no longer fit with economic historians' growing evidence that both eras saw
significant economic change and many challenges to the relationship between the
organisation of the family and the functioning of the economic system. None was
more dramatic than the demographic catastrophe of the Black Death.

The Black Death, the Golden Age and women's economic activities

The initial visitation of the Black Death in 1348–49 killed between 30 and 45
per cent of the English population. Recurrences meant that by the 1370s the
population had been halved. The result was a severe and prolonged labour shortage widely understood to have accelerated the demise of feudal relations and
provided some of the foundation stones for England's unique economic path.

The ways in which the Black Death nailed the coffin of English feudalism remain under discussion but what is not in doubt is that workers, especially but not only in agriculture, enjoyed a massive increase in both nominal and real wages as landowners struggled to recruit and retain labour. '[T]he evidence for a rise in both cash wages and real wages in the second half of the fourteenth century, coinciding with the sudden and sustained population decline … has been well established' (Penn and Dyer, 1990: 356). Phelps-Brown and Hopkins (1981) calculated that the daily wages in cash of skilled building labourers in Southern England increased by 66 per cent between the 1340s and the 1390s from 3d to around 5d per day while those of the unskilled almost doubled from around 1½d to 3d per day. It was a 'Golden Age' for the English peasantry now extensively calibrated as, for example, in Figure 11.1.

Medievalists have debated the extent to which women shared in this utopia. Some have argued that women's gains were even more marked than those of men as the labour shortage eroded the pre-existing gender division of labour. Women could now find employment in jobs which had earlier been reserved for

Figure 11.1   The real wages of unskilled farm labourers (by decade)

Notes: The real wage is computed as the annual nominal wage divided by the annual cost of a consumption basket (see Humphries and Weisdorf, 2015). The annual wage is obtained by multiplying the daily wage rate by 260 days.

Sources: Wages: Clark (2007). Cost of consumption basket: Allen (http://nuffield.ox.ac.uk/People/sites/Allen/SiteAssets/Lists/Biography%Sections/EditForm/london.xls.)

men, migrate to towns to work in the growing textile industries or commercial
service centres, and become members of an expanding class of household servants and so enjoy 'a high degree of economic independence' (Goldberg, 1986;
1992; see also Barron, 1989). It is not difficult to see this strand of the literature
in terms of a structuralist-functionalist view, with the gendered division of jobs
and the patriarchal authority of male heads of households shifting to accommodate the economy's need for labour and specifically the need for workers able
and willing to work away from home outside household divisions of labour and
lines of authority.

This rosy view did not, however, go unchallenged. Other historians argued
that whatever the implications of the Black Death for male workers, the organisation of social reproduction through the household retained women in traditional roles. '[W]omen tended to work in low-skilled, low-paid jobs ... This
was true in 1300 and it remained true in 1700' (Bennett, 1988: 278; 1996;
Mate, 1998). The rigid grip of the gender division of labour prevented women
from seizing or consolidating the opportunities created by the labour shortage.
In an influential article, Judith Bennett painted a picture not of decline from a
lost 'Golden Age' but of 'new designs embroidered on a cloth of oppression and
deprivation' and suggested that 'the presence of continuity presents us with the
discomforting possibility that the roots of women's subordination are embedded deeply in ourselves and the men around us' (Bennett, 1988: 279–80). The
sphere of social reproduction dictated norms and structures, which the economy
could only exploit not change.

A lively debate ensued about the continuities of gender subordination even
in a world where labour was at a premium, with feminist historians taking
an absolute autonomy view and arguing for the 'triumph of patriarchal structures ... over demographic crisis' (Bardsley, 1999: 29; 2001). Their opponents,
in structuralist mode, found it impossible to contemplate a situation where the
organisation of the household did not give way to the needs of the economy:
'a situation where women's labour was both excessively cheap and reluctantly
and sparingly used by farmers is hard to sustain' (Hatcher, 2001: 195; see also
Langdon, 2011; Rigby, 2000).

Empirical case studies from the medieval economy were cited in support of
both views. Caroline Barron found that for medieval London 'the picture of the
lifestyle of women ... is quite a rosy one; their range of options and prospects
differed only slightly from those of the men who shared their level of prosperity' (Barron, 1989: 47–8), though she found the position changing in the course
of the sixteenth century, when the resumption of growth in the population
militated against the employment of women, a view shared by other authors
(see also Casey, 1976; Elliott, 1981). Similarly, P. J. P. Goldberg argued that

throughout the Middle Ages women living in towns could support themselves, though he too suspected that their independence grew more precarious as the fifteenth century drew to a close (Goldberg, 1986). On the other hand, John Langdon in a detailed study of Old Woodstock through the ravages of the Black Death argued that wage structures reflected 'deeply entrenched attitudes among the suppliers and consumers of labour' which kept wages, including the gender pay gap, largely stable (Langdon, 2011: 29). The debate has simmered on, kept alive by fresh empirical interventions which support one reading or another. Even more importantly, it has been seized on by other scholars working on a larger canvas and integrated into a meta-theory of economic growth that surprisingly has women at its centre. Unfortunately, this female-centred account of growth remains trapped between an understanding of the family/household as wholly autonomous or as totally determined by the needs of the economy. The relative autonomy perspective provides a way forward.

The Black Death, the north-west European marriage pattern and the 'Little Divergence'

Demographers had long noted a difference in household functioning and structures across Europe, demarcated by an imaginary line drawn from Trieste in the south to St Petersburg in the north. John Hajnal (1965) had reported how households in the south and east refreshed their labour supplies through marriage, with young couples moving in with the groom's parents, while households in the north and west relied on 'servants', the children of other often unrelated households who circulated within the economy working on a contractual basis and acquiring skills and accumulating wages. Girls as well as boys, women as well as men and the relatively prosperous as well as the poor all participated in this circulation of labour, which according to the demographers fitted structurally with a distinct demographic regime. The widespread practice of living as a servant away from the family of origin accommodated a prolonged adolescence and fostered later marriage. While women in the south and east normally married as teenagers, those in the north and west married much later, well into their twenties, or indeed never married, with the corollary that population growth was restrained. Within this 'north-west European marriage pattern' (NWEMP), as it became known, marriage involved the formation of an independent household, a possibility dependent on prior accumulation by the young couple, requiring in turn a period of time in service earning wages and incidentally gathering experience and learning skills. The elements of the NWEMP fitted together as a structuralist-functionalist pre-industrial system: (prolonged) life-cycle service, later marriage, accumulation by servants of both sexes and the foundation on this basis of independent nuclear households.

Hajnal emphasised the ways in which women's involvement in life-cycle service broke down patriarchy. 'While in service, women were not under the control of any male relative. They made independent decisions about where to live and work and for which employer' (Hajnal, 1982: 474–5). In this sense, the hypothesis of a NWEMP is a challenge to those gender historians who saw absolutely autonomous patriarchal households as impervious to economic opportunities.

While the elements of the NWEMP all neatly interlock, combining the organisation of production and social reproduction, the system's origins and evolution were not specified. One recent intriguing hypothesis has linked the emergence of the NWEMP to the economic conditions that prevailed in those parts of Europe particularly ravaged by plague. In a key article, Tine de Moor and Jan Luiten van Zanden argued that the labour shortage that followed the Black Death resulted in 'a strong increase in real earnings especially for women ... [and] accelerated the general adoption of the NWEMP ... particularly among servants' (2010: 11). De Moor and van Zanden also linked the new economic opportunities for women and their resulting independence to the relatively favourable environment provided by north-west religious, social and political institutions.

In positing this 'girl-powered Little Divergence' (GPLD), De Moor and van Zanden were joined by powerful allies as other authors argued that women's improved position in the post-plague labour market and especially the growth of opportunities as servants in husbandry was further boosted by landowners' response to labour scarcity. The latter involved the relative expansion of *horn*, that is, pastoral agriculture in which it was argued women had a comparative advantage, versus *corn* (generically, grain) production in which it was argued they did not. The shift from arable to pastoral allegedly pushed up female wages and so boosted female labour force participation (Voigtländer and Voth, 2013). Alert readers might notice here the oscillation between a structuralist-functionalist approach in seeing women unconstrained by pre-existing patriarchal structures in their seizure of the new opportunities and an absolute autonomy biological determinism in thinking women possessed a natural advantage in pastoral agriculture and disadvantage in crop production.

Not only were the origins of the NWEMP in the post-Black Death labour market, but its spread enabled north-west Europe to escape the Malthusian trap that continued to hold other regions to subsistence levels and kick-started continuous and compounded, albeit low-level, growth. Thus Nico Voigtländer and Hans-Joachim Voth see fertility restriction emerging as an indirect consequence of the abundance of land after 1348–50. The Black Death, they argued, raised 'land-labour ratios and thus wages … raising female employment opportunities outside the peasant household' (Voigtländer and Voth, 2013: 2229). The result was an increased average age at first marriage for women which reduced fertility rates and 'in turn lowered population pressure in a Malthusian setting and helped to keep wages high'(Voigtländer and Voth, 2013: 2260). The Black Death had a silver lining in the north-west's early break with Malthusian stagnation. Women were the key agents in this great escape.

Thus marriage-regulated population and precocious escape from a Malthusian subsistence equilibrium has come to be seen as a distinctive feature of the north-west, which explains why this area began to grow in advance of the rest of Europe, and indeed the world, long before industrialisation. Yet these ideas were primarily theoretical or based on often contentious macroeconomic approaches (Clark, 2007; van Zanden, 2009; Malanima, 2009; Acemoglu and Robinson, 2012). Other empirical evidence did not always seem to justify the sharp divisions implied in the nomenclature of *divergence* (McCants, 2015). Moreover, the demographic zones do not seem to presage relative economic development in the way predicted (Dennison and Ogilvie, 2014). Yet there is an obvious empirical test. If England escaped a Malthusian trap in the post-plague era because women could earn higher wages as servants and so postponed marriage, there should be evidence in the historical record on remuneration. The problem is that, unlike men's wages which have been extensively documented (see Figure 11.1), there was no comparable wage data for women. The reasons are clear. Women's economic activities are hard to capture. Data on their remuneration is fragmentary and difficult to interpret. Women were more likely paid as part of a team, by task or in kind. Day wages, where they exist, must be compared with annual contracts that usually involved board and lodging for which a value must be imputed. Together with Jacob Weisdorf, I augmented existing collections of data put together by intrepid historians with additional archival research and compiled a wage series for women workers (Humphries and Weisdorf, 2015). Among its uses is the light it throws on the hypothesis of a GPLD.

It is relevant here that there were two distinct forms of female employment: daily wage labour, often on a casual basis, and the annual service central to the NWEMP, which usually involved living-in and so was partially remunerated in the form of room and board. We collected and processed observations related to both types of employment and so provided two separate series: (1) daily wages; and (2) the equivalent remuneration implicit in longer-term contracts (for an account of how we imputed values for board and lodging and dealt with other problems in making the annual data comparable, see Humphries and Weisdorf, 2015: 407–17). Both series relate to unskilled women defined according to the

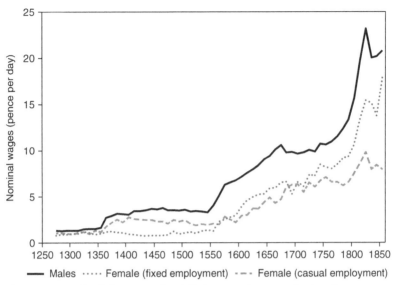

Figure 11.2   The daily wages of unskilled men and women (by decade)

Notes: This figure shows the nominal day rates of men and women by decade. Women's remunerations are divided into those paid for casual employment and those paid for annual employment. Annual and weekly payments are turned into day rates on the assumption of a five-day work week (totalling 260 working days per year).

Sources: Humphries and Weisdorf, 2015.

Historical International Classification of Occupations (HISCO) and associated social class scheme (HISCLASS). Figure 11.2 presents our main findings in terms of the evolution of both types of female wages (decadal averages are reported in an appendix to the published paper). Male wages are reproduced for comparison. The published paper (Humphries and Weisdorf, 2015) explores these trajectories in comparison with men's wages and for what they imply about the length of the working year. Here my focus is on the implications for the GPLD.

Women's wages and the GPLD

The wage trajectories in the two segments of the female labour market are very different and cast light on how both working households and landlords responded to the post-plague situation and sought to modify the range and type of women's activities, and so shift the interface between production and social reproduction to their advantage. Focusing on the post-plague era, it is clear that women's casual wages enjoyed an almost immediate boost similar though not as large as that of men, while wages for women in annual service remained stagnant, even allowing generously for the value of perquisites. The rise in casual remuneration made day labour more attractive in comparison with annual service. This gap was recognised by both contemporaries and labour historians who reported that workers in the late Middle Ages preferred employment on a daily or weekly basis because it offered the possibility of higher returns and more leisure (Bailey, 1994: 162; Dyer, 1980: 367–9; Kenyon, 1962; McIntosh, 1986; Poos, 1991: 218–20). Employers, too, would surely have been keen to take up the cheaper ex-annual worker to replace the more expensive day worker. Why movement between types of employment did not erode the gap is a key question.

One obvious consideration is that annual contracts carried with them security of employment. If women were unsure of sufficient casual work for their support, they would be prepared to accept the drawbacks of annual service. Undoubtedly this was partially the case. Several historians have expressed doubts as to whether there was enough employment throughout the calendar year to match servants' earnings in cash and kind (Hatcher, 2011; Langdon, 2011; Poos, 1991). But given that it would only have required half of the year at medieval casual rates to match the annual pay (including the value of board and lodging) in service (Humphries and Weisdorf, 2016: 418–20), young and healthy women might have been persuaded that occasional labouring jobs, in addition to seasonal work in agriculture or opportunities in cloth production, would see them through. A second consideration hinges on the types of women who inhabited the two sectors and the nature of the medieval labour market.

As the term 'life-cycle service' (Laslett, 1965) implies, annual servants were understood to be predominantly younger unmarried women. Living-in after marriage created problems for both servants and employers. Indeed, in the NWEMP it was the exclusion from lucrative service on marriage that prompted women to stay single. Although perhaps the empirical evidence suggests a less crisp mapping between marital status and labour market segment, with plenty of older and most likely married women observed working in service, in general this assumption is supported. But even if older married women were institutionally barred from annual service, they were not confined to working unpaid in the household. In our investigation of wages, we found many *mulieri* or *uxori* (older women) in casual work and so able to take advantage of the booming wages, but they did so in ways which nudged rather than challenged the organisation of social reproduction, for many such women accessed their employment through their husbands, working alongside them in husbandry, trades or crafts, or recruited by them to work for the same employer. They worked in family-based production teams transferred from the household to the fields, forests, mines, forges, building sites, gentry's houses and estates of the medieval economy via an accommodating labour market. As a result, they took the authority structures of the household into those same workplaces.

One powerful example comes from a unique source: the weekly account of an early fifteenth-century forgemaster, surviving in the records of the Durham Cursitor. The bishops of Durham, in their capacity as Earls Palatine during the Middle Ages, enjoyed the proprietorship of all mines within the bounds of the count palatine of Durham. Such mines were usually farmed out but Bishop Langley in 1408 tried the experiment of smelting and working his own iron. The resulting account roll survived and was transcribed and annotated at the end of the nineteenth century by Gaillard Thomas Lapsley (1899). The accounts record the employment of several workmen paid by the piece from December 1408 to November 1409. The men had clearly defined duties, were paid regularly and their output recorded so that both piece rates and average daily and weekly earnings can be computed. There was probably also a small body of ordinary less-skilled labourers employed under the direction of a 'forman'. Two named women were also employed performing miscellaneous unskilled but onerous tasks which varied from breaking up the ironstone (*petras frangere*) to blowing the bellows (*belowes sufflans*). Although the women's pay varied, at around 2½d per day (Lapsley, 1899: n. 11) it was slightly less than the casual rate but well above the annual rate computed as a daily equivalent according to the Humphries and Weisdorf series (2015: 431). Moreover, the work seems to have been plentiful, although the women did not work continuously.

Hiring was nepotistic. The two women who had access to this economically attractive employment were the wives of the smith and the foreman and although sometimes employed on specific tasks and paid individually, the women were more frequently employed helping their husbands, in which case they received a fixed rate of ½d per *blome*, that is unit, of iron produced. Their help most likely raised the productivity of their husbands and boosted the men's earnings. Finally, although both women feature regularly in the accounts, they did not work continuously, enjoying both the many 'festivals' – that is, idle days of the medieval calendar – and other unexplained absences. Their labour at the forge left some time for them to fulfil their domestic responsibilities in the households of the smith and the foreman.

This one example can be replicated from across the economy: in lead mines; in building repairs; in shepherding; in arable agriculture; in domestic service; and in crafts and trades (for other examples, see Humphries and Weisdorf, 2015: 411). These suggest that women accessing the Golden Age casual labour market often did so as part of a labour unit that was based on the household and so did not grant the independence that threatened patriarchal authority; and although space and time was left for women to complete unpaid work in their homes, reduced leisure relative to husbands may already have been implied in a medieval double shift. Simultaneously, the participation of such husband and wife teams within wage labour reinforced and perhaps even spread the nuclear family structures from which they emanated.

What, however, stopped younger women from seeking increasingly more lucrative employment in the casual labour market and instead apparently persisting in much less rewarding annual service? The social norms of the era discouraged younger women from hiring themselves by the day and moving from job to job (Roberts, 2005; Speechley, 1999; Whittle, 2005). Mobility and independence branded them as disreputable, even immoral. Annual service was considered more appropriate mainly because contrary to Hajnal's account (see above) it was associated with the maintenance of male authority and young female subordination. Some independent-minded young spinsters resisted the social norms and can be detected in the historical record working for day wages: the 'mayds in the craine' who worked regularly driving machinery via a treadmill on a Chester construction site; and, the women who 'puled flax' or 'brake hemp and swynglye' for the Shuttleworths of Gawthorpe (Harland, 1857: 56; 1857: 61; Rideout, 1928). Such women sought protection from sexual predation and charges of immorality as they roamed in search of employment by working in teams with other women shearing sheep, swingling hemp, digging peats, haymaking, weeding and labouring on construction sites. And often they too also carried the family's lines of authority into the labour market by working in family-based teams in order to combine attractive wages and untarnished reputations. Working alongside fathers, mothers or brothers meant that young women could access day wages while remaining within patriarchal or at least familial oversight.

Thus the post-plague labour shortage undoubtedly put pressure on the conventional social controls, but economic rationality was insufficient to break down the ways in which women were channelled into different sectors of the labour market according to their age, marital status and other circumstances and arbitrage away the casual–annual differential (see Figure 11.2). Understanding why requires attention to a missing piece of the story: the mobilisation of the repressive state apparatus. The persistently low pay of women in annual service was a consequence of the intervention of the medieval state acting in the interests of the landlords with the passing of the Ordinance and Statute of Labourers in 1349 and 1351.

Most economic historians agree that the labourers and artificers who survived the Black Death, including women, sought to take advantage of their scarcity and obtain higher wages for their labour. In England, as elsewhere the ruling class's response to the sudden increase in the peasantry's power was a mix of concession and repression, with the latter exemplified by legislation to hold wages and prices down to levels prevailing before the plague (Putnam, 1939). While the extent to which the Ordinance and Statute of Labourers was enforced remains debatable, the law's intentions were clear. Firstly, all able-bodied men and women free and bond, without definite means of support, were commanded to accept service at the rate of wages that had existed before the Black Death: the compulsory service clause. Secondly, reapers, mowers and other workmen or servants were forbidden to leave their masters within the term of their contracts, without reasonable cause or permission, and other masters were forbidden to eloign workers or employ runaways: the contract clause. Thirdly, nobody was to give or receive higher wages than were customary: the wages clause (Putnam, 1908). The provisions were intended to prevent workers from exploiting labour scarcity and holding up employers at key moments in crop production. Note that the provisions applied to women as well as men and that the contract was to be by the year or other usual term and *never by the day*.

Even if patchily enforced, these ordinances raised the costs of mobility and involved risks for recalcitrant workers, some of whom were whipped, humiliated in the stocks, returned to vindictive masters and perhaps ultimately cowed. In lists of offenders against the Statute women loom large and were singled out for harsh treatment (Penn, 1987; Putnam, 1908; Thompson, 1904). Moreover, the Statute was used against female harvest workers seeking to exploit the labour scarcity not just for taking excessive wages, but for moving from place to place (Poos, 1991). Evidence suggests that the compulsory service clause was particularly oppressive to women, for '[e]qual numbers of women and men in presentments (court records) probably translated, in the world outside the courtroom, into a practice of compulsory service that was predominantly, perhaps overwhelmingly, female' (Bennett, 2010: 23).

The Statute and Ordinance were not intended to bear down with particular force on women workers but in practice they were bound to do so for the categories they evoked were patriarchal and paternalistic and made women offenders easier to identify and charge. Moreover, these laws gave force to a suspicion of masterless persons, with unmarried women living and working on their own the most mistrusted. This legal prejudice persisted well into the early modern era when there is mounting evidence that it was the young unmarried woman who was most vigorously forced into service (Bennett, 2010; Middleton, 1988; Scott, 1973). Middleton, for example, cites Gregory King's estimate that there were 300,000 women in service in 1695 compared with 260,000 men and concludes that 'the protection which service offered against the uncertainties and irregularity of the labour market may have been extended to rather more women than men, but it did so only by reaffirming their subservient status'

(Middleton, 1988: 32). So, although the authorities' coercion of those 'out of service' back into subordinate employment, and more generally the repressive reaction to the presumption of the peasantry, was intended to maintain social order and keep general wage levels down, an incidental effect was that women, especially young women, bore the brunt of the backlash. Gender subordination was reinforced as a by-product of class struggle in this dramatic episode of English history as it was, too, in other times and places (Humphries, 1977).

Conclusions

Recent theorisations of variations in long-run economic performance draw attention to divergence within Europe – whereby the north-west, particularly England, moved ahead – and link this lead to the region's later age of marriage, and slower population growth. This interpretation has been embellished by linking the demographic pattern to life-cycle service, interpreting such service as a consequence of the Black Death, and positioning women at the centre of the account: a 'girl-powered Little Divergence' (GPLD). The model is characterised, like many which preceded it, by an inconsistent oscillation between an absolutely autonomous system of social reproduction, with biologically determinist overtones, and a completely derivative family system, which changes smoothly in response to economic opportunities. It is the latter which is emphasised in the GPLD which assumes that women who worked as annual servants enjoyed higher wages following the Black Death and that this was the cause of their delayed marriage.

A newly available series of women's wages observed in both annual and casual employment and over the very long run enables this assumption to be tested. The results are negative, for female servants' wages remained stagnant over the post-plague period providing no support for the GPLD hypothesis. If the Black Death, and women's response to it, did create the west via the GPLD it is not evident in wage patterns. Instead, the latter are interpreted as reflecting a contestation over women's roles as the relatively autonomous system of social reproduction responded to the chronic post-plague labour shortage. While workers struggled to improve their position, their responses were pattered by the conventional norms that structured family lives. While employers sought to repress assertive peasants, their clampdown reflected patriarchal ideas of dominance and subordination and was more easily imposed on younger unmarried women.

The post-plague interface between the organisation of social reproduction and the economy was not redrawn only by the needs of the economy; nor did it indicate only the continuities of patriarchy. It also reflected how people sought to seize opportunities, secure advancement, defend privilege, control subordinates and throw off oppressors – all while freighted with inherited values and constrained by pre-existing institutions. Conceptualising social reproduction as relatively autonomous requires attention to agency, class, state and history. Such a frame explains why the 'Golden Age' glittered far less brightly for women. As casual workers, they were all too often employed alongside and under the direction of husbands or fathers, their productivity and earnings subsumed in the men's remuneration. As annual servants, they struggled to evade legislation which required they work at customary wages on restrictive contracts. In the long and drawn-out struggle between landlords and workers which followed the Black Death, both sides projected patriarchal ideals of dominance and subordination and exhibited a fear of female autonomy. Not surprisingly then, despite the chimera of new opportunities and booming wages, outcomes for women were often but 'new designs embroidered on a cloth of oppression and deprivation'.

References

Acemoglu, D. and Robinson, J. A. (2012), *Why Nations Fail: The Origins of Power, Prosperity and Poverty* (London: Profile Books).

Bailey, M. (1994), 'Rural Society', in Horrox R. (ed.), *Fifteenth-Century Attitudes: Perceptions of Society in Late Medieval England* (Cambridge: Cambridge University Press), pp. 150–68.

Bardsley, S. (1999), 'Women's work reconsidered: gender and wage differentiation in late medieval England', *Past and Present*, 165, 3–29.

Bardsley, S. (2001), 'Reply', *Past and Present*, 173, 199–202.

Barron, C. M. (1989), 'The 'Golden Age' of women in Medieval London', *Reading Medieval Studies*, 15, 35–58.

Bennett, J. (1988), '"History that stands still": women's work in the European past', *Feminist Studies*, 14, 269–83.

Bennett, J. (2010), 'Compulsory service in late medieval England', *Past and Present*, 209:1, 7–51.

Broadberry, S., Campbell, B. M. S., Klein, A., Overton, M. and van Leeuwen, B. (2015), *British Economic Growth 1270–1870* (Cambridge: Cambridge University Press).

Casey, K. (1976), 'The Cheshire cat: reconstructing the experience of medieval women', in Carroll, B. (ed.), *Liberating Women's History* (Urbana: University of Illinois), pp. 224–49.

Clark, G. (2007), 'The long march of history: farm wages, population and economic growth, England 1209–1869', *Economic History Review*, 60, 97–136.

De Moor, T. and van Zanden, J. L. (2010), 'Girlpower: the European marriage pattern and labour markets in the north sea region in the late medieval and early modern period', *Economic History Review*, 63, 1–33.

Dennison, T. and Ogilvie, S. (2014), 'Does the European marriage pattern explain economic growth?', *Journal of Economic History*, 74:3, 651–693.

Dyer, C. (1980), *Lords and Peasants in a Changing Society: The Estates of the Bishopric of Worcester, 680–1540* (Cambridge: Cambridge University Press).

Elliott, V. (1981), 'Single women in the London marriage market: age, status, and mobility, 1598–1619', in Outhwaite R. B. (ed.), *Marriage and Society* (London: Europa), pp. 81–100.

Goldberg, P. J. P. (1986), 'Female labour, service and marriage in the late Medieval urban economy', *Northern History*, 22, 18–38.

Goldberg, P. J. P. (1992), *Women, Work, and Life Cycle in a Medieval Economy: Women in York and Yorkshire c. 1300–1520* (Oxford: Clarendon Press).

Hajnal, J. (1965), 'European marriage patterns in perspective', in Glass, D. V. and Eversley, E. C. (eds), *Population in History: Essays in Historical Demography* (London: Edward Arnold).

Hajnal, J. (1982), 'Two kinds of preindustrial household formations systems', *Population and Development Review*, 8:3, 449–94.

Harland, J. (1856–57), *The House and Farm Accounts of the Shuttleworths of Gawthorpe Hall in the County of Lancashire at Smithils and Gawthorpe*, parts I and II, Vols 35 and 41 (Chetham Society).

Hatcher, J. (2001), 'Women's work reconsidered: gender and wage differentiation in late medieval England', *Past and Present*, 173, 191–8.

Hilton, R. H. (1975), *The English Peasantry in the Later Middle Ages* (Oxford: Clarendon).

Humphries, J. (1982), 'Class struggle and the persistence of the working-class family', *Cambridge Journal of Economics*, 1:3 (1977) 241–258. Reprinted in Held, D. and Giddens, A. (eds), *Class Conflict and Power: A Reader* (London: Macmillan), pp. 470–91.

Humphries, J. and Rubery, J. (1984), 'The reconstitution of the supply side of the labour market: the relative autonomy of social reproduction', *Cambridge Journal of Economics*, 8:4, 331–46.

Humphries, J. and Weisdorf, J. (2015), 'The wages of women in England, 1260–1850', *Journal of Economic History*, 75:2, 405–47.

Kenyon, N. (1962), 'Labour conditions in Essex in the reign of Richard II', in Carus Wilson, E. M. (ed.), *Essays in Economic History* (London: Edward Arnold).

Langdon, J. (2011), 'Minimum wages and unemployment rates in medieval England: the case of Woodstock, Oxfordshire, 1256–1357', in Dodds, B. and Liddy, C. D. (eds), *Commercial Activity, Markets and Entrepreneurs in the Middle Ages* (Woodbridge: Boydell Press).

Lapsley, G. T. (1899), 'The account roll of a fifteenth century Iron Master', *Economic History Review*, 14, 509–29.

Laslett, P. (1965), *The World We Have Lost* (London: Methuen).

McCants, A. (2015), 'Historical demography', in Scott, H. (ed.), *Oxford Handbook of Early Modern European History, 1350–1750* (Oxford: Oxford University Press), pp. 119–44.

McIntosh, M. K. (1986), *Autonomy and Community: The Royal Manor of Havering, 1200–1500* (Cambridge: Cambridge University Press).

Malanima, P. (2009), *Pre-modern European Economy: One Thousand Years* (Leiden: Brill).

Mate, M. (1998), *Daughters, Wives and Widows after the Black Death: Women in Sussex, 1350– 1535* (Woodbridge: Boydell Press).

Middleton, C. (1988), 'The familiar fate of the famulae: gender divisions in the history of wage labour', in Pahl, R. E. (ed.), *On work: Historical, Comparative and Theoretical Approaches* (Oxford: Blackwell), pp. 21–47.

Parsons, T., and Bales, R. F. (1965), *Family, Socialization, and Interaction Process* (Glencoe, IL: Free Press).

Penn, S. A. C. (1987), 'Female wage earners in late fourteenth century England', *Agricultural History Review*, 35, 10–14.

Penn, S. A. C. and Dyer, C. (1990), 'Wages and earnings in late medieval England: evidence from the enforcement of the labour laws', *Economic History Review*, 43, 356–76.

Phelps Brown, H. and Hopkins, S. V. (1981), *A Perspective of Wages and Prices* (London, Methuen).

Poos, L. R. (1991), *A Rural Society After the Black Death: Essex 1350–1525* (Cambridge: Cambridge University Press).

Putnam, B. (1908), *The Enforcement of the Statute of Labourers During the First Decade After the Black Death, 1349–59* (London: P.S. King & Sons).

Putnam, B. (1939), 'Yorkshire Sessions of the Peace, 1361–1364', *Yorkshire Archaeological Society*, Red Series Vol C.

Richie, N. (1962), 'Labour conditions in Essex in the reign of Richard II', in Carus Wilson, E. M. (ed.), *Essays in Economic History* (London: Edward Arnold), pp. 91–111.

Rideout, E. (1928), 'The account book of the New Haven Chester, 1567–8', *Transactions of the Historical Society of Lancashire and Cheshire*, 80, 86–128.

Rigby, S. H. (2000), 'Gendering the Black Death: women in late medieval England', *Gender and History*, 12:3, 745–54.

Roberts, M. F. (1981), 'Wages and wage earners in England, 1563–1725. The evidence of the wage assessments' (Unpublished DPhil. thesis, University of Oxford).

Roberts, M. F. (2005), 'Recovering a lost inheritance: the marital economy and its absence from the prehistory of economics in Britain', in Ågren, M. and Erickson, A. M. (eds), *The Marital Economy in Scandinavia and Britain, 1400–1900* (Aldershot: Ashgate), pp. 239–56.

Speechley, H. V. (1999), 'Female and child agricultural day labourers in Someret, c. 1685– 1870' (Unpublished PhD thesis, University of Exeter).

Thompson, E. M. (1904), 'Offenders against the Statute of Labourers in Wiltshire AD 1349', *Wiltshire Archaeological and Natural History Magazine*, 33, 384–409.

Van Zanden, J. L. (2009), *The Long Road to the Industrial Revolution: The European Economy in a Global Perspective* (Leiden: Brill).

Van Zanden, J. L. (2011), 'The Malthusian intermezzo: women's wages and human capital formation between the late Middle Ages and the demographic transition of the 19th century', *History of the Family*, 16, 331–42.

Voigtländer, N. and Voth, H. J. (2013), 'How the west 'invented' fertility restrictions', *American Economic Review*, 103, 2227–64.

12

The two-child policy in China: a blessing or a curse for the employment of female university graduates?

Fang Lee Cooke

Introduction

The negative impact of the mothering role on women's participation in the labour market has been well examined in the western context, where women with childcare responsibilities often assume part-time employment or take a career break (e.g. Fagan and Rubery, 1996). Policy attention, albeit with varying level of success, has been directed to address gender inequality in employment, particularly in nation states of the European Union (see Grimshaw and Rubery, 2015; Rubery, 2013). By contrast, while a significant level of gender equality in employment in China has been achieved during the state-planned economy period, measured by the extent of women's participation in full-time employment and the relatively small gender pay gap (Gustafsson and Li, 2000; Nie *et al.*, 2002), gender discrimination has increased substantially as a result of the deepening marketisation of the economy since the 1980s in China (Cooke, 2012). In particular, labour market discrimination against women of childbearing age, especially against female university graduates, is a salient feature.

To date, female university graduates' employment in China and the longer-term impact of recent social policies on their economic and social well-being have received limited research attention outside China. Yet this is not a small cohort of the labour force with a relatively high level of human capital. Owing to the dramatic expansion of higher education (HE) since the early 2000s, some 7.7 million students graduated from HE institutions in 2016 compared with 2.12 million in 2003. In 2014, women made up approximately 52.1 per cent of undergraduate students, 51.6 per cent of postgraduate and 36.9 per cent of PhD students (The State Council of China, 2015). This has led to the oversupply of graduates who are deemed over-qualified but under-skilled by many employers who seek practical skills and work experience. A direct labour market consequence for these graduates is a prolonged period of unemployment, under-employment and a falling wage premium (Li *et al.*, 2016). According to Huang and Bosler (2014), the wage premium paid to HE graduates fell by 19 per cent since the late 2000s.

Women make up 45 per cent of HE graduates and, since the ending of the state job allocation system in the 1990s, have encountered increasing sex discrimination in employment largely due to their mothering role (Cooke, 2012). While labour regulation is in place to protect female workers against unlawful discrimination, non-compliance is the norm, even within the state sector and government organisations (Cooke, 2001). For example, in the banking sector where more than half the workforce are female graduates, branch managers often specify the number of female employees who are allowed to become pregnant each year in order to ensure staffing levels. What drives this endemic discrimination? What strategy do (some of the) female university students adopt, for example, entering motherhood early/prematurely, to enhance their employment prospects? And how may this strategy affect others concerned?

In late 2015, the Chinese government ended the one-child policy that was imposed on the nation since the early 1980s to allow each married couple to have two children (with effect from 2016) in order to address emerging social issues related to the ageing population. What impact is this new policy having on women, particularly female university graduates? It is important to note that university students are relatively young in China, even at the Masters and PhD degree level, with the majority still in their twenties upon graduation, and only a very small proportion become mothers during their study period. The relaxation of birth-control policy and the discriminatory response of employers are therefore likely to exert further pressure on young female university students. What is, then, the broader social cost of the two-child policy?

At the same time, one labour market consequence of the oversupply of inexperienced university graduates is the growth of informal employment,[1] a form of employment that already makes up over 60 per cent of employment for the national workforce. The proportion of university graduates taking up informal employment has been rising in recent years. A survey of 2,009 graduates found that 22 per cent chose self-employment (自主创业) as their preferred mode of employment, a substantial increase from just 6 per cent in 2008. This trend might reflect the decline of jobs in the labour market as a result of the Global Financial Crisis (cited in Liao and Wu, 2013). It indicates that informal employment has become an important channel to reduce graduate unemployment and is increasingly accepted (Wang *et al.*, 2016).

The new wave of employer discrimination in the light of the new birth-control (two-child) policy is likely to push more female university graduates into informal employment, with potentially negative implications for their life-time employment outcomes, including for example, job security, wage and pension income and social benefits entitlement. Given that childcare support has been relatively poor in the private sector and work–life balance initiatives to support workers with care responsibilities mostly absent, the role of the extended family is likely to become even more important than before.[2] Will this added require-ment for family support rekindle some of the traditional Chinese cultural values and what social policy implications may this have for encouraging the return to a greater emphasis of family values that have been weakened in the marketisation of the economy?

This chapter aims to address the above issues to fill some of the knowledge gaps. It argues that, given current gender norms and persistent employer dis-crimination, the recent amendment of the birth-control policy in China may paradoxically weaken women's bargaining power and position in the labour market with long-lasting effects, not just for women but for their family as a whole. It draws on interview data with professionals in the public sector and banking sector to explore how employers and female graduates are interpreting this change of policy and what it has meant for the employment opportunities of female graduates. It calls for the need to monitor the labour market effects of this policy for women in order to highlight new forms of gender discrimina-tion that may arise, and mechanisms and interventions that can be put in place to ensure that different social policies do not compromise each other, and that the enactment of one policy does not undermine the interest of a large segment of the population that it aims to protect. It has been cogently argued in the European context that it is important to contextualise policy changes within the broader social policies and approaches to care, as well as to examine employers' strategic responses to policy changes to assess the wider impact of any policy changes, and this chapter adopts a similar approach in examining the impact of the two-child policy on university women graduates' employment prospects.

Government policy and impact on university graduate employment

Two policy initiatives introduced by the Chinese government since 2014 have strong implications for women graduates' employment prospects. One is the 'Public Entrepreneurship and Innovation' and the other is the full implementa-tion of the two-child policy. The following section outlines these two initiatives.

Unemployment pressure and government initiative

Some 10 million HE graduates competed in the job market in 2016. They consist of 7.7 million university graduates in 2016, 0.3 million overseas gradu-ate returnees and 2 million unemployed graduates from previous years (Wang et al., 2016). Flexible employment (e.g. agency employment and temporary employment) and self-employment (or 'entrepreneurship' as the more sophis-ticated label) are becoming alternatives for an increasing number of university graduates (Wang *et al.*, 2016). As graduate employment is a performance indicator for universities, students are often 'encouraged' by the university to find an employer and sign an employment contract or become an entrepre-neur (self-employed) before they graduate. The latter deprives these young graduates of employment security and other social security protection, despite a small amount of start-up subsidies as a favourable policy provided by the government.

In September 2014, the Chinese Premier Li Keqiang first mentioned 'Public Entrepreneurship and Innovation' (大众创业、万众创新 'public entrepre-neurship mass innovation') at the World Economic Forum. In March 2015, 'Public Entrepreneurship and Innovation' was officially written into the Government Work Report, as a national strategy in response to the aggravating unemployment problem (The State Council of China, 2015). The State Council and local governments have subsequently introduced a series of policy measures to promote HE graduate employment and entrepreneurship. However, gradu-ate entrepreneurship as a high-profile national strategy for employment and economic growth has attracted much skepticism as to how realistic it is to expect the youngest, poorest and most inexperienced, with limited entrepreneurship training, to become successful business people in a short period of time. The encouragement of flexible employment and particularly self-employment sig-nals the end of the state commitment to formal employment for university graduates and may push those most disadvantaged in the labour market into insecure work (see Wang *et al.*, 2016).

Two-child policy and its uptake

As noted earlier, the one-child policy was enforced in the early 1980s to control the rapid population growth in China. The two-child policy was partially adopted in 2013 for married couples who are the only child of their family as an incremental policy to increase the population to address socio-economic problems associated with the care and cost of an ageing population.

From 2016 onwards, the two-child policy was implemented for all married couples.

The full implementation of the two-child policy has serious economic, institutional, social and organisational implications for the government, employers and families that require social policy attention. Several key issues are highlighted below (see Money163.com, 2016; Wang, 2016):

1) Who will guarantee women's employment rights vis-à-vis the widespread gender discrimination in the labour market without penalty to the offending employers?
2) Who will provide childcare services? Many grandparents have been looking after the first grandchild. As they grow older, they may not be able to look after the second grandchild or to look after two grandchildren together.
3) Who will finance the upbringing of the second child? The cost of living is increasing sharply in China mainly due to the rising cost of housing and raising a child (e.g. education and healthcare for a child, loss of income for the mother, and childcare cost). Couples want to provide the best milk products, best toys, best schooling and extra curriculum activities such as music, arts and sports for their child. Parents also compare and compete against each other (Cooke and Xiao, 2014).
4) Where will the child receive education (from nursery to high school)? There is a severe shortage of good-quality nurseries and schools. Parents are willing to pay high prices for their child to attend the best nursery/school they can afford, thus raising the bar of entry to schools and rocketing the housing prices of residential areas with popular schools. For those outside the nursery/school catchment area, significant resources will be needed to secure a place for the first child. For the second child this will be more challenging.
5) And, consequently, what social policy should be introduced to facilitate the implementation of the two-child policy (e.g. tax reduction for families with a second child, family allowance for nursery and maternity subsidy for employers) by reducing the burden of care?

Existing studies of the implementation since 2013 of the two-child policy for married couples who are the only child of their family revealed that a much lower proportion than anticipated of those qualified to have a second child have opted to do so. Three main reasons deter them from having a second child: financial pressure, childcare pressure and career pressure for women (Peng, 2016). According to the Third National Survey of Chinese Women's Social Position conducted in 2010, that is, before the full implementation of the two-child policy (cited in Song, 2016), women surveyed believed that having a second child would significantly reduce their employment in the urban area. Similarly, a survey published by Ganji.com revealed that 76 per cent of career women surveyed opted not to have a second child for financial reasons; 71 per cent anticipated difficulty in balancing their family and career; and 56 per cent admitted that having a second child might affect their career negatively (cited in Villarias, 2016). At the same time, some women face pressures from their family to have a second child to carry on the family line.

Impact of the two-child policy on employers

Under normal circumstances, the overhead cost for staffing is 40 per cent for an employing organisation, in addition to what is believed to be a rather heavy business tax (e.g. Peng, 2016). The cost associated with childbearing and childrearing is the main deterrent for employers to hire young women who have yet to fulfil their motherhood role (HRBar, 2016; see Table 12.1 for a summary of indicative cost). When a female employee is pregnant, the employer must continue to pay her salary and benefits, in addition to the cost of hiring

Table 12.1   A summary of indicative maternity costs for female employees in China

Three periods	Length	Cost involved	Potential problems
Pregnancy	10 months	Long-term sick pay (see below) Overall cost of temporary replacement staff	Disruption of work flow Difficulty in finding temporary replacement staff
Maternity	4 months onward	Maternity wage (including wage differential where applicable) Overall cost of temporary replacement staff	Resignation of the new mother when maternity leave is over Slow arrival of the maternity subsidies applied by the employer, causing delays in compensation
Breast feeding	8 months	Sick leave of the new mother, regular leave of absence associated with childcare (e.g. child being sick or temporary absence of childcare arrangements)	Slack performance of the mother due to legal protection of employment rights during the 'Three Periods'

Source: Adapted from HRBar, 2016.

another person to fill the place during the pregnant woman's absence from work (pregnancy checks, maternity leave, breastfeeding leave, leave of absence when the child is sick and so on). In addition, mothers of young children may be much less flexible in terms of working time due to childcare responsibilities (e.g. Li, 2015). This is particularly problematic in China where overtime may be required at short notice, often unpaid or under-paid. In addition, as China is encountering an economic slowdown, many companies are transitioning and upgrading their business. Downsizing to increase efficiency has become an inevitable part of the change, which presents a problem for employers as, by law (albeit not well enforced), they cannot reduce pay or dismiss female employees who are not working during their 'Three Periods' (pregnancy, maternity and breastfeeding), as defined in Table 12.1.

The author's interviews with several employers (both public and private sector) and female employees in public sector professional organisations in 2015 and 2016 revealed three types of behaviour from female employees during pregnancy and maternity leave that make employers wary. It should be noted at the outset that this may not be a widespread phenomenon across the country (gaming may be less possible in the private sector with performance-related pay or for low-earner families who need the wage); nor is the intention here to justify employer discrimination against pregnant women. Rather, these incidents are intended to demonstrate the two sides of the story/behaviour and how these behaviours may impact on the other party in negative ways. The first type is gaming behaviour which is the most costly and inconvenient for employers. Some women will take sick leave (paid or unpaid) once pregnancy is confirmed until childbirth in order to ensure a smooth pregnancy and take full advantage of any pay entitlements – one female employee in a public sector organisation was disclosing how she took advantage of the system for most of her pregnancy and even when she went to work for the limited days, she arrived late and left early. Then the new mother will take maternity leave and may extend the leave with sick leave or other leave of absence until the company presses her to return to work. Some mothers will then quit their job when the employer is no longer willing to keep the position open for her. In this situation, employers may lose out if the employee did not submit her application for maternity subsidy from the social security outlet. The research found that some employers resort to stopping the new mother's wage payment until the maternity subsidy arrives to avoid this loss and then will pass the payment directly to the employee on maternity leave. A second behavioural scenario that was uncovered from the interviews is that the pregnant woman will continue to work but work more slowly, forcing the employer to hire someone else to share part of her workload. A third type of behaviour reported by managers is that pregnant women may attend work but may be slack in their performance and disrupt others by chatting for prolonged periods about their pregnancy experience and so on. As a branch manager of a state-owned bank where the majority of employees are women remarked:

> Few pregnant staff work as normal to complete their task without asking for special treatment or having long periods of leave of absence. The younger generation of women are very delicate and cannot endure hardship like the earlier generations. Parents and grandparents also treat the baby a lot more preciously these days than we used to when we had several children in one family and when everybody had to work hard to make a bare living.

An employer from a private service company shared similar sentiments, pointing out the inadequate role of the state in financing the childbirth policy:

> From the government's point of view, encouraging childbirth and increasing the quality of the population is beneficial to the country's long-term development. However, employers should not bear the bulk of the cost of childbirth. Such a burden will deter employers from hiring and promoting women with childrearing responsibility. The government as the policy maker should take more social responsibility, reduce taxation for businesses which have a large female workforce, increase maternity social security benefits to the individual and the employer, and give special consideration to companies that need to carry out business restructuring and lay off their employees, including women during their Three Periods. If we hire a young female post-graduate who is typically 24 or 25 years of age, train her up and then in 2–3 years' time, she will have a child and then a second one. For those whose family financial situation is good, they may choose to quit the job and become a full-time housewife for a few years. This will be costly for the business. So we prefer to hire men.

Even in the public sector where labour costs may be less of a concern, staff shortages due to maternity may be difficult to manage for the organisation. For example, interviews with school headmasters show that the two-child policy is already having an impact on the staffing levels and the workload of the existing workforce, particularly at workplaces which are primarily staffed by women, such as banks and schools. In one of the schools, where the majority of teachers are women, three out of seven school teachers teaching the same year/grade were pregnant a few months after the enactment of the policy. Two of them have taken long-term leave to ensure a smooth pregnancy and a healthy newborn. As one of the headmasters remarked, 'the post-80s and 90s generations are physically and emotionally tender', as most of them are the only child of the family, known as the 'Little Emperor' (see also Marshall, 1997). This level of staff absence has a major impact and male teachers are facing heavier work-loads as a result because staffing levels in public schools are determined by the government and short-term replacement is difficult. This suggests the need for gender mainstreaming policies to protect against gender equality policies being derailed from other domains, as was argued in the European context (Rubery and Koukiadaki, 2016).

Impact of the two-child policy on female graduates: employer discrimination

Given the various issues highlighted above, it is perhaps not surprising that employment discrimination is one of the many challenges encountered by female university graduates (Liu, 2016), a situation that has been steadily wors-ening since the 1980s with the ending of graduate job allocation by the state (see Cooke, 2001; 2009; Woodham *et al.*, 2009). In early 2015, the National Development and Strategic Research Institute of Renmin University of China released a research report which revealed that for every one job interview invi-tation a female jobseeker received, male jobseekers would receive 1.42 inter-view invitations. After changing the gender to male on the application form, opportunities for female applicants to receive an interview invitation would increase 42 per cent (cited in Zhang, 2016).

According to a study conducted in 2015 by the All-China Women's Federation (ACWF) on female graduates in several universities in three prov-inces and municipalities including Beijing, 86.6 per cent of the women students surveyed felt that they have been discriminated against in their jobseeking pro-cess (cited in Hou, 2016). In particular, 80.2 per cent of the women studied reported the following discriminatory practices from employing organisations: 'making gender specific requirements in the job advertisement', 'refusing to accept female applicants or look at their CVs', 'denying women applicants written test or interview opportunities', 'denying women applicants second interview opportunities', 'raising the qualification requirements for female applicants' and so forth (Hou, 2016, p.9). The study further revealed that the women interviewed were discriminated against on at least 17 occasions on average (Hou, 2016).

Some employers were reported to have blatantly asked women candidates if they had plans for having a family soon or if they were considering having a second child. So much so that 'when are you planning to start a family?' has become a 'must-ask' question during job interviews with female job candi-dates (*Beijing Youth Newspaper*, 2015). If the answer was positive, then these candidates would be dropped in the recruitment selection process (Liu, 2016). It was reported that in graduate job fairs, there is a strange phenomenon in which PhD graduates are not as competitive as undergraduates, overseas graduate returnees are not as competitive as domestically grown graduates and singletons are not as competitive as those married with a child (e.g. Money163.com, 2016). With the full implementation of the two-child policy, some employers have escalated, unlawfully but without punishment, their recruitment criteria from 'married with child' to 'married with two children' (e.g. Li, 2015; Sohu. com, 2016).

The full implementation of the two-child policy has evidently further undermined female graduates' employment opportunities (*Beijing Youth Newspaper*, 2015). According to a survey report released by www.51job.com, a major online job advertisement company, on the impact of the two-child policy on women's employment, 75 per cent of the companies surveyed had increased concerns over the recruitment of female employees as a result of the two-child policy (cited in Huaxia Jingwei Net, 2016). Another survey conducted by the ACWF in 2015 also indicated that the implementation of the two-child policy for married couples who are the only child of their family has exacerbated employment discrimination against women. In addition, professional women who already have one child may be passed over for promotion when they have the second child (cited in Huaxia Jingwei Net, 2016).

Despite the existence of legislation that stipulates the employment rights of women (e.g. the Constitution; Labour Law, Safeguarding Women's Rights Law; and Employment Promotion Law), enforcement of these laws remains problematic and channels to seek remedy are ambiguous – a general problem in the implementation of labour laws in China (e.g. Cooke, 2012; Cooney *et al.*, 2014; Liu, 2016). Therefore, in reality, women's employment rights are not guaranteed for many female jobseekers.

Employer discrimination against female university graduates, an entrenched practice that has been exacerbated with the adoption of the two-child policy, has serious employment and career implications for this growing cohort of the new labour force. If the socially determined family roles of women, particularly those with care responsibilities, in western societies have to a large extent shaped women's identities as contingent and intermittent workers with undervalued occupational skill classification and therefore financial reward for many (Rubery and Grimshaw, 2015), then the marginalisation of female university graduates in the Chinese labour market is arguably a far more serious form of 'economic and social exclusion' (Rubery and Grimshaw, 2015: 328). The choice of employment mode for the childrearing graduate women in China is even more restricted to no employment, self-employment, temporary employment or agency employment – but not necessarily part-time employment on a regular basis as part-time work is uncommon for skilled jobs.

Individual strategy and impact

Individual strategy

Under the one-child policy, employers tended to favour university graduates who are already mothers instead of those who are single or newly married to avoid maternity costs and what employers referred to as other 'hassles' associated with working mothers with young children. Facing employment barriers, a small but growing number of female university graduates respond to the situation by getting married and having their child during their postgraduate studies – in China, Master degree courses are usually structured for a 2.5- or 3-year period (e.g. Sohu.com, 2016). They can then enter the job market with more competitive advantage than their counterparts who are yet to go become mothers. For many university student mothers, becoming a mother during their university education is a kind of helpless choice. However, the full implementation of the two-child policy has eroded the benefit of such a strategy, as it would be far more difficult to have two children during the postgraduate study period.

Discouraged by employer discrimination, some female postgraduate students identify with the strategy of having a child first and then seeking employment, given that it is more difficult for female postgraduates (older and closer to childbearing stage) than for female undergraduates to find employment. However, this strategy has its drawback. Those who become a mother during their postgraduate studies may have to take a year off from their studies. These 'post-graduate student mothers' face dual pressures of completing their study while going through their pregnancy and childbirth (Zhang, 2015). Early parental responsibility means that they may encounter financial difficulties and have little time to enjoy life or hone their skills and knowledge before starting a family. Pregnancy tends to distract students from their studies which means that they may not get the best result, which in turn undermines their employment prospects. Maternity may also reduce their chance to work as a research assistant for their supervisors, which is a good opportunity to gain experience and resources beneficial to their studies and future career. In short, motherhood during their postgraduate study period means that female university students are, in their mid-twenties, facing the financial, physical and emotional burden of having to raise children, develop a career and pay a mortgage at the same time (Li, 2015).

Impact on other university postgraduate students

The 'child first, employment second' strategy adopted by some female post-graduate students was initially accepted by their peers as a personal choice. However, the author's interviews with several postgraduate students and academics on their experience about living or working with these new mothers showed that such as a strategy may have its downside not only for the mothering students but also their peers and supervisors. Those sharing a dormitory – a common accommodation arrangement in Chinese universities – with the pregnant student find that their freedom of activities in the dormitory is heavily restricted – for example, by the need to keep noise down (which means no music, no visitors, no loud discussion and practically no life) and no late-night studying (as lights should be turned off) in order to create a conducive environment for the foetus to grow and the pregnant peer to rest. As noted earlier, Chinese families, coming themselves from one-child families, are very precious about their babies and do all they can to provide the best conditions for the child right from the start of the pregnancy (see also Chua, 2011; Cooke and Xiao, 2014). Requests for 'special treatment' from a pregnant student may include favourable task allocation for group assignments, exemption from housework in the dormitory, accompanying hospital visits, assistance in shopping and other errands. Emotional support is often needed. All these demands make life difficult for the young peers and reduce their tolerance level after a while.

For those new mother students living away from university, their friends may be asked to assist with all sorts of tasks such as research assistance, submitting forms, notices and thesis, and so on, often at short notice. Being absent from the campus also means that the mother student may not be pulling her weight in group activities or assignments and be resented for having an easy ride.

Impact on the family

The twin problem of graduate unemployment and the two-child policy also impacts the graduates' family in a variety of ways, including, for example, finding employment, funding for housing and childcare support. In particular, grandparents' financial and childcare support has been a crucial subsidy that enables the mother to take up full-time work and for the young married couple to sustain a living standard which goes beyond their means. However, such selfless cross-generation subsidy may have a negative effect on the grandparents, as many of them may spend most of their savings on financing their children and grandchildren, leaving themselves vulnerable to poor health (owing to childcare responsibilities) and reduced living standards. Who will provide elderly care and healthcare to them when they need it?

Policy considerations

Li (2015) argues that it is unfair to push the bulk of the childbirth cost to employers and blame them for being irresponsible when they discriminate against mothers-to-be. Given the extensive employer discrimination against mothers, to avoid staffing 'hassles' and the added burden on additional business costs, more intervention is needed from the government to prevent further deterioration of women's employment and career prospects and to safeguard women's rights and interests (Peng, 2016). This is a challenging task under the marketised economic environment. Nevertheless, what can be done to provide better childcare support and promote gainful employment for women? Peng (2016) argues that, as the most important public service provider and resource allocator, the government has a responsibility – and the ability – to resource public services to faciliate families to have children. A number of government interventions, ranging from positive incentives or facilitation to punitive mechanisms, may be considered, some of which have been adopted in western countries and have been recommended to the International Labour Organization to close the gender pay gap (e.g. Grimshaw and Rubery, 2015).

Firstly, tax reduction may be provided for families with children (Peng, 2016). In addition, better social security provision may be provided for maternity leave to reduce employers' financial burden, for example, by linking maternity leave subsidy directly to corporate tax reduction or introducing provisions whereby only those law-abiding employers will receive subsidies.

Secondly, the government should put in place better family policy for parental leave, childcare leave and carers' leave (Song, 2016). A paternity leave policy may be adopted to encourage more men to participate in the childrearing process and share in the housework. Parental leave entitlement may also be introduced after guaranteeing adequate maternity leave as a more flexible leave arrangement. Paternal and parental leave entitlments will promote a better relationship for the couple, as housework and care responsibilities are more likely to be shared, and promote greater gender equality by reducing the negative impact of maternity leave on a woman's career (Peng, 2016).

Thirdly, the government should strengthen access to early childhood education facilities and faciliate affordable private childcare through, for example, extending free school education to pre-schoolers, investing more in pre-school childhood education and improving the quality of state-funded school education to reduce parents' financial burden in sourcing good-quality (private) education for their children. In addition, the government could introduce favourable incentives (e.g. subsidies) to encourage employers and private investors to participate in childcare service provision and other education-related services (Peng, 2016).

Fourthly, affirmative action measures may be introduced, particularly in the public sector. These may include, for example, promoting good-quality flexible employment and reserving job positions to married women with children. It is important to note that these measures have their own problems and may trigger another set of disadvantaged labour market outcomes for women as has been found in the European context (e.g. Grimshaw and Rubery, 2015; Rubery, 2015). It has been observed that employers in China have been innovative in creating alternative forms of employment to overcome government regulation of particular types of non-standard forms of employment, for example using outsourcing to replace agency workers (e.g. Cooke and Brown, 2015).

Fifthly, state institutions should play a greater advocacy role to promote gender equality and the sharing of household responsibilities between wife and husband. For example, state-owned enterprises and public sector organisations can play a larger role in promoting gender equality practices at workplaces, such as promoting work–life balance initiatives and providing affordable and good-quality childcare services. As Rubery (2013) noted in the context of policy retrenchment in Europe, the public sector is not only an important source of quality employment and childcare services, but also a crucial public space to promote political ideology of gender equality and the social value of care work – not just childcare but also elderly care as the Chinese population ages. Equally, the All-China Federation of Trade Unions (ACFTU) and the ACWF, two key NGOs under the leadership of the Chinese Communist Party, can be mobilised to carry out more effective campaigns for improved childcare privision at both the policy and the operational level. Both ACFTU and ACWF are known for their welfare role.

Sixthly, state institutions should improve the anti-employment discrimination legislation and enforce compliance more effectively to safeguard women's equal employment rights. This is perhaps the toughest issue to tackle given the relatively poor record of labour law enforcement in China as noted earlier (Cooke and Brown, 2015; Cooney et al., 2014).

Finally, and more broadly, the full implementation of the two-Child policy reignites social debates of the decling tradition of family values and calls for the reconstruction of family policy and the family ethics system (Peng, 2016). In the last few decades, the structure of Chinese families has become nuclear and many familial cultural traditions have been eroded as a result of greater job mobility, the commercialisation of domestic responsibilities and changing social values. Filial piety as a virtue has been diluted by individualism of the younger generation who were brought up in a self-centred environment as the only child. The impact of the two-child policy and the ageing population mean that traditional family values need to be revitalised in order to fill the gap created by the inadequacy of the social welfare system. The tradition of mutual assistance and responsibility sharing within the family will resume in becoming the main source of security and welfare support as a pragmatic familial survival and advancement strategy in response to economic and social changes.

However, while re-emphasising the role of family as an important thread in the social fabric that underpins social harmony, the government should assess its family policy to identify what can be done to mobilise family support for the implementation of the two-child policy on the one hand, and to use the two-child policy as a facilitator to remodel family arrangements on the other (Peng, 2016). It is worth noting that while the Chinese traditional culture places strong emphasis on family values to make up for the inadequacy of the social welfare system, little has been done by the state in the family policy space to facilitate the functioning of the family self-support system. On the contrary, the weakness of the social welfare system is perhaps the outcome of a once-strong family self-support system. It is time that the government adjusts its family policy and takes remedial action to support the functioning of other social policies in a more holistic manner. Without an integrated set of social policies as a solid foundation, it will be difficult to expect families to operate in a self-sufficient manner, leaving those most at need in a vulnerable position and forcing families to adopt strategies that will render some of the social policies fruitless.

Conclusions

This chapter examined tensions in the university graduate labour market that have been intensified by different goals of the social and economic policies adopted by the Chinese government since the 1980s. Existing evidence suggests that the two-child policy exacerbates the labour market discrimination of female graduates and in part undermines the enthusiasm of married couples to have a second child. If the intention of the two-child policy is to overcome labour shortage and the social security pressures associated with an ageing population, then the increased labour costs and the consequent employment discrimination related to having a second child are severely undermining its implementation and triggering another set of social problems that may be difficult to tackle in the short term.

In particular, the full implementation of the two-child policy since 2016 will have strong implications for the employment prospects of Chinese female university graduates. Employers have become more aggressive in their recruitment screening, in a context of rising graduate unemployment and under-employment as a result of the expansion of the HE sector in the early 2000s. The adoption of the two-child policy on the one hand, and the Public Entrepreneurship and Innovation policy on the other, is likely to push graduate women into self-employment or contingency work that is characterised by employment insecurity and work fragmentation, and is under-paid and under-valued. For both individuals and the country, it is not only a waste of human capital, but also a major setback to the reasonable level of gender equality that has been achieved during the state-planned economy period (Cooke, 2012).

The current labour market conditions for female Chinese graduates, in light of the two-child policy, exemplifies Rubery and colleagues' argument regarding the importance of integrating labour market policies and social policies, particularly in the social reproduction sphere, for the policies to work effectively (e.g. Rubery and Koukiadaki, 2016). The case of the two-child policy and the revelation of both employer and female employee responses to this policy change also demonstrates the utility of Rubery's analytical approach in two ways, if we are to fully understand why this policy will have such negative implications. The first is the importance of contextualising these responses in the wider context of economic and social policies of caring and employment flexibility to help uncover deeper causes of problems in women's employment and the gender pay gap. The second is the need to put employers under the spotlight (cf. Rubery and Urwin's (2011) argument of 'bringing the employer back in') to examine women's employment opportunities to show how the everyday organisational realities are shaped by changes in macro policies and how these shape employment opportunities for women at the level of the firm in both the private and the public sector. Research on women's employment in China will benefit significantly by adopting this holistic approach.

In short, the emerging gendered pattern of contingency employment in China may mirror the path that has been travelled by several developed countries (e.g. Rubery, 2015). There are therefore many lessons to be learned for China in terms of enhancing the quantity and, particularly, the quality of graduate women's employment through effective social policy intervention in an integrative manner. Equally, what has occurred in China may have implications for other developing nations, which are at different stages of industrialisation and commercialisation but are at the same time grappling with obstructing social problems and possible solutions.

Notes

1   Informal employment includes, for example, agency employment, temporary employment, fixed-term employment, causal employment and self-employment.
2   The important role of family institutions in social reproduction and in facilitating the labour market participation of women with childcare responsibilities has been well recognised in the western context (c.f. Bosch *et al.*, 2009 on the interrelationships between employment regimes and welfare regimes, including family systems).

References

Beijing Youth Newspaper (2015), 4 December, p. 4.

Bosch, G., Rubery, J. and Lehndorff, S. (eds) (2009), *European Employment Models in Flux: A Comparison of Institutional Change in Nine European Countries* (Basingstoke: Palgrave Macmillan).

Chua, A. (2011), 'Why Chinese Mothers are superior', *The Wall Street Journal*. Retrieved on 14 September 2012, from http://online.wsj.com/article/SB10001424052748704111504576059713528698754.html.

Cooke, F. L. (2001), 'Equal opportunities? The role of legislation and public policies in women's employment in China', *Women in Management Review*, 16:7, 334–48.

Cooke, F. L. (2012), *Human Resource Management in China: New Trends and Practices* (London: Routledge).

Cooke, F. L. and Brown, R. (2015), *The Regulation of Non-Standard Forms of Work in China, Japan and Republic of Korea*, Conditions or Work and Employment Series No. 64 (Geneva: International Labour Organization).

Cooke, F. L. and Xiao, Y. C. (2014), 'Gender roles and organisational HR practices: the case of women's careers in accountancy and consultancy firms in China', *Human Resource Management*, 53:1, 23–44.

Cooney, S., Biddulph, S. and Zhu, Y. (2014), *Law and Fair Work in China* (London: Routledge), pp. 96–9.

Fagan, C. and Rubery, J. (1996), 'The salience of the part-time divide in the European Union', *European Sociological Review*, 12:3, 227–50.

Grimshaw, D. and Rubery, J. (2015), *The Motherhood Pay Gap: A Review of the Issues, Theory and International Evidence*, Conditions of Work and Employment Series No. 57 (Geneva: International Labour Organization).

Gustafsson, B. and Li, S. (2000), 'Economic transformation and the gender earnings gap in urban China', *Journal of Population Economics,* 13:2, 305–29.

Hou, J. B. (2016), 'The full implementation of Two-Child policy or exacerbating employment discrimination against women: Committee members calling for anti-discrimination in employment legislation as soon as possible', *Legal Daily*, 15 March.

HRBar (2016), 24 March 2016, http://pig66.com/weixintoutiao/zhichangren/2016–03 –24/798444.html, accessed 26 March 2016.

Huaxia Jingwei Net (2016), 'Employment discrimination against having a second child: enterprises recruitment demands married with child(ren) in recruitment', 23 March 2016, http://huaxia.com/zk/sszk/wz/2016/03/4776082.html, accessed 14 April 2016.

Li, J., Cooke, F. L., Mu, J. L. and Wang, J. (2016), 'The measurement and determinants of underpayment of wages in China: an empirical assessment of the 2003–2008 period', *Journal of the Asia Pacific Economy*, 21:1, 26–52.

Li, S. S. (2015), 'Not prepared for "Two-Child" yet, but gender discrimination in employment attacks already', *Bond Times* (证券时报), 28 December, A03.

Liao, L. P. and Wu, Y. Y. (2013), Flexible employment: the new choice of university graduates. *Beijing Education*, 4, 7–9.

Liu, J. W. (2016), 'Zhonghua Women's College Professor Sun Xiaomei representative: to accelerate the development of anti-employment discrimination law', *Guangming Daily*, 13 March.

Marshall, A. (1997), 'Little emperors', *The Times*, 29 November.

Money163.com (2016), 'Four difficult points that need to be addressed in the full implementation of Two-Child policy: who would safeguard women's employment rights', 9 March 2016, http://money.163.com/16/0309/01/BHM8JN7900253B0H.html, accessed 14 April 2016.

Nie, W., Hopkins, E. W. and Hopkins, A. S. (2002), 'Gender-based perceptions of equity in China's state-owned enterprises', *Thunderbird International Business Review*, 44:3, 353–77.

Rubery, J. (2013), 'Public sector adjustment and the threat to gender equality', in Vaughan-Whitehead, D. (ed.), *Public Sector Shock: The Impact of Policy Retrenchment in Europe* (Cheltenham: Edward Elgar), pp. 43–83.

Rubery, R. (2015), 'Austerity and the future for gender equality in Europe', *Industrial and Labor Relations Review,* 68:4, 715–41.

Rubery, J. and Grimshaw, D. (2015), 'The 40-year pursuit of equal pay: a case of constantly moving goalposts', *Cambridge Journal of Economics*, 39:2, 319–43.

Rubery, J. and Urwin, P. (2011), 'Bringing the employer back in: why social care needs a standard employment relationship'. *Human Resource Management Journal*, 21, 122–37.

Rubery, J. and Koukiadaki, A. (2016), *Closing the Gender Pay Gap: A Review of the Issues, Policy Mechanisms and International Evidence* (Geneva, International Labour Organization).

Peng, X. Z. (2016), 'Fulfilling the goal of the full implementation of the Two-Child policy requires an integrated policy match', *Exploration*, 1, 71–4.

Sohu.com (2016), 'The impact of Two-Child policy on female students', 15 April 2016, http://mt.sohu.com/20160415/n444248481.shtml, accessed 20 April 2016.

The State Council of China (2015), *Opinions on the Various Policy Measures Related to the Vigorous Promotion of Public Entrepreneurship and Innovation* (State Issue 2015, No. 32)

[国务院.国务院关于大力推进大众创业万众创新若干政策措施的意见 (国发〔2015〕32号) 11 June].

Villarias, A. (2016), 'Having second child worries many Chinese women', China Topix, 27 February 2016, http://chinatopix.com/articles/78099/20160227/having-second-child-worries-many-chinese-women.htm, accessed 14 April 2016.

Wang, X. Y. (2016), 'Following the full implementation of the Two-Child policy, what difficulties do ordinary people have?' *Daily Economic News*, 9 March, 3.

Wang, J., Cooke, F. L. and Lin, Z. H. (2016), 'Informal employment in China: Recent development and human resource implications', *Asia Pacific Journal of Human Resources*, 54:3, 292–311.

Woodhams, C., Xian, H. and Lupton, B. (2009), 'Furthering equal opportunity in China: sex discrimination and gender segregation in Chinese labour markets', *The International Journal of Human Resource Management*, 20:10, 2084–19.

Zhang, H. Y. (2015), 'Following the full implementation of the Two-Child policy, it is even more necessary to safeguard women's employment rights', *Gansu Daily*, 9 December, p. 4.

Zhang, L. X. (2016), 'Implementing the "Two-Child" policy should also share the cost of childbirth', *Trade Union Information*, 10, 17.

Part III

Convergence, divergence and the importance of regulating for decent work

13

The social reproduction of youth labour market inequalities: the effects of gender, households and ethnicity

Jacqueline O'Reilly, Mark Smith and Paola Villa

Introduction

Young people have been disproportionately hit by the economic crisis. In many European countries, unemployment rates have increased faster for youth than for prime age groups (O'Reilly *et al.*, 2015). Vulnerability to the risks of poverty and precarious employment has been compounded by increasing economic inequalities and the rise of temporary, part-time and zero-hours contracts. Gender differences between young men and women appear to have converged on several standard labour market indicators (such as employment rate, unemployment rate, share of temporary and part-time work) (Eamets *et al.*, 2015), although young women are still more likely to be 'not in employment education or training' (NEET) than young men. Where there has been a levelling in gender disparities this is largely owing to an overall decline in the male labour market and men's educational outcomes, while girls' performance has improved. Nevertheless, reduced gender inequalities in some cases are the outcome of increased overall precariousness for all young people.

Youth labour market vulnerability extends beyond simple gender differences. The context of vulnerable young women and men in the labour market varies across the European Union (EU), but similarities influencing indicators such as NEET rates, youth employment and unemployment rates, early school-leaving, and gender pay gaps are found across all countries (Gökşen *et al.*, 2016a). Vulnerability to poverty and social exclusion relates to family background, a gender segregated labour market and the role of ethnicity. The economic crisis has exacerbated these disadvantages. The interdependency of these dimensions subject young people to differing degrees of vulnerability to unemployment and precariousness in the labour market, depending on where they live and with whom.

Surprisingly, little attention has been given to bringing together some of these distinct strands of research on new patterns of vulnerability and labour market segmentation that include an understanding of the impact of different institutional environments, the legacy of parental households and the differentiated experience by gender and ethnicity (Zuccotti and O'Reilly, forthcoming). We are interested in identifying how new patterns of segmentation in youth labour markets are developing. We explore the impact on young people's trajectories, focusing on vulnerability by gender, ethnicity and parental household differences. We examine the extent to which policies for young people recognise gender differences and, ultimately, the extent to which a gender mainstreaming approach has been visible in policies to help young people find paid work.

Our analysis draws on the concept of social reproduction and economic production developed by Humphries and Rubery (1984). We consider youth trajectories in relation to the employment status of their family households across Europe for both young women and young men. Furthermore, we use the example of ethnic differences in the UK to illustrate new lines of segmentation. We then examine the extent to which policy has sought to address these inequalities.

The difficulties faced by young people cannot simply be read off in terms of particular gender, family background or ethnic characteristics. We argue that a more integrated approach can inform policy as well as trace patterns of continuity and change in the differentiated experience of young people in Europe. We draw on the results from a large-scale European research project on strategic transitions for youth labour in Europe (www.style-research.eu) and, in particular, the work of Gökşen et al., 2016a; Berloffa et al., 2015; and Zuccotti and O'Reilly (forthcoming). We examine the legacy of parental employment for young Europeans and, in the UK context, how these differences are shaped by ethnicity. We conclude by arguing that in order to understand emerging patterns of segmentation in youth labour markets a more holistic approach is required. This includes an analysis of the legacy of household differences from the sphere of social reproduction to understand how these interact with the sphere of economic production. Our analysis indicates that a more holistic understanding of the differential effects of these dimensions is required if policy initiatives are to be better targeted at making work more equal for young women and men from different family and ethnic backgrounds.

Economic production, social reproduction and youth labour market segmentation

In their seminal article, Humphries and Rubery (1984) argued that the concepts of economic production and social reproduction captured different organising principles, enabling us to understand cross-national differences in female and maternal employment. Humphries and Rubery's (1984) key argument was that the *sphere of economic production* encompassed the interaction between different societal institutions, such as collective bargaining systems, vocational and educational training (VET) systems and employment regulation. The constellation of these institutions established a particular employment logic that varied between countries and between sectors. It differentiated and segmented workers in terms of employment conditions. Employers' preferences and abilities to recruit specific types of labour drew on a range of different employment contracts. For example, while policies to support shorter working times or partial early retirement were more commonly found in traditional, industrial and male-dominated sectors, the use of part-time contracts was predominantly reserved for women in feminised sectors of the economy (O'Reilly and Fagan, 1998). This could explain why, in some countries, employers' preferences were more closely aligned with the production of well-qualified, highly skilled labour. In other countries, and in some sectors where the weakness of the VET institutions resulted in a less well-qualified supply of labour, employers were more likely to design jobs with inferior employment contracts, and for women these were often on a part-time basis. This analysis has been more widely taken up in labour market research with a more '*productivist*' focus, that is, where the attention was purely on the public sphere of economic production, as evidenced by the considerable volume of literature dedicated to discussions of the merits of the varieties of capitalism (VOC) approach. The Humphries and Rubery (1984) approach, in contrast, went beyond this narrower economic focus on 'production regimes' (Rubery, 1992, 1993).

Their innovative and significant contribution was to make a much stronger link to including a parallel analysis of the *sphere of social reproduction* (Picchio, 1992). This referred to institutions supporting the reproduction of labour, including the family as well as other significant institutions, such as school timetables and working-time norms. The organisation of these institutions, essential to the way in which the sphere of social production was structured, affected the forms and levels of female labour market participation and the patterns and organisation of consumption and leisure. Humphries and Rubery argued that we could not assume a symbiotic 'fit' between these two spheres of economic production and social reproduction. Instead, they argued, a degree of autonomy existed between them. One of the advantages of their analysis was that it could potentially identify contradictions and sources of change, particularly in relation to the forms and levels of female labour market participation.

During the 1980s and 1990s this perspective enabled researchers to go beyond the traditional scope of labour market analysis that was largely centred on the employee–employer relationship, either at the micro- or at the macro-level. Instead, the analytical framework based on economic production and social reproduction provided a conceptual bridge that had links with developing approaches in comparative social policy and welfare state studies. This allowed researchers to make connections between how state policies shaped labour supply through education and training as well as through the provision (or not) of childcare services. It allowed an understanding of how, and on what terms, women's labour supply was constituted in different societies (O'Reilly, 1994).

The early debate on the role and position of women within the production system put the family at the core of the analysis (Kenrick, 1981; Picchio, 1992). This literature conceptualised the family and the labour market as social institutions, with attention focused on their role in the reproduction of labour power. In this framework, the state plays a fundamental role in the reproduction of labour, its action affecting standards of living (i.e. economic well-being) and shaping the legal structures regulating the reproduction and employment of the labour force. The state's intervention takes place through the distribution of benefits and the provision of services, but also through legal structures, in the regulation of both the system of social reproduction (i.e. family law) and the labour market system (i.e. employment legislation).

A key tenet of the literature on social reproduction is that the labour force is not homogeneous. Individuals differ substantially, not only in terms of education and skills but also in terms of personal characteristics and the position they occupy in the social structure of the labour market (Villa 1986: 261). Their position in the labour market must therefore be explained with reference to the existing economic and social differences in the system of social reproduction. This implies that differences in the economic and social status of workers (by gender, by age or by ethnic group) are a reflection of (1) the social and economic position of the individual's family (crucial in determining access to entry jobs, hence occupations and career advancements); and (2) the position workers occupy within the family and how this can affect their transition to adulthood.

Despite the insights this approach has provided to understanding female labour force participation, this kind of analysis has not been applied to youth labour markets. Conventionally, analysis of youth labour markets has given more attention to skill production systems and VET or to the type of labour market transitions young people can make on entering employment. More conservative-leaning approaches have focused on supply-side characteristics as those requiring a change of attitude on the part of either the young person or their family and peers. Yet Humphries and Rubery's sphere of social reproduction could be extended to encompass the way in which households and gender relations support transitions into employment from the educational system. In fact, very little attention has been given to providing a systematic comparison of how the characteristics of parental households are associated with youth labour market transitions (Berloffa et al., 2015), or the interaction of household characteristics with ethnic differences (Zuccotti and O'Reilly, forthcoming). Yet an adapted framework from that initially proposed by Humphries and Rubery (1984) can provide an innovative insight into the appearance of new forms of inequality in youth labour markets in Europe and its contribution to labour market segmentation theory. This more holistic approach allows us to integrate both the impact of households on youth transitions and the types of segmented labour markets they can access.

The evidence suggests that labour market experience for young people varies greatly across European countries. Moreover, these differences have been on the increase during the economic crisis. School-to-work transitions vary in terms of entry speed into employment, the time required to acquire job stability and the quality of employment. First-time jobs are often rather unstable (e.g. temporary contracts) or characterised by short durations (e.g. training contracts). For some youth, these 'flexible' contracts act as ports of entry into stable jobs, but for others they tend to become traps, leading to frequent spells of unemployment experienced between precarious jobs (Leschke, 2012). Some young people withdraw from the labour market for prolonged periods of time because they are discouraged in their attempts to find work, have caring responsibilities or return to education. NEET status for those who are unemployed or inactive is therefore a frequent phenomenon among some young people, and one that has increased manifold with the Great Recession (Bell and Blanchflower, 2011; Karamessini and Rubery, 2014). These differences in youth school-to-work transitions may be explained by cross-country differences in educational and training systems, employment policy and labour market institutions, and general macro-economic conditions. However, in addition to individual and country characteristics, we argue that family background also plays an important role in determining the type of trajectories experienced by young individuals, especially in Mediterranean and some Eastern European countries.

For some young people, unemployment is a frictional experience; for others, long-term exposure is part of a generational legacy (O'Reilly et al., 2015). The experiences of the parents of today's children shape the opportunities of young people through the transmission of resources and cultural capital (Warmouth *et al.*, 2014). We know from social mobility research that parental unemployment can become an 'unintended' legacy for their own children, depending on where they live and how the economy around them has changed in recent decades (MacDonald *et al.*, 2013; Macmillan, 2014).

The growing polarisation of households between the 'work-poor' and the 'work-rich' was brought to the attention of policy-makers in the mid-1990s (Anxo and O'Reilly, 2001; Gregg and Wadsworth, 1994, 2001). In the UK, for example, a range of policies during the 1990s sought to address this disparity and reduce the proportion of workless households. However, since the onset of the economic crisis of 2008–09, the proportions of work-poor households have been on the increase, particularly in countries hard-hit by the crisis (Berloffa *et al.*, 2015: 8; Gregg *et al.*, 2010).

The growth of jobless households co-existed with an increase in households with two working parents. Many commentators have evidenced the decline of the traditional 'male breadwinner' household model (Crompton, 1999), alongside a rise in non-traditional and single-parent families. The unequal distribution of paid work across these different household types not only illustrated growing levels of inequality, but also the potential exacerbation and extension of these inequalities for younger generations (Atkinson, 2015). The inclusion of household effects on labour market outcomes brings together the argument made by Humphries and Rubery (1984), with implications for identifying new lines of labour market segmentation and its inclusion in theoretical approaches.

Gender, youth labour market transitions and parental household characteristics

Gender differences in youth labour markets and school-to-work transitions are frequently under-estimated and it is often implicitly assumed that gender gaps only open up around parenthood so that younger generations are largely unaffected (Plantenga *et al.*, 2013). These gaps reflect segregation of educational and training choices as well as processes in the labour market – including employer behaviour – which serve to reinforce gender roles and stereotypes that subsequently produce occupational gender segregation.

The analysis conducted by Gökşen and colleagues (2016a), based on the European Union – Survey on Income and Living Conditions (EU-SILC) dataset, demonstrate that gender gaps for young people exist across almost all measures of educational and labour market statuses used to assess vulnerable outcomes. Their cross-national evidence suggests that gender differences open up early in the life course and that the policy environment across European countries is not well adapted to addressing these gender differences in the youth labour market. The extent of these vulnerabilities varies across different school-to-work regimes but is nevertheless present across unemployed and precarious employment statuses. Gökşen and colleagues (2016a) compare five country types: (1) universalistic (Denmark and the Netherlands); (2) liberal (United Kingdom); (3) employment-centred (France and Belgium); (4) sub-protective (Spain, Greece and Turkey); and (5) post-socialist countries (Slovakia). These country types represent different institutional environments and school-to-work transitions regimes for young people (Walther, 2006). They find that transitions are somewhat smoother and more predictable in systems where the education and training system has already differentiated young people both horizontally and vertically into tracks leading to different labour market destinations; but significant gender and country-specific differences remain. Transitions are found to be more fluid where the flows of information between education and labour market are continuous and extensive and gender gaps smaller, as in the case of employment-centred regimes (France and Belgium); yet migrants fair less well (Gökşen et al., 2016a: 35–6). In regimes where education systems are less stratified and where linkages between education and labour market are weaker, transitions seem to be more interrupted and gender gaps larger (for example, in the UK).

Using the lens of social reproduction we are also interested in understanding how households' characteristics affect youth transitions. Using the EU-SILC cross-sectional data, Berloffa and colleagues (2015) focus on mapping the significance of this trend across 29 European countries (27 EU countries, plus Norway and Switzerland) for different categories of youth (aged 16–24) living in the family of origin.[1] They were interested in identifying whether there was a generational legacy of parental worklessness on employment patterns of young people today. Their analysis found that young people growing up in workless households are more likely to be unemployed. Indeed, across all European countries the likelihood of young people being unemployed was much higher if they came from a work-poor household (see Table 13.1). Using data from 2005 and 2011, they show how during the Great Recession this higher likelihood of being unemployed increased across all country groups, apart from in Eastern Europe, albeit this occurred at different rates.

The results in Table 13.1 show how the risk of being unemployed for young people was generally higher in traditional breadwinner and work-poor households, and that these risks increased between 2005 and 2011. In the Nordic countries youth unemployment has increased most among traditional breadwinner families, and remained high among those where no one worked. In English-speaking and Continental countries, while the children of working single parents

Table 13.1   Unemployment rates of young people (16–24) living in the family of origin by the employment status of parents and group of countries, 2005 and 2011

	Year	Two-parent household, both parents work (work-rich)	Two-parent household, only one works	Single-parent household, parent works	One- or two-parent household, none of the parents work (work-poor)
Nordic	2005	0.15	0.13	0.29	0.31
countries	2011	0.34	0.45	0.33	0.49
English-	2005	0.06	0.09	0.22	0.18
speaking countries	2011	0.14	0.16	0.25	0.42
Continental	2005	0.14	0.15	0.24	0.28
countries	2011	0.10	0.17	0.16	0.33
Mediterranean	2005	0.21	0.27	0.27	0.33
countries	2011	0.38	0.44	0.36	0.51
Eastern	2005	0.27	0.35	0.33	0.44
European countries	2011	0.25	0.33	0.24	0.37

Notes: The 29 countries have been grouped as follows: Nordic (DK, FI, NO, SE); English-speaking (UK, IE); Continental (AT, BE, CH, DE, FR, NL); Mediterranean (CY, EL, ES, IT, MT, PT); Eastern European (BG, CZ, EE, HR, HU, LT, LV, PL, RO, SI, SK).

Source: Data drawn from Berloffa *et al.* (2015: table 4.1a) based upon calculation on EU-SILC cross sectional data 2005, 2011.

were most vulnerable in 2005, it is those coming from work-poor households who were subsequently hit hardest. The disparities between household types were less apparent in Mediterranean countries in 2005. But, by 2011, they had increased substantially; the risk of being unemployed for Mediterranean youth had risen more for those from the work-poor households, as well as those from traditional breadwinner households. Despite this aggregate fall in unemployment across Eastern Europe, young people from traditional breadwinner households and the work-poor were at the highest risk of being unemployed in 2011 (Table 13.1).

Further multivariate analysis by Berloffa and colleagues (2015) demonstrates that young people living in households where both parents work generally have a lower probability of unemployment/inactivity, with some differences across country groups and over time. In particular, living with a working father, all things being equal, reduced the probability of not working in all country groups in 2005. However, six years later, paternal employment plays a significant role only in Continental and Mediterranean countries. Maternal employment has an additional, and often larger, effect in Mediterranean and English-speaking countries on the likelihood of their children also being in employment.

In their analysis of the EU-SILC data Berloffa and colleagues also differentiate between the effects of parental employment status on sons' and daughters' employment probabilities (Berloffa *et al.*, 2015; tables 5.2 and 5.3). Sons' status is significantly affected by both parents working. In particular, in English-speaking countries, living with two working parents has a hugely positive effect on the probability of employment; in Mediterranean countries, parental employment significantly reduces the probability of young people's unemployment and inactivity. In Continental and Nordic countries, the effects were different before and during the crisis. In Continental countries, sons of a working mother are less likely to be unemployed in both years, while the role of the father emerges only for the youngest cohort (i.e. during the crisis), helping to reduce the probability of unemployment and inactivity for their sons. In Nordic countries, sons of a working father were less likely to be unemployed before the crisis (in 2005); and sons of a working mother were more likely to be employed during the crisis (in 2011).

For daughters, both paternal and maternal employment is associated with a lower likelihood of being unemployed or inactive in Mediterranean and Continental countries. In Nordic countries, in 2005, the employment condition of both parents is significantly correlated with their daughters' only, helping to lower the probability of her being unemployed or inactive. On the contrary, in English-speaking countries, young women's employment status depends only on their mother's employment status, and only for 2011.

These results provide empirical evidence of an intergenerational persistence of worklessness. The effects of the crisis show that inequalities in the risk of worklessness associated with the parental occupational structure fell in Nordic countries, remained almost unchanged in Continental countries and rose in English-speaking and Mediterranean countries. The gendered effects are also clear, with a positive intergenerational correlation between fathers and sons but, once controlled for mothers' working conditions, this correlation is small in almost all country groups (the exception being the Mediterranean countries). Similarly, young women with a mother who had been employed were less likely to be inactive. This association is highest in the Nordic countries than elsewhere. It also decreases over time in all countries, apart from the Mediterranean group. These results clearly indicate how family legacies continue to have a long-term impact on the early labour market outcomes for young people. These findings also illustrate the value of examining youth transitions using an adapted approach proposed by Humphries and Rubery (1984). This approach goes beyond examining the trajectories of isolated individuals, but links their outcomes to the household and employment opportunities of their parents, within the institutional settings set up by the state that shape the legal structures regulating the social reproduction and employment of the labour force (Humphries and Rubery, 1984; Villa, 1986). Taking this approach a step further, we were also interested in examining how these effects vary by household characteristics as a vector for reinforcing segmentation or protecting young people against the risk of poor employment prospects.

Ethnicity, gender and work-poor households

These differential experiences of young people in terms of gender and household effects identified above can also vary by ethnicity. The examination of ethnic groups across the EU is frequently framed in terms of migration, rather than an analysis of native-born, non-white population. Such cross-national comparisons of native ethnic differences are complex because of the varied ethnic composition of national populations, as well as the limited availability of substantial comparable data. For example, Gökşen and colleagues (2016b) had to rely on county of birth in order to identify ethnic variations using the EU-SILC data; second-generation youth were not identifiable and migrants from a variety of national origins were amalgamated. Nevertheless, they found strong evidence of disadvantage by comparing the intersectionality of youth, gender and 'migrant' status. A summary of their results for unemployment and NEET status is presented in Table 13.2. Here we see the gender and ethnicity gaps in relation to EU-born young men are evident in all countries, and these gaps have been exacerbated, in most cases, by the onset of the economic crisis. Exceptions include the case of the Netherlands where the situation of non-EU youth improved over time and in the UK where non-EU-born youth tended to fair better than men born in the EU. The same was not true for young women who were more likely to be NEET. Similarly, NEET rates for non-EU-born women improved in France and Belgium but remained much higher than for EU-born men.

Here we extend the analysis of Gökşen and colleagues (2016a) for ethnicity and Berloffa and colleagues (2015) for household impacts on youth transitions using the UK as an example case based on the work of Zuccotti and O'Reilly (forthcoming). The UK data have the advantage of including more nuanced detail around ethnic minority groups that is not available in other EU countries, as well as allowing us to include more detailed evidence related to parental

Table 13.2   Ratio of unemployment and NEET rates in eight European countries, broken down by EU/non-EU country of birth and gender (youth 16–29 years)

	Pre-crisis, 2005–08				Crisis/austerity, 2011–13			
	EU-born men	EU-born women	Non-EU-born men	Non-EU-born women	EU-born men	EU-born women	Non-EU-born men	Non-EU-born women
Unemployment								
DK	1.00	1.41	2.08	1.08	1.00	0.93	n/a	0.80
NL	1.00	1.45	5.91	7.86	1.00	0.74	2.34	2.32
FR	1.00	1.08	1.51	1.56	1.00	0.90	1.23	2.14
BE	1.00	1.13	2.36	2.72	1.00	0.92	3.23	2.33
SK	1.00	1.07	n/a	n/a	1.00	0.97	n/a	n/a
UK	1.00	0.63	0.62	0.80	1.00	0.69	0.78	0.90
ES	1.00	1.32	1.37	1.86	1.00	1.02	1.43	1.10
EL	1.00	1.57	0.51	1.60	1.00	1.04	1.07	0.94
NEET								
DK	1.00	1.52	1.57	2.82	1.00	1.18	0.05	2.64
NL	1.00	2.07	3.73	6.32	1.00	1.20	1.06	1.80
FR	1.00	1.51	1.51	3.91	1.00	1.01	1.04	3.57
BE	1.00	1.42	2.47	4.55	1.00	1.12	3.13	3.69
SK	1.00	1.50	n/a	n/a	1.00	1.30	n/a	n/a
UK	1.00	1.73	0.85	2.20	1.00	1.33	0.89	1.72
ES	1.00	1.39	1.45	2.72	1.00	0.99	1.48	1.56
EL	1.00	1.51	0.62	2.78	1.00	1.01	1.49	1.66

Source: Data drawn from Gökşen et al. (2015: tables 3.3 & 3.5) based upon calculation on EU-SILC cross sectional data 2005, 2011.

households and their employment levels. For example, the analysis developed allows us to distinguish between ethnic minorities who were born in the UK or came here when they were very young and more recent adult migrants to the UK.

By using a multi-dimensional, intersectional approach combining household and personal characteristics with labour market outcomes, together with the inclusion of ethnic minority status, we can develop a more holistic analysis as proposed by Humphries and Rubery. It also moves this approach towards a more intersectional analysis. Intersectionality stemming from the critical standpoint of African-American feminists has been advocated to examine multiple disadvantages and inequality (Cho et al., 2013; Collins, 2015; Crenshaw, 1991). Rather than focusing on one dimension or comparing bimodal inequalities of race, gender or class separately, the concept of intersectionality captures discrete combinations of multiple sources of disadvantage, which themselves reflect differentiated locations of power, domination and discrimination. Applied intersectional analysis focuses on differences *between* categories, such as between ethnic groups, as well as *within* categories of class, gender and ethnicity. While this concept has been extensively discussed in radical feminist forums, McBride and colleagues (2015) and Mooney (2016) suggest the application of an intersectional approach to empirical examination in the field of labour studies is well overdue. An intersectional approach also brings to the fore new sets of inequalities and how the effects of disadvantage translate for young men and women of different ethnic groups (Crawford and Greaves, 2015). This approach generates a more differentiated reading of the effects of labour market segmentation and the interaction of ethnicity, gender and parental household employment status associated with the likelihood of young people becoming NEETs.

The cross-European analysis of households from Berloffa and colleagues (2015) shows that the legacy of parental worklessness continues to touch young people. This pattern is also found in the UK; young people who come from a work-poor household where no adults in their household were working when they were aged 14 have a much higher rate of being NEETs today compared to those coming from any other family type. However, this effect varies in its intensity in terms of both gender and ethnicity.

When comparing Indian and Bangladeshi young men raised in workless households, Zuccotti and O'Reilly's (forthcoming) analysis of UK data reveal that they do noticeably better than their equivalent white British counterparts: they are much less likely to become NEET. Adult Indian and Bangladeshi men having parents with a low occupational status still have a higher chance of acquiring a service-class position than their white British counterparts (Zuccotti, 2015), even after controlling for education and other social background characteristics.

African men raised in single-parent households where that parent is working had more chance of being in either education or in employment compared to their white British male counterparts coming from a similar household. For young women, a different pattern revealed itself: white British and Caribbean young women were more successful at finding work than was the case for young white British and Caribbean men – they were the least successful at integrating into employment in the UK.

Young Caribbean men raised in two-earner households were more likely to be NEET compared to their white British counterparts. Young Caribbean men do not gain from the advantage of having both parents in employment. This may in part be due to difficulties in transferring dominant cultural capital in terms of social networks and habitus to enable them to find formal employment (Rafferty, 2012), which in turns affects educational and labour market opportunities. In contrast, the very low NEET rates found among young Indian and Bangladeshi men show that having had workless parents does not necessarily have the same expected negative effect for these young people.

By examining gender differences, Zuccotti and O'Reilly (forthcoming) do not find evidence that Pakistani and Bangladeshi women were less likely to be NEET than white British women among those raised in one-earner households. Knowing, however, the very high levels of unemployment and inactivity of Pakistani and Bangladeshi women, Zuccotti and O'Reilly (forthcoming) estimated a model excluding full-time students from the analysis finding that for young Pakistani women the penalty for those raised in one-earner households became more evident than for other ethnic groups. For those who do not manage to continue in further education, employment opportunities are reduced. For those who studied, the chances of obtaining employment and a higher occupational status are greater, although not necessarily equivalent to those of their white British counterparts. Educational attainment clearly makes a bigger difference for some non-white ethnic groups than appears to be the case for white British boys.

Zuccotti and O'Reilly (forthcoming) argue that we cannot simply read off from a selection of disadvantaged categories that these automatically determine the likelihood of being NEETs. Labour market segmentation for young people involves a complex set of mechanisms related not only to patterns of employer discrimination, the organisation of the VET system, but also to family characteristics and clearly some of the effects through the education system. Some of the explanation for the effect of parental worklessness on young generations has focused on (1) the transmission of attitudinal differences; (2) regional disparities in available jobs; (3) the effects of the benefits system generating a culture of dependency; and (4) differences in the cultural and social capital of parents. High parental expectations among ethnic minorities might lead to a direct motivation to participate in education and/or employment, which can counterbalance the disadvantages of their social origins.

Taken together these findings from our European comparison of the household effects on the labour market opportunities for young men and women, and how these pan out in different trajectories for young people from different ethnic backgrounds in the UK, illustrate new lines of labour market segmentation that have received negligible attention using an intersectional approach to date. They also illustrate how the effects of families vary between different communities of young people. There are universally comparable outcomes for young people coming from disadvantaged, work-poor families in that their entry into the labour market is more difficult. However, when we compare these for different ethnic groups and for young women and men, we can observe that transitions into employment are shaped by a complex system of mechanisms. For these reasons, policy interventions need to be more clearly targeted for the vulnerable groups that this analysis identifies.

Conclusions

This chapter demonstrates the interaction of the gendered dynamics of the youth labour market and the interrelationship with ethnicity and the sphere of social reproduction. Segmentation remains a powerful tool for understanding the challenges that young people face in the labour market. Here the interaction between gender, ethnicity and parental households shed light on new contours of segmentation that are often overlooked by researchers and policy-makers. By integrating the role of parental household into the early labour market experiences of young people, particularly during a crisis, we illustrate how an extension of the Humphries and Rubery (1984) framework of social reproduction acts in the dynamics of segmentation of the youth labour market with variable consequences by gender and ethnicity.

The evidence we bring together here from a large-scale European project[2] highlights the emergence of gender gaps in labour market experiences early on in the economic lives of young people, in line with other studies that consider gender differences, confirming the higher rates of NEET (Berg, 2015; McDowell, 2002) or extended periods of precariousness experienced by young women (Anxo et al., 2005). We also show how similar household effects have differential outcomes for different ethnic groups in the UK. However, there are a wider range of factors that shape outcomes for young people in the labour market (Reinecke and Grimshaw, 2015) and the studies briefly reported in this chapter demonstrate how the characteristics of the household provides yet another influence extending Humphries and Rubery's sphere of social reproduction to their influence on the youth labour market.

The analysis of the policy environment towards young people underlines that policy towards youth labour markets is often gender blind and there is limited evidence of consistent gender mainstreaming. Gökşen and colleagues (2016b) found that although the typologies of different welfare and school-to-work regimes captured some of the variation in national transitional systems, they also leave substantial variation unaccounted for. This partly relates to the absence of a comprehensive categorisation of school-to-work transitions, but also specific role of gender differences within these institutional environments.

Studies that consider ethnic comparisons are even slimmer on the ground. The analysis of the policy environment towards young people demonstrates the importance of considering the country-specific institutional environment when analysing youth labour markets.

Given the gender gaps identified in the labour market data, policies could be more efficient if they recognised gender and ethnic differences in youth labour markets. For example, school dropout rates for boys, segregation of training opportunities for girls and the interaction of gender and ethnicity in educational choices do not receive sufficient attention in more aggregate analysis. Although there is some evidence of good practice that recognises gender differences at the margins and indeed the intersectionality of youth, gender, ethnicity and other forms of vulnerability these policies are very much the exceptions (Knijn and Smith, 2012).

It is perhaps not surprising that policy towards youth has a small gender-sensitive component given the low level of gender mainstreaming in policy-making more generally (Smith and Villa, 2012). Long-term gender inequalities need to be addressed earlier, as once they emerge they tend to grow and become entrenched. The role of households in perpetuating, or protecting against, the consequences of segmentation requires a comprehensive policy approach addressing the multitude of factors that affect youth labour market access.[3] Our analysis illustrates new lines and trajectories in the segmentation of youth labour markets along the lines of gender, household and ethnic. These new forms of segmentation can, in part, be traced back to some of the effects of household patterns of employment and how these affect young people's opportunities in contemporary labour markets. As Rubery (2015) notes, the main thrust of labour market policy has failed to recognise the impact upon increasing segmentation of youth, largely by deregulation at the margins of the labour market. Unfortunately, the Great Recession has only served to exacerbate these gendered and ethnic lines of segmentation.

Acknowledgements

The research leading to these results has received funding from the European Union's Seventh Framework Programme for research, technological development and demonstration under grant agreement no. 613256. Further details about the research project on Strategic Transitions for Youth Labour in Europe (STYLE) are available on the STYLE project website: www.style-research.eu.

Notes

1　The 29 countries have been grouped as follows: Nordic (DK, FI, NO, SE); English-speaking (UK, IE); Continental (AT, BE, CH, DE, FR, NL); Mediterranean (CY, EL, ES, IT, MT, PT); Eastern European (BG, CZ, EE, HR, HU, LT, LV, PL, RO, SI, SK).

2　STYLE: Strategic Transitions for Youth Labour in Europe (www.style-research.eu).

3　To some extent the UK policy on 'Troubled Families' could be seen as an example of such a 'linked-up' approach. This programme, introduced in the UK after the summer riots in 2011, attempts to address families facing multiple disadvantages and helps ensure that young people from these backgrounds are not 'left behind'. However, the reputed success of this programme has been questioned as being 'too good to be true' (Crossley 2015); and Bawden (2016) claims that 'cash-strapped councils' have had an incentive to manipulate the evidence to prove their success. Nevertheless, this kind of policy illustrates attempts to move towards more targeted approaches to address multiple lines of segmentation.

References

Anxo, D. and O'Reilly, J. (2001), 'Regulating Working Time Transitions', in Schmid, G. and Gazier, B. *Full Employment and Labour Market Dynamics: Social Integration by Transitional Labour Markets* (Cheltenham: Edward Elgar) pp. 339–64.

Atkinson, A. (2015), *Inequality: What can be done?* (Cambridge, MA: Harvard University Press).

Bawden, A. (2016), 'The troubled families scheme has failed – this is the folly of payment by results', *Guardian*, 9 August, https://www.theguardian.com/commentisfree/2016/aug/09/troubled-families-programme-failed, accessed 9 August 2016.

Bell, D. N. and Blanchflower, D. G. (2011), 'Young people and the Great Recession', *Oxford Review of Economic Policy*, 27:2, 241–67.

Berloffa, G., Filandri, M., Matteazzi, E., Nazio, T., Negri, N., O'Reilly, J., Villa, P. and Zuccotti, C. (2015), 'Work-poor and work-rich families: Influence on youth labour market outcomes', *STYLE Working Papers*, WP8.1, http://style-research.eu/wordpress/wp-content/uploads/ftp/STYLE-Working-Paper-WP8_1.pdf (CROME: University of Brighton: Brighton).

Cho, S., Crenshaw, K., Williams and McCall, L. (2013), 'Toward a field of intersectionality studies: theory, applications, and praxis', *Signs*, 38:4, 785–810.

Collins, P. H. (2015), 'Intersectionality's definitional dilemmas', *Annual Review of Sociology*, 41:1, 1–20.

Crawford, C. and Greaves, E. (2015), *Socio-Economic, Ethnic and Gender Differences in HE Participation*, BIS Research Paper No.186 (Department for Business, Innovation and Skills: London).

Crenshaw, K. (1989), 'Demarginalizing the intersection of race and sex: a black feminist critique of antidiscrimination doctrine, feminist theory and antiracist politics', *The University of Chicago Legal Forum,* 140, 139–67.

Crenshaw, K. (1991), 'Mapping the margins: intersectionality, identity politics, and violence against women of color', *Stanford Law Review,* 43:6, 1241–99.

Crompton, R. (1999), *Restructuring gender relations and employment: the decline of the male breadwinner* (Oxford and New York: Oxford University Press).

Crossley, S. (2015), *The Troubled Families Programme: The Perfect Social Policy?,* Briefing No. 13 (Centre for Crime and Justice Studies, November), https://crimeandjustice.org.uk/pub lications/troubled-families-programme-perfect-social-policy, accessed 9 August 2016.

Eamets, R, Humal, K, Beblavý, M, Maselli, I, Bheemaiah, K, Smith, M., Finn, M. and Leschke, J. (2015), *Mapping Flexibility and Security Performance in the Face of the Crisis,* STYLE Working Papers, No. 10.1 (Brighton: University of Brighton).

Gökşen, F., Filiztekin A., Smith, M., Çelik Ç., Öker I. and Kuz S. (2016a), *Vulnerable Youth & Gender Mainstreaming,* STYLE Working Papers, WP4.3, http://style-research. eu/publications/working-papers STYLE WP10.2 (Center for Research on Management and Employment (CROME): Brighton: University of Brighton), http://www.style-research.eu/wordpress/wp-content/uploads/ftp/D4_3_030316_FINAL.pdf

Gökşen, F., Yükseker, D., Filiztekin A., Öker, I., Kuz, S., Mazzotta, F., and Parisi L. (2016b), *Leaving and Returning to the Parental Home during the Economic Crisis,* STYLE Working Papers WP8.3 (Center for Research on Management and Employment (CROME): Brighton: University of Brighton), http://www.style-research.eu/word press/wp-content/uploads/2015/03/STYLE-Working-Paper-D8.3-Leaving-and-re turning-to-the-parental-home-during-the-economic-crisis.pdf

Gregg, P. and Wadsworth, J. (1994), 'More work in fewer households?', discussion paper (London: National Institute of Economic and Social Research).

Gregg, P. and Wadsworth, J. (2001), 'Everything you ever wanted to know about measuring worklessness and polarization at the household level but were afraid to ask', *Oxford Bulletin of Economics and Statistics,* 63, 777–806.

Gregg, P. and Wadsworth, J. (2003), 'Workless households and the recovery', in Dickens, R., Gregg, P. and Wadsworth, J. (eds), *The labour market under New Labour: the state of working Britain* (Hampshire: Palgrave Macmillan) pp. 32–9.

Gregg, P., Scutella, R. and Wadsworth, J. (2010), 'Reconciling workless measures at the individual and household level. Theory and evidence from the United States, Britain, Germany, Spain and Australia', *Journal of Population Economics,* 23:1, 139–67.

Humphries, J. and Rubery, J. (1984), 'The reconstruction of the supply side of the labour market: the relative autonomy of social reproduction', *Cambridge Journal of Economics,* 8:4, 331–46.

Karamessini, M. and Rubery, J. (2014), *Women and Austerity: The Economic Crisis and the Future for Gender Equality* (London: Routledge).

Kenrick, J. (1981), 'Politics and the construction of women as second-class workers', in Wilkinson, F. (ed.), *The Dynamics of Labour Market Segmentation* (London: Academic Press,) pp. 167–92.

Knijn, T. and Smith, M. (2012), 'European Union and member states' youth policies agendas', in Knijn, T. (ed.), *Work, family Policies and Transitions to Adulthood in Europe* (Basingstoke: Palgrave Macmillan).

Leschke, J. (2012), 'Has the economic crisis contributed to more segmentation in labour market and welfare outcomes', European Trade Union Institute (ETUI) Research Paper, Copenhagen Business School.

McBride, A., Hebson, G. and Holgate, J. (2015), 'Intersectionality: are we taking enough notice in the field of work and employment relations?', *Work, Employment & Society*, 29:2, 331–41.

MacDonald, R., Shildrick, T. and Furlong, A. (2014), '"Benefits Street" and the myth of workless communities', *Sociological Research Online*, 19:3, 1, http://www.socresonline.org.uk/19/3/1.html.

McDowell, L. (2002), 'Transitions to work: masculine identities, youth inequality and labour market change', *Gender, Place and Culture*, 9:1, 39–59.

Macmillan, L. (2014), 'Intergenerational worklessness in the UK and the role of local labour markets', *Oxford Economic Papers*, 66:3, 871–89.

Mooney, S. (2016), '"Nimble" intersectionality in employment research: a way to resolve methodological dilemmas', *Work, Employment & Society*, 30:4, 708–18.

O'Reilly, J. (1994), 'What flexibility do women offer? Comparing the use of, and attitudes to, part-time work in Britain and France in Retail Banking', *Gender, Work and Organisation*, 1:3, 138–49.

O'Reilly, J. and Fagan, C. (eds) (1998), *Part-time Prospects: International Comparisons of Part-Time Work in Europe, North America and the Pacific Rim* (London and New York: Routledge)

O'Reilly, J., Eichhorst, W., Gábos, A., Hadjivassiliou, K., Lain, D., Lesckhe, J., McGuinness, S., Mýtna Kureková, L., Nazio, T., Ortlieb, R., Russell, H. and Villa, P. (2015), 'Five characteristics of youth unemployment in Europe: flexibility, education, migration, family legacies, and EU policy', *SAGE Open* (23 March 2015), http://sgo.sagepub.com/content/5/1/2158244015574962.

Picchio, A. (1992), *Social Reproduction: The Political Economy of the Labor Market* (Cambridge: Cambridge University Press).

Plantenga, J., Remery, C. and Ludovici, M. S. (2013), *Starting Fragile Gender Differences in the Youth Labour Market* (Luxembourg: Publications Office of the European Union).

Rafferty, A. (2012), 'Ethnic penalties in graduate level over-education, unemployment and wages: evidence from Britain', *Work, Employment & Society*, 26:6, 987–1006.

Reinecke, G. and Grimshaw, D. (2015), 'Labour market inequality between youths and adults: a special case?', in Berg, J. (ed.), *Labour Markets, Institutions and Inequality: Building Just Societies in the 21st Century* (Cheltenham and Geneva: Edward Elgar and International Labour Organization).

Rubery, J. (1992), 'Productive systems, international integration and the single European market', in Castro, A., Mehaut, P. and Rubery, J. (eds), *International Integration and Labour Market Organisation* (London: Academic Press).

Rubery, J. (2015), 'The UK production regime in comparative perspective', paper presented to the International Conference on Production Regimes in an Integrating Europe, WZB, Berlin, July 1993.

Rubery, J. (2015), 'Austerity and the future for gender equality in Europe', *ILR Review*, 68:4, 715–41.

Schoon, I. (2014), 'Parental worklessness and the experience of NEET among their offspring: evidence from the Longitudinal Study of Young People in England (LSYPE)', *Longitudinal and Life Course Studies*, 5:2, 129–50.

Smith, M. and Villa, P. (2012), 'Gender equality and the evolution of the Europe 2020 strategy', in Blanpain, R., Bromwich, W., Rymkevich, O. and Senatori, I. (eds), *Labour Markets, Industrial Relations and Human Resources Management in Europe: From Recession to Recovery* (Kluwer) pp. 3–23.

Villa, P. (1986), *The Structuring of Labour Markets: Steel and Construction Industries in Italy* (Oxford: Oxford University Press).

Walther, A. (2006), 'Choice, flexibility and security in young people's experiences across different European contexts', *Young,* 14: 2, 119–39.

Zuccotti, C. V. (2015), 'Do parents matter? Revisiting ethnic penalties in occupation among second generation ethnic minorities in England and Wales', *Sociology,* 49:2, 229–51.

Zuccotti, C. and O'Reilly, J. (forthcoming), 'Ethnicity, households and gender effects on becoming NEET: An intersectional analysis', *Work, Employment and Society*.

14

Labour policies in a deflationary environment

Annamaria Simonazzi

Introduction

National models of employment, production and welfare both mediate and respond to multiple pressures for change associated with various external and internal challenges: increased globalisation, deregulation and financialisation of markets, technological change, the ageing of the population and migration flows. The analysis of these challenges, their effect 'in maintaining, reshaping, revitalizing or indeed destabilizing national employment models', as well as the interlocking nature of institutions has been at the centre of Jill Rubery's research (Bosch, Lehndorff and Rubery, 2009: 2). The possibility of spillover or domino effects from employment to welfare, family and the production spheres increases the scope of change and suggests the need for a multifaceted approach involving macroeconomic, labour and social reproduction objectives (Rubery, 2015).

The Eurozone crisis has rekindled the debate on how to respond to short- and long-term change and to the hardships that it produces. The countries worse hit by the sovereign debt crises, in particular, have been the targets and laboratory of an unprecedented interventionism in the sphere of labour and industrial relations.[1] A problem of competitiveness, and specifically of labour cost competitiveness, has been diagnosed for their illness, hence the need for 'employment friendly reforms' to spur productivity and competitiveness. Labour and welfare reforms inflicted on, or self-inflicted by, various countries have been pursued within a deeply recessionary macro-environment. Indeed, internal devaluation has become a functional substitute for currency devaluation, and austerity-oriented fiscal policies are used to complement and reinforce the structural reforms. Consequently, the landscape of industrial relations has deeply changed and the 'European social acquis', rooted in social dialogue and public systems of social protection, is everywhere in retreat. A 'toxic austeritarism' (Hyman, 2015) 'has left little or no margin for domestic democratic institutions and social actors, downgraded from political to executive subjects' (Leonardi, 2016).

The long crisis and the policies that have been implemented in response raise questions that transcend a single country to encompass the European institutions. This chapter addresses two issues, analysed from the point of view of the Italian case. The first, relates to the increasing inequality in the labour market. As observed by Rubery (2015: 2), mainstream economics' failure to find a 'direct correlation between regulation and macro employment performance and growth ... changed the terms from performance to social justice issues ... [E]mployment regulation was still considered harmful because it favoured insiders over outsiders.' In Italy, the increasing dualism of the labour market has been depicted as an insider–outsider problem, created by the 'excessive' protection of standard employment relations. Consequently, the recent legislation aimed at reducing the regulation of the labour market has been presented as a necessary step towards greater equality. The second issue relates to the search for viable models to address the challenges of technological change in a globalised and competitive environment. Here again, the decade-long stagnation of Italian productivity has been ascribed to the insufficient flexibility and excessive protection of the labour market. This chapter also contrasts the short-term competitiveness effects of austerity/flexibility policies with the long-term efficiency effects deriving from a greater commitment of both the employer and the employed workforce. The view of social policy as a productive factor is embedded in the conviction that sustained growth and decent working conditions are the result of the interactions between macro-policies and labour outcomes, and great risks can spring from neglecting the systemic consequences of generalised, pan-European austerity.

The construction of a dualistic labour market

We can distinguish three phases in the development of Italy's labour policies in recent decades. In the first, in the early 1990s, agreements were targeted mainly at achieving wage flexibility; in the second, from the mid-1990s to the mid-2000s, legislation aimed at increasing labour market flexibility through the liberalisation of a wide range of atypical contracts; since then, and especially since 2011, the legislation turned to target the 'dualism' in the labour market.

Until the outbreak of the crisis, labour market reforms in Italy had mostly targeted new hirings (the so-called flexibility at the margin), while the firing rules for regular contracts were left substantially untouched. This policy was originally justified as a means of promoting the participation of youth and other hard-to-employ to the labour market (Rubery and Piasna, 2016). Between 1995 and 2007, despite a mediocre rate of growth of GDP, more than 3 million jobs were created (what has been called growth-less job creation), with flexible employment, characterised by fixed-term contracts, involuntary part-time and bogus self-employed, accounting for most of it. On top of these, and often inter-mingled with them, Italy also witnessed a great number of informal workers in the shadow economy. New hiring has taken place mainly through temporary work contracts, and the share of youth in temporary contracts is significant (Figure 14.1). At the end of 2012, only 21 per cent of new hiring contracts were open-ended, while 58 per cent were fixed-term, 9 per cent collaboration contracts,[2] 3 per cent apprenticeship contracts and other precarious contracts (temporary work agencies) accounted for the remaining 9 per cent (Table 14.1). In an economic slowdown, precarious workers are the first to be made redundant, though workers with an open-ended contract are far from shielded.

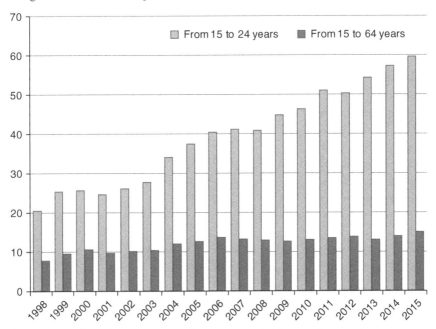

Figure 14.1   Share of temporary employment in total Italian employment by age group, 1998–2005 (%)

Source: Fana *et al.* (2016).

Table 14.1   Hiring and firing by type of contract, 2012

	Hiring		Firing	
	Number	%	Number	%
Premanent contracts	1,788,830	20.9	2,202,341	25.3
Temporary contracts	5,011,019	58.4	4,664,905	53.6
Apprenticeships	277,496	3.2	211,828	2.4
Collaboration contracts	756,582	8.8	832,111	9.6
Other	745,247	8.7	791,384	9.1
Total	**8,579,174**	**100.0**	**8,702,569**	**100.0**

Notes: 'Other' includes agency contracts and job on call also in the public sector.

Source: ILO (2015).

Since the mid-2000s, labour policies moved in somewhat contradictory ways; they aimed at reducing the dualism in the labour market by reducing the firing costs of open-ended contracts and promoting, through regulation and subsidies, the conversion of certain types of atypical contracts, while, at the same time, favouring the growth of other non-standard forms of employment.

Under the concurrent pressure of the markets and EU governors,[3] the Monti government launched the first attack on the protection of regular employment. The *Legge Fornero* (Law 92/2012) of 2012 aimed at addressing labour market dualism by acting on the firing and hiring costs of different types of contracts. On the one hand, it reduced the cost of individual dismissal, weakening the effectiveness of the 'Articolo 18' of Law 300/1970, which regulates firing conditions on open-ended contracts;[4] on the other, it tried to limit employers' use of 'false' self-employment and 'collaboration contracts' and to create incentives for the greater use of apprenticeship contracts. Finally, it reformed the system of unemployment benefits, extending the coverage to some forms of precarious contracts.

In 2014, Law 78/2014 (*Decreto Poletti*) removed the need to justify the use of fixed-term contracts, while still maintaining some limitations: a firm could not have more than 20 per cent of its total workforce on a fixed-term contract,[5] and each contract could only be renewed for a maximum of three years.

Finally, in 2015, the Renzi government adopted two different policies that also aimed to reduce labour market dualism and foster 'regular' employment by acting on two fronts: lowering firing costs of open-ended contracts and providing a generous subsidy for permanent hiring. Firstly, a broad-ranging enabling law (the so-called Jobs Act) involved the regulation governing dismissals, simplification of contracts and labour law procedures, reformed unemployment

benefits and active and passive labour market policies, and improved reconciliation between work and family life. The Jobs Act abolished workers' reinstatement rights in case of dismissal (except for discriminatory reasons), replacing
it with a monetary compensation (amounting to two months' pay per year of
work, reduced to half for firms with less than 15 employees). It introduced a
new standard open-ended contract for new hires, which reduces the level and
the uncertainty of firing costs for all new permanent contracts in firms with
at least 15 employees (the 'contratto a tutele crescenti', or 'graded security
contract'). Finally, while eliminating some forms of atypical contracts, such
as project work contracts, it increased the maximum amount of revenues
that can be received in vouchers from €5,000 to €7,000 per year, thereby
de facto incentivising the most precarious type of contract (see Chapter 8).
Secondly, a measure passed in the 2015 Budgetary Law provides a sizeable
temporary rebate of non-wage labour costs (up to €8,060 per year for three
years) to new permanent hiring of workers who, in the previous semester, did
not hold an open-ended position. These incentives are not targeted to specific
groups of workers, nor are they contingent upon firm-level net job creation,
that is, firms can use the subsidy to convert a temporary contract into a permanent one.

Assessment of the success of the new law is necessarily still preliminary.
Using microdata for Veneto, Sestito and Viviano (2016) conclude that the
two measures contributed to double the monthly rate of conversion of fixed-
term jobs into permanent positions. However, around 40 per cent of the new
total gross hires with open-ended contracts occurred because of the incentives, whereas 5 per cent can be attributed to the new firing regulations. Fana
and colleagues (2016) also find that the increase in permanent contracts was
mostly due to the conversion of temporary contracts into permanent ones.
Excluding transformations, new permanent contracts (net of dismissals) were
only 20 per cent of the total contracts activated during the first nine months of
2015, with a high share of involuntary part-time contracts. A dominant effect
of fiscal incentives, especially for big firms, is also detected by the analysis of
the Central Statistical Office (Istat, 2016: 190–3). If the new firing rules made
firms less reluctant to offer permanent job positions to yet untested workers, the opportunity of benefiting from the incentives in case of a conversion
certainly boosted temporary hiring, which came to be concentrated at the
very end of the period set for claiming the subsidy. The high rate of subsidised
conversions also raises the issue of the size of the dead-weight loss implicit in
these subsidies.

The insider–outsider debate

Flexibility policies were first advocated as the necessary response to the low job creation of the 1980s. In those years, 'jobless growth' and 'Eurosclerosis' were imputed to the rigidity of the labour market. Deregulation, it was argued, would lead to a net creation of jobs. Similarly, ten years later, the 'growth-less job creation' was credited to the labour market reforms. A lively debate on the employment effects of employment protection legislation (EPL) has accompanied these reforms. If the 1994 Organisation for Economic Co-operation and Development (OECD) Jobs Study (OECD, 1994) concluded that job creation relies on efficient markets, free from institutional constraints, ten years later the 2004 OECD Employment Outlook drew more cautious conclusions. Noticing the general tendency of labour policies towards 'easing the recourse to temporary forms of employment while leaving existing provisions for regular or permanent employment practically unaltered' (OECD, 2004: 63), the report concluded that the net impact on employment is ambiguous. In fact, EPL leads to two opposite effects: it reduces exits from the labour market while making entry more difficult. Thus, it concluded, employment cannot increase without economic growth, but differences in the strictness of EPL for regular and temporary jobs respectively might lead to the rise in the incidence of temporary work for groups in a weaker labour market position, such as youth, prime-age women and low-skilled workers. In view of this, facilitating the use of temporary employment while not changing EPL for regular employment may aggravate labour market duality and negatively affect the career and productivity of those trapped in temporary jobs.

Of the two options to reduce dualism – increase protections for temporary workers or reduce protections for regular employment – eventually the latter prevailed in Italy. With dualism worsening, the debate about increasing inequalities in the labour market intensified. Various arguments, ranging from the insider–outsider to the intergenerational conflict, have converged on attributing the precariousness of the 'outsiders' to the protection of the 'insiders' and have thus been instrumental in orienting the policies towards the reduction of protection. After decades of policies aimed at reducing the supposed rigidity of the labour market, compounded by austerity measures implemented in the crisis, the increasing precariousness of ever-greater segments of the workforce produced by these policies has been used to argue for the need to eliminate the excessive protection of insiders that unfairly discriminates against outsiders.

Yet was the Italian labour market as rigid as commonly maintained? The indicators of labour turnover have never validated the official accounts of an overly rigid Italian labour market. Research on turnover had demonstrated the co-existence of a very high index of turnover with a high share of job positions with long tenure. Contini and Trivellato (2005) argued that this apparently contradictory evidence could be explained by the dichotomy between two different models of employment – extremely mobile and extremely stable workers – that were combined in the index. While the youth account for most of the turnover, there are also plenty of workers in other age brackets in perennial flux. Among them, women, low-educated people and employees in small firms, low-tech segments of the value chain or traditional reservoirs of irregular work (agriculture, commerce, construction, services). These workers experience long spells of unemployment, often longer than the periods spent in employment. Core workers' protection had to do more with professional skills, experience and the firm's specific capabilities, making them valuable to the firm, than with EPL. As labour market segmentation theory has long made clear, multiple factors lead to the differentiation of employment conditions and rewards and it is worker–capital divisions, rather than employment regulation, which are the main source of inequalities in the labour market (Rubery and Piasna, 2016).

With increasing competition from low-cost countries in 'mature' products, and the swift path of technological change, even core male workers employed in sectors no longer protected from competition have come to be increasingly exposed to the risk of dismissal and unemployment (Istat, 2016: 129). Meanwhile, the protection of regular employment has been gradually eroded. An indication of the decreasing degree of rigidity of the labour market is provided by the OECD index of EPL (to be interpreted with caution owing to doubts about the reliability of the indicator). The index for Italy fell from 3.82 in 1990 to 2.26 in 2013, and compares not too unfavourably with an index of 2 for Germany and 3 for France (Table 14.2). Firing difficulties, which have a great weight in the indicator, have been further reduced in 2015 (as explained in the previous section). Moreover, thanks to a policy approach of levelling-down equalisation, in

Table 14.2   Employment protection legislation (OECD index), selected countries 1990; 1992; 2007; 2013

	Italy	France	Germany	Spain	Portugal	Greece
1990	3.82	2.7	2.92	3.65	4.1	3.62
1999	3.19	2.98	2.34	2.8	3.7	3.62
2007	2.38	3.05	1.93	2.68	3.49	2.62
2013	2.26	3	2	2.31	2.5	2.07

Source: OECD (2017).

Table 14.3 Index of protection for open-ended contracts (EPRC) and ratio of temporary contracts (EPT) over EPRC, 2013

	Italy	France	Germany	Spain	Portugal	Greece
EPRC	2.79	2.82	2.98	2.28	2.69	2.41
EPT/EPRC	0.97	1.33	0.59	1.39	0.87	1.21

Notes: Employment protection for regular contracts (EPRC); Employment protection for temporary contracts (EPT).

Source: OECD (2017).

2013 the index no longer indicates the existence of dualism in the Italian labour market (Table 14.3). The striking difference with Germany may be due to both the reduced protection of regular employment in Italy and the great increase in the precariousness of the secondary labour market in Germany.

What can be concluded from the results achieved by labour market deregulation in terms of employment and growth? One tenet of labour market segmentation theory is that flexibility is much more easily achieved by policies that support growth, when job opportunities are plenty and workers move between jobs. Data on gross labour turnover (hiring and firing) confirm this proposition. Labour turnover in Italy was high at the beginning of the last decade before the reforms that tackled insiders' protection, but in fact fell during the crisis when turnover mostly involved dismissals (Table 14.4). Once dismissed, adult workers face greater difficulties in re-entering the labour market (Simonazzi and Villa, 2007). The absence of effective retraining and activation policies makes these workers subject to the loss of human and social capital, increasing the risk of long-term unemployment; in 2015, 68.4 per cent of total adult unemployed were unemployed for more than 12 months, compared to 55.5 per cent of unemployed youth (Istat, 2016: 133). The absence of a correlation between labour market flexibility and macroeconomic employment performance raises the question of the social and long-term (growth) effects of these policies.

Inequalities, unemployment, precariousness, poverty

Job quality

The deep and prolonged economic crisis has taken a toll on the labour markets, with a fall in employment rates, dramatic increases in unemployment

Table 14.4   Gross turnover (hiring and firing/quitting) by firm size and region – Italy, manufacturing

	Total	20–49	50–199	200–499	Over 500	North-West	North-East	Centre	South
2003	29.9	34.2	30.6	27.4	25.8	23.8	31.5	30.0	34.2
2004	26.1	25.5	27.7	24.8	25.7	20.9	29.2	28.3	37.2
2005	24.0	25.4	24.4	23.2	22.3	18.3	24.7	26.7	35.3
2006	25.7	26.5	27.0	24.3	23.8	20.7	26.1	27.7	37.0
2007	26.9	26.1	29.8	27.5	24.2	22.0	28.6	30.3	38.8
2008	24.1	23.5	25.5	23.2	23.3	20.1	24.9	26.4	34.6
2009	17.5	17.4	19.2	17.0	16.1	15.2	17.0	17.8	28.0
2010	18.8	18.9	20.4	19.4	16.5	15.9	19.4	18.2	27.7
2011	18.5	19.3	19.7	17.7	16.7	15.5	18.4	18.2	27.3
2012	17.2	17.8	18.8	15.4	15.8	14.2	16.5	18.3	27.3
2013	16.1	16.4	16.8	14.0	16.2	13.0	16.2	16.5	25.2

Source: Checchi and Leonardi (2015) on Bank of Italy data.

and its duration. Between 2007 and 2014 unemployment doubled, from 6 to 13 per cent, only partly mitigated by a massive use of short-time schemes and wage redundancy funds. Employment and inactivity rates are now among the worst of the whole EU. While employment conditions have worsened especially for youth, deterioration is common to all age groups. The unemployment rate, which has increased across all age groups, reached a peak of 35.5 per cent in the 15–24 age bracket and is 9.7 per cent for the traditional male breadwinner category (the age bracket 35–49) (Table 14.5). The number of NEETs is also especially worrying: 2.3 million aged 15–29 in 2015, 96 per cent of which are in the age bracket 18–29. Their share increased from 17.7 per cent in 2008 to 25 per cent in 2013 (down to 22.3 per cent in the second quarter of 2016) (Istat, 2016b: 115).

The crisis has also affected those who remained in employment, remarkably worsening the quality of existing jobs and the level of pay. The OECD has developed a framework to assess the quality of jobs, structured around three main dimensions: earnings quality, labour market security and quality of the working environment. It is no wonder that all programme/crisis countries – Estonia, Greece, Hungary, Italy, Poland, Portugal, the Slovak Republic, Spain – do relatively badly in two or all of the three dimensions of job quality, and none performs well in at least one of these dimensions (OECD, 2016). Conversely, Germany and the Nordic countries are among the best performers (at least two out of three dimensions). Outcomes on job quality across socio-economic groups

Table 14.5   Employment and unemployment rates by sex, area, age, citizenship and education, 2016

	Employment rate (%)			Unemployment rate (%)		
	Total	Male	Female	Total	Male	Female
Total	57.7	66.9	48.5	11.5	10.6	12.8
Area						
North	66.3	73.8	58.8	7.4	6.5	8.6
Centre	62.3	70.6	54.3	10.4	9.4	11.6
South	44.0	56.1	32.1	19.3	17.6	22.1
Age						
15–34	40.6	46.3	34.7	21.4	20.2	22.9
15–24	17.2	19.5	14.7	35.5	35.1	36.1
25–34	61.0	70.2	51.7	16.9	15.4	18.9
35–49	72.8	83.7	62.1	9.7	8.3	11.5
50–64	58.3	70.0	47.2	6.2	6.2	6.2
Citizenship						
Italian	57.5	66.5	48.4	11.1	10.4	12.2
Foreign	59.5	71.1	49.3	15.0	13.0	17.4
Education						
Primary	43.1	55.3	29.7	15.8	14.4	18.5
Diploma	64.6	73.9	55.4	10.8	9.4	12.5
Graduate	78.6	83.6	74.8	6.2	5.0	7.2

Source: Istat (2016b).

confirm the evidence on labour market inequalities. The worse off are youth and low-skilled workers. Not only do they have the poorest performance in terms of employment and unemployment rates, but they also have the worst outcomes with respect to job quality: lower earnings quality, considerably higher labour market insecurity and higher job strain (especially the low-skilled).

The dynamics of wage inequality depicted in the OECD job quality index must be seen against a context of falling 'average' earnings. Additionally, most of the jobs lost during the crisis were predominantly low-paid (Istat, 2015: 157). These two factors result in a deceptive increase in earnings quality. In effect, like all other 'crisis' countries (but also the UK, see Blundell *et al.*, 2014), between 2010 and 2016 Italy suffered a reduction in real wages (Figure 14.2). An important factor has been the increasingly low levels of entry wages for newly hired young workers, due to the diffusion of atypical and apprenticeship contracts for first-job seekers (Figure 14.3). There is a persistent wage penalty, of the order of 11 per cent, associated with working under a temporary contract. Checchi

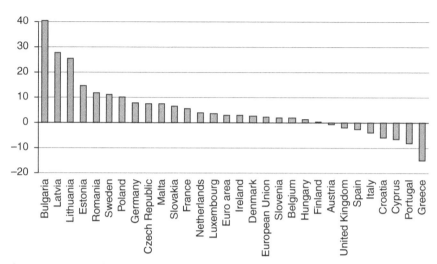

Figure 14.2 Development of real wages, 2010–16 (%)

Source: AMECO Database. Consumer Price deflator.

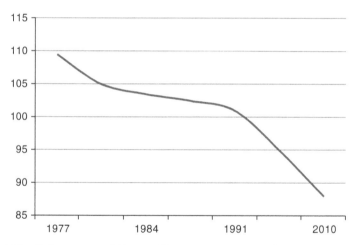

Figure 14.3 Relative wage of 30 year olds to average wage – Italy (%)

Source: Checchi and Leonardi (2015), based on Bank of Italy survey on household incomes.

and Leonardi (2015) have estimated that it mostly affects workers in the two bottom quintiles, while workers in the top quintile are less penalised. Moreover, this penalty is halved when individual fixed effects are included, suggesting that labour market flexibility increases wage differentials partly by sorting individuals according to their unobservable characteristics and partly by changing the wage for less-qualified occupations. This indicates that there are at least two types of temporary workers: the 'professionals', who take advantage of temporary contracts to increase their market power by enlarging the set of potential employers; and the 'precarious', who do not succeed in achieving a permanent job because they do not have the abilities demanded in the labour market. This same difference determines the probability to move out of a temporary contract to an open-ended one. Checchi and Leonardi conclude that whenever a legislative reform expands the share of workers under temporary contracts then, other things being constant, an increase in earnings inequality should be expected.

Welfare state retrenchment

The deregulation of the labour market ('flexibility at the margin') has been accompanied by partial reform of the so-called 'shock absorber' systems. A truly universal unemployment benefit scheme and income-support schemes are still in the making in Italy. The existing unemployment benefit system is based on two pillars: the unemployment benefit (divided into ordinary and reduced contributions) and the *cassa integrazione* (a short-time work scheme that keeps the worker attached to the firm, divided into ordinary, extraordinary and exceptional). The Fornero reform improved the first pillar, addressing two structural issues of the unemployment insurance benefits system: the low level and the short duration of benefits for workers on standard contracts, and the low coverage of workers with non-standard contracts. For workers on standard contracts the reform increased the replacement rate to 75 per cent of the previous wage and the maximum duration to 12 months (and to 18 months for those over 55), leaving unchanged at 52 full-time weeks the eligibility conditions. For workers on non-standard contracts, the replacement rate was increased to 75 per cent of the wage for a maximum duration of half the number of weeks of contributions. Eligibility criteria were reduced to 13 weeks of contributions in the previous 12 months. As a result, the number of workers covered increased by about 800,000 between November 2012 and November 2013. Nevertheless, the reform left other aspects of the system unchanged, such as the lack of social assistance available to jobseekers who have exhausted the eligibility period for unemployment benefits (ILO, 2015). As for the second pillar, the reform slightly revised eligibility conditions and involved the social partners, through the bilateral funds, in the funding of the benefit extended to all firms with more than 15 employees. The Jobs Act further revised the unemployment insurance system, setting new conditions for the renamed unemployment benefit (NASPI), a new provision (ASDI) to cover unemployed workers in distressed economic conditions who had exhausted the period (up to 18 months) of normal unemployment benefit, and a special benefit covering atypical workers ('collaborators', as defined in Note 2) (DIS-COLL).[6]

Active labour market policies (ALMPs) have always had a secondary role in Italy. With the crisis, the traditional difficulty in running efficient Public Employment Services (PES) and activation programmes for jobseekers has proved challenging. Thus Italy prioritised hiring incentives, which are easy to implement, even though in most cases the literature identifies significant dead-weight losses associated with this type of programme. Consequently, most ALMPs consisted in introducing and/or modifying the eligibility requirements for employment subsidies, according to what were deemed the categories of worker in most need of employment opportunities at that particular time (ILO, 2015: 61–70). These policies contrast with empirical results suggesting that employability of dismissed workers increasingly relies on both training and availability of jobs. The same report emphasises the point that no ALMP, no matter how efficient, can work if the economy is not growing. Since reforms in the labour market have been accompanied by draconian cuts in the budget, little room has been left for compensatory, active or passive, labour policies or welfare expenditure. Budget constraints were added to the notorious scarce efficiency of PES in reallocating labour towards equally scarce job opportunities. In an ever-deteriorating macroeconomic context, increased flexibility could do little to counteract the massive unemployment created by the crisis and the subsequent austerity policies. That is why, starting from these premises, it is difficult to speak of 'security'.

Pension reform

At the peak of the crisis, the Monti government also implemented a pension reform, which increased the minimum retirement age to 66 years, eliminating all forms of flexibility. Having fixed the calculation of pension benefits strictly according to contributions paid, it introduced an unnecessary rigidity with regard to retirement age. Precipitously and rigidly applied to respond to the urgent need to reduce spending and appease the financial markets (and the EU and German authorities), this reform left several short-term and long-term problems open. If, according to international assessment (International Monetary Fund and World Bank), after the Fornero reform the Italian pension system had become the most rigorous of EU systems, it was also the least adequate in terms of pension income and the most ineffectual with respect to the broader objectives of productivity, growth and employment. Two main trade-offs, which derive from the interrelation between the pension system, the labour market and the welfare state, threaten its long-term sustainability. Firstly, by

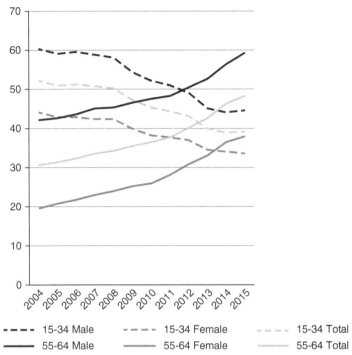

Figure 14.4   Employment by age and gender, 2004–15 (%)

Source: Istat (2016: 132).

increasing the retirement age among older workers, the reform had a negative effect on youth unemployment (Figure 14.4). By slowing down the substitution between workers of different ages, this might have had an impact also on productivity, if young workers are more attuned with new technologies. Secondly, by allowing atypical workers with low pay and fragmented work careers to be inadequately covered, the new contribution-based system has set in motion a 'pension time bomb' when these people reach retirement age. This problem is especially severe for women, who are more exposed to the risk of fragmentation of careers because of a poor reconciliation policy (Simonazzi, 2015). Subsequent laws attempted to respond to these problems by gradually extending the coverage to larger sections of atypical workers and re-introducing some flexibility in retirement age.

The interaction between the crisis and the labour and pension reforms has produced conflicting effects on the female employment rate. While occupational segregation sheltered women (relative to men) from the first effects of the crisis, subsequently female employment has suffered the effects of the fiscal crisis because of an over-representation in public sector employment. While the pension reform forcibly sustained the employment rate of older women, overall the crisis has brought the slowly increasing long-term trend of the female participation rate (which is still far behind the European average) to a halt.

To conclude, since the crisis growth eluded expectations, unemployment grew as did precariousness and insecurity. Income inequality and poverty increased. Social expenditure and social investment (education, research and development, health and care, training and active labour market policies) have all been drastically curtailed because of the fiscal compact. While real earnings stalled and mobility among income classes may not have decreased substantially, intergenerational mobility – measured across occupational groups (Simonazzi and Barbieri, 2016) and income groups (Franzini and Raitano, 2013) – has certainly decreased. The next section briefly discusses the long-term impact on growth.

Flexibility, productivity and growth

Structural reforms have their roots in the approach of mainstream economic theory that links the market mechanism with efficiency and productivity. According to this view, the problem with 'crisis countries' is a lack of cost competitiveness owing to excessive wage and labour protection. In 2004, the OECD Employment Outlook (OECD, 2004: 63) argued that a reasonable degree of EPL 'may foster long-term employment relationships, thus promoting workers' effort, co-operation and willingness to be trained, which is positive for aggregate employment and economic efficiency'. However, the 2016 OECD Employment Outlook (OECD, 2016) turned this argument on its head; well-designed structural reforms of product and labour markets may entail costly adjustments in the short run, but in the long-run the greater productivity of a more efficient allocation of labour will prevail again. Micro-economic factors buttress the long-run relationship (for a survey of the empirical research, see Boeri et al., 2015). In fact, by increasing firms' costs of dismissal, employment protection has a negative impact on productivity at the firm level: it lowers workers' effort (poor work performance or absenteeism) because there is less threat of lay-off, and it discourages firms from experimenting with new technologies with higher mean returns but also higher variance. The report concludes that the high employment and wage losses associated with greater flexibility in regulation governing the dismissal of workers on regular (open-ended) contracts would be reversed in a few years. The short-run costs are claimed to be less acute in countries with significant labour market dualism (measured as the share of fixed-term employment in total employment), and they would be smaller if reforms are implemented in the upswing, though it is in a depression that they are politically more enforceable (OECD, 2016). This view has legitimised the inclusion of structural reforms as a pre-condition in any agreements between the European Commission (EC) and programme or crisis member countries.

The results of these studies have not gone unchallenged. The short-run costs have been re-assessed and found to be neither small nor transitory, even for flexible labour markets such as the US one (Autor et al., 2016). The analysis of long-term effects of labour reforms on productivity and growth has been challenged on two grounds. Firstly, the model is based on the hypothesis of a smooth and efficient reallocation of labour. The assumption of a (full) employment equilibrium pre-empts any serious consideration of the costs of adjustment. Secondly, a truly dynamic analysis must consider the effects of employment relations on the factors determining innovation and competition. Specifically, competition increasingly relies on the quality and complexity of products, rather than on their price (Simonazzi et al., 2013). To be successful, firms must innovate their products, processes and organisation. To this end, a skilled and cooperative workforce is as essential as the firm's commitment to invest in its labour force. If arm's-length labour relations can make cost competitiveness profitable in the short run, this strategy may not pay in the long run. An increasing stream of literature has supported the view that labour market institutions that favour cooperation between workers and firms prove essential in sustaining growth and innovation (Addison et al., 2015; Fana et al., 2016).[7] The Italian experience provides support to this view, even if on the negative side. Concern for 'excessive' regulation of the labour market has diverted attention from the structural problems at the origins of the stagnation of the Italian economy. Deregulation of the labour market has been preferred to an alternative strategy based on investing in people in combination with an industrial policy aimed at strengthening and upgrading the industrial structure. The result has been slow growth and stagnant productivity, a segmented labour market and an impoverished workforce.

Deregulation and austerity policies in Italy have impacted on macroeconomic performance also via their effects on income inequality. The unions' weakened bargaining power has resulted in low or negative real wages. More decentralised and individualised wage settings have increased wage dispersion and polarisation. Together, these factors have affected the rate of growth of domestic demand (consumption and investment). With the fiscal compact barring public expenditures, only exports have been left to counter the recession. By sustaining the share of wages and reducing inequality, industrial relations targeting a more equal society might have contributed to economic sustainability, thereby sustaining growth.

Conclusions

Since the crisis, within the European Monetary Union framework, austerity measures and structural reforms (i.e. labour and wage flexibility) have been the only instruments admitted to address macroeconomic imbalances. Drastic cuts in social investment and 'internal devaluations' have magnified the dualism in the labour market and increased inequality and poverty. The Italian experience does not support the view that, if sufficiently flexible, labour markets adjust quickly to shocks, so that, in the long run, the benefits of flexibility outweigh the short-run adjustment costs.

No degree of labour flexibility can provide an adequate response to the multiple challenges represented by technological, organisational and social changes. These changes call for coordinated responses in the production, employment and social spheres. The diverse experiences of European countries over the recent decades highlight the role of social policy as a productive factor. In Sweden, technological change has been tackled within a cooperative climate in industrial relations; new forms of work organisation and generous policies favouring the upgrading of skills and the improvement in the quality of work have turned the challenge of technical change into an opportunity (Anxo, 2016). Conversely, Germany seems to have co-opted only one part of the labour force, leaving a large proportion of low-skilled or fragile workers behind (Lehndorff, 2015). Finally, in the Southern European countries, the structural reforms implemented in the crisis have eroded labour rights and weakened labour unions, reinforcing a 'low road' of wage cuts and precarious work that has priced out any alternative attempt of profiting from technological innovation. Wage moderation and low wages could not counter the effects of productivity decline; on the contrary, they are at the root of the productivity problem (Ciccarone and Saltari, 2015; Tronti, 2013).

This chapter has argued in favour of a different model in which unions, firms and the state can interact to devise a long-term industrial policy capable of fostering those organisational changes and those patterns of innovation that better respond to a shared social model. This calls for a complete reboot of the European and national approaches towards macroeconomic, labour and social policies.

Notes

1   See Schulten and Muller (2014) for an analysis of labour market deregulation policies in the EU.
2   'These contractual arrangements ... provide a contractual framework for individuals who are not formally employees of the firm and yet provide their regular working services (material or immaterial – i.e. consultants) to firms that often utilize them as normal employees. Compulsory pension and other social contributions are lower for these workers, which makes their labour costs lower than those of regular employees. As a result, many firms make great use of this type of arrangement' (ILO, 2015: 33).
3   See the confidential letter sent on 5 August 2011 by European Central Bank (ECB) President Jean-Claude Trichet and his designated successor, Bank of Italy Governor Mario Draghi, to the Italian head of government, demanding fiscal tightening and sweeping reforms before the ECB stepped into the market to ease mounting pressure on Italian bonds (Il Sole 24 Ore, http://24o.it/eHYLu).
4   This law protected workers from invalid lay-offs, requiring reinstatement in several cases. Law 92/2012 weakened this protection but did not completely abolish it. For a considerable set of cases, in fact, both the obligation of recourse to the courts in case of disputes over a dismissal and the possibility of workers' reinstatement were preserved.
5   Specific exceptions permitted by the law and sectoral collective agreements can allow deviation from this rule.
6   For detailed information, see: http://www.nuovi-lavori.it/index.php/sezioni/504-jobs-act-cambia-i-sussidi-di-disoccupazione?highlight=WyJzdXNzaWRpIiwiZGlzb2NjdXBhemlvbmUiXQ.
7   Differences in systems of innovations and industrial relations can explain differences in empirical results. For instance, it is argued that in the US skills are scouted mostly in the market, while in the European systems they are chiefly nurtured within the firm. This difference may explain why the empirical literature has found that firms' innovative dynamics are associated with centralised bargaining systems in the European economies (Addison et al., 2015) and with decentralised bargaining mechanisms and flexible labour markets in the USA (Menezes-Filho and Van Reenen, 2003). See Fana and colleagues (2016) for a review.

References

Addison, J. T., Teixeira, P., Evers, K. and Bellmann, L. (2015), *Collective Bargaining and Innovation in Germany: Cooperative Industrial Relations?*, IZA Discussion Paper Series No. 7871 (Bonn: Institute for the Study of Labor).

Anxo, D. (2016), 'Upskilling to avoid jobs' polarisation and growing income inequalities: the Swedish experience', *Economia & Lavoro*, 50:2, 13–24.

Autor, D. H., Dorn, D. and Hanson. G. H. (2016), *The China Shock: Learning from Labor Market Adjustment to Large Changes in Trade*, NBER Working Paper, No. 21906 (Cambridge, MA: National Bureau of Economic Research).

Blundell, R., Crawford, C. and Wenchao, J. (2014), 'What can wages and employment tell us about the UK's productivity puzzle?', *The Economic Journal*, 124:576, 377–407.

Boeri, T., Cahuc, P. and Zylberberg, A. (2015), *The Costs of Flexibility-Enhancing Structural Reforms. A Literature Review*, OECD Economic Department Working Papers, http://www.oecd-ilibrary.org/economics/the-costs-of-flexibility-enhancing-structural-reforms_5jrs558c5r5f-en, accessed 18 March 2017.

Bosch, G., Lehndorff, S. and Rubery, J. (2009), 'European employment models in flux: pressures for change and prospects for survival and revitalization', in Bosch, G., Lehndorff, S. and Rubery, J. (eds), *European Employment Models in Flux* (London: Palgrave Macmillan), pp. 1–56.

Checchi, D. and Leonardi, M. (2015), *Labour Market Measures in Italy 2008–13: The Crisis and Beyond* (Geneva: International Labour Organization).

Ciccarone, G. and Saltari, E. (2015), 'Cyclical downturn or structural disease? The decline of the Italian economy in the last twenty years', *Journal of Modern Italian Studies*, 20:2, 228–44.

Contini B. and Trivellato U. (2005), 'Dinamiche e persistenze nel mercato del lavoro italiano: una sintesi', in Contini B. and Tivellato U. (eds), *Eppur si muove* (Bologna: Il Mulino), pp. 13–84.

Fana, M., Guarascio, D., and Cirillo, V. (2016), 'Did Italy need more labor flexibility? The consequences of the jobs act'. *Intereconomics*, 51:2, 79–86.

Franzini, M. and Raitano, M. (2013), 'Economic inequality and its impact on intergenerational mobility', *Intereconomics*, 48:6, 328–35.

Hyman, R. (2015), 'L'austeritarismo e l'Europa: quali vie per resistergli', *Quaderni Rassegna Sindacale*, 3, 65–110.

ILO (International Labour Organization) (2015), *Inventory of Labour Market Policy Measures in the EU 2008–13: The Crisis and Beyond*, Synthesis report (Geneva: International Labour Organization).

Istat (Istituto Italiano di Statistica) (2015), *Rapporto annuale* (Rome: Istat).

Istat (Istituto Italiano di Statistica) (2016a), *Rapporto annuale* (Rome: Istat).

Istat (Istituto Italiano di Statistica) (2016b), *Il mercato del lavoro*, 12 September, http://www.istat.it/it/files/2016/09/Mercato-del-lavoro-II-trim_2016.pdf?title=Il+mercato+del+lavoro+-+12%2Fset%2F2016+-+Testo+integrale+e+nota+metodologica.pdf, accessed 18 March 2017.

Lehndorff, S. (2015), 'Model or liability? The new career of the "German model"', in Lehndorff, S. (ed.), *Divisive Integration: The Triumph of Failed Ideas in Europe – Revisited* (Brussels: European Trade Union Institute).

Leonardi, S. (2016), 'Trade Unions and collective bargaining in Italy in the years of the crisis'. Forthcoming in Lehndorff, S., Dribbusch, H. and Schulten, T. (eds.), *A Rough Landscape – European Trade Unions in Times of Crises* (Brussels: European Trade Union Institute).

Menezes-Filho, N. and Van Reenen, J. (2003), 'Unions and innovation: a survey of the theory and empirical evidence', in Addison, J. T. and Schnabel, C. (eds), *International Handbook of Trade Unions* (Cheltenham: Edward Elgar), pp. 293–334.

OECD (Organisation for Economic Co-operation and Development) (1994), *The Jobs Study* (Paris: OECD).

OECD (Organisation for Economic Co-operation and Development) (2004), *Employment Outlook* (Paris: OECD), http://www.oecd.org/els/emp/34846856.pdf.

OECD (Organisation for Economic Co-operation and Development) (2016), *How Good Is Your Job? Measuring and Assessing Job Quality* (Paris: OECD), http://www.oecd.org/std/labour-stats/Job-quality-OECD.pdf, accessed 18 March 2017.

OECD (Organisation for Economic Co-operation and Development) (2017), *Indicators of Employment Protection* (Paris: OECD), http://www.oecd.org/employment/emp/oecdindicatorsofemploymentprotection.htm, accessed 18 March 2017.

Rubery, J. (2015), *Re-regulating for Inclusive Labour Markets*, Conditions of Work and Employment Series No. 65 (Geneva: International Labour Organization).

Rubery, J. and Piasna, A. (2016), *Labour Market Segmentation and the EU Reform Agenda: Developing Alternatives to the Mainstream*, Working Paper No. 10 (Brussels: European Trade Union Institute).

Schulten, T. and Müller, T. (2014), 'European economic governance and its intervention in national wage development and collective bargaining', in Lehndorff, S. (ed.), *Divisive Integration: The Triumph of Failed Ideas in Europe – Revisited* (Brussels: European Trade Union Institute), pp. 331–63.

Sestito, P. and Viviano, E. (2016), 'Hiring incentives and/or firing cost reduction? Evaluating the impact of the 2015 policies on the Italian labour market', *Questioni di Economia e Finanza*, 325.

Simonazzi, A. (2015), 'Italy: continuity and change in welfare state retrenchment', in Vaughan-Whitehead, D. (ed.), *The European Social Model in Crisis: Is Europe Losing its Soul?* (Cheltenham: Edward Elgar and Geneva: International Labour Organization), pp. 339–85.

Simonazzi, A. and Barbieri, T. (2016), 'The middle class in Italy: reshuffling, erosion, polarization', in Vaughan-Whitehead, D. (ed.), *European Middle class Disappearing – Evidence in the World of Work* (Cheltenham: Edward Elgar and Geneva: International Labour Organization), pp. 245–70.

Simonazzi, A., Ginzburg, A. and Nocella, G. (2013), 'Economic relations between Germany and southern Europe,' *Cambridge Journal of Economics*, 37:3, 653–75.

Simonazzi, A. and Villa, P. (2007), 'Le stagioni della vita lavorativa e il tramonto del 'sogno americano' delle famiglie italiane', in Villa, P. (a cura di) *Generazioni flessibili* (Roma: Carocci Editore).

Tronti, L. (2013), 'Riforme della contrattazione, produttività e crescita: un dialogo tra economisti', *Economia & Lavoro*, 47:3, 7–70.

15

Uncertainty and undecidability in the contemporary state: the dualist and complex role of the state in Spanish labour and employment relations in an age of 'flexibility'

Miguel Martínez Lucio

Introduction

When discussing the state and labour regulations, the debate tends to focus on the role of the law. From a sociological, or politico-sociological, perspective it is often the case that we like to complement such an approach with a greater sensitivity to other forms of representation at the level of the state, such as the role of 'social dialogue' and the role of the various state entities and authorities such as labour inspectors. There is a tendency sometimes to see the state as one factor in an array of social and institutional relationships, but this tends to obscure the more complex role of the state. In addition, the interests of the state and the way it aligns to specific social actors can also be much more complex and even contradictory, especially in terms of balancing economic and political imperatives when it comes to questions of efficiency and legitimacy (Offe, 1984). The state is, as we know, not merely the political arm of some dominant economic and social elites (although it can be), but a complex and even contradictory space, an ensemble of institutions balancing representative, interventionist and institutional dynamics (Jessop, 1982, 2002). The state can therefore be seen as 'a relatively unified ensemble of socially embedded, socially regularised, and strategically selective institutions, organisations, social forces, and activities organised around (or at least involved in) making collectively binding decisions for an imagined political community' (Jessop, 2002: 40). The state can therefore be interpreted, as far as Jessop is concerned, at various levels of activity such as modes of political representation; internal articulation of the state apparatus in the forms of modes of intervention and their realisation; political projects articulated by different social forces regarding such forms of representation and intervention; and broader hegemonic projects that attempt to legitimise the state in relation to economy and society (Clark, 2001; Hyman, 2008; Jessop, 2002: 42; for a further discussion, see MacKenzie and Martínez Lucio, 2014). To this extent, the question of coordination of such levels and different approaches in public policy and state agencies politically and organisationally is one we need to be alert to (Crouch, 1993). What is more, the state intervenes not just in social spaces but also in ideological ones where specific issues, sensibilities and even national debates develop and configure the nature and impact of state policies (Locke and Thelen, 2006). Within these social and ideological spaces the question of gender and equality is a significant dimension which is often missing, but which, when added to any analysis, will allow us to evaluate more clearly the extent and failings of labour rights and policy – as Jill Rubery and her colleagues' work points out (Fagan and Rubery, 1996; Humphries and Rubery, 1984; Rubery, 2011; Rubery and Fagan, 1995). These insights on the ambivalence of regulation and employment relations contribute to the approach this chapter takes in terms of looking at the inherent ambivalence in questions of regulation and state policy in relation to different groups of workers and social agendas. The ways in which working time, pay systems and training are structured needs to be understood in terms of their contradictory effects; and while the issue of gender is just a part of this chapter the relevance of such studies is that they ask us to focus on different state or regulatory projects and how they intertwine and even contradict each other. Meardi and colleagues (2016) have similarly argued that a gender-sensitive perspective has enriched discussions on the state in labour and employment relations and broadened the way in which we seek to evaluate the role of the state across different agendas.[1]

This approach is important for this chapter because the state in Spain has had a series of competing projects and strategies – not to mention narratives – which have led to a contradictory set of agendas and developments that have increasingly been at odds and in conflict with each other. Hence, we need to understand the way in which the state has developed and responded to competing challenges and issues through its complex and varied institutional make-up. To appreciate this, we must also place the question of the state in relation to work and employment in a historical context so we can see how these specific issues have emerged; how the state has been responsible or not for such issues in the past, and if so in what form and through what means; how it has responded to them through various projects and different apparatus; and what kinds of narratives and sensibilities, if any, have emerged to frame discussions. This allows us to appreciate the difficulty in clearly delineating any uni-linear or mono-causal narrative of the Spanish state as either 'progressive' and social or simply 'regressive' and neoliberal. In many senses, the state in responding to the development of a market-oriented economy and globalisation on the one hand is also developing social agendas and political forms of rights at work on the other; many observers have stated that the tensions between these since the 1970s is quite acute. The challenge of establishing a system of rights and regulations after the Francoist regime and of creating organised and established approaches to regulation during the decline of the more organised and Keynesian state approaches within Europe (Lash and Urry, 1985) has meant that strategic initiatives have been important in ensuring – or trying to ensure – the effective reach of that regulation. After discussion of this subject, this chapter focuses on the way 'social dialogue' (a slightly ambivalent term generally, and no less so for Spain) from above and forms of intervention and labour market policies from below have been used to sustain what has arguably emerged as a fairly successful system at one level, but one which has also presided over extensive labour market fragmentation.

Constructing the public sphere in the realm of work and employment

In a comparative study of the impact of austerity on Southern European economies since 2008, Koukiadaki and colleagues (2016) have argued that those normally right-wing and/or elite European Commission-based commentators and politicians criticising the lack of labour flexibility in Greece, Portugal and Spain have tended to ignore the fact that these systems emerged from oppressive regimes where you would not have anticipated the eventual levels of institutional trust and joint working that has overseen labour relations and work-related issues more generally after those periods of authoritarianism. The relative economic success that the Spanish system saw in formal terms, and its far-reaching coverage in terms of collective bargaining, is something that, in 1981, one would not have easily foreseen. In this respect, any analysis has to be mindful of the perspectives and predictions that shape our assumptions and views.

The case of the Spanish state was one where the formal reach and role of state organisations were fairly extensive in terms of industry and political life during the Francoist dictatorship from the late 1930s to the mid-1970s. The paternalistic nature of the state in some sense had a Fordist and authoritarian-regulation perspective and was politically supportive of employer interests. However, in such a context the detailed organisation of work-related issues – the *ordinanzas laborales* (labour ordinances) come to mind, as does the state-led system of worker representation through the vertical unions – means that the arena of workers' rights consisted of elements which in turn configured some of the later legacies of the regime and post-regime period. This curious background became a focus of engagement later in relation to state resources for organised labour and questions of job classifications. This meant there was a tension between the formal state concern with order in labour relations (pre- and post-1975) and the more decentralised realities that existed in the actual arenas of labour relations, which had to be resolved in the political domain (Molina, 2006). This and the historical context bring to the fore the argument that the state is involved in the labour-relations arena in curious ways (Molina, 2014). In fact, the role of the political is important in terms of resolving the limitations of the state in Spain during certain periods (Martínez Lucio, 1998), yet contrary to Molina's seminal work (see 2014, inter alia) I would emphasise the much more contradictory nature of state projects and the vacillation or ambivalence in state trajectories as salient factors. In addition, the systematic and strategic features of the state seemed limited to a short-term and deferential approach to finance capital and to the informal practices of employers (Banyuls and Recio, 2009). The state was also relatively inegalitarian in terms of labour market policies and inclusiveness for a long period of time – committed to a highly gendered and hierarchically paternalist view of work and the role of women (Lopez and Santos del Cerro, 2013).

Yet the first decade or so of the post-Francoist years saw the development of a system of formal collective and individual rights which underpinned trade union representation and which ensured – what appeared then to be – a robust set of constitutional rights for workers through the construction of a collective voice, the establishment of majority representation and the power of unions through systems of works councils and collective bargaining (for a reflection on that earlier period, see Baylos Grau, 1999; see also Alonso, 1999 and 2007). The development of election-based works councils (*comites de empresa*), trade union branches (*secciones sindicales*) and principles of collective bargaining representatives contributed to a system which was one of the highest in Europe in these terms, although it had one of the lowest memberships. This allowed joint regulation to develop, although, as suggested in parts of this chapter, in some cases there are question marks over matters of implementation and the role of the social content of collective bargaining.

Within the others spheres of the state, beyond that of the area of the law, the development of the public sector has been significantly developed and modernised in areas such as education and health, with systems of labour relations of a more structured nature being enhanced (leaving aside for the time being the question of austerity) in terms of employment stability and collective voice, even with the functionary status of the individual employment relation. Public sector labour relations have seen relatively important improvements in terms of female worker inclusion and the development of what could be termed 'good employment relations and conditions'. In this respect, this has been an important signalling feature of the role of the state in questions of work and employment, although the push to greater flexibility and wage controls since 2008 has suggested a susceptibility and lack of significant political influence by trade unions. What is more, the ongoing extension of the state labour inspectorate and its integrated and professional orientation have been seen as a basis for the innovation and renewal of state roles (Benavides *et al.*, 2009: Meardi *et al.*, 2012; Sesé *et al.*, 2002). The use of elaborate information systems and joint working with social partners become features of some aspects of the labour inspectorate, although resourcing has always been a concern for the trade unions in relation to their views of this aspect of the state, especially when compared to certain other European cases (Morillas *et al.*, 2013). In some regional-national states (*autonomias*) within Spain the link between state organisations and social partners was more advanced at key points with this space assisting in the coordination of these different roles.

Nevertheless, a body of collective and individual rights emerged after the mid to late 1970s in a context of extensive industrial restructuring and labour market change. The role of systematic and detailed policies to withdraw public subsidies and restructure key industries was a key feature of the Socialist government's industrial policies in the 1980s. For some this represented a more market-oriented approach to industry and development (Smith, 1998). The extent of redundancies was extensive and involved a range of compensation programmes and welfare support services which allowed some space for trade unions, employers and managers to mitigate some of the negative aspects of the changes. The cost of laying people off or making them redundant was relatively higher in Spain when compared to other parts of Europe, and, for example, in some key industries such as steel there were exceptional payments and support provided to specific communities along with retraining initiatives. This restructuring strategy, which was met by various mobilisations and strikes by the trade unions, was nevertheless resolved through complex micro-level negotiations between the main actors over the conditions and support for restructuring (Martínez Lucio, 1998); for some, this has meant that the trade union role has been more engaged in facilitating change, as in telecommunications, although this led to a labour relations culture of monetising and focusing on the quantitative aspects of change as opposed to the qualitative ones (Rodriguez Ruiz, 2015). It also led to labour relations success being viewed as avoiding conflict and facilitating downsizing, albeit with significant remuneration for those affected in the more organised and unionised parts of industry and the economy. In this respect the nature of 'social' dialogue was skewed around particular agendas in the 1980s, establishing a particular language of restructuring. The main trade unions argued for a broadening of this agenda although the reality of different circumstances forced compromises and a dialogue based on negotiated restructuring and downsizing. The state's key ministries in relation to employment and industry – working with regional autonomous governments – were focused on this *reconversion*. However, much debate has focused on the cost of restructuring and of the payment to workers in high-profile sectors, but as trade unions and progressive economists attempted to point out, the nature of the welfare state in terms of unemployment payments and social benefits remained limited although there were some improvements.[2] Working alongside these strategies was the state's conciliation and mediations service, which allowed for individual negotiations to take place between workers and their organisations during moments of change and thus, while on occasions it did lead to higher redundancy payments, also meant that the process could be fast-tracked and avoid collective mechanisms of regulation (Martínez Lucio and Blyton, 1995). Hence, individual mechanisms of regulation were developed to bypass or 'parallel' collective frameworks creating a curious set of dual universes of regulated and deregulated realities.

Another feature of the state which limited the impact of the collective and newly formed individual framework of rights at work was the question of the under-funded nature and limited reach of the judicial system in relation to work and employment issues. The slow and complex nature of the judicial system meant that cases concerning health and safety or wages, and not just redundancies, would take considerable time and thus lead to greater use of informal and individualised – and non-regulated – solutions between employers and workers. In effect, this would create – perhaps – a form of voluntarism and a more deregulated culture even if the system was more regulated in theory. This was sustained by an emergent political discourse that steadily consolidated itself by extolling the Anglo-Saxon approach to regulation and organisational management.[3] The current post-2008 austerity crisis also led to a series of reforms in terms of collective bargaining that further facilitated management's opt-out or modifications of collective agreements in certain circumstances (see Rocha, 2014; Fernandez Rodríguez *et al.*, 2016).

In addition, since the 1980s the state has steadily facilitated the development of specific forms of temporary and agency contracts. For some this has meant a dualist state policy which has led to some of the highest levels of numerical flexibility in Europe and a push to a more fragmented social and economic context in

terms of work and employment (Sola *et al.*, 2013).[4] For others, this represents
a situation where Spain has seen the emergence of an insider–outsider labour
market (Dubin and Hopkin, 2014). Hence, the state has deliberately created
counter spaces to the collective space of dialogue and regulation it has overseen,
creating a dualism which has been regulated by different sets of organisations,
both public and private. For Prosser (2015), Spain is part of a set of countries
where such changes are as much about liberalisation of labour markets and not
just dualist tendencies. In terms of gender, ongoing equality measures have not
been able to stem the dualist traits within the economy in terms of the position
of women (Lux and Wöhl, 2015). Miguelez and Recio (2010) have pointed to
the way in which labour market inclusion policies intended to benefit women
in Spain have not been fully complemented with policies that have created
more family and working-time support. In terms of social expenditure, the
country is still below the European norm (Miguelez and Recio, 2010). Even
before the 2008 austerity crisis, the Spanish labour market was uneven and
exhibited dualist characteristics. There had been substantially high levels of temporary contracts and there operated an informal dimension of work in sectors
such as construction and especially agriculture. Young workers and women had
historically found it difficult to get contracts in permanent core employment
(Fernandez *et al.*, 2016; Fernández Rodríguez and Martínez Lucio, 2014), and
these core sectors were not a main employment sector for immigrant workers
either. Sectors such as agriculture, hospitality, domestic service and construction sectors have also been prone to higher levels of outsourcing and temporary
contracting that have created a more precarious experience for migrant workers and the organisation of that employment. In addition, the unemployment
rate in the past few years for immigrant communities has regularly been above
40 per cent. Hence any discussion of the labour market needs to account for the
complex and sometimes contradictory roles of social reproduction (Humphreys
and Rubery, 1984). The understanding of the role of the state in this regard in
relation to labour and employment relations needs to be broadened. What is
more, equal opportunities approaches must be more clearly linked to systems
of labour market organisation, policy and public discourses (Fagan and Rubery,
1996; Rubery and Fagan, 1995).

While trade unions have involved groups such as migrants through various
social inclusion strategies – in some cases with the help of state resources –
the overall system of welfare and social service support has been constrained
and uneven. We need to comprehend that these economic and social regulatory characteristics counter many of the political initiatives that emerge
from various social and state sources in relation to the politics of inclusion.
In addition, the extent of ongoing social and organisational hurdles in Spain is

very apparent, especially for non-EU migrants due to the sectors they work in as well (Solé and Parella, 2003). There are serious mismatches in the labour market in terms of immigrants and their skills, for example (Fernández and Ortega, 2008).

To this extent, while the level of collective bargaining coverage was high for the past 20 to 30 years, most workers in sectors such as construction and agriculture relied on agreements signed at the national and provincial levels, with these being known for their limited content and authority in real and effective terms (Martínez Lucio, 1998). In addition, the labour market saw the entrance of immigrant workers in those sectors which had a weaker tradition of union organisation and regulatory coverage: hospitality, construction, domestic service and retailing (Cachon, 2007). These are sectors that were disproportionally affected by the economic crisis in the post-2008 period but they were already poorly protected in terms of labour market regulation and policy in Spain.

Yet the irony is that this growing dualism – coupled with the changing social character of the labour market in terms of younger workers, women and ethnic minorities who are mainly in poorly paid and insecure jobs – has meant that the state has had to respond to these forms of development by creating informational and support services for marginalised workers and intervening on questions of training and development alongside social organisations and trade unions (see Martínez Lucio and Connolly, 2012). One could argue that trade unions have been linked to various state bodies and representative structures, although you could not claim that Spain has a strong corporatist system of labour relations – however, as discussed later, a debate on this does exist. The link to the political parties is much more flexible but relations with the main right and left parties up until this time were fluid, with the left relatively united in terms of social dialogue (for some, the two majority trade unions had had too strong an institutional social dialogue relationship with the right-wing *Partido Popular* from the late 1990s up until 2003): 'Stronger state–union relations in Spain result in more inclusive political action and servicing towards immigrants by Spanish unions. By contrast, the multicultural, pluralist nature of the UK labour market and public sphere result in British trade unions paying more attention to linguistic diversity and community organizing' (Meardi *et al.*, 2012: 19). Yet sectors such as agriculture, hospitality, domestic service and construction have been prone to higher levels of outsourcing and temporary contracting, which has created a more precarious background for the migrant worker experience and labour organisation. The fragmentation of the economy has led to a growing disconnect between marginalised workers and trade unions – regardless of the institutional efforts of the latter. Increasing government strategies of neoliberal reform, in terms of limiting the workers covered by sector agreements and collective bargaining more generally, and of limiting the ability of trade unions to challenge management attempts at restructuring over the past decade, have undermined the regulation of employment. In effect, the state is caught trying to limit and contain some of the problems it creates through the dualist legacy it has developed.

The question of social dialogue in Spain: overcoming challenges from above?

While the level of participation in terms of representation at the state level with regards to trade unions and employer organisation is not as embedded as that of certain Nordic countries, the level of political exchange between the three main 'actors' (to use the language of the corporatist and neocorporatist debates) is intriguing and for some this has represented an important feature of the past 40 years (Guillén Rodríguez and Gutiérrez Palacios, 2008). The role of social dialogue in some form or another has been considered by various commentators to be a significant feature of Spain's political dimension and labour relations system. In the face of possible conflict – both industrial and political – there has been a view that the Spanish system has a capacity for reconciliation and realism which tends to underpin the main features of emerging democracy; this could be due to the memory of authoritarianism and the civil war, and it may also be due to the relatively inclusive nature of the nation-building projects since the early 1980s with their focus on Europeanisation, modernisation and 'technological progress'. Between 1982 and 2010 (and in some respects up to 2015) the main forces of the parliamentary left and right have managed to create a language of progress which has been significant in framing national industrial debates, and at the heart of such approaches has been the focus on the importance of 'democratic consolidation' (Linz and Stepan, 1996). Within this context, the development of the state has been a key feature of nation-building around the main aspects of health, education and transport. There have been question marks over the nature of that development and the extent to which it has been premised on an uncoordinated and unregulated set of developments in terms of the construction and banking industrial sectors; however, in discursive terms, the 30 years referenced previously was marked, broadly speaking, by certain features of consensus.

In terms of social dialogue, there is a range of scholars who argue that this has been sustained by a flexible but continuous – even if interrupted at times – system of national agreements of a neocorporatist nature. Such agreements have varied from tripartite national agreements on wages and employment through to specific agreements on questions of training and working conditions (Gonzalez Begega, 2015; Guillén Rodríguez and Gutiérrez Palacios, 2008). There has been a shift from the tripartite stabilisation and reform-type agreement to the more specific and focused agreements between employers and major trade unions, with the trade unions managing through their relative power to sustain a system of dialogue (Molina and Rhodes, 2011). What is more, trade unions have taken to political exchange in terms of institutional roles and regulation as it is less of a risk than bargaining over restructuring and change – as was the case in the 1980s (Molina, 2006) – and this can also guarantee a supportive framework for a coordinated collective bargaining system (Molina, 2005). In effect, the focus of bargaining has also moved to a supply-side orientation, as it has in issues such as training, which we discuss in the next section.

Hence, there is a curious flexibility to the system of representation and it has become an interesting framework for other levels of labour relations regarding the role of the political in labour relations (see Hamann, 2011). In fact, during the period of austerity and the crisis of joint regulation resulting from the nature of labour reforms driven by the right-wing government (2010–15), irrespective of the presence of short general strikes and political tensions, there have been many instances of negotiation and discussion in relation to various aspects of labour relations (see Gonzalez Begega et al., 2015) – the system in effect 'goes down' at certain moments, to use a computing term, but it has an ability to 'reboot' and revert to negotiation quite swiftly according to such authors in some cases.

What is more, there are various ministerial and functional forms of tripartite engagement in areas such as migration policy and equality. The emergence of forums for the discussion of legislation and the use of public resources has been a visible part of the state's structure, which has also reproduced itself at the level of regional autonomous states, although the politics and general orientation of those levels can limit or enhance such dialogue. The role of the *Consejo Economic y Social* as a national informative and consultative body that includes a range of organisations has been important in sustaining forms of dialogue across the different spheres and interests of society, although it was late in being developed by various governments. This informational political exchange allows for a range of dialogues to exist across various dimensions of the state.

However, there are views that this system is primarily strategic in orientation and not as embedded as would first appear (Martínez Lucio, 1998; Roca, 1991). The argument is that the nature of social dialogue has been more about implementation and less about high-level policy formulation. There has not been any consistent engagement in terms of more strategic economic issues or a focus on employment (and within that specific aspects of employment). The more permanent or fixed forms of dialogue such as the *Consejo Economico y Social* have not really had the impact some would desire in strategic terms. Some critical voices have argued much of this may be due to the nature of social democracy in Spain, which has been enthralled with marketisation. There is a view that there is a trade-off between strategy and structure – that the collective voice of workers has been strategically restricted to specific times and in terms of specific spaces (Martínez Lucio, 2000) in order to limit the constraints on the evolution of a more globalised and marketised capitalist economy.

In fact, Molina (2007) has argued that for all the grandiose edifice of '*concertación*' it has not quite brought in a tightly articulated system of labour relations, and, in reality, it is more fragmented than at first imagined. The sector level of bargaining has been an uneven feature of Spain and it depends on what sector you look at (Fernandez et al., 2016). A recent study by Sola and colleagues (2013) has shown ongoing reforms of the labour market and ever greater flexibility and change, which, while in some cases concerted and negotiated, have not quite eroded the ever dualist nature of the labour market and work. In part this is due to the nature of the left in Spain until recently and the way in which, in the 1980s, the Socialists did not institutionally embed labour voice (Sola et al., 2013). In effect, the state has used its complex structures to locate labour voice in specific ways and in a strategic manner that have allowed broader economic debates to be limited and perhaps more closed than some observers would prefer to acknowledge. In all fairness, one could argue that trade unions and employers' organisations may have had resource issues when it came to playing a fuller role in terms of supporting and implementing public policy relevant to them; but any study of the discourse of the years when the Socialists were in power would find few references supporting the importance and value of organised labour to society, even if the legislation was developed to conform with the Western European norm. What is more, the state building project was complex since it balanced economic, social and political imperatives in a manner that did not emphasise a deep role for organised labour and long-term planning.

The supply-side state and regulation: overcoming the challenges from below?

A major feature of the role of the Spanish state in terms of labour relations and work more generally has been the emergence of a supply-side state. If the space for proactive strategic engagement with social actors such as trade unions was not systematically developed as discussed earlier, it was the question of supporting the quality of work and workers in terms of training that was seen to be the main focus of regulatory activity and engagement beyond collective bargaining. The question of vocational training and general skills development has seen the emergence of key tripartite foundations that have been central to distributing funds and development training in these areas of activities. Within the European Union – especially in some of the most advanced economies and political systems – the role of social dialogue in relation to training has been seen as important due to the role social partners can play in developing new forms of training and qualifications relevant to a more service- and information-based economy (Stuart, 2007). There are two ways of viewing these types of developments at the macro and micro level. The first sees this as a new space for the rethinking of regulation and organisational roles around the fusing of broader economic roles and a new portfolio of flexible work (Castells, 1986). The second is more critical and argues that this represents a fragmented and reactive role around productivity coalitions – a form of micro-corporatism at best and business unionism at worse (Alonso, 2001) – which is about the potential exploitation of workers. Nevertheless, within Spain, from the 1990s onwards, the state began to expand these new institutional roles in terms of labour relations representation and intervention. At the regional and autonomous government level the role of local state bodies in facilitating inward investment and longer-term planning did see a space for social dialogue in some aspects (Almond *et al.*, 2014).

The context was clear: in the mid-1990s nearly half the workforce had no qualifications (Homs, 1999). The relative exclusion of female and younger workers from the core of the labour market also presented a set of challenges for the state and the nascent system of labour relations in the 1980s – and through to the 1990s as well (Pérez-Díaz and Rodriguez, 1995) – well before the challenge of integrating migration during later decades and dealing with training agendas at that time. The emergence of new systems of qualification, greater attention to access, ongoing support for businesses, and the strategic role of trade unions as facilitators and training bodies was key to this formal state response (Rigby, 1999). Part of the problem is that the employer classes especially at the micro level have not been systematic in developing coherent approaches to learning and training within their workplaces – particularly smaller firms (Castillo *et al.*, 2000; Crespo and Sanz 2000) – hence, social dialogue and neocorporatist institutions have formed a key part of this portfolio of state engagement, especially at the sector level (Rigby, 2002), and in relation to new groups of workers such as immigrants at the local municipal level as well (Aragon Medina *et al.*, 2009). The regional dimension of the state has been equally important in recreating such new roles and forms of dialogue. The argument is that the social actors can

complement the limited reach of the state and create new spaces for its intervention on such matters, fine-tuning this intervention in relation to changing
demands, especially beyond the rigid and formal scope of the state's regulation
of standard qualifications and learning. This represents a new form of intervention that has drawn the Spanish state into European and supranational dynamics.
For the trade union movement, it was a chance to enact roles which were not
voluntarily being developed by employers in many cases, and to support the
social state and manage specific arenas in the absence of a tradition of coherent
intervention and attempts to deal with marginalised workers (Martínez Lucio,
2008). The renewal of trade unionism – its modernisation – was such that it was
conditioned by this *historic obligation* due to the limited nature of aspects of the
state and capital and Spain.

The problems with this new sphere of regulation and joint intervention have
nevertheless been significant. Firstly, these new roles bring new questions of
capacity as wide-ranging projects and agendas are engaged with which require a
systematic set of structures and internal regulations – let alone cultural changes
especially within the aims and activities of trade unions. The way in which these
new functions link to the other roles in such organisations becomes a serious
question. There is the possibility that the role of the state in learning is integrated but not critically developed, opened up or driven by a more emancipa-
tory view. The agenda is for inclusion into a pre-established system of learning.
In the UK this has brought significant discussions as to the remit of trade unions
to deploy public funds for broader and skill-based agendas (see McIlroy and
Croucher, 2013; Rainbird and Stuart, 2011). Hence the question is not just
related to Spain but is broader in terms of labour relations. However, questions
over the use or regulation of state funds themselves are a matter which has led
trade unions to limit their engagement with such post-industrial shifts in terms
of state policy – a period of limiting the use of such spaces has been clear due to
a public and political critique of such funding (one which the author believes fails
to appreciate the imperative on trade unions to enact training and the ways in
which they have ensured a greater scope for learning compared to what would
have been the case without their initiatives).

In terms of broader state policy on work and employment, the main problem is that such training or broader employment policies have not always been
located in terms of a more proactive innovation and technology strategy (Recio
and Banyuls, 2004), regardless of the social-democratic hype and rhetoric in
the 1980s regarding the role of new technology and post-industrial possibilities. According to Carvajal Muñoz (2002), such developments in training have
focused on soft skills and the enhancing of social control over workers – linking
to a state interest in a pliable post-industrial workforce. So, irrespective of the

inclusion of trade unions, employers and others in such processes, there has not been a broader remit of social and economic renewal according to the more critical voices, and this has shaped a specific type of inclusion.

The regulatory gaps and inconsistencies of the role of the state and the regulation of work

The role of the state in Spain must therefore be located in a context where economic and social changes have not fitted any one general pattern of economic development and transition (Molina and Rhodes, 2007). There has been a range of developments which suggest that the state in general has had to manage a fragmented terrain but has also contributed to that fragmentation, given the manner in which economic development has been framed.

In structural terms, while the state has been able to create a semblance of dialogue and political exchange at some levels – as noted earlier – there have always been concerns about the strategic, partial or momentary nature regarding this dialogue, as noted earlier. The problem is that embedding that dialogue at the level of state intervention and state welfare policies has been fairly constrained beyond the question of training, which in turn has its critics. Furthermore, the attempt to balance the creation of a 'European' welfare and social state has been limited by the more market- and competition-oriented features of economic policy; it is as if there is a dual transitional process and competing demands or imperatives (Martínez Lucio, 1998). What is more – as Miguelez and Recio (2010) point out – the welfare dimension and more proactive labour market aspects of the state have not systematically complemented the more formal systems of rights developed by the state since the 1970s. We have also seen sectors such as retailing evolve (Royle and Ortiz, 2009) – and traditional sectors such as agriculture change – and these have been increasingly developed beyond the effective regulatory reach of the project of formalisation and democratisation of labour relations, in part due to the nature of employers in such sectors.

In political terms, this ambivalence has come to the fore in terms of the response to the Global Financial Crisis after 2008 which was based on curtailing the role of the state, limiting welfare support in what is already an uneven social system in terms of social security and unemployment benefit, and in particular focusing obsessively on the reform of collective bargaining, effectively limiting its remit (Rocha, 2014). In effect, this has emphasised the inconsistencies of the state and created greater gaps in terms of its coverage and remit. It has also opened the door to a more coercive state discourse based on the undermining of collective entities as in the anti-union discourse of the *Esperanza Aguirre*-led right-wing Madrid regional government in previous years – although it must be said that there are inconsistences and that there are still competing visions of the state.

What we do know though is that the trade union project led by the larger unions to enact regulation and to support the state from below in the light of its inconsistencies has been undermined. The state relies on political involvement and support from civil society – especially one which seeks an ideological hegemony, as any good Gramscian will know. In Spain, trade unions took a decision to engage and support key state roles around services to immigrant workers and communities, training programmes and inspection as they were confronted with a fragmented and less-coordinated employer class and state system on such matters which was not consistent socially (Martínez Lucio, 2007). Yet the last five years have seen a serious challenge to this project on the ground due to limitations in funding and problems with credibility and, in extreme cases, malpractice. This has exacerbated the crisis and the inconsistencies of the state.

Conclusions

The role of the state in Spain since the 1970s has therefore been complex and multifaceted, and has been configured by a range of factors, both structural and strategic. One can begin to judge the nature of the state from various political and historical perspectives. Much will depend on one's starting point and where one's analytical focus or gaze falls when starting the story of the Spanish state in relation to labour relations.

On the one hand, there is a narrative which is mindful of the very deep challenges facing the state, and the way the inefficiencies of the curiously and quite expansively industrialised Spanish economy under the Franco regime had to be transformed and renewed in the context of the industrial crisis of the 1970s and 1980s – and how a system of social dialogue had to be constructed in very politically challenging circumstances. Within this context, a form of social dialogue – that somewhat broad term – and political exchange emerged that was able to configure a relatively coordinated set of joint regulations and regulatory processes in terms of employment conditions. Within this context there has been a regularity in terms of agreements and negotiations – a strategic ability to overcome structural challenges (Roca, 1991; Gonzalez Begega *et al.*, 2015). Trade unions have been brought into new roles and formal arenas which have sustained a system of maturity in terms of regulation.

On the other hand, there is a view that social dialogue has been truncated and uneven. The increasing decentralisation of the state in territorial terms has not necessarily exacerbated this as it has depended on the economic and social policies of the autonomous governments in questions.[5] There is a belief though that the inclusion of a social voice at such a level has been uneven and rarely consistent. What is more, the 1980s are seen as a period when the opportunity for labour inclusion – and the development of a systematic counterpoint to the narrative and fetishising of post-industrial narratives – could have created a more balanced and deeper system of social dialogue and change. The relentless pursuit of industrial change in terms of '*la recoversion industrial*' and the emergent stigmatising of trade unions as political actors configured a system which was more attuned to marketisation even when the state was developing itself significantly (Smith, 1998).[6] Much has been bound up with the nature of the social democratic tradition in Spain – and the crisis of the left overall beyond it – which contributed to a stigmatising of the 'protected worker' and his or her 'protecting organisations' as a discourse limiting broader social engagement (Fernández Rodríguez and Martínez Lucio, 2014). The related problem is that, as Rubery's work has consistently shown, the question of social reproduction, gender and equality remains a major challenge in the way we conceptualise the role of regulation and the way we provide broader narratives of the limitations of contemporary public policy and social partner actors regardless of their rhetoric of 'inclusion'.

However, as we know, history is rarely made in a context of our choosing. The social democratic agenda of the 1980s and 1990s established a model of development and piecemeal accommodation to a neoliberal set of agendas which configured the general imbalances in terms of the state roles which later governments simply formalised. Hence Spain can be seen as a case of competing projects of change where the social dimensions of the state had to be developed at a time when the market and neoliberal policies were in the ascendancy (Alonso, 2007; Martínez Lucio, 1998). Academically, we need to broaden the lens of our analysis in historical and regulatory terms; we need, as Jessop (1982 and 2002) has reminded us, to focus on the broader and sometimes contradictory role of the state itself in terms of different apparatus and different political projects. As my colleague has noted, also in relation to the role of the state in the current context of austerity, we need to be also mindful of believing that the state will be easily reconfigured into a 'neoliberal' or 'withdrawn state' in terms of the economy as the emerging social tensions and contradictions in social and employment terms will draw aspects of the state back into new roles (Rubery, 2011). Perhaps given the role of the coercive and juridical spheres of the state in the current context it will be a more direct form of state role, but it will also be one that will not escape new social agendas so easily as they take the shape of new voices and movements *in and against* the state. In this respect, a greater degree of fragmentation of the state is likely and a more dualist social context. This in turn forces us to think of the state in broader terms and realise its contradictory features.

Notes

1   An earlier version of this chapter was published in *Sociología de Trabajo* Spring/Primavera 2016 45–67: 'Incertidumbre, indecisión y neoliberalismo emergente. El papel dual y complejo del Estado Español en las relaciones laborales y de empleo.' I would like to thank Carlos Fernández Rodríguez for his comments on the earlier version and his support.
2   All this was happening at a time when trade unions were having to consolidate their legitimacy and when membership had declined since the peaks reached soon after the death of Franco (Jordana, 1996).
3   For a discussion of the impact of neoliberal Anglo-Saxon language and methods in management read Ferner and Quintanilla (1998) and Ferner and colleagues (2001).
4   Although much depends on how you define numerical flexibility and what the legal framework for temporary contracting is.
5   It is beyond the scope of this chapter to review the importance of the Basque state in its ability to inculcate stronger forms of social engagement and dialogue; greater attention in future is needed in terms of internal comparative analysis within Spain.
6   To be able to open a more systematic debate on this key period, the nature of industrial policy in the 1980s and early 1990s would have to be studied carefully and the financial accounts of key companies (public and private) that were closed or 'restructured' would have to be scrutinised closely. The extent and role of subsidies and the use of the discourse of Europeanisation being associated with the removal of them would have to be considered. The author's opinion, as someone who studied labour relations in Spain during this period and who was also present during the equivalent processes in the UK at that time, would be to question the economic assumptions of that period and the critique of state support for what were officially considered to be failing industries.

References

Almond, P., Menendez, M. G., Gunnigle, P., Lavelle, J., Balbona, D. L., Monaghan, S. and Murray, G. (2014), 'Multinationals and regional economies: embedding the regime shoppers?', *Transfer: European Review of Labour and Research*, 20:2, 237–53.
Alonso, L. E. (1999), *Trabajo y Ciudadanía: Estudios Sobre la Crisis de la Sociedad Salarial* (Madrid: Trotta).
Alonso, L. E. (2001), 'New myths and old practices: postmodern management discourse and the decline of Fordist industrial relations', *Transfer,* 7:2, 268–88.

Alonso, L. E. (2007), *La Crisis de la Cuidadanía Laboral* (Barcelona: Anthropos).

Aragon Medina, J., Alba Arteaga, L., Haidour, M. A., Martinez Poza, A. and Rocha Sanchez, F. (2009), *Las Políticas Locales para la Integración de los Inmigrantes y la Participación de los Agentes Sociales* (Madrid: Catarata).

Banyuls, J. and Recio, A. (2012), 'Spain: the nightmare of Mediterranean neoliberalism', in S. Lehndorff, *A Triumph of Failed Ideas: European models of capitalism in the crisis* (Brussels: European Trade Union Institute), pp. 199–217.

Baylos Grau A. P. (1999), 'La intervención normativa del Estado en las relaciones laborales colectivas', in Carlos Prieto Rodríguez, C. and Miguélez Lobo, F. (eds), *Las relaciones de empleo en España* (Madrid: Siglo XXI), pp. 239–58.

Benavides, F. G., García, A. M., Lopez-Ruiz, M., Gil, J., Boix, P., Martinez, J. M. and Rodrigo, F. (2009), 'Effectiveness of occupational injury prevention policies in Spain', *Public Health Reports,* 124 (Suppl. 1), 180–7.

Carvajal Muñoz, R. M. (2002), 'Los cursos de formación ocupacional para desempleados en cuatro municipios de la comarca sierra sur sevillana: ¿formación para la inserción laboral o intercambio de intereses entre organizaciones participantes?', *Rev. Témpora 5* (Mayo).

Castells, M. (1986), *Nuevas Tecnologias, Economia y Sociedad en Espana,* Vol. 1 (Madrid: Alianza Editorial).

Castillo, J. J., Alas-Pumariño, A. D. L., Bono, A. D., Fernández, J., Galán, A. and Santos, M. (2000), 'División del trabajo, cualificación, competencias', *Sociología del Trabajo: Revista Cuatrimestral de Empleo, Trabajo y Sociedad,* 40, 3–50.

Crespo, J. and Sanz, I. (2000), 'La formación continua en España: implicaciones de política económica', *Papeles de economía española,* 86, 280–94.

Dubin, K. A. and Hopkin, J. (2014), 'A crucial case for flexicurity: the politics of welfare and employment in Spain', in Clegg, D. and Graziano, P. (eds), *The Politics of Flexicurity in Europe: Labour Market Reform in Hostile Climes and Tough Times* (Basingstoke: Palgrave Macmillan).

Fagan, C. and Rubery, J. (1996) 'The salience of the part-time divide in the European Union' *European Sociological Review,* *12*(3), 227-250.

Fernández Rodríguez, C. J., Ibañez Rojo, R. and Martínez Lucio, M. (2016), 'Austerity and collective bargaining in Spain', *European Journal of Industrial Relations*, 22:3, 267–80.

Fernández Rodríguez, C. J. and Martínez Lucio, M. (2014), 'El discurso del despido libre en España: una reflexión sobre el papel de los mitos y los prejuicios en las políticas de empleo', *Cuadernos de Relaciones Laborales*, 32:1, 191–219.

Fernández, C. and Ortega, C. (2008), 'Labor market assimilation of immigrants in Spain: employment at the expense of bad job-matches?', *Spanish Economic Review*, 10:2, 83–107.

Ferner, A. and Quintanilla, J. (1998), 'Multinationals, national business systems and HRM: the enduring influence of national identity or a process of "Anglo-Saxonization"', *International Journal of Human Resource Management*, 9:4, 710–31.

Ferner, A., Quintanilla, J. and Varul, M. Z. (2001), 'Country-of-origin effects, host-country effects, and the management of HR in multinationals: German companies in Britain and Spain', *Journal of World Business*, 36:2, 107–27.

Gonzalez Begega, S., Balbona, D. L. and Guillén Rodríguez, A. M. (2015), 'Gobiernos y sindicatos ante la reforma del estado del bienestar.¿ Ruptura del diálogo social en la periferia de la eurozona?', *Revista de economía crítica*, 20, 102–19.

Guillén Rodríguez, A. and Gutiérrez Palacios, R. (2008), 'Treinta años de pactos sociales en España: un balance', *Cuadernos de Información económica*, 203, 173–80.

Hamann, K. (2011), *The Politics of Industrial Relations: Labor Unions in Spain* (London: Routledge).

Humphries, J. and Rubery, J. (1984), 'The reconstitution of the supply side of the labour market: the relative autonomy of social reproduction', *Cambridge Journal of economics*, 8:4, 331–46.

Hyman, R. (2008), 'The State in industrial relations', in Blyton, P., Heery, E., Bacon, N. and Fiorito, J. (eds), *The Sage handbook of Industrial Relations* (London: Sage), pp. 258–83.

Jessop, B. (1982), *The Capitalist State* (Oxford: Martin Robertson).

Jessop, B. (2002), *The Future of the Capitalist State* (Cambridge: Polity).

Jordana, J. (1996), 'Reconsidering union membership in Spain, 1977–1994: halting decline in a context of democratic consolidation', *Industrial Relations Journal*, 27:3, 211–24.

Koukiadaki, A., Tavora I. and Martínez Lucio, M. (2016), 'Continuity and change in joint regulation in Europe: structural reforms and collective bargaining in manufacturing', *European Journal of Industrial Relations,* 22:3, 221–34.

Lash, J. and Urry, S. (1987), *The End of Organised Capitalism* (Oxford: Polity).

Linz, J. J. and Stepan, A. C. (1996), 'Toward consolidated democracies', *Journal of Democracy*, 7:2, 14–33.

Locke, R. M. and Thelen, K. (1995), 'Apples and oranges revisited: contextualized comparisons and the study of comparative labor politics', *Politics and Society*, 23, 337–68.

Lopez Díaz, E. and Santos del Cerro, J. (2013) 'La mujer en el mercado laboral español', *Economía española y Protección Social*, 5, 145–67.

Lux, J. and Wöhl, S. (2015), 'Gender Inequalities in the Crisis of Capitalism: Spain and France Compared', in Ebenau, M., Bruff, I. and May, C. (eds), *New Directions in Comparative Capitalisms Research* (London: Palgrave Macmillan), pp. 101–17.

McIlroy, J. and Croucher, R. (2013), 'British trade unions and the academics: the case of Unionlearn', *Capital and Class*, 37:2, 263–84.

MacKenzie, R. and Martínez Lucio, M. (2014), 'The colonisation of employment regulation and industrial relations? Dynamics and developments over five decades of change', *Labor History*, 55:2, 189–207.

Martínez Lucio, M. (1998), 'Spain: regulating employment and social fragmentation', in Ferner, A. and Hyman, R. (eds), *Changing Industrial Relations in Europe*, 2nd edn (Oxford: Basil Blackwell).

Martínez Lucio, M. (2007), 'Trade unions and employment relations in the context of public sector change: the public sector, "old welfare states" and the politics of managerialism', *International Journal of Public Sector Management*, 20:1, 5–15.

Martínez Lucio, M. (2008), '¿Todavía organizaciones del descontento?: los retos de las estrategias de renovación sindical en España', *Arxius de sociologia*, 18, 119–33.

Martínez Lucio, M. and Blyton, P. (1995), 'Constructing the post-Fordist state? The politics of labour market flexibility in Spain', *West European Politics*, 18:2, 340–60.

Martínez Lucio, M. and Connolly, H. (2012), 'Transformation and continuities in urban-struggles: urban politics, trade unions and migration in Spain', *Urban Studies*, 49:3, 669–84.

Meardi. G., Donaghey, J. and Dean, D. (2016), 'The strange non-retreat of the state: implications for the sociology of work', *Work, Employment and Society*, 30:4, 559–72.

Meardi, G., Martín, A. and Riera, M. L. (2012), 'Constructing uncertainty: unions and migrant labour in construction in Spain and the UK', *Journal of Industrial Relations*, 54:1, 5–21.

Miguélez, F. and Recio, A. (2010), 'The uncertain path from the Mediterranean welfare model in Spain', in Anxo, D., Bosch, G. and Rubery, J. (eds), *The Welfare State and Life Transitions: A European Perspective* (Cheltenham: Edward Elgar).

Molina, Ó. (2005), 'Political exchange and bargaining reform in Italy and Spain', *European Journal of Industrial Relations*, 11:1, 7–26.

Molina, Ó. (2006), 'Trade union strategies and change in neo-corporatist concertation: a new century of political exchange?', *West European Politics*, 29:4, 640–64.

Molina, Ó. (2007), 'State and regulation of industrial relations in Spain: old wine in a new governance bottle?', *South European Society and Politics*, 12:4, 461–79.

Molina, Ó. (2014), 'Self-regulation and the state in industrial relations in Southern Europe: back to the future?', *European Journal of Industrial Relations*, 20:1, 21–36.

Molina, Ó. and Rhodes M. (2011), 'Spain: from tripartite to bipartite pacts', in Avdagic, S., Rhodes, M. and Visser, J. (eds), *Social Pacts in Europe: Emergence, Evolution, and Institutionalization* (Oxford: Oxford University Press), pp. 174–202.

Morillas, R. M., Rubio-Romero, J. C. and Fuertes, A. (2013), 'A comparative analysis of occupational health and safety risk prevention practices in Sweden and Spain', *Journal of Safety Research*, 47, 57–65.

Offe, C. (1984), *Contradictions of the Welfare State* (Cambridge, MA: MIT Press).

Pérez-Díaz, V. and Rodriguez, J. C. (1995), 'Inertial choices: an overview of Spanish human resources, practices and policies', in Locke, R. M., Kochan, T. A. and Piore, M. J. (eds), *Employment Relations in a Changing World Economy* (Cambridge, MA: MIT Press), pp. 165–96.

Prosser, T. (2015), 'Dualization or liberalization? Investigating precarious work in eight European countries', *Work, Employment and Society*, 30:6, 949–65.

Rainbird, H. and Stuart, M. (2011), 'The state and the union learning agenda in Britain', *Work, Employment and Society*, 25:2, 202–17.

Recio, A. and Banyuls, J. (2004), 'Employment without technology? The paradox of the Spanish Labour Market', *Economia et Lavoro*, 38:1, 115–37.

Rigby, M. (2002), 'Spanish trade unions and the provision of continuous training: partnership at a distance', *Employee Relations*, 24(5), 500–15.

Roca Jusmet, J. (1991), 'La concertación social', in Miguélez, F. and Prieto, C. (eds), *Las Relaciones Laborales en España* (Madrid: Siglo XXI), pp. 361–79.

Rocha, F. (2014), 'Crisis and austerity policies in Spain: towards an authoritarian model of industrial relations', in Rocha, F. (ed.), *The New EU Economic Governance and its Impact on the National Collective Bargaining Systems* (Madrid: CCOO), pp. 175–204.

Rodríguez-Ruiz, Ó. (2015), 'Unions' response to corporate restructuring in Telefónica: locked into collective bargaining?', *Employee Relations*, 37:1, 83–101.

Royle, T. and Ortiz, L. (2009), 'Dominance effects from local competitors: setting institutional parameters for employment relations in multinational subsidiaries; a case from the Spanish supermarket sector', *British Journal of Industrial Relations*, 47:4, 653–75.

Rubery, J. (2011), 'Reconstruction amid deconstruction: or why we need more of the social in European social models', *Work, Employment and Society*, 25:4, 658–74.

Rubery, J. and Fagan, C. (1995), 'Gender segregation in societal context', *Work, Employment and Society*, 9:2, 213–240.

Sesé, A., Palmer, A. L., Cajal, B., Montaño, J. J., Jiménez, R. and Llorens, N. (2002), 'Occupational safety and health in Spain', *Journal of Safety Research,* 33: 4, 511–25.

Smith, W. R. (1998), *The Left's Dirty Job: The Politics of Industrial Restructuring in France and Spain* (Pittsburgh, PA: University of Pittsburgh Press).

Sola, J., Alonso, L. E., Fernández Rodríguez, C. J. and Ibañez Rojo, R. (2013), 'The expansion of temporary employment in Spain (1984–2010): neither socially fair nor economically productive', in Koch, M. and Fritz, M. (eds), *Non-Standard Employment in Europe. Paradigms, Prevalence and Policy Responses* (Basingstoke: Palgrave), pp. 67–83.

Solé, C. and Parella, S. N. (2003), 'The labour market and racial discrimination in Spain', *Journal of Ethnic and Migration Studies*, 29:1, 121–40.

Stuart, M. (2007), 'Introduction. The industrial relations of learning and training: a new consensus or a new politics?', *European Journal of Industrial Relations*, 13:3, 269–80.

16

Work and care regimes and women's employment outcomes: Australia, France and Sweden compared

Dominique Anxo, Marian Baird and Christine Erhel

Introduction

The objective of this chapter is to analyse how national care regimes interact with the employment regime to influence female employment outcomes. We do this with a comparative analysis of Australia (population 24 million), France (62 million) and Sweden (9.5 million), three advanced market economies that have distinct and contrasting employment and care regimes. For the employment regime, we focus on paid work across the life course and we focus on parental leave and childcare as indicative of the care regime. The chapter draws on the theoretical framework developed by Rubery and colleagues (1999, 2001) and Rubery (2002). This theoretical tradition emphasises that the gender division of labour between employment and unpaid care and domestic work is structured by the articulation of family policies and the organisation of employment and working time, as well as other elements of the welfare state regime such as the taxation system. This approach has drawn attention to important societal differences in the shape and degree of gender inequalities. Comparative studies of time (see, for example, Anxo *et.al.,* 2011) have clearly shown that the gender division of labour between paid work, care and domestic activities is strongly dependent on prevailing societal norms and the institutional and societal contexts.

Australia is regularly referred to as a liberal welfare state even though the Australian system does not fit easily into the standard Esping-Andersen (1990) typology. For most of the twentieth century Australia had a centralised mechanism to set wages and working conditions, leading to Australia also being referred to as the (male) wage-earners' welfare state. As a consequence, the provision of leave entitlements has been a result of the industrial relations system rather than welfare policies (Baird, 2005). Having had a strongly oriented full-time male breadwinner/female carer model, the care and employment regimes in Australia have not kept pace with the social changes in female education levels, gender roles and expectations nor with the demographic changes in the workforce. This has resulted in an 'institutional lag' and, since the turn of the millennium, the need for a fresh focus on work and family policies (Baird and Williamson, 2009).

In terms of social protection models, France belongs to the Continental model, including quite high levels of social redistribution and a well-developed family policy. Until the 1970s, it was characterised by a male breadwinner model, encouraging mothers' inactivity through the tax system and through the under-development of formal childcare for younger children (under the age of three). The necessity to increase employment rates to finance social protection, as well as the increase in women's education level, has led to a progressive development of childcare, although some incentives to maternal inactivity remain in public policies. Gender equality at work (in terms of wages, but also employment conditions and job quality) has also emerged as a policy goal over recent years, partly influenced by European gender equality policies.

Often presented as the ideal type of social democratic welfare state (Esping-Andersen, 1990), Sweden emphasises the principles of universalism, egalitarianism and individual rights. The Swedish model is also founded on a strong political commitment to the goal of full employment. Sweden stands out as providing one type of societal system based on high employment rates, with only a small gender gap; a high incidence of dual-earner households; extensive and generous family policies; strong welfare support systems for childcare, parental leave and elderly care; and egalitarian wage structures, including relatively low gender wage inequality. Furthermore, the overall political context, which is characterised by gender mainstreaming combined with high female involvement in the political process and institutions (government bodies, parliament and labour market organisations), creates an institutional set-up conducive to a more balanced gender division of labour and responsibilities over the life course.

Two propositions guide the chapter: the first is that policies relating to care are changing in Organisation for Economic Co-operation and Development (OECD) countries, even in national regimes that are very different (such as Australia, France and Sweden); the second is that policies do impact on women's labour market activity across the life course in relation to both overall participation and hours of work. To consider these propositions, the chapter proceeds in the following way. The first section of the chapter considers women's key social and labour market features in each of the countries, highlighting current employment outcomes. The second section provides an overview of the work and care policy regimes in each country, with a focus on parental leave, child-care and hours flexibility. This section demonstrates the different policy trajectories of each of the three countries to date. For consistency, OECD data are used where possible, mainly from the family database (OECD, 2016b), supplemented by official country-specific statistics. We conclude with a discussion of the relationship between the policy regimes and female employment outcomes, suggesting some similar policy issues and trends are occurring in Australia and France, but not to the same degree in Sweden, the country with the longest history of gender equitable policy goals.

Female and maternal employment rates

In this first section, we characterise the three countries and their employment regimes using a gender perspective, building on empirical evidence about gender gaps in employment rates, working time, earnings and job quality.

For the past 40–50 years, two of the most salient features and persistent trends in Sweden, France and Australia have been the rising education levels of women and the increased feminisation of the labour force, with a related shift from the single male breadwinner household towards the dual-earner household. This feminisation of the labour force has occurred despite very different policy frameworks in each of the three countries. Both France and Australia have experienced a gradual and marked growth in female employment from around the late 1980s. The trend shows that for the prime working age population (25–64) in 2014 the employment rates for women in both France and Australia is approximately 68 per cent, with the surge in female employment beginning early in the 1980s for France and a few years later for Australia.

Sweden stands out as the exception among the three countries, with female employment rates consistently higher since the 1970s. In 1985, for example, the female employment rate in Sweden was 79 per cent compared to France at 54 per cent and Australia at 44 per cent. By 2014, the Swedish female employment rate was still higher at 81 per cent, although France and Australia are narrowing that gap as their female employment rates grow. Interestingly, as Table 16.1 shows, education outcomes for women are considerably higher than for men and higher than the OECD average in Australia and Sweden yet, as we later discuss, this investment is not reflected in higher employment rates or pay outcomes for Australian women.

Observing these trends, it would seem therefore that the economic and social shifts of the 1980s in all three countries, including more human capital

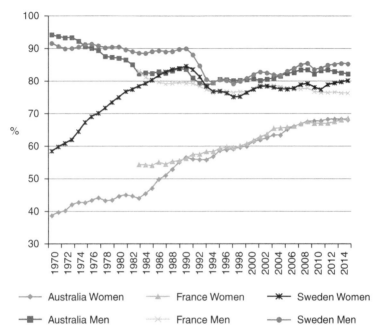

Figure 16.1   Female and male employment rates in Australia, France and Sweden 1970–2014 (%)

Source: OECD, 2016d

Table 16.1   Percentage of population with tertiary education by gender for individuals aged 25–64, 2014

	Men	Women
Australia	38	45
France	30	34
Sweden	33	45
OECD-34 average	32	36

Source: OECD (2016e): Table CO3_1_Educational attainment by gender.

investment for women and economic and industry restructuring from manufacturing to services, are associated with increases in female employment rates. Shifts in government objectives are also noteworthy. The need to increase employment rates in order to finance social protection has been an incentive for national policies to encourage female labour force participation in Sweden and France (see Rubery *et al.*, 2001; Rubery 2002). In Australia, the need to increase female employment rates has been driven by the perceived need of governments to increase the size of the labour market and gross domestic product.

By international standards, Sweden is characterised by high employment rates at the two ends of the age distribution, high employment continuity over the life course and relatively low gender disparities in labour market integration. This has not been the case for Australia and France. In Sweden, neither couple formation nor childbirth impacts on women's employment rates, with the latter positively correlated to female labour market participation (Anxo *et al.*, 2011). The main impact of childbirth in Sweden is therefore a combination of a period of parental leave followed by a temporary reduction of working hours to long part-time hours while children are young (preschool children) rather than a reduction of employment rate.

In France, maternal employment stands at a relatively high level, above the OECD average. However, important barriers and disincentives to employment remain for mothers, especially for the lower qualified. Indeed, in terms of mothers' activity rates, important differences emerge according to the age and the number of children. Labour market participation is lower for mothers of young children and decreases with the number of children. In 2013, 78.6 per cent of mothers of one child (aged 0–14) were active, as well as 73.1 per cent of mothers of two children, but only 53 per cent of mothers of three or more children.[1] Part-time employment is also more developed for mothers of young children, and at least partly results from constraints in the availability or the cost of child-care. In France, 15.1 per cent of women still declare that their inactivity or part-time work is due to a lack of care services (Eurostat, Compendium 2010).[2]

Lower maternal employment rates are the distinguishing feature of female employment in Australia (see Table 16.2). Relative to other OECD nations, Australian maternal employment rates for mothers with a child under 15 are

Table 16.2   Population and female and maternal employment rates, 2015

Country	Population	Female employment rate 25–64 (%)	Maternal employment rate child <15* (%)
Sweden	9.5 million	80.7	83.1
France	62 million	68.2	72.4
Australia	24 million	68.7	63.5
OECD average		63.3	66.8

Note: *Year 2013 for Australia

Source: Employment rate: OECD (2015). Maternal employment rate: OECD (2016e), Data for Chart LMF1.2.A. Maternal employment rates.

lower, at 63.5 per cent compared with the OECD average of 66.8 per cent. The rate is even lower for mothers of children younger than three years. In Australia, female employment has been closely associated with family formation. The major shift in the last four decades has been that, rather than withdrawing completely from the labour market after childbirth, Australian women move to part-time hours (Baird, 2016).

To summarise, despite some convergence among the three countries in terms of increasing female employment rates, there continues to be considerable divergence in relation to maternal employment rates for women with children under the age of 15. Sweden stands out with relatively high maternal employment rates. It is in relation to maternal employment therefore that we see the impact of the differing policy frameworks most profoundly, which we discuss in the next section.

Figure 16.2 displays the age–employment profiles of men and women in the three countries. As illustrated, Australia, compared to France and Sweden, exhibits the largest gender gap in employment rates across the life course. In contrast to the two other countries, Australia also shows a slight decrease in the female employment rate during the period of childbearing (around two percentage points between 25 and 39 years old). Sweden has the highest female employment rates across the life course and exhibits the smallest gender employment gap with, as in France, high employment continuity over the life course. In 2013, according to the OECD (2016b), Sweden had also the highest incidence of dual full-time earner couples: 45.6 per cent compared to 41.4 per cent in France and only 23.4 per cent in Australia.

One of the most interesting developments in these countries since the 1970s is that children are no longer associated with a permanent or temporary withdrawal from the labour market. The continuity of female employment patterns conceals, however, large gender disparities in working time. Motherhood still implies a significant reduction of female labour supply. The presence of young preschool children significantly increases the incidence of part-time work, implying a significant reduction of working time. This is most pronounced in Australia, where 48 per cent of mothers work less than 35 hours (with the vast majority of these working less than 30 hours), compared to 31 per cent and 35 per cent in France and Sweden respectively (see Table 16.3). In France only a small proportion of women work less than 35 hours. The share of short part-time work (1–19 hours) is low in Sweden and France (less than 10 per cent), contrasting with Australia with a share of short part-time work above 20 per cent. By contrast, for men in all three countries, fatherhood entails an increase of labour supply in terms of both participation and working hours.

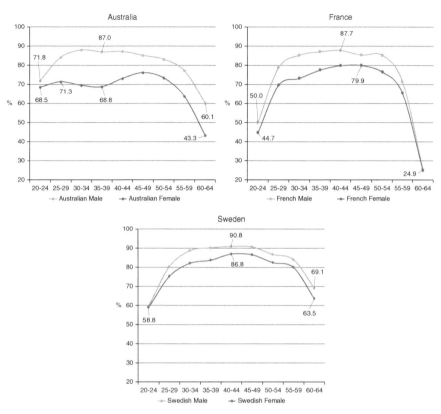

Figure 16.2   Age–employment profile in Australia, France and Sweden, 2014

Source: OECD (2016a).

Table 16.3   Working time distribution among Australian, French and Swedish women with at least one child under 14 years of age, 2014 (%)

Working-time band	Australia	France	Sweden
1 to 19 hours	21.0	9.1	8.2
20 to 29 hours	17.4	13.2	10.1
30 to 34 hours	9.7	8.7	16.4
35 to 39 hours	23.4	46.3	17.4
40 hours or more	28.5	22.7	47.8

Source: OECD (2016a).

Job quality and gender gaps

Job quality has been introduced among policy goals at the international level since the 2000s, and has received attention in the comparative literature, together with the development of specific indicators (Davoine *et al.*, 2008; Green *et al.*, 2013). Job quality is usually considered as a multi-dimensional concept, including pay and earnings, employment quality and the type of contract, training opportunities and working conditions. Here we focus more specifically on wage and part-time employment for which gender gaps are particularly important, before presenting a more global perspective on job quality by gender on the basis of OECD data.

As noted above, part-time work has been developing in the three countries since the 1990s, for mothers of young children but also more generally for women. In 2015, 38 per cent of employed Australian women were working part-time, well above French and Swedish female part-time employment rates (22.3 per cent and 18 per cent respectively). The gender gap in part-time employment rates is higher in Australia and in France than in Sweden (almost 24 per cent in Australia, 15 per cent in France and 7 per cent in Sweden in 2015).[3] The links between part-time and job quality are ambiguous, as they can be seen as a way to reconcile family and work or as a constraint for women, resulting either from insufficient childcare or from bad labour market conditions. The concept of involuntary part-time work may help differentiate between these different situations, although it mainly reflects labour market and care constraints. According to OECD data, involuntary part-time amounts to 39.2 per cent of part-time employment in France for women and has been strongly increasing since 2012 (in a context of high-level unemployment), whereas it stands at lower levels in Australia (25.5 per cent) and in Sweden (28.4 per cent). Thus involuntary part-time does not directly connect with the level of part-time rates; in the Australian case part-time may be considered by women as a way to stay in the labour market when then have children, whereas most French women would prefer to work full-time in a more regulated labour market (with a 35-hour legal working time) and in a context of quite well-developed childcare. However, part-time work has a direct incidence on women's earnings and gender pay gaps, and may also affect future career prospects.

Given existing OECD data, it is only possible to compare gender pay gaps of full-time employees. According to OECD data (Table 16.3), the three countries have persistent pay gaps, with the gender pay gap being highest in Australia. Additionally, according to OECD data, the gender wage gaps stand at

Table 16.4   Gender gap in median earnings of full-time employees

	2000	2006	2012/2013*
Australia	17.2	16.7	18*
France	14.6	14.0	13.7
Sweden	15.5	14.6	15.1
OECD average	18.2	16.1	15.2

Note: *Year 2013 for Australia

Source: OECD (2014)

a relatively high level for tertiary educated workers in all three countries, even for the prime-age cohorts (35 to 44).

The causes of the persistence of gender pay gaps are varied, but as argued by Rubery and colleagues (2005), the wage structure of economies and labour market segregation are understood to be important contributors, and more so than individual characteristics, such as educational attainment. Sweden is a pronounced example of this; from the early 1970s up to the early 1990s, the creation and development of a modern and encompassing welfare state and the related expansion of public sector employment in Sweden contributed not only to the feminisation of the labour force and the increase of the overall employment rate, but also to the upgrading of the job structure in Sweden. By contrast, although Australian women have high educational attainment, it also has a highly sex-segregated labour market which may explain the relatively higher gender pay gap in Australia.

To characterise women's employment position, it is also important to adopt a job quality perspective, that goes further than a wage perspective and includes other dimensions of job quality, such as employment conditions (especially job security) and working conditions (such as, physical constraints, stress). When disaggregated by gender, such analyses show that women are generally disadvantaged in terms of employment conditions but that men experience more onerous working conditions on average (Fagan and Burchell, 2002).

Several multi-dimensional indicators of job quality have been developed over recent years, but here we refer to the OECD index as it is the only one that includes information for Australia. The OECD job quality index is composed of three main dimensions (Cazes *et al.*, 2015): earnings quality is measured by an index that accounts for both the level of earnings and their distribution across the workforce; labour market security takes into account both the coverage of unemployment benefits and their generosity; and quality of the working environment is measured by the incidence of job strain, which is a combination of high job demands and limited job resources.

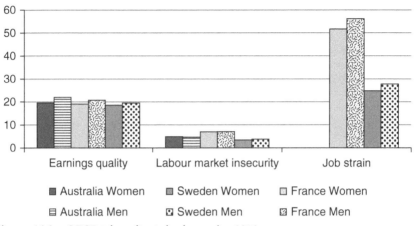

Figure 16.3   OECD job quality index by gender, 2010

Note: Earnings quality in USD PPS and labour market insecurity and job strain in %

Source: OECD (2016c).

For all three countries, the results confirm that women are penalised in earnings quality (level and distribution), whereas their protection against unemployment is very similar to men's. Job strain is higher in France than in Sweden
for both men and women, but its level is higher for men in both countries.
(Australia is not included in the job-strain index.) This is related to the type of
jobs that men hold; as noted above they are over-represented in the industrial
manufacturing sector. However, according to national data for France, working conditions have been declining for women: 58 per cent of muscular-skeletal
disorders hit women (42 per cent men) and stress at work (resulting from high
demands and low autonomy, following the Karasek model) affects 28.2 per cent
of women (19.6 per cent of men) (Lemière, 2013). Similarly, for a larger set
of European countries, Burchell and colleagues (2007) also found a reduction in
gender gaps in exposure to some physical risks. The OECD index does not take
into account the problem of involuntary part-time employment that concerns
more women than men, as mentioned above.

Job quality gaps are observed throughout the life course. According to a
French study, young women, even the well-educated, face a lower job quality
when they enter the labour market (the gender wage gap amounts to 20 per
cent for a Master's degree and above); older women (over 50) tend to make
more frequent transitions towards inactivity (Lemière, 2014). These differences
by gender tend to persist despite a general and significant increase in women's
education levels in all three countries.

In summary, the three countries have experienced an overall increase in education and female employment rates, continued occupational and industry segmentation and persistent gender pay gaps in favour of men. The divergence in women's employment between Australia, France and Sweden is evident in rates of maternal employment and part-time working hours. In this respect, Australia stands in sharp contrast to Sweden and France, with lower maternal employment and considerably shorter part-time work hours. These patterns may be explained, at least in part, by the policy regimes in each of the countries, which we discuss next.

Policies and work-care regimes

The differences in labour market outcomes for women have to be understood in relation to the nation's institutions and public policies, including parental leave, childcare and flexible work policies, as well as social and fiscal policies and labour market regulations. The differences in the care regimes in the three countries are summarised in Table 16.5 below. Sweden exemplifies the dual earner-carer model, whereas in France and Australia institutional arrangements favour

Table 16.5   National policy frameworks compared

	Parental Leave	**Childcare**	**Flexible work**
Australia	12 months per parent of unpaid parental leave with 18 weeks paid for mothers and 2 weeks ring-fenced for fathers/ same-sex partners	Fragmented childcare system for preschool children (aged <5), some government subsidy and mix of formal and informal care	Right to request (RTR) flexible work arrangements for parents and carers
France	Two years' leave with an allowance, extended by a year if fathers share the care	Government subsidies for formal care for children aged <3 and free preschool for all children aged 3–5	Right to request part-time in the public sector. In the private sector depends on collective agreements
Sweden	480 days' parental leave with payment, 90 days ring-fenced for each parent	Publicly financed childcare facilities for children aged 1–5	Large possibilities of reversible time options over the life course through statutory regulations and collective agreements

a maternalist model, with policies only more recently encouraging fathers' involvement in care.

Australia

The current care regime in Australia has emerged relatively recently. Although community and political debates relating to parental leave and childcare policies have been high on the agenda in Australia for the past 20 years, it was not until the election of the Labour government in 2007 that any substantial reform was introduced. Previous governments had adopted a neoliberal, market-based philosophy, relying on individual employer–employee negotiations or employer–union bargaining. This situation resulted in polarised outcomes in the labour market. Higher-skilled workers in certain industries and with higher bargaining power had better entitlements than lower-skilled, less-powerful workers. For example, in relation to employer provision of paid parental leave, women in the finance and higher education sectors were much better off than those in the retail or hospitality sectors (Baird *et al.,* 2009).

The childcare system in Australia is complex and under review. The delivery of formal childcare and school education is the responsibility of the state and local governments, but funding is from a mix of state and federal governments. Preschool education (that is under five years) tends to also be organised at the state level, and out-of-school-hours care is generally a local or state government responsibility. Formal childcare for 1–3 year olds is even more mixed, being offered between private and public providers; and although public expenditure on childcare has been increasing, it still remains at less than 1 per cent of GDP (OECD, 2016b). Approximately 30 per cent of preschool-age children attend formal childcare services in Australia (Australian Government, 2014) and for working families, grandparents provide the bulk of informal childcare for children aged 0–12. There is a commitment to provide access to one year of preschool education for all children; however, this has not yet been achieved. The review of the childcare system has a focus on early childhood education *and* care and, as well as concerns about the provision of adequate and quality childcare, there is debate about the availability of trained care workers, including 'nannies', and their working conditions.

Australia's paid parental leave system is also a relatively recent policy innovation. Introduced by the federal Labour government in 2011, it provides for 18 weeks' pay at the national minimum wage. Eligibility is wide and covers those with the equivalent of one day's work a week for the ten months prior to birth. Self-employed women can also access the scheme. Use of the scheme, however, is inflexible and the 18 weeks must be taken in one block and before the child's first birthday. Although called parental leave, the scheme is aimed at the primary carer and has been overwhelmingly used by mothers (Whitehouse *et al.*, 2015). The paid parental leave scheme is underpinned by a right to unpaid parental leave in the labour legislation, the Fair Work Act. Unpaid parental leave has been available to women since 1979, to adoptive parents since 1980 and to men since 1990, and each parent is now eligible to 12 months' unpaid parental leave and a job guarantee, or up to 24 months for one parent. In addition, employers may supplement the government scheme with their own paid parental leave scheme. Approximately 50 per cent of employers do this, although provisions are more generous in certain sectors such as finance and education. Public sector employees also have access to between 12 and 14 weeks paid parental leave at replacement wages, which can be taken in addition to the 18 weeks noted above. In 2013, a modest scheme of two weeks' pay at the national minimum wage was introduced for fathers and same-sex partners. This might be seen as the first policy step to directly address gender role behaviour and an attempt to encourage fathers to share the care load.

Although it can be argued that parental leave and childcare policies are now embedded in the macro-policy framework, aspects of the policies remain highly contested. For example, the current government is proposing to reduce the paid parental leave scheme and the proposed changes to the childcare and tax transfer system remain unresolved. Income tax in Australia is based on individual incomes, whereas many welfare benefits are based on family income. Combined with the costs of childcare this creates a disincentive for women with young children to return to work. Furthermore, there is ongoing disagreement about the best way to resolve Australia's dilemma of low maternal employment rates, with an explicit aim of the federal government to increase female participation rates (see Baird and O'Brien, 2015).

Overall, in relation to work and family public policies, Australia has shifted ground in the past 10 years from a conservative neoliberal position to a greater focus on the role of government in addressing labour market and gender equality needs. It is important to note that the policy rhetoric is typically couched in business case arguments rather than equity goals or welfare needs. More attention is also being paid to the deficit of women in leadership positions and the persistent gender pay gap, with the government's Workplace Gender Equality Agency taking a lead in this regard. Reporting on gender participation and pay gaps in firms with 100 or more employees is obligatory, but targets rather than quotas are the preferred method of addressing the leadership gap.

There continues to be significant gender gaps in the labour market and these are of concern to all stakeholders – individuals, employers, unions and governments. As noted above, the participation and employment rates of women, and especially of mothers, are lower than men's, there is a large gap in terms of hours of work, and there remains a significant gender pay gap and care gap between men and women. While there are major public policy debates under-way, there is also a considerable debate among employers and in the labour movement about how best to reconcile the pressures of working and family lives for men and women.

However, work and family public policies tend to remain maternal in focus and there is little attention to shifting the dominant male full-time worker/female part-time worker model to a more shared-work and care model.

France

France is characterised by a well-developed childcare system that has been expanding through a diversification of childcare for children under the age of three (including childminders and different forms of private childcare). However, several features of the French social protection and tax system are still inherited from the male breadwinner model that was predominant until the end the 1970s. After a brief description of the components of the French 'model', and of some persistent contradictions, we focus on new trends in gender and employment policies that focus on labour market inequalities.

The French childcare system is based on free pre-primary school starting at the age of three (and two for a minority of children) and on a set of subsi-dised childcare solutions for younger children. Indeed, the originality of the French childcare system for young children (0–3) is that its growth relies on the development of both public 'collective' childcare and 'individual' childcare (childminders working at their home, or at parents' home). All these childcare types are sustained by public financing, including 'individual' childcare arrange-ments for which parents benefit from specific allowances (income-related) and tax cuts. The result of this system is that 99.6 per cent of children aged 3–5 go to school on a full-time basis, and that 49.7 per cent of children aged 0–2 are enrolled in formal childcare or preschool services.[4] For younger children, the growth in childcare supply results mainly from the development of childminder and individual childcare.

However, despite the development of childcare, French social and labour market policies are inherited from the male breadwinner model, and are still wavering between a goal of protection for women (and mothers) and incentives to work. Firstly, as far as mothers of young children are concerned, the French family policy provides inconsistent incentives for some women; although wom-en's labour market participation is a policy goal, low-wage (i.e. low-qualified) mothers with two or more children are encouraged to stop working or to take a part-time job through the parental leave programme. This parental leave can be quite long (three years until 2014; two years since 2015), which creates difficulties in returning to work (even when the working contract is maintained). A reform implemented in January 2015 introduced an incentive to 'share' the leave between the two parents: the allowance is now limited to two years, unless the father also takes a leave (in which case the allowance can be received until the child is three years old).

Secondly, the French tax and social policy system is family-based and creates an incentive for the specialisation of one spouse in market activities if he/she has a higher income. In practice, 75 per cent of women earn less than their husband, which places them in a situation where their incentive to work or to increase their working hours is lower (Lemière, 2014). Major social policies are also family-based, such as the minimum income – the *Revenu de Solidarité Active* (RSA). The RSA is work-oriented and provides a differential allowance for beneficiaries who are working (under a certain income threshold). Although the issue of individualised income tax is not yet a priority (and still a debated issue), gender equality has been promoted to a major policy goal over recent years.

The law on 'real equality between men and women' *(loi pour l'égalité réelle entre les femmes et les hommes)* was voted in in July 2014. It includes two important and quite innovative tools, in addition to the reform of parental leave (already mentioned above). Firstly, it creates an obligation for firms to bargain on the topic of gender equality at work (wages, careers, access to training). Firms who do not comply will be unable to contract with public administrations. Secondly, it reinforces existing quotas that nominations for directors in public administrations and CEOs for large firms should include at least 40 per cent of women after 2017 (to reach an actual share of 40 per cent in firms over 250 employees in 2020).

Other recent measures were intended to improve women's labour market situation, although they were not gender-specific. Concerning part-time work, the social partners and the government introduced a threshold for part-time jobs of 24 hours a week in 2013 (the reform *Accord National Interprofessionnel*), to avoid the development of part-time with limited number of hours worked (less than 25 hours) in France. However, there are many limits to its actual implementation, as the employer can depart from the minimum 24 hours if the employee agrees. Besides, branch-level social bargaining can also modify the 24-hour threshold and introduce a lower minimum duration, which happened in 48 industries (until March 2015), so that 44 per cent are now covered by an industry agreement setting a shorter minimum duration.[5] As a consequence of this bargaining process, the 24-hour threshold adopted in 2013 can be expected

to have only a limited impact on part-time duration in France and on the incidence of part-time contracts including those with less than 25 hours for women.

To encourage work–family reconciliation, childcare is still in a process of
development, with some efforts to reduce territorial inequalities. Thus French
policy has evolved over the last 10 years; it is now focusing both on work–family
reconciliation and on gender equality in the job, mixing services supply, social
dialogue and quota policies for nominations.

Sweden

The Swedish childcare regime is a mixed system of outsourcing and insourcing
(in-house provision). During the first two years of age the majority of children
are cared for in the home within the framework of a generous and flexible
parental leave system (see below). After the leave period, childcare is mainly
provided by day-care centres. Childcare in Sweden is highly subsidised and
financed and administered by local authorities, with parents co-financing childcare activities by paying a fee. The continuous growth of publicly financed childcare facilities has contributed to the growth of female labour supply. In the early
1970s, only 30 per cent of preschool children (1–5 years old) were enrolled in
public-financed childcare compared to 83 per cent in 2015. Since the mid-1990s
Swedish municipalities have the obligation to provide childcare facilities for
working fathers and mothers.

The Swedish parental leave programme, introduced in 1974, has clearly
sustained the feminisation of the labour force and contributed to the changes
in women's behaviour in the labour market, specifically halting their withdrawal from the labour market. The length of parental leave was initially
six months but was successively extended to 16 months (480 days) in the
1990s, with full job security on return.[6] The level of compensation is 80 per
cent of gross earnings for the first 390 days. For the remaining 90 days, parents
receive a flat rate of 180 SEK.[7] It is interesting to note that the parental leave
system is one of the few social/citizen rights that is not fully individualised.
In order to favour a more equal gender distribution of absence, a designated
non-transferable leave benefit of a month for each parent was introduced in
1993, a second month was introduced in 2002 and a third in 2016. This rule
constitutes, therefore, a strong incentive for fathers to use their right to parental leave for at least 90 days. The gender division of parental leave remains,
however, unevenly distributed; in 2015, 74 per cent of the total number of
net compensated days were taken by mothers (see Swedish Social Insurance
Agency, 2016).[8]

Since the amount of income-related benefits is based on the income during the six months immediately preceding the birth of the first child, this constitutes a strong economic incentive for parents to be gainfully employed and work full-time prior to childbirth. This benefit system has, therefore, a great influence on labour market behaviour and working-time patterns for presumptive parents. Typically, young, childless, cohabiting, employed women and men work full-time before childbearing in order to maximise their income level during parental leave. Also worth noting is the fact that their working time increases smoothly in order to maximise pension benefits after retirement.[9] This strategy appears to be an efficient tool to secure women's labour market integration, foster employment continuity and improve gender equal opportunities.

The question of how to raise men's take-up rates of extended leave and other working-time adjustments over the life course and bring about a stronger involvement of men in unpaid domestic and care activities is a crucial political issue and could provide a policy instrument for reducing gender inequality in the division of labour and income development over the life course.

To a considerable extent, the positive employment outcomes in the Swedish economy during the last three decades, particularly the high and growing female employment rate, are clearly related to the creation of a modern welfare state; strong public involvement in the financing and provision of healthcare, social care, childcare and education; and the related expansion of public employment. An individualised taxation system in a context of high average and marginal tax rates has also reinforced the dual breadwinner model.

Conclusions

Rubery (2011) convincingly argued that researchers and policy-makers should not take for granted 'the argument that regulation hinders outsider groups such as women' and urges us to examine more closely 'how gender differences may interact in specific and varying ways with employment and social regulations'. In this chapter, we have canvassed the impact on women of differing labour market and care regime forms of regulation and show that there is indeed a difference between men's and women's employment outcomes, which may be said to advantage the 'insiders', that is, men. Taking a closer look *within* gender, however, we also show that by comparing the data on female and maternal employment, hours of work and job quality in each of the countries, the interaction of care and employment regimes influence women's and mother's employment outcomes differently. Australia's lower maternal employment rates and high part-time work rates reflect that country's strongly regulated industrial male breadwinner legacy and less-developed parental leave and childcare regime. In France, the regime has produced relatively high employment rates for women and mothers, although with some inequalities among mothers but there are still clear gender wage and job quality gaps. By contrast, Sweden's long-term gender equity approach and supporting parental leave and childcare policy regime are reflected in high employment rates and longer hours of work for Swedish women, including mothers, over the life course.

The interaction of care and employment regimes is ever more significant as women's labour market attachment increases. At the same time, care regimes are in transition in each of the countries, and especially so in Australia and France. Australia appears most concerned with female labour market attachment, but from an economic rather than a social or gender equality perspective. It also has the most market-oriented care regime of the three countries. France sits in the middle, with a mixed welfare-economy orientation, and Sweden is the most gender equitable and welfare-oriented country. Our overview suggests that some policy change is occurring in Australia and France, both in response to, and leading to, a modest decline in the pervasiveness of the traditional male breadwinner model. Policies such as providing leave for parenting, addressing childcare demands and encouraging fathers to actively participate in care are becoming more evident, although the emphasis on changing gender roles is still in its infancy in France and nascent in Australia. By contrast, policies to encourage more gender equitable care outcomes have been a feature of the Swedish system for many years.

Our analysis demonstrates that the institutional context and the interaction of national care regimes with the employment regimes in each of the countries have influenced female employment outcomes. Furthermore, social context is important. For instance, attitudes to motherhood and increasing education rates of women in all three countries suggest the need to pay more attention to the interaction of regulation with social norms and trends. The comparison of Australia, France and Sweden shows that, despite differing policy regimes, common across all three countries are persistent gender pay gaps and the continued dominance of female caregiving. While this situation remains, the reduction of gender difference and inequality remains elusive under both welfare-oriented and more market-oriented regimes. As Rubery (2011: 1104) has eloquently said: 'what is required is both a more gendered analysis of institutions and a more social analysis of gender as the starting point for the more positive task of analysing how reregulation could be used to reduce gender difference and inequality.'

Notes

1   All the figures cited here come from DREES (Direction de la recherche des études, de l'évaluation et des statistiques), except when another source is indicated; data available at http://www.data.drees.sante.gouv.fr/ReportFolders/reportFolders.aspx?sCS _referer=&sCS_ChosenLang=fr.

2   Care services might also correspond here to elderly care. Note that the average proportion in the EU stands at a higher level (27.9 per cent).

3   Figures: OECD (2016a).

4   OECD Family database (2016b).

5   Ministère du Travail, de l'Emploi et de la Formation Professionnelle: 'Bilan de la loi de sécurisation de l'emploi du 14 juin 2013 au 03 avril 2015' (Review of the law on employment security), http://travail-emploi.gouv.fr/IMG/pdf/CONFERENCE_THEMATI QUE_DU_3_AVRIL_2015_-_Bilan_de_la_loi_de_securisation_de_l_emploi.pdf.

6   The parent leave system is associated with full employment guaranty and the employment contract is not suspended during the work absence.

7   Parents not in employment before the birth or adoption of their child are entitled to a flat rate of 180 SEK (1 SEK = 0.11 Euro; 1 Euro = 9.15 SEK).

8   The incidences of fathers taking parental leave and the average duration of the father's absence have, however, continuously increased since the introduction of the parental leave system: from 1 per cent of compensated days in the mid-1970s to 26 per cent in 2015 (corresponding to around 80 working days of absence; see Swedish Social Insurance Agency, 2016).

9   It should also be stressed that the Swedish pension system takes into consideration the diversity in patterns of labour market integration over the life course and the uneven distribution of risks by limiting the cost of necessary work interruptions linked to parenting, care activities and involuntary employment disruptions such as unemployment, disability or sickness. The time that workers devote to higher education, to small children or to national military service, as well as absence due to unemployment and sickness, also gives rise to pension rights. In other words, future entitlements to a pension are currently not only related to work history and earnings but are also linked to other forms of activity and periods of benefit receipt, including parental, unemployment, sickness and partial disability benefits.

References

ABS (Australian Bureau of Statistics) (2015), Gender Indicators, Australia, August 2015, Cat. No. 4125.0, http://abs.gov.au/ausstats/abs@.nsf/Lookup/by%20Subject/4125.0~Aug %202015~Main%20Features~Attainment~6153, accessed 30 January 2016.

Anxo, D., Mencarini, L., Pailhé, A., Solaz, A., Tanturri, M. L. and Flood, L. (2011), 'Gender differences in time-use over the life course: a comparative analysis of France, Italy, Sweden, and the United States', *Feminist Economics*, 17:3, 159–95.

Australian Government (2014), 'Childcare and early childhood learning', *Productivity Commission Inquiry*, 1:73, 89.

Baird, M. (2005), 'Parental leave in Australia: the role of the industrial relations system', *Law in Context: Work, Family and the Law*, 23:1, 45–64.

Baird, M. (2016), 'Policy tensions: women, work and paid parental leave', in Hancock, K. and Lansbury, R. D. (eds), *Industrial Relations Reform: Looking to the Future* (Sydney: Federation Press).

Baird, M. and O'Brien, M. (2015), 'Dynamics of parental leave in anglophone countries: the paradox of state expansion in the liberal welfare regimes', *Community, Work and Family*, 18:2, 198–217.

Baird, M and Williamson, S. (2009), 'Women, work and Industrial relations in 2008', *Journal of Industrial Relations,* 51:3, 331–46.

Baird, M., Frino, B and Williamson, S. (2009), 'Paid maternity and paternity leave and the emergence of equality bargaining in Australia: an analysis of enterprise agreements, 2003–2007', *Australian Bulletin of Labour,* 35:4, 671–91.

Burchell, B., Fagan, C., O'Brien, C. and Smith, M. (2007), *Working Conditions in the European Union: The Gender Perspective,* Report (Dublin: European Foundation for the Improvement of Living and Working Conditions).

Cazes, S., Hijzen, A. and Saint-Martin, A. (2015), 'Measuring and assessing job quality: the OECD Job Quality Framework', OECD Social, Employment and Migration Working Papers, No. 174 (Paris: Organisation for Economic Co-operation and Development) http://dx.doi.org/10.1787/5jrp02kjw1mr-en.

Davoine, L., Erhel, C. and Guergoat-Larivière, M. (2008), 'Monitoring employment quality in work: European Employment Strategy Indicators and beyond', *International Labour Review*, 147:2–3, 163–98.

Esping-Andersen, G. (1990), *Three Worlds of Welfare Capitalism* (Princeton: Princeton University Press).

Fagan, C. and Burchell, B. (2002), *Gender, Jobs and Working Conditions in the European Union*, Report (Dublin: European Foundation for the Improvement of Living and Working Conditions).

Fagan, C. and Rubery, J. (1996), 'Transitions between family formation and paid employment', in Schmid, G., O'Reilly, J. and Schomann, K. (eds), *International Handbook of Labour Market Policy and Evaluation* (Cheltenham: Edward Elgar), pp. 348–78.

Green, F., Mostafa, T., Parent-Thirion, A., Vermeylen, G. and Van Houten, G. (2013), 'Is job quality becoming more unequal?', *Industrial and Labor Relations Review*, 66:4, 753–84.

Lemière, S. (2013), *L'accès à l'emploi des femmes: une question de politiques*, Rapport d'une mission sur l'emploi des femmes réalisée à la demande du ministère des Droits des Femmes.

Lemière, S. (2014), 'Le partage entre emploi et famille et entre femmes et hommes: une question de politiques', *Regards croisés sur l'économie,* 15, 230–44.

OECD (Organisation for Economic Co-operation and Development) (2014), Employment Database, OECD.Stat, http://stats.oecd.org/index.aspx?queryid=54751, accessed 21 September 2016.

OECD (Organisation for Economic Co-operation and Development) (2015), Labour Force Statistics 2015, OECD.Stat, http://stats.oecd.org/Index.aspx?DataSetCode=STLABO UR, accessed 21 September 2016.

OECD (Organisation for Economic Co-operation and Development) (2016a), 'Labour Market Statistics: Labour Force Statistics by Sex and Age: Indicators. OECD Employment and Labour Market Statistics (database), http://dx.doi.org/10.1787/data-00310-en, accessed 19 May 2016.

OECD (Organisation for Economic Co-operation and Development) (2016b), 'Family Database', http://oecd.org/els/soc/oecdfamilydatabasethefamilysupportcalculator.htm, accessed 30 May 2016.

OECD (Organisation for Economic Co-operation and Development) (2016c), 'Job quality indicators', http://oecd.org/index.aspx?Datasetcode=JOBQ, accessed 13 May 2016.

OECD (Organisation for Economic Co-operation and Development) (2016d), Family Database, http://www.oecd.org/social/family/database.htm, accessed 22 September 2016.

Rubery, J. (2002), 'Gender mainstreaming and gender equality in the EU: the impact of the EU employment Strategy', *Industrial Relations Journal*, 33:5, 500–22.

Rubery, J. (2011), 'Towards a gendering of the labour market regulation debate', *Cambridge Journal of Economics*, 35:6, 1103–26.

Rubery, J., Grimshaw, D. and Figueiredo, H. (2005), 'How to close the gender pay gap in Europe: towards the gender mainstreaming of pay policy', *Industrial Relations Journal*, 36:3, 184–213.

Rubery, J., Smith, M., Anxo, D. and Flood, L. (2001), 'The future of European labour supply: the critical role of the family', *Feminist Economics*, 7:3, 33–69.

Rubery, J., Smith, M. and Fagan, C. (1999), *Women's Employment in Europe: Trends and Prospects* (London and New York: Routledge).

Swedish Social Insurance Agency (2016), 'Statistics on children and parental leave', https:// forsakringskassan.se/wps/portal/statistik/barnochfamilj/foraldrapenning, accessed April 2016.

Whitehouse, G., Baird, M., Alexander, M. and Brennan, D. (2015), 'Australia country note', in Moss, P. (ed.), *International Review of Leave Policies and Research 2015*, available at: http://leavenetwork.org/lp_and_r_reports/, accessed 8 July 16.

17

Minimum wages and the remaking of the wage-setting systems in Greece and the UK

Maria Karamessini and Damian Grimshaw

Introduction

The steady encroachment of a more neoliberal set of market principles among advanced capitalist countries has not necessarily been accompanied by a declining role of the state. This is as true with respect to the state's role in wage-setting as it is in other areas of economic governance, such as social transfers, product market regulation and corporate governance (Streeck, 2014). Since the economic crisis, government minimum wage policy has played an increasingly interventionist role in many countries, albeit with divergent goals, including responding to falling living standards, adjusting unit labour costs, compensating for falling welfare budgets and substituting for collective wage negotiation. Such interventions may adapt the minimum wage up or down, reflecting (and shaping) a constellation of competing interests and political and economic conditions, as well as pay equity goals (Grimshaw and Rubery, 2013; Rubery, 2003).

Theoretical ideas about the crowding out of participative wage-setting (Aghion *et al.,* 2011), legitimation of marketisation processes (Koçer and Visser, 2009) and a neoliberal shift (e.g. Baccaro and Howell, 2011; Hermann, 2014; Hyman, 2015) are helpful in revealing both the underlying reasons for state interventions in minimum wage fixing and the interrelationship with national industrial relations systems and conditions of employment. In this chapter, we develop these ideas through a comparative empirical analysis of two countries that are to some extent at the opposite ends of Europe's minimum wage policy approaches observed since the economic crisis: Greece and the UK.

Minimum wage policy in Europe since the economic crisis

At the onset of the global financial and economic crisis, 20 of the 27 European Union (EU) member states had a generally applicable statutory minimum wage. With Croatia, which joined the EU in 2013, and Germany, which adopted a national minimum wage in 2015, by 2016, 22 of the 28 EU member states possessed statutory minimum wage systems.

Since the beginning of the crisis, many countries have sought to contain the impact of minimum wages on average wage developments and labour costs, especially those where austerity policies were scrutinised by the Troika. However, a significant number of countries have continued to rely on minimum wage increases to conduct their wage policy (ILO, 2015a). The contrasting approaches reflect new momentum in old debates about the role of minimum wages in labour markets, fuelled by evidence of a slowdown in real-wage growth, persistent high shares of working poor and long-run increases in earnings inequality (OECD, 2015). The introduction of a statutory minimum wage in Germany in 2015 further triggered debates across Europe, especially in countries without a statutory minimum wage (Eurofound, 2016). However, in most of these countries (for example, in Austria, Finland and Denmark) there was a consensus among the main actors to stick to the collectively agreed sector or occupational minima. In Italy, the government included the possibility of introducing a statutory minimum wage in the reform of its Jobs Act, but decided not to implement it for the time being, following criticism from the trade unions. In Cyprus, where a statutory minimum wage applies to nine occupations, the employer organisations insist that this should be abolished or drastically reduced (Eurofound, 2016). Although, the combination of sector minimum rates and high levels of collective bargaining coverage can, at least from a pay equity perspective, be regarded as a functional equivalent to a statutory national minimum wage (Garnero et al., 2015), the long-standing erosion of bargaining coverage well before the economic crisis, its significant retreat during the latter in many countries (ILO, 2015b) and the expansion of low-wage sectors in most economies bring minimum wage policy back on the European agenda.

The most important changes in minimum wage policy during the crisis took place in those EU countries that had to ask for financial assistance from international institutions.[1] In exchange, they had to implement economic adjustment programmes dictated and supervised by their creditors. A key macroeconomic tool was to use minimum wage cuts as a mechanism to depress wage settlements through the whole economy. For example, Ireland reduced its hourly minimum wage by 1 euro (around 12 per cent) in early 2011 in response to Troika pressures, although quickly reversed this decision after strong union campaigns. The Greek government was pressured even further by the Troika and implemented a radical 22 per cent cut in its national minimum wage. Similarly, in implementation of their loan agreements, Latvia, Lithuania, Bulgaria, Portugal and Spain (as well as Greece and Ireland) all imposed freezes of their minimum wage for several years. All the above countries increased the minimum wage once the period of freeze was over – the last being Ireland in 2016 – while the freeze is still ongoing in Greece. This is why no other EU country except Greece has experienced a decrease in the nominal value of a minimum wage over the eight-year period 2008–16 (Figure 17.1).

It follows, therefore, that Europe witnessed contrasting trends in the real value of minimum wages. Of the 15 countries with trend data for 2008–15 (Figure 17.2), it increased significantly in eight (as much as 35 per cent in Poland), stagnated in six countries (Czech Republic, Spain, the UK,

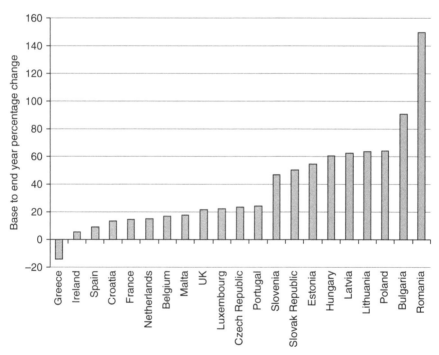

Figure 17.1   Change in monthly minimum wages at current prices, national currency 2008–16

Source: Eurostat database online (extracted 21 August 2016).

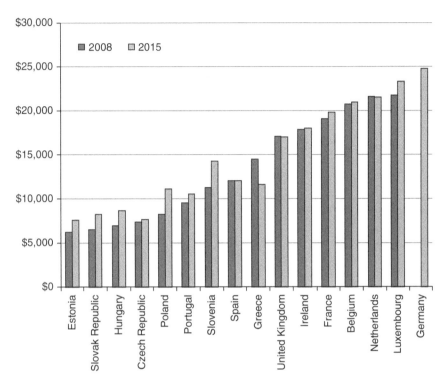

Figure 17.2   Real annual minimum wages, 2008–15, at 2014 prices (US$ PPP)

Source: OECD statistics online (extracted 21 August 2016).

Ireland, Belgium and the Netherlands) and dropped in one country (Greece, by 20 per cent).

During the period 2008–15, median wages increased less so than minimum wages in all EU countries with a statutory minimum wage, except Ireland where the opposite occurred, and in France, Belgium and Spain the national minimum wage and median wage grew at the same pace. In Greece, the minimum wage reduced more than median wages. As a result of the above trends, the relative minimum wage – as measured by change in the Kaitz index – decreased in Greece and Ireland, remained stable in France, Belgium and Spain, and rose in the other EU countries shown (Figure 17.3). The developments in the relative minimum wage have therefore narrowed earnings inequalities at the bottom end of the wage distribution in countries where the Kaitz index increased since the beginning of the crisis and widened earnings inequalities in the few where it has fallen –namely, Greece and, especially, Ireland.

Overall, the different patterns can be collected into four groups of change

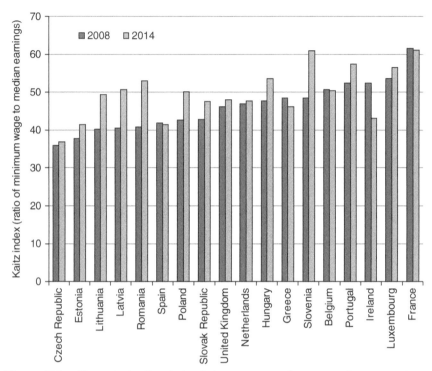

Figure 17.3 Change in the Kaitz index (minimum wage relative to median earnings), 2008–14

Source: OECD statistics online (extracted 21 August 2016).

over the period 2008–15 according to trends in real minimum wages and relative minimum wages (Table 17.1). The largest group of countries – seven of the 15 countries for which we have complete data – have experienced upwards trajectories in both the real and relative values of their minimum wages. A second group of five countries, among them the UK, experienced either limited change (flat trend) in both values or upwards change in one of either real or relative values. A third group experienced a drop in one of the indicators, experienced by Ireland during the period shown. And, finally, Greece occupies the group in which both real and relative values fell significantly during the period.

Explaining state policy towards minimum wage fixing

Evidence of divergent minimum wage trends reviewed above is further complicated by a likely variety of economic and political thinking that underpins the

Table 17.1   Patterns of change in real minimum wages and Kaitz index, 2008–14/15

		Kaitz index		
		Down	**Flat**	**Up**
Real MW	**Up**	C. ---	B. ---	A. Estonia, Hungary, Luxembourg, Poland, Portugal, Slovakia, Slovenia
	Flat	C. Ireland	B. Belgium, Czech Rep., France, Netherlands, Spain	B. UK
	Down	D. Greece	C. ---	C. ---

Notes: Up is for rises of 5%+ (Real minimum wage (MW)) or 1.5+ points (Kaitz) and Down is for falls of more than −5% or −1.5 points. The cells are grouped into four categories, A–D; '—' signifies no country examples.

Source: Figures 17.2 and 17.3.

Table 17.2   Five frames for understanding state policy towards wage-fixing

		Collective bargaining:		
		Dismantle	**Mostly neutral**	**Supportive**
Minimum wage	**Raise**	Crowding-out (Aghion *et al.*, 2011)	Legitimation (O'Connor, 1973)	Participative distribution (Sen, 1999)
	Neutral			Collective self-regulation (Kahn-Freund, 1959)
	Cut	Neoliberal shift (Howells, 2015)		

policy approaches. If we consider theoretical rationales for state interventions to raise or cut the minimum wage, then we can identify five possible frames of analysis, each of which considers the intersection with collective bargaining (Table 17.2). It may be, as the writings of Aghion and colleagues (2011) suggest, that states intervene to raise the minimum wage as a direct response to a per-ceived erosion of trust and cooperation in labour markets (especially between workers and employers). The problem is that there is a strong tendency for a self-perpetuating dynamic such that, on the one hand, the higher minimum wage under stringent state control discourages the formation of trust (by limit-ing opportunities for workers and employers to build experience at cooperating in wage bargaining) and, on the other, sustained experience of non-cooperation generates demand by citizens for stronger state intervention in setting minimum wage standards (Aghion *et al.*, 2008). In other words, the active state-controlled minimum wage policy in this view crowds out collective forms of wage negotiation (for the case of France, see Gautié, 2011). Some states may even seek purposefully to undermine the foundations for collective wage bargaining while simultaneously actively raising the minimum wage; this is in other words a strongly non-participative approach to distribution.

A second frame of analysis is that states are in fact responding to the problem of legitimation as identified in O'Connor's (1973) early study on the fiscal crisis of the state. The idea is that any capitalist state must respond to dual pressures both to foster private capital accumulation and to legitimise (to citizens) the unequal and destabilising effects of accumulation through policies of income redistribution and social protection; it can be interpreted as a struggle between providing for market justice and social justice. As capitalism becomes more and more disorganised in a race to accumulate, then raising the statutory minimum wage may bolster support for (or subdue resistance against) the liberalisation project (Koçer and Visser, 2009). Unlike the crowding out frame, the thesis of legitimation is (in our interpretation) ambivalent about the procedure for raising the minimum wage: it may be achieved through trusting, tripartite forms of social dialogue – deliberative negotiation rather than stringent state control – since the distributive result is what matters for legitimation. There is a limit to redistribution of course, since it must not constrain employer profitability in this perspective; similar to flexicurity packages of reforms post-crisis, states pare back protections while sustaining full respect for the imperative of business flexibility (Heyes, 2013). Moreover, it may also be complemented by deregulatory labour market policies that provide employers with 'exit options', by strengthening employer discretion to adjust other employment conditions (Jaehrling and Méhaut, 2013).

We describe a third more positive policy frame as 'participative distribution', inspired by the writings of Sen and the Webbs on the potential for virtuous circles between equality and development. This type of policy action suggests a state finely attuned to the intricacies of a strongly complementary institutional setting, involving tripartite consideration of the conditions for, and effects of, minimum wage rises, a strong and coordinated trade union role in collective bargaining (in low-wage sectors especially), highly engaged employers (e.g. as members of industry associations) and quite possibly a proactive, egalitarian approach to issues of pay equity.

At the other end of the spectrum, 'neoliberal shift' describes the purposeful actions of a nation state (or pan-national authority) designed both to reduce the wage floor and to curtail the reach and effectiveness of collective bargaining in a determined effort to shrink labour's share of national income, possibly to depress real wages in an effort to boost competitiveness and also to accelerate labour market deregulation. In Howells' critical analyses (2015, 2016) there is a sense that stronger state actions, via a raft of legal regulations, are intended to incrementally disembed markets from society –to undo welfare rights, to shift the balance of public and private governance of economic activity, and in particular to rule out collective interference over employment organisation. The restrictive control of minimum wage policy alongside a dismantling of collective bargaining has the effect of substituting legal regulation for collective regulation. This is in direct opposition to our fifth frame of analysis shown in Table 17.2, that of collective self-regulation, or 'collective laissez-faire' to use Kahn-Freund's description of post-war UK where social partners assume full authority for wage-fixing backed up by state support for participative (that is, collectively negotiated) standards (see also Bosch and Lehndorff, chapter 2, this volume).

In the following analysis, we apply these different policy frames to the cases of Greece and the UK. In particular, we argue that in response to an attack on pre-vailing institutions (rather than incremental, path dependent change) Greece has experienced a radical change in minimum wage policy approach from one char-acterized by 'collective self-regulation' to its opposite form, that of 'neoliberal shift'. The UK, by contrast, appears set on a 'crowding out' policy approach, as we explore below.

Greece: minimum wage policy as 'neoliberal shift'

Greece is currently living through its ninth year of recession during which GDP has fallen by 26 per cent, disposable income by 30 per cent and the aver-age wage by 26 per cent, while unemployment reached more than a quarter of the labour force (27 per cent) and the risk of poverty or social exclusion more than one in three of the population (36 per cent). Since the eruption of the sovereign debt crisis in late 2009, Greek governments have been obliged to implement three Economic Adjustment Programmes (EAP), under the super-vision of the Troika and currently the Quartet,[2] as a prerequisite for the loans granted in 2010, 2012 and 2015 by Eurozone partners and the International Monetary Fund.

Prior to 2012, Greece's minimum wage was determined by national-level col-lective bargaining and was a core feature of its wage-setting system. In 2012 and 2013, the Greek government introduced radical changes in the determination of the minimum wage as a final step in the complete recasting of the pre-crisis wage-setting system. The government first bypassed the national collective bargaining by unilaterally imposing a lower statutory minimum wage (and a new subminimum for workers aged under 25 years old) and then abolished collective bargaining on minimum wages altogether. State intervention in minimum wage policy is only one component of the neoliberal attack on labour rights that has been orchestrated under the first two EAPs adopted in 2010 and 2012 respectively (Karamessini, 2012). The attack had two core goals: (1) to reduce nominal unit labour costs and restore losses in price competitiveness after Greece's entry in EMU; and (2) to recast the wage determination system in order to make wage developments conducive to export-led growth.

Minimum wage policy pre-crisis: 'collective self-regulation'

Before 2012, the national minimum wage was an integral part of collective bargaining and a key instrument of wage determination in Greece, which was one of three EU countries (with Belgium and Estonia) to set the national minimum wage through bipartite negotiations (Schulten, 2012). National-level bargaining on the minimum wage was a core element of the post-war collective bargaining system established in 1955. The General Confederation of Greek Labour (GSEE) and peak employer organisations regularly signed the National General Collective Agreement (NGCA), which not only determined the minimum wage but also set the floor for various employment conditions and workers' rights. National-level bargaining on sectoral or occupational minima was the second most important feature of the Greek collective bargaining system. Company-level bargaining was added after 1974 and improved upon sector and occupation minima.

While for most of the post-war period minimum wages were fixed jointly by employers and unions, there were periods of state intervention. In 1982, the government raised the national minimum wage by 48 per cent (23 per cent in real terms) with subsequent annual adjustments fixed by inflation-linked indexation. This indexation system was abolished in 1990. At the same time, a new law on 'free' collective bargaining replaced compulsory state-controlled arbitration, effective since 1955, with independent third-party mediation and arbitration.

The Greek wage-setting system of the 1990s and 2000s combined bipartite negotiation of a national minimum wage with relatively high collective bargaining coverage (65 per cent in 2009). The latter was achieved through both the regular use of extension mechanisms by the Minister of Labour and a system of articulated, multi-layered and coordinated collective bargaining. As in Spain during the 1990s and much of the 2000s, the national minimum wage operated in 'distant coexistence' with the basic wage rates negotiated in collective agreements (Grimshaw and Bosch, 2013: 59) such that its coverage in the official labour market was very low: less than 1 per cent of employees in firms with 10 or more employees were paid up to 105 per cent of the minimum wage in 2010 (OECD, 2015: figure 1.13) and this rate would remain low even if employees from small firms were included. However, national bargaining on the national minimum wage was extremely important in two respects. First and foremost, minimum wage increases functioned as a minimum standard for national sector – and occupation-level bargaining. Depending on their bargaining power and the particular conditions in their industry or occupation, unions customarily set their target increases somewhere between minimum wage increases and those achieved by the most powerful public utilities and banking federations. This customary union bargaining behaviour explains the uninterrupted fall of the Kaitz index from the early 1980s right up to the crisis years (Figure 17.4). In the late 1990s, the bargaining rounds between management and the strong unions in public utilities and banking were decoupled from the bipartite fixing of the national minimum wage. A basic mechanism of articulated bargaining and wage drift was thus broken (Ioannou 2000). However, public utilities and banking remained in the 2000s – as in the 1980s and the 1990s – the strongholds of the

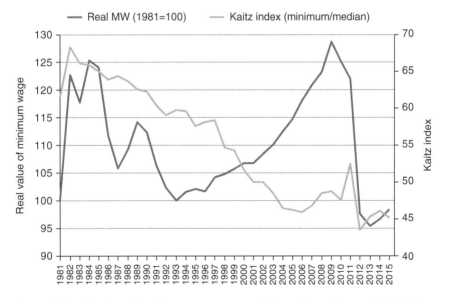

Figure 17.4   Trends in the real minimum wage and Kaitz index in Greece, 1981–2015

Notes: MW refers to minimum wage.

Source: OECD statistics online (extracted 21 August 2016).

union movement and dominated the leadership of GSEE. General strikes supported by these unions were often used to reinforce GSEE's bargaining power during negotiations on the minimum wage. A second reason for the importance of the national minimum wage during the 1990s and 2000s was that it constituted a reference point for individual bargaining on pay in the relatively large informal labour market, similar to evidence in other countries of the 'lighthouse effect' of minimum wages (Boeri *et al.*, 2010).

Alongside constant and robust productivity growth, the above-described wage-setting system allowed for an uninterrupted increase in both the real minimum wage (Figure 17.4) and the real compensation per employee in the period 1993–2009 equal to 29 per cent and 53 per cent, respectively (in cumulative terms). The multi-layered and coordinated system of collective bargaining led to important wage inequalities, especially between the public and private sectors, but at the same time reinforced the middle of the wage distribution through national bargaining on sector and occupational minima and established relatively low inequality in the bottom half of the wage distribution; the pre-crisis Kaitz level was still higher than the EU average in 2008 (Figure 17.3). As for the real value of the minimum wage (purchasing power), this was also above the EU average at that time (Figure 17.2).

Minimum wage policy, internal devaluation and deregulation of the wage-setting system

Reducing labour costs in the business sector of the economy was one of the key goals of the first EAP (2010–11) that considered it central to the process of internal devaluation intended to boost price competitiveness and reduce the external deficit. This goal became an explicit and quantified target under the second EAP (2012–15), which necessitated a 15 per cent reduction. To achieve it, the first EAP imposed measures designed to decentralise collective bargaining (Dedoussopoulos *et al.*, 2013; Ioannou, 2012; Karamessini, 2012, 2015; Koukiadaki and Kokkinou, 2015), including suspending the extension of collective agreements by the Minister of Labour to non-signatory firms, ensuring that firm-level agreements prevail over sector and occupational agreements by abolishing the 'favourability' clause and allowing 'associations of persons' (non-union organisations usually set up by employers) to sign firm-level collective agreements instead of unions.

Despite the reforms, the pace of wage reductions during 2010 and 2011 was deemed too slow. The Troika and the Greek government pinned the blame on continued rises in the national minimum wage (equal to inflation for the Eurozone region), which had been agreed by the NGCA in July 2010. In their view, such rises conflicted with the goal of labour cost reduction (Kanellopoulos, 2015). The government launched a tripartite dialogue to discuss national minimum wage developments compatible with boosting competitiveness and preserving employment. But the Troika considered the results of this dialogue unsatisfactory since they did not ensure 'the quick responsiveness of wages to the fall in economic activity' (European Commission, 2012: 38). Koukiadaki and Kokkinou summarised the views of the social partners as follows:

> 'During the discussions, the employers' associations opposed the reduction of the minimum wage but were in favour of a three-year freeze in wage and maturity increases and the reduction in social insurance contributions. On the other hand, the GSEE [unions] rejected any change in relation to wage costs and stated that the discussion should focus only on non-wage costs.' (2015: 145)

The stalemate led the Troika and the government to design, in 2012, a series of measures building on two pillars: an immediate and drastic reduction of wage floors and the completion of the 2010–11 reforms to radically recast the wage-setting system. The 2012 measures can be grouped as follows:

- Legislative reduction of the minimum wage by 22 per cent followed by a freeze until the end of 2016.
- Introduction of a lower minimum wage for young people under the age of 25 years, at 87 per cent of the reduced minimum wage followed by a freeze until the end of 2016.
- Further dismantling of the collective bargaining system through the reduction to three months of the after-effects of collective agreements and freedom to negotiate individual contracts thereafter; the elimination of unilateral recourse to arbitration and its restriction to ruling only the basic wage; the freeze of all seniority bonuses provided by law or collective agreements; and the removal of 'tenure' from all existing labour contracts.
- Invitation to social partners to simplify the NGCA by establishing a single-rate statutory minimum wage and to abolish the multiple minimum wages according to type of work, education, marital status and seniority. The subsequent failure of the National Committee for Social Dialogue, set up in September 2012, to agree a reform led to a government-imposed (following consultation) national minimum wage from January 2017, which is said to be fully compatible with a decentralised and individualised system of industrial relations.

These decisions were taken with the goal of encouraging sizeable reductions in nominal wages across the whole economy and thereby generate the 15 per cent

Table 17.3 Wage developments, Greece 2008–15

	Annual rates (%), nominal	
	Minimum wage	**Average wage***
2008	3.4	3.7
2009	5.8	3.1
2010	2.7	−2.0
2011	6.8	−3.8
2012	−21.4	−3.0
2013	0.0	−7.0
2014	0.0	−2.1
2015	0.0	−1.7

Notes: * Nominal compensation per employee; total economy.

Source: Authors' calculations from Eurostat online minimum wage database; European Economy, Statistical Annex, Spring 2016 for average wage.

contraction of labour costs specified in the second EAP as needed to reverse losses in labour cost competitiveness of domestic production during 2000–09. Having increased by 10 per cent between 2008 and 2011, the nominal minimum wage fell abruptly by 22 per cent in 2012 and remains at the same nominal level at the time of writing (mid-2016). Adjusted for prices, the real value of the minimum wage fell by 24 per cent between 2010 and 2015, bringing to an end a long period since the mid-1990s of steady real gains in the wage floor for the Greek workforce (Figure 17.4). Average nominal earnings data show annual declines of between 2 and 7 per cent during 2010–15 (Table 17.3), resulting in a cumulative loss of 18 per cent.

As well as forcing through major cuts in nominal wages across the whole wage distribution, the reduced minimum wage and the new subminimum for youth (with the notoriously high 'adult' age of 25 years old) were also explicitly intended by the authors of the second EAP (European Commission, 2012: 38) to (1) send a strong signal to employers and unions bargaining wages in other sector- and firm-level agreements (2) reduce informality and undeclared work by pulling the latter into the formal labour market; and (3) widen differentials at the bottom end of the wage distribution, thought to price out of employment the low-skilled who might receive payments at or above the minimum wage. In fact, because average earnings have been in continuous freefall since 2010 (owing to the depressed macroeconomic climate and the dismantled collective bargaining system), the bottom half of the wage distribution has become more compressed following the one-off minimum wage cut in 2012.

Table 17.4   Wage inequality indicators, Greece 2004–14

	2004	2007	2009	2011	2012	2013	2014
Kaitz index	46.5	46.8	48.7	52.5	43.5	45.3	46.1
Low pay incidence	20.0	15.1	15.1	12.3	11.8	13.9	17.9

Notes: The incidence of low-paid workers is defined as the share of full-time workers earning less than two-thirds of gross median earnings of all full-time workers.

Source: OECD statistics online (data extracted on 21 August 2016).

We can identify four successive periods (Tables 17.3 and 17.4): (1) 2007–09 – the Kaitz index increased as a rising minimum wage outpaced average wages; (2) 2009–11 – the Kaitz index again increased but this time owing to steady growth in the minimum wage alongside falling average earnings; (3) 2012 – the one-off cut in the minimum wage produced an unprecedented nine-point drop in the Kaitz index; and (4) 2012–14 – as the nominal value of the minimum wage was frozen in 2012 and average wages have declined each year since, the Kaitz index increased, which is absolutely contrary to the desired goals of the second EAP.

During this period, the *deregulation of the wage-setting system* has led to the *individualisation of wage bargaining* and, ultimately, under conditions of mass unemployment, to a compression of wage differentials towards the minima. It is noteworthy that the number of sector and occupational collective agreements and arbitration awards has fallen from 101 in 2009 to 23 in 2015, while the coverage of employees by collective agreements fell from 65 per cent in 2009 to 40 per cent in 2013 (ILO, 2015b); forthcoming data will undoubtedly reveal an even lower rate. Moreover, the institutional deregulation identified with the 'neoliberal shift' in Greece has caused not only huge wage devaluation, but also a rising share of low-paid workers since 2011 (Table 17.4) even when we use an indicator that refers to a depressed median wage.

Under the third EAP (2015–18) a commission of high-level international experts was formed in March 2016 to make independent recommendations and other reforms in industrial relations. The commission has not concluded with a unified proposal. Nevertheless, a majority of its members have recommended a return to bipartite negotiations of the national minimum wage with automatic *erga omnes* effects, but only after consultation with an independent group of experts, and the replacement of the special minimum wage for youth by experience-based subminimum wages for a maximum of two years (Hellenic Republic, Ministry of Labour, Social Security and Social Solidarity 2016: 2–3).

The UK: a case of 'crowding out'?

The UK is quite different: the government intervened in 2016 to raise the minimum wage over a medium-term period in order both to arrest the stagnant trend in real earnings growth and to reduce public expenditures on in-work benefits claimed by many millions of low-wage workers. At the same time, however, the UK policy approach shares similarities with Greece in the policy interactions with participative forms of wage-fixing, albeit displaying a passive disconnect with collective bargaining rather than an outright 'frontal assault', as Marginson (2014) puts it for Greece. We explore these issues here.

Prior to its introduction of a national statutory minimum wage in 1999, the UK had, for several decades, applied a complex system of minimum wage protection that was jointly regulated by unions and employers without state intervention. These 'Wages Councils' (founded in 1909 as 'Wages Boards') operated in 66 sectors at their peak, covered around 3.5 million workers and fixed overtime and holiday entitlements as well as wage rates (Burgess, 2006). The government abolished them in 1993 as part of a wider deregulatory labour market policy approach.[3] The problem, however, was that it left a considerable hole in wage protection, since the 1980s had witnessed a significant drop in collective bargaining coverage; the near-comprehensive collective bargaining structures of the period 1950–80 had quickly collapsed to a minority of the private sector workforce already by the early 1990s (Brown, 2010: figure 11.1). As such, the early-twentieth-century rationale for the introduction of Wages Councils – namely, that many workers were employed in sectors without collective representation and deserved protection from wage exploitation – was once again true and paved the way for unions' newfound positive support, leading eventually to a government determination to establish (under the Labour party) a national statutory minimum wage (effective from 1999).

Nevertheless, while the policy approach was inclusive of employers and unions in the process of minimum wage-fixing – via the reputable, independent Low Pay Commission (see Brown, 2009) – it was not accompanied by policies designed to prop up collective bargaining or to establish stronger 'participative standards' in the UK labour market.[4] Collective bargaining coverage continued to decline during the 2000s (down to an estimated 16 per cent in the private sector by 2015). From the outset, therefore, the minimum wage policy approach generated a clear risk that wages would cluster around a single regulated wage rule at the very bottom of the wage distribution (Grimshaw, 2010). Figure 17.5 displays the characteristics of the UK's 'isolated' minimum wage policy visually, showing the falling private sector collective bargaining coverage (from an

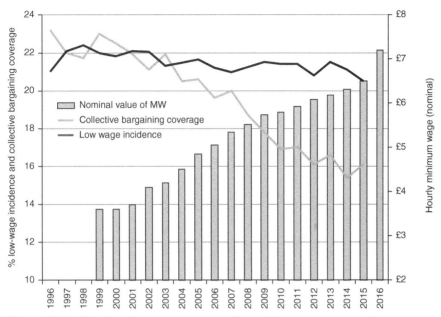

Figure 17.5   Trends in the minimum wage, collective bargaining coverage (private sector) and the incidence of low pay in the UK, 1996–2016

Notes: Low-wage incidence defined as share of employees earning less than two-thirds median gross hourly earnings; MW refers to minimum wage.

Source: Annual Survey of Hours and Earnings for low-wage incidence (authors' estimates from published data); private sector collective bargaining data from BIS (2016: table 2.4b).

already very low level), the steady rise (except the crisis years) in the minimum wage and the persistent high share of the low-wage workforce, averaging around 21–22 per cent throughout the 20-year period shown.

Compared to the situation in Greece (see Figure 17.4), the pre-crisis decade of real minimum wage gains in the UK looks similar in terms of the positive upwards trend, although the UK delivered higher real gains overall: OECD data show that for 2000–09 the real minimum wage recorded a 33 per cent rise in the UK (Figure 17.6) compared to 21 per cent in Greece. Thereafter, of course, the two country narratives are completely divorced. While the UK slowed down minimum wage rises during the crisis, which translated into a cumulative 5 per cent real cut from peak to trough (2009–13), the minimum wage in Greece went into a tailspin following the Troika's instructions, amounting to a 26 per cent real cut in the same period (OECD data). Trends in each country's relative minimum wage value also differ, with a notably steady upwards trend

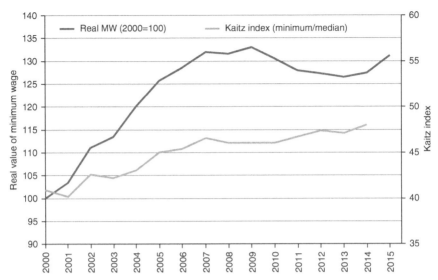

Figure 17.6   Trends in the real minimum wage and Kaitz index in the UK, 2000–15

Note: MW refers to minimum wage.

Source: OECD statistics online (extracted 6 October 2016).

in the UK (from 41 per cent to 48 per cent of median earnings) and a fluctuating trend in Greece punctuated by the steep drop in 2012 (from 53 per cent to 44 per cent of median earnings). What seems clear for the UK, therefore, is that low-wage workers have benefited from a relatively reliable statutory minimum wage instrument. It delivered large-scale gains during the good economic times, did not over-react during the crisis (although Greece is not necessarily a fair comparator) and has gradually shifted the position of the wage floor upwards relative to the wage distribution's mid-point; 2014 data place the UK just below the OECD 18-country average – Kaitz measures of 48 per cent and 50 per cent respectively (see Figure 17.3 above).

Nevertheless, the persistently high share of low-wage employment suggests all is not well in the UK's labour market. If the wage floor is rising against median earnings and the share of workers earning between the minimum wage and a threshold of two-thirds of median earnings is high and stable, it would appear that the rising minimum wage is not generating a sufficiently strong ripple effect in the bottom half of the wage structure. Instead, it seems that in the UK's weak and perforated industrial relations context – absent of other wage standards set for example by industry collectively bargained rates – the statutory minimum wage acts as a dominant 'external key rate' for many employers and proves far more important than productivity or human capital factors in wage-setting. Bryson and Lucchino (2014), for example, find almost one in three UK workplaces mention the minimum wage as an influence on their largest occupational group. The result is that very strong 'wage contours' around the minimum wage are generated in many segments of the labour market (after Dunlop, 1957). We would expect the UK to mirror to a large extent the situation in the USA. There, research finds evidence of minimum wage contours in several sectors, suggesting wage structures for many occupational groups are more closely tied to minimum wage trends than other factors such as changing skills and work experience (Levin-Waldman, 2002; Rodgers *et al.*, 2004).

We interrogate the UK data here by examining what has been happening with levels of pay just above the minimum wage for male and female workers – namely, at earnings up to 10 per cent, 20 per cent and 30 per cent higher than the minimum wage. Table 17.5 presents earnings data for these three 'wage contours' for the period 1999–2012. Three findings are significant.

1) The 2003–12 period of a rising minimum wage (nominal and Kaitz, see above) was consistent with a growing concentration of both men and women in all three low-wage contours shown. This strongly supports the thesis that the minimum wage became an increasingly dominant 'external key rate' during the period. It also points to weak wage spillover effects (see also Dickens and Manning, 2015; Stewart, 2012).[5]

2) The three observed minimum wage contours are far more strongly embedded for women than for men; in 2012, 15 per cent of women and 8 per cent of men (adults) were paid in the first wage contour of very low wages (minimum wage plus 10 per cent, equivalent to a gross hourly wage of £6.08–£6.69 at the time); and at the second wage contour (minimum wage plus 20 per cent) we find almost a quarter of all women employed (23 per cent) and one in seven (14 per cent) men.

3) There has been a diminishing of the gender divide since 2003. For example, while in 2003 women faced almost three times the likelihood as men of being paid in the second wage contour, by 2012 this had reduced to less than twice the risk. However, the risk for both groups increased significantly and by a similar size in terms of numbers affected: both witnessed a rise of approximately 1 million (1.01 million male workers and 0.98 million female workers) paid in the second wage contour (minimum wage plus 20 per cent) over this nine-year period.[6]

Furthermore, the increasing segmentation of low-wage workers in minimum wage contours during the pre- and post-crisis periods have exerted a significant

Table 17.5 Minimum wage contour trends in the UK: the share of female and male employees in pay bands above the minimum wage, 1999–2012

	1999	2003	2008	2012
First wage contour				
(MW + 10%)				
Women	11.9%	9.5%	12.7%	15.0%
Men	4.1%	3.2%	5.7%	8.4%
Second wage contour				
(MW + 20%)				
Women	20.7%	16.7%	20.4%	23.2%
Men	7.6%	6.0%	9.7%	13.6%
Third wage contour				
(MW + 30%)				
Women	27.7%	24.9%	26.4%	30.1%
Men	11.3%	10.0%	13.2%	18.4%
Minimum wage as %	47.6%	47.5%	52.4%	54.2%
of median pay				
Median pay as %	MW+110%	MW+111%	MW+91%	MW+84%
of minimum wage				
% women paid below median pay	61%	60%	58%	57%
% men paid below median pay	39%	40%	42%	43%

Notes: MW refers to minimum wage; the minimum wage level in April for each year was £3.60 (1999), £4.20 (2003), £5.52 (2008) and £6.08 (2012); data referring to the three tiers refer to adults aged 22+ (1999-2008) and 21+ (2012); median pay refers to all employees on adult rates (male, female, full-time, part-time) and was £7.57 (1999), £8.85 (2003), £10.54 (2008) and £11.21 (2012) (gross hourly, overtime excluded, nominal.

Source: ASHE earnings data (ons.gov.uk), 'Distribution of low paid jobs by 10p bands' and 'Annual Survey of Hours and Earnings: Table 1 All employees'; authors' original compilation.

downwards drag on median earnings. Adjusting for prices (using the Retail Price Index), real wages for the UK workforce came to a standstill in the period 2003–08, rose during the crisis year of deflation in 2009 and then went into freefall (dropping 10 per cent) until 2015 when they picked up a little. While other factors were certainly in play, it is notable that GDP per capita increased substantially in 2003–08 and, after a fall in 2008–09, resumed at a fairly steady rise thereafter (Grimshaw and Rafferty, 2016: figure 11). As such, we need to look at factors other than long-standing problems of slow productivity growth, weak capital investment and poor innovation performance that are features of the UK's private sector. Our suspicion is that the near-absence of other regulatory arrangements for wage-setting, especially collective bargaining, denies workers and employers an important 'beneficial constraint' (Streeck, 1997). If workers had more 'voice' in negotiating and defending wages (as in France and Germany, for example) then this would allow them to leverage minimum wage gains further up the wage distribution (Grimshaw *et al.*, 2014). Instead many low-wage employers appear to be responding by fusing job grades at lower levels, collapsing customary wage differentials between supervisory and non-supervisory grades and using the minimum wage as a standard rate rather than as a floor against exploitation.

As well as acting as a drag on median earnings, a high share of workers in low-wage jobs imposes a significant cost on the welfare state in the form of in-work benefits ('tax credits' in the UK). Partly in response to this issue, the government introduced a new higher adult minimum wage (for workers aged 25 plus as in Greece) fixed initially in 2016 at approximately 7 per cent higher than the rate for 21–24 year olds. More radically, the government said it would *require* the Low Pay Commission to raise the new premium adult rate to £9.00 (from the 2016 £7.20 rate) or 60 per cent of median earnings by 2020.[7] This intervention is significant for two reasons. Firstly, for the first time since the establishment of the tripartite Low Pay Commission in 1999, the government has asserted control over the fixing process, thereby strengthening government power and diminishing the voice of employer and trade union organisations. Secondly, it sets what appears to be a very ambitious target for the wage floor, which ought to contribute to reducing the share of workers in low-wage employment.

As estimations in Figure 17.7 show, the two targets generate very different results: the £9 target would take the minimum wage above the low-wage threshold by 2018, while the 60 per cent target would set in train a slower set of annual rises converging with where the previous minimum wage would have been by 2020. However, it is understood that the £9 target has been quietly shelved and that when the Low Pay Commission makes its report in October 2016 it will recommend a 2017 rate in line with the 60 per cent target.[8] As such, it will continue the past trajectory of minimum wage rises with a slow closing of the gap between the wage floor and the low-wage threshold. Nevertheless, without complementary policy reforms to strengthen participative standards, the high share of workers paid in narrow wage contours above the minimum wage is unlikely to change.

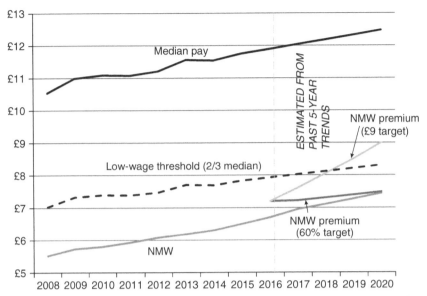

Figure 17.7   Projected minimum wage trends with alternative 2020 targets (nominal value)

Notes: Median pay is for all employees, gross hourly pay excluding overtime, nominal value; NMW is the national minimum wage (adult rate) for April each year; projected median pay for 2016–20 applies the annual average rise recorded for 2010–15 (1.2%) and the projected NMW trends assume steady rises in rates during 2017–20.

Source: Annual Survey of Hours and Earnings.

Conclusions

While in 2012 the Greek government cut the minimum wage by 22 per cent as a main plank of its wage devaluation policy approach in a context of relentless economic recession, the UK minimum wage enjoyed small but steady rises during employment recovery, followed by a potentially radical statutory intervention that promises to deliver a succession of minimum wage rises during the period 2016–20 in an effort to cut welfare benefits paid to poor workers. Our two-country analysis has revealed diverging effects on labour costs and the shape of the wage distribution. In Greece, the real value of the minimum wage today is below its level recorded in 1981, according to the OECD's purchasing parity measure; this is an extraordinary indictment of the country's economic management since the 2008 crisis under Troika control. The share of low-wage employment has increased, but this is secondary in significance to the plummeting real value of earnings for all workers. The UK's pay problems are different. Here we find a rising wage floor and a flat trend in real median earnings, coupled with a persistent high share of low-wage employment and a growing concentration of workers, especially high among women, paid within 'wage contours' just above the minimum wage.

A key failing in both countries' minimum wage policy approaches is their isolation from potentially complementary wage-setting institutions, namely collective bargaining. The Troika-led interventions in Greece were designed to dismantle long-standing processes of bipartite negotiation in minimum wage-setting by substituting unilateral state action for social partner regulation. We characterised this policy approach as a 'neoliberal shift'. The policy goal was to establish low-level coverage of collective bargaining and individualised industrial relations and to fix the minimum wage as a safety net via a frontal assault against collective bargaining and labour rights at large. It should be stressed, though, that the Tsipras government managed to place the revival of collective bargaining as a core plank of industrial relations reforms under the third EAP. As a result, it has been recently agreed between the government and the Quartet that both the favourability clause in collective agreements and the extension mechanism will be restored in September 2018. In the UK, the radical 2016 policy reform diminished the remit of the tripartite Low Pay Commission by unilaterally fixing the 2020 adult rate so that scope for interaction with social partners in fixing the minimum wage is reduced. The weak presence of collective bargaining in the UK's private sector workplaces means the role of social partners in the minimum wage-fixing process had been important. As such, this statutory intervention acts to 'crowd out' participative decision-making over wages. Both countries therefore have witnessed ruptures to pre-existing intersections with the national industrial relations model, although this is of a far greater scale in Greece and as the result of far more explicit concerted actions. The contrasting cases support the need for better policy approaches that engage with collective bargaining and participative minimum wage fixing processes since these facilitate a more robust approach to sustaining real wage gains and a pay equity approach that supports a wider approach of making work more equal.

Notes

1 The so-called Troika comprises the European Central Bank (ECB), the European Commission (EC) and the International Monetary Fund (IMF).
2 Namely, the EC, ECB, IMF and the European Stability Mechanism (ESM).

3 With the exception of the Wages Council for agriculture, which was abolished some years later in 2013 (again by a Conservative government).

4 See Chapter 2 in this volume for a full elaboration of the notion of 'participative standards'.

5 While the studies by Stewart (all sectors) and by Dickens and Manning (elderly care sector) find no evidence of wage spillovers from minimum wage rises in the UK, Butcher and colleagues (2012) find spillovers up to the 25th wage percentile. The difference is explained by the different time periods examined and the different counterfactual wage distributions used in models (McKnight et al., 2016).

6 During the period 2003–12, the total male workforce increased from 11.44 million to 12.46 million and the total female workforce from 11.14 million to 12.25 million (as recorded in the ASHE earnings database).

7 In its revised remit for the Low Pay Commission, the government states: 'The Government estimates that the level of the combined national minimum wage and the premium in April 2016 will be 55 per cent of median earnings and has set out an ambition that this should continue to increase to reach 60 per cent of median earnings by 2020, subject to sustained economic growth. The Government's objective is to have a National Living Wage of over £9 by 2020' (BIS, 2015: 2).

8 The 60 per cent target is likely to be estimated against median earnings for workers aged 25 and over, which raises the median slightly and therefore raises the eventual minimum wage by 2020 compared to the line plotted in Figure 17.7.

References

Aghion, P., Algan, Y. and Cahuc, P. (2008), *Can Policy Interact with Culture? Minimum Wage and the Quality of Labor Relations*, National Bureau of Economic Research (NBER) Working Paper, w14327.

Aghion, P., Algan, Y. and Cahuc, P. (2011), 'Civil society and the state: the interplay between cooperation and minimum wage regulations', *Journal of the European Economic Association*, 9:1, 3–42.

Baccaro, L. and Howell, C. (2011), 'A common neoliberal trajectory: the transformation of industrial relations in advanced capitalism', *Politics and Society*, 39:4, 521–63.

BIS (Business, Innovation and Skills) (2015), *National Minimum Wage: Low Pay Commission 2016* (London: Department for Business, Innovation and Skills).

BIS (Business, Innovation and Skills) (2016), *Trade Union Membership 2015: Statistical Bulletin* (London: Department for Business, Innovation and Skills).

Boeri T., Garibaldi P. and Ribeiro M. (2010), *Behind the Lighthouse Effect*, IZA (Institute of Labour Economics) Discussion Paper No. 4890 April 2010 (Bonn: Institute of Labour Economics).

Bryson, A. and Lucchino, P. (2014), *The Influence of the National Minimum Wage on Pay Settlements in Britain*, Report for the Low Pay Commission, London.

Butcher, T., Dickens, R. and Manning, A. (2012), *Minimum Wages and Wage Inequality: Some*

Theory and an Application to the UK, CEP Discussion Paper 1177 (London: London School of Economics).

Dedoussopoulos A. with V. Aranitou, F. Koutentakis, M. Maroupoulou (2013), *Assessing the Impact of the Memoranda on Greek Labour Market and Labour Relations,* Working Paper No. 53, Governance and Tripartism Department (Geneva: International Labour Office) http://www.ilo.org/ifpdial/information-resources/publications/WCMS_232796/lang--en/index.htm, accessed 6 September 2016.

Dickens, R. and Manning, A. (2015), 'Spikes and spill-overs: the impact of the national minimum wage on the wage distribution in a low-wage sector', *The Economic Journal*, *114*:494 (2004) C95–C101.

Eurofound (2016), *Statutory Minimum Wages in the EU 2016*, European Observatory of Working Life, http://www.eurofound.europa.eu/observatories/eurwork/articles/working-conditions-industrial-relations/statutory-minimum-wages-in-the-eu-2016

European Commission (2012), *The Second Economic Adjustment Programme for Greece*, European Economy Occasional Papers No. 94 (Brussels: Directorate-General for Economic and Financial Affairs Publications) ec.europa.eu/economy_finance/publications/occasional_paper/2012/ pdf/ocp94_en.pdf.

Garnero A., Kampelmann, S. and Rycx, F. (2015), 'Minimum wage systems and earnings inequalities: does institutional diversity matter?', *European Journal of Industrial Relations,* 21:2, 115–30.

Grimshaw, D. (2010), 'The UK: Developing a progressive minimum wage in a liberal market economy', in D. Vaughan-Whitehead (ed.), *The Minimum Wage Revisited in the Enlarged EU* (Cheltenham: Edward Elgar and Geneva: International Labour Organisation).

Grimshaw D., Bosch, G. and Rubery, J. (2014), 'Minimum wages and collective bargaining: what types of pay bargaining can foster positive pay equity outcomes?', *British Journal of Industrial Relations,* 52:3, 470–98.

Grimshaw D. and Rubery, J. (2013), 'The distributive functions of a minimum wage: first- and second-order pay equity effects', in Grimshaw, D. (ed.), *Minimum Wages, Pay Equity and Comparative Industrial Relations* (London: Routledge), pp. 81–111.

Hellenic Republic (2016), Ministry of Labour, Social Security and Social Solidarity, *Extract from the recommendations of the Commission of Independent Experts, as summarised by its President, Prof. Jan van Ours*, Press Release, Athens, www.ypakp.gr/uploads/docs/9946.pdf, accessed 30 September 2016.

Hermann, C. (2014), 'Structural adjustment and neoliberal convergence in labour markets and welfare: the impact of the crisis and austerity measures on European Economic and Social Models', *Competition & Change*, 18:2, 111–30.

Heyes, J. (2013), 'Flexicurity in crisis: European labour market policies in a time of austerity', *European Journal of Industrial Relations*, 19:1, 71–86.

Howell, C. (2015), 'The changing relationship between labor and the state in contemporary capitalism', *Law, Culture and the Humanities*, 11:1, 6–16.

Howell, C. (2016), 'Regulating class in the neoliberal era: the role of the state in the restructuring of work and employment relations', *Work, Employment and Society*, 30:4, 573–89.

Hyman, R. (2015), 'Three scenarios for industrial relations in Europe', *International Labour Review* 154:1, 5–14.

ILO (International Labour Organization) (2015a), *Inventory of Labour Market Policy Measures in the EU 2008–2013: The Crisis and Beyond* (Geneva: ILO), http://www.ilo.org/wcmsp5/groups/public/---dgreports/---inst/documents/publication/wcms_436119.pdf.

ILO (International Labour Organization) (2015b), *Trends in Collective Bargaining Coverage: Stability, Erosion or Decline?*, Policy Brief No. 1: Labour Relations and Collective Bargaining, ILO, www.ilo.org/global/topics/collective-bargaining-labour-relations/publications/WCMS_409422/lang--en/index.htm, accessed 6 September 2016.

Ioannou, C. (2000),'Social pacts in Hellenic industrial relations: Odysseus of Sisyphus?', in G. Fajertag and P. Pochet (eds), *Social Pacts in Europe: New Dynamics* (Brussels: European Trade Union Institute).

Ioannou C. (2012), 'Recasting Greek industrial relations: internal devaluation in light of the economic crisis and European integration', *The International Journal of Comparative Labour Law and Industrial Relations,* 28:2, 199–222.

Jaehrling, K. and Méhaut, P. (2013), 'Varieties of institutional avoidance: employers' strategies in low-waged service sector occupations in France and Germany', *Socio-Economic Review*, 11:4, 687–710.

Kahn-Freund, O. (1959), 'Labour law', in Ginsberg, M. (ed.) *Law and Opinion in England in the 20th Century* (Devon: Stevens).

Kanellopoulos, K. (2015), 'The effects of minimum wages on wages and employment', in *Economic Bulletin,* 41, Bank of Greece, Athens, 7–30.

Karamessini, M. (2012), 'Sovereign debt crisis: an opportunity to complete the neoliberal project and dismantle the Greek employment model', in S. Lehndorff (ed.), *A Triumph of Failed Ideas: European Models of Capitalism in the Crisis* (Brussels: European Trade Union Institute). www.etui.org/content/download/21029/175754/file/C8+12+A+triumph+of+failed+ideas+WEB.pdf.

Karamessini, M. (2015), 'The Greek social model: towards a deregulated labour market and residual social protection', in Vaughan-Whitehead, D. (ed.), *The European Social Model in Crisis: Is Europe Losing its Soul?* (Cheltenham: Edward Elgar and Geneva: International Labour Organization).

Koçer, R. G. and Visser, J. (2009), 'The role of the state in balancing the minimum wage in Turkey and USA', *British Journal of Industrial Relations*, 47:2, 349–70.

Koukiadaki, A. and Kokkinou, C. (2015), 'The Greek system of collective bargaining in (the) crisis, in Koukiadaki, A., Tavora, I. and Martinez Lucio, M. (eds), *Joint Regulation and Labour Market Policy in Europe during the Crisis* (Brussels: European Trade Union Institute).

Levin-Waldman, O. M. (2002), 'The minimum wage and regional wage structure: implications for income distribution', *Journal of Economics,* 36:3, 635–57.

McKnight, A., Duque, M. and Rucci, M. (2016), *Creating More Equal Societies: What Works?*, Evidence Review for DG Employment and Social Affairs (Brussels: European Commission).

Marginson, P. (2014), 'Coordinated bargaining in Europe: from incremental corrosion to frontal assault?', *European Journal of Industrial Relations,* 21:2, 97–114.

O'Connor, J. (1973), *The Fiscal Crisis of the State* (New York: St Martin's Press).

OECD (Organisation for Economic Co-operation and Development) (2015), 'Recent Labour Market Developments with a Focus on Minimum Wages', *Employment Outlook 2015* (Paris: OECD).

Rodgers, W. M., Spriggs, W. E. and Klein, B. W. (2004), 'Do the skills of adults employed in minimum wage contour jobs explain why they get paid less?', *Journal of Post Keynesian Economics*, 27:1, 38–66.

Rubery, J. (2003), *Pay equity, minimum wages and equality at work* (Geneva: International Labour Organization).

Schulten, T. (2012), 'European minimum wage policy: a concept for wage-led growth and fair wages in Europe', *International Journal of Labour Research*, 4:1, 85–104.

Sen, A. (1999), *Development as Freedom* (Oxford: Oxford University Press).

Stewart, M. B. (2012), 'Wage inequality, minimum wage effects, and spillovers', *Oxford Economic Papers*, 64:4, 616–34.

Streeck, W. (1997), 'Beneficial constraints: on the economic limits of rational voluntarism', in Rogers Hollingsworth, J. and Boyer R. (eds), *Contemporary Capitalism: The Embeddedness of Institutions* (Cambridge: Cambridge University Press), pp. 197–219.

Index